# Social Policy in Canada

# Social Policy in Canada

Ernie Lightman

OXFORD
UNIVERSITY PRESS

# OXFORD
### UNIVERSITY PRESS

70 Wynford Drive, Don Mills, Ontario M3C 1J9
www.oupcanada.com

Oxford University Press is a department of the University of Oxford.
It furthers the University's objective of excellence in research, scholarship,
and education by publishing worldwide in

Oxford    New York

Auckland    Cape Town    Dar es Salaam    Hong Kong    Karachi
Kuala Lumpur    Madrid    Melbourne    Mexico City    Nairobi
New Delhi    Shanghai    Taipei    Toronto

With offices in

Argentina    Austria    Brazil    Chile    Czech Republic    France    Greece
Guatemala    Hungary    Italy    Japan    Poland    Portugal    Singapore
South Korea    Switzerland    Thailand    Turkey    Ukraine    Vietnam

Oxford is a trade mark of Oxford University Press
in the UK and in certain other countries

Published in Canada
by Oxford University Press

**National Library of Canada Cataloguing in Publication Data**

Lightman, Ernie S
Social policy in Canada : who benefits, who pays?/
Ernie Lightman.

Includes bibliographical references and index.

ISBN-10: 0-19-541648-1    ISBN-13 978-0-19-541648-0

1. Canada–Social Policy.
2. Public Welfare–Canada–Finance.
I. Title

HN103.5.L54 2002      361.6'1'0971      C2002-903446-9

Cover design: Brett Miller
Text design: Valentino Sanna, Ignition Design and Communications

6  7  8  –  11 10 09
Printed in Canada

**Mixed Sources**
Product group from well-managed
forests, and other controlled sources
www.fsc.org  Cert no. SW-COC-002358
© 1996 Forest Stewardship Council
FSC

# CONTENTS

# List of Tables

# List of Figures

I am very pleased as well as honoured to have been asked to introduce Professor Ernie Lightman's book. Having been his friend and colleague in both teaching and writing about social policy for a quarter of a century (both of us within schools of social work), I have become well acquainted with his intellectual rigour, progressive economic and social analysis (for an economist!), and social activism. His book has been eagerly awaited. Now that it is here, I can assure its readers that it is both timely and of profound importance. I have no doubt it will prove to be a seminal text to a broad range of upper-level social science and professional education students—including social work, social policy, public administration, human services, and health care—as well as to faculty, policy analysts, community activists, and the general public.

At the start of the twenty-first century social policy analysis in Canada needs a shot in the arm and Professor Lightman's *Social Policy in Canada: Who Benefits? Who Pays?* provides it. The fact is that social policy has fallen off the political agenda and social welfare has become an abused and neglected subject. A highly doctrinaire economic discourse prevails and the mantra of economic growth and privatization is repeated endlessly as the only way forward. While it is correct that health and education are accorded a high degree of priority in today's business-dominated politics, the political legitimacy of social policy is at a very low ebb. In short, the post-World War II social contract—full employment with economic growth, universality, and a guaranteed social minimum—has been broken and not replaced.

The implications of market-driven economic policy in Canada are clear for all to see: significant hunger, wretched homelessness, increasing inequality, growing numbers of desperate women, individuals, and families struggling to make ends meet, and an increasing reliance on charity to fill the void left by social program cutbacks. This is an alarming scenario for future generations of Canadians. Indeed, one must now observe that in the post-11 September world, while our borders may well be secure (and perhaps we are all a little safer), the struggle for social and economic justice is far from won. Thankfully, Professor Lightman's text points us in the right direction in claiming priority attention for social policy informed by a discerning and understandable economic analysis grounded in the insights of that discipline, but informed also by a compelling concern for human welfare and social well-being.

In lucid prose Professor Lightman engages the hard questions about the relationship between economic and social policy and the challenges facing a decimated welfare state.

He argues that economic policy should be seen as a subset of social policy, a radical viewpoint, considering the predominant neo-liberal economic paradigm that engulfs us all. In making the case for the primacy of social policy and the choices that must be addressed by those favouring a more just and caring Canadian society, he directs our attention to the need not only to understand the expenditure side of the redistribution question but also, and importantly, revenue generation and the choices that undergird the question of who pays. There is no other book in Canada that combines within it a detailed discussion of both allocation and revenue generation.

In the current context of our time, several features of the book are particularly noteworthy. First, Professor Lightman provides a new definition of social policy set in a structural context and rooted in the idea of interdependence. In this he follows in the Titmussian tradition. However, he argues that social policy is conceptually distinguishable from economic policy in that social policy rejects the notion of indifference among individuals, which is the hallmark of the latter. While noting that his definition of social policy is normatively neutral he nonetheless, in my view, is asserting the critically important idea that as human beings we live our lives in societies and not merely as isolated individuals or discrete units of labour power. In other words, there is more to life and social well-being than the satisfaction of individual preferences. Indeed, he is absolutely correct to argue that economic policy 'should be subject to the same analytical and value-based assessments as are social policies.'

Second, Professor Lightman, in accepting that market society will be with us for a long time to come, addresses the question of how best to ensure that all members of the community might exercise free choice and benefit from living in such a society. How to make the market work better is a central theme of the text and one that needs the urgent attention of those who do not see minimalist government, privatization, and the spur of poverty as the only set of policy prescriptions available. The point Professor Lightman makes is that vulnerable and dependent people need to be empowered so that they might exercise their full rights and responsibilities as capable consumers in today's society. This requires a commitment to social inclusion and their full participation in decision-making and substantive policy initiatives directed at redressing 'inequalities in wealth, income, and human resources'.

Third, the text is important, as the chapters on taxes and user fees (frequently neglected in social policy analysis) will be especially beneficial to students and people in the community who are interested in these areas. Indeed, the chapter on gambling and charities breaks new ground in Canadian social policy literature.

The main reason why I believe this is a critical and timely publication is that it skilfully prepares the ground for a much-needed debate about a new social contract in Canada: one that is propelled by the urgency of a fresh dialogue about progressive social policy and the contributions that economics can make. This debate is as much about the substance of social inclusion, progressive policy outcomes, and the need for an economics centred in the Canadian people and environment as it is about ways of furthering dialogue between labour and corporate interests, the community and the state. The need to look to European models and not to that of the United States is a critical consideration. In Canada we have a long way to go, but Professor Lightman is pointing us in the right direction.

Perhaps the most significant aspect of the book is that it is written by an economist, and one who has spent his career educating social workers. It is good to know that the hegemony of classical economic thinking in our world is being challenged and that the claims of social policy are being advanced by an economist who has taken the road less travelled. As Professor Lightman notes, Canadians have opportunities to make choices. He has provided a foundation for better choices, thus making an important contribution to an expanded understanding of social policy and hence to a more equal and inclusive society.

**Graham Riches**
Professor and Director
School of Social Work and Family Studies
University of British Columbia
Vancouver, BC

Late in the autumn term, 1999, I received an individualized form letter from the president of the University of Toronto. He congratulated me on having made it to the university's 'Twenty-Five Year Club' and invited me to a reception where I'd receive official recognition. My first reaction was surprise. Twenty-five years ago I'd have given huge odds that I wouldn't last in my department. Students (and, even more, colleagues) in my early years had similar sentiments.

I began to think about the University of Toronto and the changes it had undergone since I entered as an undergraduate in 1963—from what we thought of as a 'community of scholars' with a social conscience, to a highly efficient fundraising machine with marked anti-union tendencies. Just like a large multinational corporation. I began as a colleague (student category), grew into a colleague (faculty category), and ultimately evolved into simply an employee. On balance, I didn't much like these later transitions in my alma mater and employer. Then I remembered that at the official reception the 25-year awards would be presented by a major financial backer of various neo-conservative causes and supporter of the Conservative government in Ontario. So I decided to ignore the awards ceremony.

The invitation did start me thinking retrospectively, about the parallels between my career and the welfare state in Canada. I was born right around the time when Ottawa sent out the first baby bonus cheques, the first of our important social programs. As I grew up, other initiatives were added: first there was Old Age Security (OAS) and hospitalization in the 1950s; medicare, the Canada Pension Plan (CPP), and the Canada Assistance Plan in the 1960s. By the early 1970s, as I left graduate school at Berkeley to take up my first real job as a faculty member at the London School of Economics, the fundamentals of our post-war welfare state were in place. Perhaps one of the reasons that my generation was always so self-confident and optimistic about the future was the existence of a reasonable set of social supports to back us up. We didn't really worry about boring issues such as unemployment.

It began to crash after the 1973 Yom Kippur war between Israel and her Arab neighbours, and the ensuing world oil crisis and global inflation. The social programs we had come to count on were removed, downsized, off-loaded, or merely gutted. At first the process occurred 'by stealth' (to use Ken Battle's memorable phrase), but after the election of the Chrétien government in 1993 there was a full frontal assault on every social initiative we had held so dear. The OAS, paid for out of current taxation, had been declared an unbearable burden for future generations, a smaller working population. So they cut back entitlement to OAS. The same demographic bulge led to fears about a crisis in CPP payments, so they raised the premiums. Through underfunding and bad planning, medicare began to fray at the edges. Our prospects for old age and retirement began to look distinctively less favourable than they had a decade earlier. By the turn of the twenty-first century, there wasn't much left of what we had built so assiduously; just the prospect of further economic and social integration with the American empire where, of course, they don't believe in social programs at all. From the welfare state optimism inherited from Britain to the rugged Darwinianism of US imperialism, all in one fast half-century.

I was trained as an economist, and I approach the study of social policy from that perspective. When I first began to teach in a school of social work, many students wondered what an economist was doing in a place that focused on meeting needs. Today, after two terms of hard-right Conservative government in Ontario and with a business-oriented federal government seemingly in place forever, most students understand the importance of connecting social welfare to the systems and programs through which we pay for them.

This book is not a text on the social policy process, the models and actors and stakeholders who interact to produce programmatic outcomes (see Wharf and McKenzie, 2000, especially ch. 3; Graham, 2000, ch. 6; Rice and Prince, 2000; Banting, 1979). Nor is it a detailed history of Canada's welfare state experience, which is fully covered by others (Guest, 1998; McGilly, 1998; Rice and Prince, 2000; Chappell, 1997; McBride and Shields, 1997). I do not focus on the role of the social work profession (Carniol, 2000; Mullaly, 1997), nor do I enumerate specific programs (McGilly, 1998; Clark, 1998). I do not follow the approach common to many texts of presenting discrete chapters on specific substantive areas, such as health or housing (Turner, 2001; Hick, 2001).

This book is a detailed exploration, within the Canadian context, of the mechanisms and tools of transfer and redistribution that are central to all aspects of social policy. I develop a new conceptual model of social policy, initially by distinguishing it from economic policy, and subsequently by arguing that economic policy should properly be viewed as a subset of social policy. The opposite view—that social policy is a small and relatively insignificant component of the economic world—is of course the dominant discourse today in both popular and governmental contexts. I reject this common hierarchy and its associated message that the promotion of economic growth through the private market is (and should be) the overriding aim of public policy in Canada.

Instead, I place economic policy under the broader umbrella of social policy and, in so doing, argue that the pre-eminence of classical economistic thinking is misguided; that our 'economic policies' should be subject to the same analytical and value-based assessments as our 'social policies'; and that there are no inexorable outcomes in public decision-making. The famous phrase of former British Prime Minister Margaret Thatcher that There Is No Alternative (TINA) to her economic and social policies is nothing more, and nothing less, than her own value-based perspective on how the world ought to be ordered. The ideas have no greater innate validity than my personal views that there are many alternatives to current neo-liberal economic and social policies, and that we are ultimately free to choose the paths we wish to follow.

In developing my case, I challenge many of the common (but unarticulated) assumptions of classical economics—narrow premises that have been so influential in the production of current social policy thinking and practice, but premises that are also often fundamentally irrelevant to the real world about us. In Part II of this book I present my definition of social policy (Chapter 2) and explore its relation to the economic market (Chapter 3). In Part II, I develop also a model of redistribution in which there are two distinct vectors: the allocation of benefits—how are they distributed, who gets what and in what form (discussed in Part III, Chapters 4, 5, and 6); and the generation of resources—who pays, and when (examined in Part IV, Chapters 7, 8, and 9). Part V summarizes the major ideas of the book and takes a look at what the future might hold for social policy in Canada, and abroad.

While much traditional social policy considers only the allocation side of the model, a critical analysis of Canada's welfare state (and its current dilemmas) and an understanding of the redistributive cycle must also include issues of finance and generating resources. There are few, if any, textbooks in Canada or the United States—though there are some in Britain (Glennerster, 1985; LeGrand, 1992) and elsewhere (Healy, 1998)—that attempt to link, in a systematic way, issues in the delivery of programs and benefits with the mechanisms of finance and payment. This book is designed to help fill that gap.

Although the ideas in this book link more closely to economics than to the other mainstream disciplines, this is not a textbook in the economics of social programs. I attempt to show that the basic questions asked by economics often are important, and that certain key concepts of the discipline are relevant in seeking answers. All needed theory and concepts are developed in this book and no prior knowledge of economics is required or assumed. Certainly, nothing herein will be unfamiliar to the student who has taken an introductory course in economics, and for those who have not, the few technical discussions are explained, or can be skipped without losing the greater import of the discussion.

In his book, *Structural Social Work*, Bob Mullaly describes working to change the system from within and working to change it from without. The latter category, of course, is more radical, as it involves fundamental structural and systemic change in the society, perhaps beyond the confines of crude market capitalism. To change from within means to accept (though not embrace) the current socio-economic system and to work for change in a more incremental fashion. My book falls primarily into the category of change from within.

But the two categories are not mutually exclusive, and while we are working to make the tax system fairer, we can simultaneously—if we so desire—also work to overthrow capitalism. And perhaps our chances of actually achieving concrete progress are greater if we don't entirely forget about the tax system. As my more radical but always supportive partner Leah points out, this is not a book about revolution, but it may contain information of value to any aspiring revolutionaries who care to read it.

A fundamental premise of my work is that there is much room for manoeuvring and incremental progress within existing social structures. We can't, for example, fight to change the tax system unless we understand it better. And we can't do much of anything unless we appreciate certain simple economic principles. We always have to ask not only about the delivery of services, but also about cost and financing. I continually ask the question, 'How are we going to pay for this?' I point out that resources are always finite, and we have to choose priorities. We can't eliminate child poverty and cut taxes and establish shelters for abused women all at the same time. A single dollar can be spent only once. At times I have sounded like the Grinch who stole Christmas.

One of the major conclusions of the book is to advocate a welfare society and to affirm the need to strengthen the capacities of people—particularly vulnerable people—to live and function as autonomous beings in a market society. To do this entails a major role for the state (and the federal government) not only to ensure people have adequate incomes and other resources to exercise freedom of choice, but also to assist them with personal supports and social benefits as desired.

## ACKNOWLEDGEMENTS

Amazingly, this book was written without financial aid for research assistance. Funding agencies give grants for research studies, which may result in a book (as part of a strategy to communicate results), but they don't generally give support for books per se. Fortunately, I was able to call upon good friends and former students—the categories are not mutually exclusive—who helped me tremendously. I discovered also that most of those mind-numbing data-collection tasks we used to send research assistants to do in the library can now be done easily and quickly from my own study, thanks to the Internet. My cynicism about technology has diminished considerably during the past year.

I'd like to thank many friends and colleagues who gave so generously of their time and ideas: Michael Birenbaum, Derek Hum, Patrick Johnston, Teri Kay, Jon Kesselman, Joe Manion, Ian Morrison, Jane McMichael, Sheila Neysmith, Malcolm Stewart, Gordie Wolfe, Kim Zapf, and Paul Zarnke. Particular thanks go to Pedro Barata, Luann Good Gingrich, Andy Mitchell, Bob Mullaly, Graham Riches, and Richard Shillington, each of whom took the time and effort to read parts (or all) of the manuscript and provided me with invaluable feedback. Graham Riches and Howard Glennerster have long urged me to actually commit to this project. Megan Mueller from Oxford University Press offered support and enthusiasm from the first day I spoke to her about a book, and Charis Wahl again showed her incredible skill in helping cut the length of the manuscript by some 20,000 words. Gilles Seguin shortened my work effort dramatically because of his personal Web site on Canadian social welfare. And I'd especially like to thank my close friend and colleague Graham Riches for agreeing to write the Foreword.

Finally, deep thanks to the two significant women in my life: my partner, Leah Cohen, and our daughter, Naomi Lightman. Without their tolerance for my sometimes extended disappearances into the computer room, without their unquestioning love and support at all times and in all circumstances, I would never have managed to begin—let alone, complete—this book.

*To the memory of my father, Ned Lightman, who worked harder throughout his life than I ever shall, and was so very proud of whatever I managed to achieve.*

# Introduction

In Part I (Chapter 1) we position our study, both historically and within the Canadian setting. A central focus of our inquiry will be issues of redistribution, and so we begin with a brief discussion of what can realistically be expected from a social change process, given the constraints of a capitalist (or market) economy.

To ground the discussion in the real world about us, we immediately proceed to an empirical examination of income redistribution in Canada over the last decade—what has been accomplished in terms of redressing inequality, and where we stand today. We examine two distinct aspects of this redistribution:

- cash transfers from government to individuals (which includes most social programs such as the Canada Child Tax Credit, Old Age Security, and social assistance); and
- cash transfers from individuals to government (primarily through the personal income tax), which provide the means to pay for our social programs.

We thus see there is a cycle of redistribution (to be explored more fully in Part II), in which money is drawn from individuals to government, and then returned from government to (other) individuals. Together, they constitute the redistributive process that is central to the analysis of this book. Without examining both parts of this cycle, the study of social policy is partial and incomplete.

We find that for those at the bottom of the income scale, transfers from government often exceed their earnings from paid work, and therefore constitute an essential supplement to their primary incomes. For those at the top, income tax significantly reduces after-tax incomes, thereby generating the resources to pay for social programs and also narrowing the income gap between rich and poor. Though the gaps remain wide, they would be far wider without active government involvement, both through its delivering of social benefits and through its raising of revenue through the income tax.

We also look at wealth in Canada, noting it is far more unequally distributed than incomes: we cannot understand poverty without also examining wealth ('the rich are rich because the poor are poor'). The extent of inequality in Canada, both in incomes and in wealth, will be surprising to many, and as we proceed through our study this inequality offers a continual reminder of the goals—and limits—of social policy practice within a market economy.

We then take a broad overview of half a century of welfare state activity in Canada, beginning at the end of World War II. We do not present a detailed chronology of events, but instead ask two fundamental questions: Why did we build a welfare state in the first instance? And why, after the early 1970s, did we with so little resistance pull it all down? We suggest two competing explanations for both the building phase and the subsequent demolition—one relates to motivations of altruism and collective caring, and the other to motives of self-interest. These two concepts provide the basis for the conceptual model of social policy that we develop in Part II of the book.

As part of our introduction, we also highlight the influence of John Maynard Keynes in the development of Canada's post-war welfare state (also known as the Keynes-Beveridge welfare state). We see the limits of the Keynesian model when faced with global inflation (and *stagflation*) in the 1970s and the shift away from Keynes in the 1980s. Nevertheless, we argue that the basic approach of Keynes—that the economy is not a self-regulating entity (as promoted by classical economics) and that government has an active role to play in economic life—remains timely and relevant today, at the dawn of the twenty-first century.

We also set the context internationally, by situating Canada alongside the other major industrialized countries: we find that welfare state activity, however measured, shows Canada to be significantly ahead of the United States and Japan, but a distinct laggard compared to the major Western European countries. Anti-welfare state rhetoric in Canada—much of it grounded in narrow comparisons between our tax levels and those of the United States—would lose much impact if only we could refocus our perspective a little and look across the Atlantic at what the countries of the European Community have achieved.

# CHAPTER ONE

# Setting the Context

*Social policies have often operated as the poor person's economic policy.*
Miller and Rein (1975: 18)

*Economic policies have usually operated as the rich person's social policy.*
Ernie Lightman, 2002

## INTRODUCTION

Once upon a time, long, long ago, Canada had no welfare state, and no social pro-grams. Parents were expected to look after their children, who, in turn, would care for their aging parents. Families constituted the basic operational units of society with lit-tle outside support or assistance. For those truly in need—the young widow with small children—the community would rally with food hampers and other acts of voluntary caring, guided by the precepts of the Elizabethan (and later, the Victorian) Poor Laws, which sharply distinguished between the deserving poor and the non-deserving poor. Only the former warranted public compassion.

In those days, immigration to Canada was overwhelmingly white and able-bodied, primarily from northern and central Europe and the United States. Government was small and non-intrusive. Its major functions were national defence and the ensuring of law and order. Its primary source of income was customs duties levied on imports. Income taxes had not yet been invented.

The economy was assumed to be self-regulating, and government had no particular role to intervene or to stabilize. If there was unemployment, it was merely a temporary aberration that would expeditiously correct itself.

Of course, all was not self-correcting: families were not always able to cope on their own. Child neglect and abuse occurred, as did spousal battering, while there were no public mechanisms to address or even name these problems. Hunger was widespread, as were illness and disease. Industrialization and urbanization, over time, led to the weakening of the traditional nuclear family without anything much to replace it. Non-white immigrants, though few in number in the early years, were subject to widespread discrimination; Aboriginal peoples were exploited and abused with impunity. Psychiatric or developmental disabilities were managed within the family or the asylum located, if possible, away from the population centres, far out of sight. Sexual diversity was neither discussed nor openly accepted. Difference, in all its forms, was barely tolerated and certainly not acknowledged as legitimate or appropriate.

Even the self-regulating economy turned out to be a myth. The Great Depression of the 1930s proved conclusively that the market, left to its own devices, would not create full employment. Only the onset of World War II, in 1939, brought the Great Depression to an end. The new economic ideas of John Maynard Keynes, providing a theoretical rationale for active interventionist government, were readily embraced in Whitehall and subsequently in Ottawa. A new post-war social consensus argued that we, as a society, could do better than we had done before. The individualism that had informed economic and social life before the war was superseded by (or at least joined with) new ideas about collective responsibility. Over a quarter-century we introduced a vast array of social programs in Canada—family allowances for children; old age security for seniors; hospitalization and medical insurance; public pensions; and non-demeaning aid to the poor. We came to see that government could be an agency for the betterment of society.

However, government could be directed towards other goals as well. We discovered that the income tax system could be a highly effective and efficient way to redistribute income from the rich to the poor; but it could also quietly send money the other way, up the income scale. Details of the tax system could be manipulated to serve the interests of the rich and powerful. When federal finance ministers announced cuts to capital gains taxes (as Paul Martin did twice in 2000), they were representing the interests of their own economic class.[1]

In addition, social programs, originally intended to focus on the needs of the vulnerable, could be turned around to protect the class interests of the powerful. Public education, though generally of a high quality and widely accessible at the lower levels, remained largely the tax-supported preserve of the middle class and rich at the post-secondary levels.

Medicare, largely funded through taxes, offered to everyone a wide range of services without user fees, but access to specialist care remained problematic for the poor; and open-ended (hence, costly) services such as psychiatry are disproportionately utilized by the rich. Programs that served only the poor, such as social assistance, came under relentless attack from those who neither need nor use their benefits. The sense of collective responsibility that marked the earlier days of Canada's welfare state increasingly has been replaced by an individualism in which the powerful use state mechanisms to meet their own needs, while blaming the vulnerable for having fallen into states of dependency.

In the beginning, social programs compensated the poor, to offset their inability to cope in the market economy. Today, many social programs, particularly the tax system, increasingly accommodate the economic (and psychological) priorities of the rich, and to some extent, of the middle classes, at the expense of the poor and marginalized.

## DISTRIBUTION AND REDISTRIBUTION

The welfare state in both Britain and Canada never was intended to replace the structures built on fundamental notions of individualism and private responsibility. It was a limited complement to market capitalism, and not a substitute. A properly functioning labour market was always seen as essential for the development of effective social programs.

It is assumed that the vast majority of the population will address their income needs through paid work, in a context of full employment and good wages. This *primary distribution* of resources occurs without direct governmental involvement. For those unable to cope in the private market, particularly those excluded through no fault of their own, *secondary* or *redistributive* government social programs come into play—but only *after* the primary distribution of the market has been found deficient. Individuals may be unable to secure gainful employment; they may earn too little to meet their family needs or be unable to work due to responsibilities of caring for children or elderly parents; or they may be unable to provide for future contingencies such as illness or old age. In such situations, government has a legitimate role—to aid, support, and supplement.

In the context of the post-war welfare state, government is not solely the provider of income support for the casualties of the private market. Instead, the optimal role for government is to facilitate or ensure that conditions maximize meaningful employment opportunities. At times, this entails direct action to create jobs; at all times, it means support for programs that enhance persons' abilities to meet their own needs. Medicare creates a healthy workforce, and a healthy workforce is a productive workforce. High-quality public education or child care directly improves effectiveness in the workplace. Assaults by governments on public education or medicare will yield a clear and predictable deterioration of employment, productivity, and living standards.

This emphasis on jobs and job creation (primary distribution) raises questions. First, an emphasis on employment may alter collective social priorities so that only programs that enhance employability are seen as legitimate. For example, child care in Canada has been increasingly conceptualized as an aid to employment, like work boots or protective equipment. At the federal level, the Canada Child Tax Benefit (CCTB) provides income support to most families with children, yet these benefits are often denied to households on social assistance (not in the paid workforce). Provincially, access to child care support may be linked to participation in work, either as training or as workfare. This process is known as the *commodification* of benefits, the linking of social entitlements to participation in the workforce and the devaluing of social programs as useful in their own right.

Second, implicit in commodification is an assumption that the distribution of income and other work rewards is fair, just, and proper and that interference in this 'natural' outcome should be minimal. Secondary redistribution, which usually involves government, is deemed to be less legitimate because it usually appropriates private resources through coercive taxation. Yet, in reality, the distinction between primary and secondary distribution is artificial. A set of subjective and changeable prior conditions influences the context within which the primary employment occurs. For example, capital accumulation occurs within a legal framework that tends to value property rights more highly than the rights of people. Thus, the right of landlords to do what they wish with their real estate takes precedence over the right of the lessees to adequate and secure housing. We could envisage, if we chose to, an alternate legal framework in which the rights to housing or to food or to a good job supersede the right to dispose of one's resources privately without interference.

> *In short, the premise that the primary distribution of jobs and rewards is some-*
> *how natural and just, while the secondary redistribution is interventionist and*
> *unjust, is false. Both primary and secondary distribution (and redistribution)*
> *are subject to the ideological framework within which all economic and social*
> *activity takes place.*

Third, the emphasis on jobs translates into an emphasis on economic growth without regard to the nature or implications of that growth. Yet, growth often pollutes; it alters the environment and affects our ecosystems; growth may entail only low-quality and insecure employment and result in unequal distribution of the spoils of economic growth. While government has an important role to aid and support job creation, it has an equal or greater obligation to monitor and influence the nature and consequences of that growth. Government must ensure that all have equal access to quality jobs, and that racism, sexism, ableism, ageism, and homophobia do not deny opportunities to some. Indeed, some argue that the cost of growth has been too high; instead of focusing on job creation, we should refocus on job-sharing, and on lower levels of growth in exchange for an improved quality of life. We must also address the proliferation of mindlessly repetitive jobs that are deeply alienating to the worker: such work may not meet the financial or psychological needs of workers, thereby severing the presumed link between paid work and the meeting of one's needs privately.

Fourth is a crucial distinction between the meeting of needs for income and of a range of other needs. While Canadians today presume that the former will usually be met through individual employment, we have collectively decided that other needs *should not* be met through the private market. Primary and secondary education or insured medical services, for example, are not assumed to be private responsibilities (though fees are becoming an increasingly significant burden for many); we pay for the bulk of these programs collectively through our taxes. Opinions differ as to which needs should be met outside the market, and also as to how to pay for them, but most of us do generally agree that certain non-income-related needs should be provided on a non-market basis.

Finally, there will always be exceptions to the assumption of private responsibility to meet income needs. People unable to meet their needs, permanently or on a short-term basis, for reasons beyond their control may become marginalized and excluded from concrete entitlements or from full participation in society. Again, we have a collective obligation to respond to these processes of social exclusion.

In sum, there are three issues to bear in mind concerning distribution and redistribution in Canada:

- Most people in Canada are assumed to meet their income needs through paid employment, the *primary distribution* of resources. Government's role with respect to this primary distribution is to facilitate the creation of adequate jobs with suitable compensation, and, on occasion, to create these jobs. Government also is to ensure equity goals are attained so that all have access on fair and equitable terms.
- Some people cannot meet their income needs through paid work because they are unable to secure suitable employment with adequate compensation. In such cases, government's role is to redistribute resources and opportunities, largely funded

through the taxation system. This is known as *secondary redistribution*. It should come into play only when the system of primary distribution fails, or is inadequate.
- For all people, there are non-income-related needs for which collective decisions have been made to utilize non-private market allocation. In these cases, the role of government is central: to determine both funding arrangements and delivery issues to meet these needs.

## INCOME INEQUALITY IN CANADA

Tables 1.1 and 1.2 and Figure 1.1 contain important information about the primary and secondary distribution of incomes in Canada. They enable us to understand what the market has produced in terms of unequal incomes resulting from differential access to regular, stable, and quality work; they also show what government has, and has not, accomplished in terms of narrowing the wide gaps between the rich and poor in Canada.

The tables present information on income *quintiles*: each quintile represents 20 per cent of the relevant population. If all incomes in Canada were distributed so that all individuals had the same income, each quintile would contain both 20 per cent of the population and 20 per cent of total income. However, incomes are not equally distributed and the quintiles reveal the extent of inequality in income distribution, and the relation of the incomes of the rich to those of the poor.

In the tables of income distribution, the first, or lowest, quintile contains data on the poorest 20 per cent of the population. The second quintile, the second-poorest 20 per cent of the population, includes those we often refer to as the working poor, while the middle quintile, as the names implies, covers the middle 20 per cent of incomes. The upper two quintiles encompass those incomes above and far above the average.

The information in the tables is presented in constant 1998 dollars so historical comparisons can be made apart from the effects of inflation. We see in these data that government has two distinct roles: it spends and it taxes. Several income measures are used, so that we can see the distinct and independent effects of both government spending policies (reflected in the system of transfers), and of government revenue-generating activities (shown in the taxation data). The 'before' data show primary distribution, what people actually earned from labour market activity; the 'after' data show secondary distribution, as affected by both the tax system and government transfer programs.

Table 1.1 shows average incomes, using the different definitions, for the lowest and the highest quintiles, for both 1989 and 1998, so that changes over the decade can be readily observed. Market incomes (primary distribution) in Canada are extremely unequal, and this inequality has increased over the past decade.

### Market Incomes

- In 1989, the poorest 20 per cent of the population received 2.6 per cent of all income in Canada, while the wealthiest 20 per cent earned 46 per cent. The ratio of rich to poor was 17.6, that is, for every dollar earned by someone in the lowest quintile, someone in the highest quintile earned $17.60.

**Table 1.1  Average Income and Income Shares, Canada, 1989–1998**
(1998 constant dollars)

| Quintile | Average Market Income | Share of Total Income | Average Market Income | Share of Total Income | $ Change |
|---|---|---|---|---|---|
| | 1989 | | 1998 | | 1989–1998 |
| Lowest | $5,837 | 2.6 | $3,993 | 1.8 | $–1,844 |
| Highest | $102,941 | 46.3 | $109,116 | 50.1 | $6,175 |
| Ratio High/Low | 17.64 | | 27.33 | | |
| | Average Transfer Payments | | Average Transfer Payments | | |
| Lowest | $6,535 | 23.8 | $6,696 | 21.4 | $161 |
| Highest | $3,969 | 14.5 | $4,258 | 13.6 | $289 |
| Ratio High/Low | 0.61 | | 0.64 | | |
| | Average Total Income | | Average Total Income | | |
| Lowest | $12,372 | 5.0 | $10,689 | 4.3 | $–1,683 |
| Highest | $106,910 | 42.5 | $113,374 | 45.5 | $6,464 |
| Ratio High/Low | 8.64 | | 10.61 | | |
| | Average Income Tax | | Average Income Tax | | |
| Lowest | $913 | 1.9 | $671 | 1.4 | $–242 |
| Highest | $24,914 | 52.5 | $27,768 | 56.3 | $2,854 |
| Ratio High/Low | 27.29 | | 41.38 | | |
| | Average After-Tax Income | | Average After-Tax Income | | |
| Lowest | $11,459 | 5.7 | $10,018 | 5.0 | $–1,441 |
| Highest | $81,996 | 40.6 | $85,606 | 42.8 | $3,610 |
| Ratio High/Low | 7.16 | | 8.55 | | |

NOTE: Market income includes earnings from participation in the paid labour force, as well as private pension income. In 1998, 87 per cent of all market income for Canadian families came from employment. Government transfers cover a range of social programs, including income from Employment Insurance (EI); Old Age Security (OAS); Canada and Quebec Pension Plans (CPP/QPP); the Guaranteed Income Supplement (GIS) and Spouse's Allowance (SA), both of which are targeted to low-income seniors; the Canada Child Tax Benefit (CCTB); provincial social assistance; Workers' Compensation benefits; and a number of other smaller government programs. Total income is the sum of market income plus government transfers. Average income tax includes both federal and provincial income taxes. Average after-tax income is total income minus income taxes payable.

SOURCE: Statistics Canada (2000a).

- A decade later in 1998 the wealthiest 20 per cent of the population earned 50 per cent of all income in Canada, while the lowest quintile earned just 1.8 per cent. The high-low ratio had grown to 27.3, an increase of 55 per cent in our measure of inequality.
- On average, individuals in the lowest quintile earned less than $4,000 in market income in 1998, a decrease in constant dollars of $1,800; individuals in the top quintile earned on average $109,000 in market income, an increase in constant dollars of $6,175 from 1989. Over the decade, then, the incomes of those at the top increased modestly in constant dollars, while the incomes of those at the bottom declined by nearly a third: the gap between rich and poor widened by more than one-half over the decade.

## Transfer Payments

Government transfer payments improved all incomes during the decade. The poorest quintile received 24 per cent of total transfer payments in 1989, just slightly in excess of their 'equal' share (which would have been 20 per cent, as they comprise 20 per cent of the population); those in the top quintile received 14.5 per cent. Over the decade, the share of all transfer payments received by both top and bottom groups dropped, with the greatest increase in share going to those in the middle quintile (not shown in the table). In 1998, on average, the transfer payments received by the top quintile were just under two-thirds (64 per cent) of the value of those received by the bottom quintile.

Overall, cash transfer payments from government, while slightly skewed down the income scale, did little to narrow the income gaps resulting from the primary distribution of market incomes: the poorest quintile in 1998 obtained little more than their proportionate share of all transfers; the largest share (27 per cent) went to the second quintile, the working poor; and the two upper quintiles together received some 30 per cent of the total.

At the same time, the transfer system did prevent the poorest Canadians from falling even farther behind those in the higher quintiles. While the market incomes of the poorest dropped substantially during the decade, the average transfer payments did grow, albeit modestly. By 1998, the poorest quintile received $6,696 from transfers and $3,993 from work; just under two-thirds (63 per cent) of their total income came from government transfers. During a decade when their incomes from work dropped substantially, the poorest Canadians depended increasingly upon government transfers, which increased only slightly in dollar terms, but were essential, given their reduced total incomes.

## Income Taxes

Income taxes have proven to be far more effective than transfers in narrowing the gaps between rich and poor, and have shown increased impact through the decade. In 1989, those in the lowest quintile paid just over $900 on average in income taxes, while those at the top paid roughly 27 times as much. (The wealthiest quintile of Canadians paid 52 per cent of all income taxes in Canada.) By 1998, average income taxes for those at the bottom had dropped by a quarter, so that they paid only 1.4 per cent of all income taxes in Canada. Tax levels for the top quintile had increased on average by just over 10 per cent, so that they were now paying 56 per cent of all income taxes.

## Final Incomes

After all income taxes and transfers, the average incomes of the poorest 20 per cent of Canadians still dropped by more than $1,400 in constant dollars over the decade, a decrease of about one-eighth. The average incomes of the top quintile grew by more than $3,600, an increase of about 4 per cent. The poorest 20 per cent of the population received only 5 per cent of total income after all taxes and transfers in 1998, while those at the top held 43 per cent of the total. The gap between top and bottom widened over the decade, rising from a ratio of 7.2 in 1989 to 8.6 in 1998.

## Incomes by Decile

Comparable calculations by Yalnizyan (1998) utilized deciles (in which the population is divided into 10, rather than five, groupings), thereby showing the relation of the incomes of the very rich to those of the very poor.[2] Using constant 1996 dollars, she reported that the ratio of average market incomes of the top decile compared to those at the bottom was 20.6 in 1973; but by 1996, this ratio had increased to a startling 314.34. In dollar terms in 1996, the average market income in the top decile was $136,737 but only $435 in the bottom decile. These findings illustrate how the market on its own has not only failed to reduce inequities but in fact has widened dramatically the gaps between rich and poor in Canada. The implications for policy suggest action to redress the glaring inequities in the primary distribution of incomes, while also using the tax and transfer systems to narrow the gaps.

**Table 1.2  Income Shares, by Quintile, 1998**

| Shares of Total Income (%) | | | |
|---|---|---|---|
| Quintile | Market Income | Total Income | After-Tax Income |
| 1 | 1.8 | 4.3 | 5.0 |
| 2 | 7.4 | 9.9 | 11.0 |
| 3 | 15.1 | 16.0 | 16.7 |
| 4 | 25.5 | 24.3 | 24.4 |
| 5 | 50.1 | 45.5 | 42.8 |

SOURCE: Statistics Canada (2000a).

## Incomes for Five Quintiles

Table 1.2 and Figure 1.1 show in table and graph form the shares of each of the five quintiles in 1998. For the bottom two quintiles, government transfers are more important than market incomes. Income taxes further increase their shares of the final pie, though proportionately less than did the transfers. Those in the third and fourth quintiles are less affected by the combined tax and transfer systems, with the former increasing its final share by just over 10 per cent, and the latter dropping by just over 4 per cent. The top quintile experiences a 15 per cent drop in its total after-tax share, though it does continue to hold more than 40 per cent of total income in Canada.

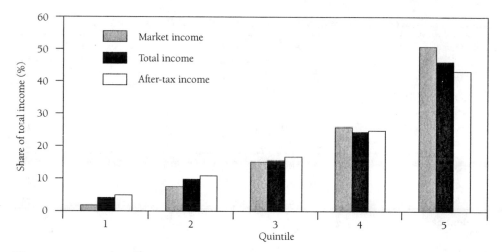

**Figure 1.1  Income Shares by Quintile, 1998**

The simple conclusion is that the welfare state interventions in Canada have been, and continue to be, important. While government transfers are now the major source of total income for those in the lowest quintile, the income tax system remains the most progressive of the measures directed towards increased equality. Transfers have kept the poorest Canadians from falling off the radar screen entirely as their market incomes have shrunk towards zero, while income taxes drawn largely from the upper income groups have provided the resources necessary for redistribution. However, as Jackson et al. (2000) have observed, 'The evidence shows that the rising economic tide of the 1990s did not lift all boats. If the gap in market incomes continues to rise, and if governments fail to rebuild income support programs, then poor and working-class families in Canada face the prospect of falling even farther behind in the years ahead.'

Table 1.3 and Figures 1.2 and 1.3 show the impact for 1998 of the tax and transfer systems on different types of families.

- The average family—the *economic family*, defined by Statistics Canada as two or more persons living in the same dwelling and related by blood, marriage, common law, or adoption—had an average market income more than two and one-half times that of the average unattached individual. After tax, the gap narrowed somewhat, as the family paid more taxes than it received in transfers, while for unattached individuals, transfers exceeded tax. The income ratio of families to individuals declined modestly, from 2.7 to 2.3.
- Elderly families' market incomes were just over one-third (38 per cent) those of the average non-elderly families. However, the seniors received government transfers ($19,000) almost equal to their market incomes ($23,000), while non-elderly families received fewer transfers and paid nearly 20 per cent of their total income in taxes. On an 'after tax and transfer' basis, the ratio of non-elderly to elderly incomes dropped substantially, from 2.6 to 1.4. Clearly, social policy in Canada has been effective in narrowing income disparities between elderly and non-elderly families.

## Table 1.3  Sources of Income, Selected Family Types, Canada, 1998

| Family Types | Average Market Income | Average Government Transfers | Average Total Income | Average Income Tax | Average Income After Tax |
|---|---|---|---|---|---|
| Economic Families (2+ persons) | $55,224 | $6,892 | $62,116 | $12,489 | $49,626 |
| Unattached Individuals | $20,758 | $5,027 | $25,784 | $4,718 | $21,067 |
| Ratio Families: Unattached | 2.7 | | | | 2.3 |
| Elderly Families | $23,482 | $18,878 | $42,360 | $6,309 | $36,051 |
| Non-Elderly Families | $60,429 | 4,994 | $65,243 | $13,468 | $51,776 |
| Ratio Non-Elderly: Elderly | 2.6 | | | | 1.4 |
| 2-Parent Families with child(ren) | $65,766 | $4,277 | $70,043 | $14,969 | $55,074 |
| Female-Headed, Lone-Parent Families | $19,242 | $7,953 | $27,195 | $2,771 | $24,424 |
| Ratio: 2P:FHLPF | 3.4 | | | | 2.3 |
| *Two-Parent Families* | | | | | |
| One-Earner | $48,206 | $6,345 | $54,552 | $12,691 | $41,860 |
| Two-Earners | $68,033 | $3,496 | $71,530 | $15,439 | $56,090 |
| Ratio 2E:1E | 1.4 | | | | 1.3 |
| *Elderly* | | | | | |
| Elderly Male, Unattached | $14,124 | $12,347 | $26,471 | $4,173 | $22,299 |
| Elderly Female, Unattached | $8,649 | $11,724 | $20,372 | $2,277 | $18,095 |
| Ratio M:F | 1.6 | | | | 1.2 |
| *Non-Earners* | | | | | |
| Non-Elderly Male, Unattached | $2,754 | $6,792 | $9,546 | $635 | $8,911 |
| Non-Elderly Female, Unattached | $3,592 | $6,221 | $9,813 | $759 | $9,054 |
| Ratio F:M | 1.3 | | | | 1.0 |

SOURCE: Statistics Canada (2000a).

- The average market income for two-parent families was more than three times that of female-led lone-parent families. However, the female-headed family received nearly double the amount of government transfers received by the two-parent unit, and also paid considerably less taxes. On an 'after tax and transfer' basis, the female-headed family had an average income of $24,424, under half (44 per cent) of the $55,074 income of the two-parent family.
- Comparing two-parent families that have one and two earners also indicates that the differential narrows after taxes and transfers. The market income of the average one-earner family was 71 per cent that of the two-earner unit; the former received nearly double the transfers of the latter, while the two-earner family paid about 22 per cent more taxes. On an after-tax basis, the income of the average single-earner family rose to 75 per cent of that of the two-earner unit.

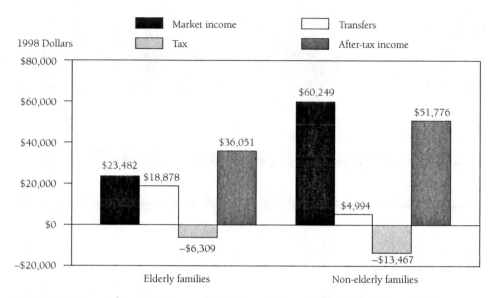

**Figure 1.2  Transfers and Taxes, Elderly and Non-Elderly Families, 1998**
SOURCE: Statistics Canada (2000a).

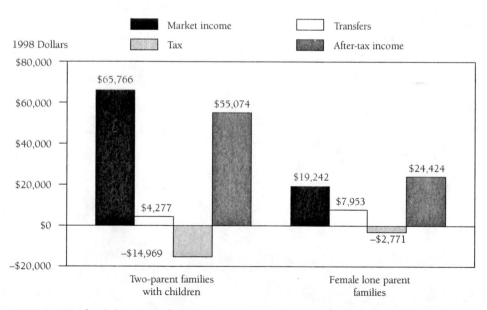

NOTE: In 1998, female lone-parent families earned only a small fraction of average market income (29.3%), but a larger proportion of average after-tax income (44.3%) as compared to two-parent families.

**Figure 1.3  Taxes and Transfers, Female Lone-Parent Families and Two-Parent Families, 1998**
SOURCE: Statistics Canada (2000a).

- Unattached individuals inevitably receive more in transfers than they pay in taxes. The market income of the elderly male was nearly two-thirds greater than that of the elderly unattached female. Both received virtually the same government transfers, but the male paid nearly double the taxes. On an after-tax basis, the ratio of incomes dropped from 1.6 to 1.2. For both men and women, government transfers constitute an important share of total income, more than 50 per cent of the total for women; and the combined effect of progressive taxation and virtually equal transfers narrows the gap in final incomes to 20 per cent.
- Among non-elderly, non-earners, incomes are low. The market incomes of women are 30 per cent greater than those of men. Although the men receive greater transfer payments, for both groups transfers greatly exceed market incomes. Government transfers comprise 71 per cent of total income for males and 63 per cent for the women. After taxes and transfers, the incomes of women and men were virtually identical.

## Gini Coefficients

Another common measure of income inequality is the *Gini coefficient*, a single indicator that is used to compare different populations or time periods. Its value ranges from 0, the case of perfect equality, when all individuals or reporting units receive the same incomes, through to 1, the case of perfect inequality, where all income is held by one of the units. Higher values thus denote greater degrees of inequality.

Figure 1.4 shows, in graph form, the Gini coefficients for Canada covering the years from 1980 to 1998 (Canada, 2001e). On the diagram are market income, total income, and after-tax income, for all economic families and unattached individuals combined.[3]

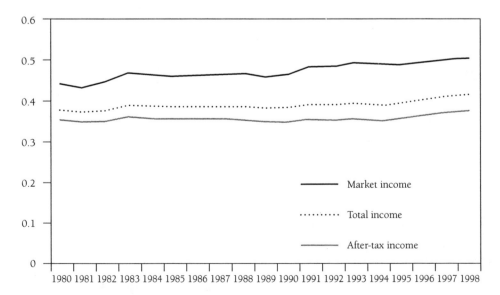

**Figure 1.4  Gini Coefficients, Canada, 1980–1998**

The data show significant growth in inequality in market incomes over the time period, with this inequality rising by 15 per cent, from a value of 0.441 in 1980 to 0.506 in 1988.[4] For total income there was slightly less growth in inequality, from 0.382 to 0.417, while on an after-tax basis, the coefficient rose more modestly, from 0.356 to 0.378. What these figures suggest are two conclusions: by whatever measure one uses, income inequality increased in Canada between 1980 and 1998; second, both taxes and transfers served to reduce the extent of inequality below what it otherwise would have been.

Though the annual data are not reported here in table form, we can also observe that until the mid-1990s, the tax and transfer systems served to ameliorate rising inequality in market incomes to some extent (note the relatively flat after-tax line in Figure 1.4); after that time, however, the federal and provincial cuts have reduced the redistributive impact of taxes and transfers, so that inequality has risen substantially in the last few years. These observations are fully consistent with what we have reported above, and serve to summarize the trends in income inequality in simple graphic form.

## WEALTH AND INCOME

While we have reasonably good information in Canada on people's incomes, we know far less about their wealth. The terms 'stock' and 'flow' are used to distinguish these two concepts. Wealth is an asset, the resources from which we can generate a flow of income. Income is what we receive from our economic activity and any government transfers. Our wealth consists of what we possess, such as a house or car, and it is usually viewed as the total value of all assets minus any liabilities or debt. To study wealth we would want to look at both assets and liabilities.

We study incomes regularly, but surveys of wealth in Canada are infrequent. Prior to a 2001 report by Statistics Canada (using data for 1999), the previous survey occurred in 1984. It is important to study wealth because, as Yalnizyan (1998) says, 'in a democracy, the distribution of power is tied to the distribution of wealth' and wealth is far more unequally distributed than is income. Wealth is also a primary means through which inequalities are sustained on an intergenerational basis. In Canada we have had no inheritance tax since 1972; as a result, the wealth that people amass in their lifetimes can be passed on to their children substantially untouched. Government gets nothing directly. Yet the end of one's life is the best time for government to take a modest share to redress some of the more extreme inequalities because (in the words of a friendly accountant) 'arguably, in many cases, the government has done more for individuals through their lifetimes than have their children, yet it is the latter who get it all.' And because wealth can generate a continuing flow of income, wealth will surely amplify existing inequalities of income.

To redress these extreme inequalities of income without some constraint on the wealth that produces income would be difficult indeed. Yet, alone among the OECD (Organization for Economic Co-operation and Development) countries, we do not tax wealth in Canada. The Canadian Centre for Policy Alternatives has estimated that an annual tax of 0.33 per cent on all wealth (total assets) in Canada—compared to a range of 0.35 per cent to 0.74 per cent in the other OECD countries—would generate revenue for government of $3.1 million for the year 2000–2001. Additionally, Yalnizyan (1998) has estimated that if we used the OECD average for taxes on inheritances, it would yield in excess of $2 *billion*. (We note that while a wealth tax could be collected annually, an inheritance tax affects an estate only at the point of death.)

According to Statistics Canada, the total assets of Canadians in 1999 amounted to almost $2.9 trillion.

- The single most important non-financial asset for Canadians was their principal residence, which accounted for about 38 per cent of total assets.
- Approximately 60 per cent of families owned their own homes: among those 55 to 64, the figure rose to three-quarters, while for those under 35, the rate dropped to 36 per cent. Real estate, cars, and home furnishings accounted for 58 per cent of total wealth.
- The most important financial asset was a Registered Retirement Savings Plan (RRSP), which represented 12 per cent of all assets. (The value of employer-sponsored pension plan benefits was not used in this survey to calculate assets.) RRSPs, stocks, bonds, and mutual funds comprised 29 per cent of total assets.
- Total debt of Canadians was $458 billion. Three-quarters of this consisted of mortgages; loans on owned vehicles amounted to about $29 billion, or 6 per cent of the total.
- Student loans (3 per cent of total debt) and credit card debts (also 3 per cent of the total) each exceeded $14 billion.

Overall, Canadians had $16 in debt for every $100 in assets, but the distribution of that debt varied across the population:

- Lone-parent families, most of which are headed by women, had a debt burden of approximately $29 for every $100 of assets, nearly double the national average.
- Younger people experienced the highest levels of debt. Family units headed by a person under 25 owed $31 for every $100 of assets, but the debt burden for those in this age group who didn't own their principal residence soared to $53 for every $100 in assets. Statistics Canada attributes this largely to high levels of student loans.
- Seniors had the lowest levels of debt, primarily because they had paid off most of their debt (including mortgages) while accumulating assets.

The data in Table 1.4 confirm that the wealth of families in Canada is distributed in a highly unequal manner.

- The median net worth of all families in 1999 was $81,000 but the poorest 10 per cent of families were actually in a negative position, with net worth estimated at minus $2,100.
- The highest decile had average net worth of $703,500: more than half (53 per cent) of all wealth in Canada was held by the wealthiest 10 per cent of the population.[5]
- The net worth of the wealthiest decile was on average 335 times that of the poorest decile.

A limited historical perspective was possible between the 1999 findings and those of 1984:

**Table 1.4  Distribution of Net Worth, by Decile, 1999**

| Deciles (family units ranked by net worth) | | Total Net Worth | Median Net Worth |
|---|---|---|---|
| | % | $ | $ |
| All family units | | 100 | 81,000 |
| Lowest | 10 | — | –2,100 |
| Second | 10 | — | 3,100 |
| Third | 10 | 1 | 14,300 |
| Fourth | 10 | 2 | 35,500 |
| Fifth | 10 | 3 | 64,700 |
| Sixth | 10 | 5 | 101,500 |
| Seventh | 10 | 8 | 152,600 |
| Eighth | 10 | 11 | 220,800 |
| Ninth | 10 | 17 | 338,100 |
| Highest | 10 | 53 | 703,500 |

— Amount too small to be expressed.

SOURCE: Statistics Canada (2001).

- Overall median net worth for all family units increased about 11 per cent, from $58,400 in 1984 to $64,600, in constant 1999 dollars.
- This increase was not shared equally by all family units: median net worth of family units in the highest 20 per cent of the population increased 39 per cent to $403,500, while the family units in the lowest 20 per cent of the population remained relatively unchanged. Clearly, the gap in wealth between the richest and the poorest of Canadians has widened dramatically over the 15-year period largely through growth among the wealthy.

# HALF A CENTURY OF SOCIAL WELFARE IN CANADA

A history of the development of Canada's welfare state is detailed elsewhere (Guest, 1997; McGilly, 1998; Black, Bryden, and Strain, 1997; Chappell, 1997; Blake and Kesheny, 1955; Teeple, 1995). We shall focus on a number of specific questions:

- Why did Canadians create a welfare state (1945–73)?
- Why did we thereafter retreat and pull back (1973–98)?
- Where are we now, in terms of social equity, and what has been the role of social programs?
- How does Canada compare internationally in terms of equity and social programs?
- What does the future portend?

## Why Did We Build Our Welfare State?

There are two general reasons why a society would create a social welfare system: the altruism motivation, and the self-interest motive.

### Altruism

Benevolence or mutual caring and a sense of social solidarity and community are held to be part of the how and why a welfare state is created. Often they are discussed in historical terms. The welfare state of Canada was deeply influenced by the British experience, both during the Great Depression and as a result of World War II. Rich and poor alike sought shelter from the German bombing in the London underground when the house of a rich person was as likely to be bombed as the house of a pauper.

The British welfare state was born in 1945 when the voters elected the first Labour government, notwithstanding the massive national debt incurred to win the war. The affordability argument—'we cannot *afford* major social spending'—that became so prominent in later years was nowhere to be seen, in spite of the huge accumulated wartime debt.

This British experience carried over to Canada, where the experience of the Great Depression was still fresh in many people's minds. Senior bureaucrats in the Department of Health and Welfare in Ottawa had studied under Keynes at Cambridge and were deeply influenced by the writings of Beveridge and, in Canada, Leonard Marsh. There was little dissent when the first social programs—Unemployment Insurance and Family Allowances—were introduced in Canada.

In recent years, however, questions have been raised. Reisman (1977), for example, has questioned the unique cause-effect relation between the British war experience and the welfare state; he points out that Scandinavia remained on the periphery of the war, but had highly developed social welfare institutions. America, on the other hand, fought in the war, but had no welfare state. This questioning, then, led to new explanations, based on more structural considerations.

### Self-Interest

The stronger version of the self-interest argument is placed firmly within a structural or Marxist tradition and focuses on the use of power: capitalism, on its own, will necessarily and inevitably widen the gap between the rich and poor. Those who own the means of production exercise power over those who have nothing but their labour. Workers will be paid as little as possible and the surplus value (profit) will be appropriated by the owners (capitalists). The gap gradually widens, as the workers remain at or near subsistence levels, while the capitalists become ever wealthier.

At some point, however, social stability is threatened; the capitalists fear an uprising from the masses of the poor. Hence, there is a need and a rationale for modest social welfare measures, to 'buy off' the workers and maintain social peace. But these social welfare measures will always be provided at the minimum level needed to maintain social stability and, as a result, will never amount to a substantial benefit for the workers. According to Marx, violent revolution, to socialize the means of production and eliminate the capitalists, was the only way to bring about true welfare throughout society.

Many later writers in the same tradition were uncomfortable with the idea of inevitable violent revolution, either because they did not see it looming on the horizon, or because they simply did not like the idea itself. They argued that it was possible to bring about a measure of welfare to the state through the organized actions of workers (trade unions), in a peaceful and non-revolutionary manner.

According to this analysis, capital and labour (unions) in Canada tacitly or explicitly agreed to the 'post-war consensus'. In exchange for providing workplace peace, labour would receive a share of the sustained economic growth that began in 1945. The trade-off, in simple terms, was relative labour harmony in exchange for a share of the continually growing economic pie. For many years thereafter, Canada (outside Quebec, where the forces of nationalism were at play) had little severe labour-management conflict. There were, of course, inevitable disputes over the precise shares of the pie, but as long as the economy was growing, everyone could continue to be better off. Today we would call this a 'win-win' situation.

The Canadian union movement generally supported new social welfare measures as part of the division of the economic pie. Through its formal link with the New Democratic Party (NDP), and, more loosely, with its predecessor, the Co-operative Commonwealth Federation (CCF), the union movement worked for the expansion of social programs, despite some ambivalence about government social welfare initiatives extending to everyone benefits that had been secured for union members through collective bargaining. If benefits were provided to all, the appeal of union membership might decline, and the hard-fought collective bargaining victories would be less appreciated (and less needed) by the rank and file.

## Why Did We Shrink Our Welfare State?

We could begin a discussion of why Canada's welfare state was substantially dismantled after 1973 by arguing that the sense of altruism across the community ended or changed in a fundamental way, or that the post-war consensus came to an end. These are valid, but there are other reasons as well.

### The End of Altruism and Changing Values in Canada?

Though the welfare state programs were cut back dramatically after the 1970s, there is considerable evidence, as reflected in public opinion polls (Lightman, 1991; Conference Board of Canada, 2000), that Canadians continued to want and value their social programs. At the same time, much of the media, several provincial governments, and opposition parties in Ottawa argued strongly in favour of individualism and self-interest and against collective responsibility.

The media in Canada are more tightly controlled than those of any other significant democracy. The message they conveyed through the decades of cutbacks after the 1970s was one of fiscal rectitude, deficit reduction, and cuts in government spending. The backdrop for it all was the supposed imperative of globalization and the need for international competitiveness. In the 1990s, the message began to approximate a moral crusade against government, adopting the American view that government social spending serves only to deny individuals the right to spend their own money as they wish. Greed and self-interest, at the expense of a broader social perspective, came back into style. The media undoubtedly shaped the public discourse and the message was heard by the federal government, which introduced massive tax cuts prior to the 2000 election.

### The End of the Post-War Consensus

The post-war consensus between capital and labour in Canada was premised on an ever-expanding economic pie to be shared by the two parties. However, the 1973 Yom Kippur war between Israel and her Arab neighbours led to dramatic increases in world oil prices, which in turn spelled the end to a quarter-century of economic growth. Suddenly, the economic pie was no longer expanding. A larger share for labour meant less for capital, and vice versa. A 'win-win' situation became a zero-sum game: the gains of the winners equal the losses of the losers. The relations between capital and labour shifted from mutual accommodation to conflict, and in a conflict, power often determines the outcome.

Welfare state programs were a casualty of this shift. With a constant or even shrinking economic pie, no longer was there surplus growth to fund new initiatives, or even to support those already in place. The welfare state came to be seen as an unaffordable luxury.

### The Politics of Federalism in Canada

The election of the separatist Parti Québécois government in 1976 marked a fundamental change in the Canadian federal system. The Liberals, under Pierre Trudeau, moved to redefine federalism in a manner that would be attractive to Quebecers. Removing Ottawa from areas held to be within provincial jurisdiction permitted the provinces to develop their own social programs according to local priorities, and limited the federal role to that of transfer agent, passing on cash and taxation capacity.

The federal Department of Finance also wanted to extricate Ottawa from direct service provision. Ottawa would provide money (and taxation power) so the provinces would be free to deliver services as they wished. The result would be a vastly downsized federal government, with dramatically reduced program responsibility.

Many federal-provincial arrangements for social and health services—the Canada Assistance Plan (CAP), Established Programs Financing (EPF), and the Canada Health and Social Transfer (CHST)—dealt with dollars, taxation capacity, and program parameters. The Social Union Framework Agreement (SUFA) of 1999 was fundamentally different, focusing on process: before Ottawa could introduce a new social program, the approval of at least six provinces was required, including the major players.

While the Prime Minister praised SUFA as a 'new departure', others saw the effect of SUFA as tying Ottawa's hands, effectively ensuring no new social programs would be undertaken on a Canada-wide basis. To put it most bluntly, SUFA essentially ended Ottawa's role as the dominant player in the federal state.

## THE MACROECONOMIC CONTEXT: KEYNES AND AFTER

The Unemployment Insurance Act, implemented in 1941, marked the failure of classical economics (though it was not widely recognized as such). Previously, economists and policy-makers held that labour was a commodity like shoes or apples: if there were shoes that no one wanted to buy, the asking price for shoes was too high; if the suppliers of shoes lowered their prices, all shoes would ultimately be purchased. Likewise, if there was labour that no one wanted to hire (i.e., *unemployment*), the price of labour (*wages*) was too high; if the suppliers of labour (*the workers*) would lower their asking prices (*reduce wages demands*), all labour would ultimately be bought (*unemployment would disappear*).

Through the years of the Great Depression, wage levels dropped in the vain hope of reaching that elusive 'market-clearing' wage at which employers would hire all those seeking work. However, as wages dropped so too did purchasing power, as unemployed workers had no money with which to buy things. The result was not more jobs (as the economists predicted), but fewer jobs, as less and less labour was needed to produce the goods that people could afford to buy.

The Unemployment Insurance Act recognized that the market, left to its own devices, would not create full employment: government had a crucial role in alleviating hardship. In this way, the Act marked the acceptance of Keynesian thinking into policy-making circles in Canada.

## Keynesianism

The work of John Maynard Keynes represented a fundamental transition in economic and political thought. Reflecting on the experience of the Great Depression, Keynes argued that government had a crucial role to play in regulating the economy, as the private market, on its own, would not suffice.

When an economy was plagued by unemployment, Keynes's solution was for government to increase overall spending power in that economy: reduced taxes (leaving people with more money to spend), or direct government spending (buying goods or services). The net effect would be that government would inject more money into the economy. People would have more money, which they would spend, and in turn, jobs would be created to produce the commodities desired. The result might well be an increased government deficit as spending would exceed revenues, but unemployment would thereby be addressed.

When full employment was reached, further increases in spending power could not create additional jobs (by definition, as there was already full employment), and more goods and services could not be produced in the short term. Instead, prices would rise to ration the available goods and services, and wages would also increase, as there were more jobs than workers. The combined effect would be inflationary. Thus, once the point of full employment was reached, additional growth in aggregate demand (overall purchasing power) was undesirable, as it would translate directly into inflation. When full employment was reached and inflation became a threat, government should create a surplus (i.e., draw in more revenue than it spends) by raising taxes and/or cutting direct government spending. This would reduce overall purchasing power in the economy and thereby lessen the inflationary pressure. Over the course of the business cycle, expansion and contraction should roughly offset each other, leading to neither chronic surpluses nor deficits. (This latter statement was an assumption, or perhaps a hope, more than an empirical certainty.)

The economics of Keynes was complemented by the work of Lord Beveridge, who outlined a post-war welfare state for Britain. Today, Beveridge's ideas would be considered incremental, yet, in the context of the times, they represented a great stride forward. The 'Keynes-Beveridge' welfare state produced the new and important social programs that followed World War II.

## The Limits of Keynesianism

The onset of inflation and chronically growing federal deficits in the 1970s revealed serious weaknesses in the Keynesian model. First, Keynes had largely focused on a closed domestic economy, one without substantial foreign trade. He did not particularly consider the impact of externally induced inflation. Yet, after the Yom Kippur war of 1973, dramatic increases in world oil prices, over which Ottawa had no control, led to widespread inflation.

In a time of recession, Keynes's model worked with great effectiveness. The increased demand resulting from massive government spending to fight World War II did, in fact, end the Great Depression, and in the post-war period, Keynesian initiatives were able to prevent a return to the earlier levels of unemployment.

However, during the 1970s, a new phenomenon, *stagflation*—low or stagnant economic growth, accompanied by high inflation—appeared. Government decision-makers frankly did not know how to respond, as Keynes had not addressed the problem of simultaneous unemployment and inflation. Was the central problem unemployment (suggesting increased spending) or inflation (suggesting the opposite)?

By the early 1980s the fight against inflation became the governmental priority, even at the price of increased unemployment. However, governments lacked the political will to either raise taxes or significantly cut spending. The economics of Keynes faltered in Canada on the rocks of political pragmatism and electoral expedience and not because of any conceptual deficiency in the model. After 1984 fiscal policy was dramatically de-emphasized as a regulator of the economy. In its place was put monetary policy, control over interest rates, as determined by the Bank of Canada.[6]

Monetary policy is much simpler and easier to understand. The Bank of Canada has discretion, within a range, to increase or reduce interest rates. Increases in rates make borrowing money more expensive, slowing or stopping a variety of economic activities. Primary among these is construction, as both building activities and sales and mortgage rates are highly sensitive to interest rate changes. Increased interest rates create unemployment, as economic activity slows, which leads to reduced purchasing power and therefore reduced inflation. As the Bank of Canada is to operate at arm's length from the government of the day, short-term political expedience should be a relatively minor concern. Along with this, however, goes a lack of democratic accountability and control when decision-making authority is devolved to a non-elected bureaucracy.[7]

This failure of fiscal policy to severely cut government spending partially protected social programs through the 1970s and 1980s. Programs were cut at the margins, but there was no frontal assault on the welfare state. Monetary policy determined that inflation would be attacked through high interest rates and growth in unemployment, rather than by directly cutting program spending.

## Towards a Balanced Budget

The election of 1993 returned the Liberals to office, with reduction of the federal deficit at the top of its agenda. Paul Martin, the Finance Minister, was determined to use fiscal policy as an effective complement to monetary policy. The sweeping cuts in his 1995 budget represented the final, massive assault on Canada's social programs. Martin combined federal transfers under CAP and EPF into one new federal program, the Canada Health and Social Transfer (CHST). More significant than the organizational arrangement was an associated cut in federal transfers to the provinces of $6–$7 billion annually.

Ottawa eliminated its deficit, but at the direct expense of the provinces, which in turn off-loaded their responsibilities to municipalities and the public at large. Deregulation and privatization increased: costs were cut, but so were service levels in education, health, and welfare.

By the 1998 budget, the deficit was gone. Ottawa was able to claim it had gotten its fiscal house in order, conveniently overlooking the two major contributory factors to the elimination of the deficit—the cuts in transfers to the provinces (which from the perspective of the taxpayer is merely an accounting shift and not a real cut) and the massive surpluses in the Employment Insurance (EI) account (resulting from restrictions on EI eligibility without corresponding reductions in premiums). In each of fiscal years 1997–8 and 1998–9, there was an EI surplus in excess of $7 billion, which was used to help eliminate the federal deficit. Without these EI transfers (which some called 'theft'), neither year would have seen a federal budgetary surplus.

Figure 1.5 shows the dramatic changes in government spending and taxes in Canada over a longer period of time. Of particular importance is the massive drop in government spending after the early 1990s to conquer the deficit. We are still coping with the impact of the huge spending cuts that have resulted in deteriorating services across the country.

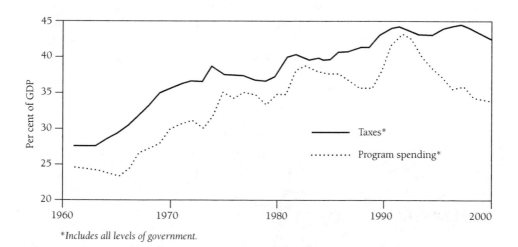

*Includes all levels of government.

**Figure 1.5  Taxes and Government Spending in Canada, 1960–2000**
SOURCE: Canadian Auto Workers (2000).

## Post-11 September

The first federal budget produced after the terrorist attacks in the US of 11 September 2001 clearly reflected new priorities in Ottawa. Most obviously, defence and security concerns took precedence over everything else, comprising the major part of the $7.9 billion in new spending. Quickly put to the side were any social agenda that may have been percolating quietly along with anticipated future tax cuts and debt reduction. Even the prospect of a deficit resulting from all the new spending became an acceptable option.

More interesting for our purposes than the form or direction of the increased spending was the fact that Ottawa was spending once again. Prior to 11 September, there were signs that the Canadian economy, following that of the United States, was slowing down dramatically, possibly heading in the direction of recession. The new spending announced in the 10 December budget would likely serve as an anti-recession measure, injecting spending power into the economy, in the classic Keynesian manner. Just as the massive spending of World War II pulled the world economy out of the Great Depression of the 1930s, so in similar manner the new spending of 10 December could be expected to create growth and stimulate the Canadian economy.

Though it would not be acknowledged as such in Ottawa, the post-11 September budget marked the end of reliance on monetary policy as the primary tool of government economic policy. Repeated interest rate reductions had proven inadequate to counter the forces of looming recession. As well as marking a return to traditional fiscal policy, the budget also nullified the existing conventional wisdom that tax cuts were the only acceptable form of fiscal policy. As we saw earlier, tax cuts and direct government spending may have similar macroeconomic impacts, in that they both inject more spending power into the hands of consumer and businesses, but prior to 11 September, only tax cuts were seen as politically viable.

Had the government chosen to undertake massive new social spending, its actions would have been roundly condemned by the business community and provincial governments. But war makes spending by government not only acceptable, but even essential. And within the classic Keynesian paradigm that spending marks a return to increased government spending, an approach to fiscal policy not contemplated in Ottawa for many years.

Tom Walkom (2001) has observed:

> Martin knows that if he runs a deficit in order to, say, set up a national pharmacare plan, all the usual suspects will hammer him.
>
> But when he runs a deficit trying to protect Canadians from some guy in a cave in Afghanistan, he will receive only praise.

# SUPPLY-SIDE ECONOMICS

Another approach to economic management has been found at the provincial level in Canada—in the *Common Sense Revolution* of Ontario's Conservative Party in 1995, and repeated in *A Fair Deal for British Columbia*, the 2001 election manifesto of the BC

Liberals. Known as *supply-side economics*, the ideas first came to prominence during the Reagan years in the United States, and are based more on ideology than on economics. They argue the desirability of reducing both government spending and taxation by the same amount, a process that would shrink the size of government and simultaneously 'free up' space for the private sector. The assumption is that if government vacates an area, the for-profit sector will replace it, in a way that is more efficient, more effective, less costly, and generally more desirable overall.

The supply-side case is weakened by the fact that it has received no credible professional endorsement. Nor has it been demonstrated anywhere that it can work in practice. Suppose taxes and spending are both cut by one dollar. The spending cut reduces economic activity by a dollar. Offsetting this is the tax cut of one dollar, but not all of this dollar will be spent, as some portion is normally saved; when the tax cut favours the rich (as happened with the immediate post-2001 election cuts in BC), the share of taxes saved will be higher than if the tax cuts favoured the poor (who tend to spend all of any increase in disposable income). As well, the Canadian Centre for Policy Alternatives in BC estimated (CCPA-BC, 2001) that nearly a third of the increase in both employment and GDP resulting from the BC tax cuts would drain away to Ontario, because of the large amounts of goods and services imported from the east.

The result is that equal tax and spending cuts are not neutral, but instead will reduce economic activity overall, as the increased spending resulting from tax cuts is less than the reductions due to the spending cuts. The overall effect is *contractionary*, a process more likely to create recession than growth.[8]

The real attraction of the supply side to its supporters lies not in its economic impact; rather, the appeal is that it reduces the size of the state. The approach is premised on a belief that government should be reduced as an end in itself, and supply-side economics merely offers a superficially attractive vehicle to legitimate the ideology. As an economic theory, the supply-side approach is void, both empirically and conceptually.

# THE INTERNATIONAL CONTEXT

There are two main ways in which countries are compared in terms of their efforts towards creating the welfare state. The first groups into 'clusters' or 'regimes' states containing the same general conditions and compares them. The second compares countries directly, examining specific programs or tax levels (which pay for the social programs).

## Welfare 'Regimes'

The most important recent categorization of welfare states was that of Gosta Esping-Andersen (1988), who presented three welfare state 'clusters' determined by three 'essential criteria': the quality of social rights; social stratification; and the relation of state, market, and family. The three clusters were:

- *Social democratic*: Norway and Sweden, possibly complemented by Denmark and Finland. These countries favoured universalist values.

- *Corporatist*: Austria, France, Germany, and Italy, favouring work-oriented approaches based on individualist values.
- *Liberal*: The United States and Australia, based on the market. Canada was presented as an 'archetypical example' of the liberal model, perhaps by process of elimination. Canada is certainly not a corporatist state; nor a true social democracy.

Any such scheme of categorization is approximate only, and differences within categories can be more important for policy purposes than the differences between groupings. After the publication of Esping-Andersen's work, a number of writers questioned the suitability of placing Canada in the same pigeonhole as the United States (O'Connor, 1989).

Esping-Andersen's analysis was published in 1988, and much has occurred in the intervening years. Canada has moved much closer to the United States, particularly since the Free Trade Agreement. Esping-Andersen's classification of Canada as a pure liberal state was perhaps premature in 1988, but appears to have been largely validated by events since that time.

## Comparing More Precisely

Direct comparisons of countries confirms Canada to be somewhere between the United States and most of Western Europe in terms of its welfare state activity.

Figure 1.6 records government revenues as a share of gross domestic product (GDP) for various countries, from 1984 to 2002 (estimated). Canada ranks almost precisely in the centre. Sweden's is the highest share, well above the other countries at the peak: 60 per cent of total GDP went to government in the form of taxes and non-tax revenues.[9] At the bottom are Japan and the United States. There has been a gradual, but fairly consistent, increase in the share of GDP going in taxes (and non-tax revenues) in the US since 1984, rising from 28.3 per cent to 31.5 per cent estimated for 2002. The trend line for Canada has been fairly constant since 1990, at around 40 per cent, above the average for the entire OECD, but below the estimates for the Euro zone countries (mainly the original members of the European Community, excluding the UK). The downward dip for Canada in the most recent years places us below the UK, reflecting the predicted impact of Canadian government spending cuts along with post-Thatcher increases in the UK under Tony Blair.

Figure 1.7 shows the extent of the so-called 'tax burden'—the total taxes paid (including social security contributions)—for three prototypical single earners in various countries in 1997, the latest year for which data are available. Figure 1.8 provides comparable information for married earners. In Figure 1.7, Canada's tax rate closely approximates that of the United States.[10] In relation to other countries, Canada is at the midpoint, below the Nordic countries but higher than Japan and slightly higher than the UK. For the low-earning single parent with two children, Canada's tax (and social security) rate, at only 4.4 per cent, is among the lowest of all reporting countries. For the married Canadian worker with two children (Figure 1.8), at the average wage, personal taxes amount to 18.2 per cent of gross earnings: this compares to a figure of 19.8 per cent for the G-7 average (the major industrialized countries) and 14.9 per cent average for the OECD countries. Overall, Canada's tax rates are very close to those of the US, above those

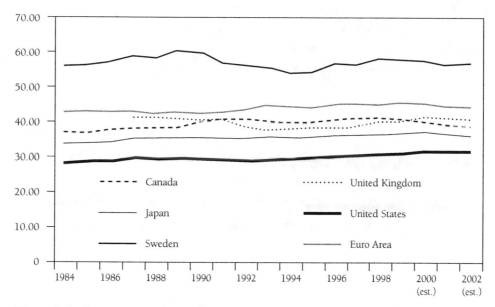

**Figure 1.6  Government Tax and Non-Tax Receipts as a Share of GDP, 1984–2002 (est.), Various Countries**

SOURCE: Derived from OECD (2000a).

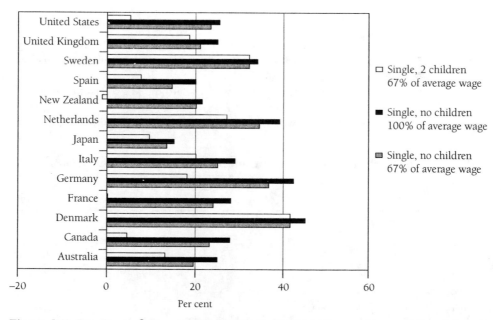

**Figure 1.7  Per Cent of Gross Wage Earnings Paid in Income Tax and Employees' Social Security Contributions, 1997, Single Earner**

SOURCE: OECD (1998).

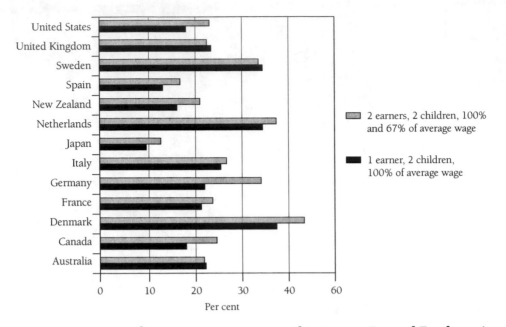

**Figure 1.8 Per cent of Gross Wage Earnings Paid in Income Tax and Employees' Social Security Contributions, 1997, Married Earner**

SOURCE: OECD (1998).

of Japan, but well below those of the major western European countries: the average worker pays 18.2 per cent of gross earnings in Canada, but 25.5 per cent in Italy, 23.5 per cent in the UK, and 21.4 per cent in France.

The evidence does not support the view that Canadians are overtaxed—even in comparison to the United States. Moreover, these tables do not reflect what taxpayers receive in exchange for their taxes, which, in Canada, includes social and health services.

**Table 1.5 Distribution of Income and Child Poverty Rates, Various Countries**

| | Top/Bottom Decile | Bottom as % of Middle | Top as % of Middle | Child Poverty Rate(%) |
|---|---|---|---|---|
| US | 6.44 | 34 | 219 | 22.7 |
| Canada | 3.93 | 47 | 185 | 13.9 |
| UK | 4.56 | 46 | 210 | 17.9 |
| Germany (W) | 3.84 | 46 | 177 | 8.7 |
| France | 4.11 | 45 | 185 | 7.5 |
| Netherlands | 3.05 | 57 | 173 | 4.1 |
| Sweden | 2.78 | 57 | 159 | 2.7 |
| Industrial Country Average | 3.53 | 52 | 181 | na |

SOURCE: Smeeding (1999).

Table 1.5 shows the ratio of the incomes (after taxes and transfers) of the top 10 per cent of the population relative to the bottom decile for a number of developed countries, using data from the Luxembourg income studies. It also shows the incidence of child poverty in each of the countries. Not surprisingly, the income gap is widest in the United States, where the top 10 per cent earn about 6.5 times that of the bottom decile, followed by the UK where the top/bottom ratio is about 4.5. In Canada, the ratio is just under 4, close to that of West Germany, and above the average for the industrialized countries (3.53) but far greater than the Netherlands or Sweden.

In terms of child poverty, Canada has a rate of about 14 per cent, meaning one in seven children lives below the poverty line. This rate is better than that of the US (nearly one in four) and the UK (18 per cent). But Canada lags far behind the other industrial countries, which have made clear policy choices to alleviate child poverty. The rates range from under 3 per cent in Sweden to less than 9 per cent in West Germany.

**Table 1.6**
**National Poverty Rates, Various Countries, Before and After Taxes and Transfers**

|  | All Households | | Two-Adult Working Families with Children | |
|---|---|---|---|---|
|  | *Before* | *After* | *Before* | *After* |
| US | 25.3 | 17.7 | 15.4 | 12.7 |
| Canada | 22.9 | 11.2 | 12.6 | 6.4 |
| Germany (W) | 22.1 | 5.5 | 3.1 | 1.5 |
| France | 34.5 | 8.2 | 18.7 | 2.1 |
| Sweden | 33.9 | 6.5 | 9.6 | 1.4 |

SOURCE: OECD, cited in Jackson et al. (2000: 43).

Table 1.6 shows the national rates of poverty for all households in a number of OECD countries, both before and after taxes and transfers. (Poverty is defined as income less than half the median for the country.) In terms of primary distribution, the poverty rate in Canada, at 23 per cent, is slightly below that of the US (25 per cent), slightly above that of Germany (22 per cent), but significantly less than those of France or Sweden, which exceed one-third. The impact of taxes and transfers make a dramatic difference in each country. In the US, such programs as exist reduce poverty rates by about a third, from 25 per cent of the population to under 18 per cent. In Canada, taxes and transfers cut poverty rates by about half, from 23 per cent to 11 per cent. The Western European countries, however, experience dramatic reductions, clearly the result of conscious policy choices to address poverty. In Germany, France, and Sweden, the rate declines by about three-quarters. The net effect is that the rate of household poverty in Canada at 11 per cent (one in nine households), is significantly better than that of the US, but noticeably worse than the other OECD countries.

# Indicators

Other measures assess the impact of welfare state programs across different countries, without limiting the focus to relative incomes.[11]

### The Human Development Index (HDI)

The United Nations (UN, 2001) produces a Human Development Index (HDI) based on three indicators:

- longevity, as measured by life expectancy at birth;
- knowledge, as educational attainment, measured by a combination of the adult literacy rate and combined gross primary, secondary, and post-secondary enrolment; and
- standard of living, as measured by gross domestic product (GDP) per capita.

The UNDP says HDI is 'a very imperfect measure' and the agency underlines that HDI is only a 'partial' measure of the full scope of human development. Nevertheless, there is a certain prestige attached to a high ranking on the HDI. For several years, Canada was highest, with politicians claiming Canada to be 'the best place in the world to live'. In July 2001, Canada dropped to third place, behind Norway and Australia.[12]

It is important to remember that the HDI records scores on four indicators only, and is not a comprehensive measure of anything. Even these indicators are imperfect: GDP per capita reports on the overall average standard of living, but does not address issues of distribution or equity: average GDP per capita can be high because the rich are very rich and pull up the averages, a situation fully compatible with extensive poverty.

### The Human Poverty Index (HPI)

The United Nations also produces a Human Poverty Index (HPI) in industrialized countries, which 'concentrates on deprivations in four dimensions of human life, quite similar to those reflected in the HDI':

- longevity, as measured by the probability at birth of not surviving to age 60;
- knowledge, as measured by the adult functional illiteracy rate;
- standard of living, as measured by the percentage of people living below the income poverty line;[13] and
- social inclusion, as non-participation or exclusion from society, measured by long-term unemployment.

On the HPI scale, Canada places much lower. Of the 18 industrialized countries for which there is data, Canada places eleventh: one in six Canadians lacks functional literacy skills, and as of 2000, 12 per cent of the population lived below the income poverty line used by the UN.

The two indices together suggest that for those at the top, life is very good, so that the overall averages, as recorded in the HDI, rank very high; however, Canada's poor performance on the HPI suggests there are many who do not share in the spoils of growth and development.

## LOOKING AHEAD

The data that we have just examined suggest several conclusions regarding social programs in Canada: First, the initiatives of our welfare state have led to a distinct narrowing of the gap between rich and poor. Primary distribution of resources and incomes, the result of labour market activity, is highly uneven in any capitalist society and over time, the gap widens. Social welfare measures, consciously introduced, narrow the differentials between rich and poor, and they certainly did so to some extent in post-war Canada.

The retreat from the welfare state, which began after 1973 and continued to the end of the century, widened the gap. In the absence of meaningful social welfare interventions, unconstrained capitalism again rewards the rich and ignores the poor. At the dawn of a new century, Canadians will have to decide if, and in what way, we wish to rebuild social cohesion and narrow the ever-widening gap. In the final chapter of the book, we shall explore some implications for the future.

Chapter 2 develops a theoretical definition of social policy, derived from the literature, and based on the links between economics and social policy. We shall examine the redistributive cycle, emphasizing that the study of social policy necessarily entails attention to both sides of social policy activity. We first ask, 'Who gets what?' (how benefits are delivered, Chapter 4); 'What do people receive and in what form do they receive them?' (Chapter 5); and 'Who receives benefits?' (Chapter 6). Then we focus on payment: 'How do we pay for the activities of the welfare state? Who pays what and in what form?' (Chapters 7 to 9)

To look at only one side—at allocation without regard for generating resources, or at budgetary issues without analyzing how the money is spent—necessarily results in a partial view. It is the hope that this book's look at both sides will result in a fuller understanding of social policy choices in Canada today.

## NOTES

1. The sometimes considerable personal holdings of finance ministers are held in blind trusts, so that they have no direct knowledge of specific investments. At the same time, there is surely an awareness that their personal holdings would inevitably benefit from cuts in capital gains taxes. There is no overt conflict of interest, but rather an indirect class-based conflict.

2. Deciles are important because they report information on income distribution within quintiles: the situation of the richest 10 per cent of the population is very different from that of the 10 per cent below them; likewise, the poorest 10 per cent are significantly behind the second-poorest 10 per cent. By referring to groupings of 20 per cent, the quintiles lose this detailed information—but they are more readily available and for a longer period of history. Yalnizyan's time horizon is different from that in Table 1.1, covering a longer period, from 1973 to 1996.

3. All these terms are defined in the same way as earlier.

4. In general, any changes of 0.01 or greater are deemed to be statistically significant.

5. By way of comparison, the top 10 per cent of families in the United States hold about two-thirds of all personal net worth, according to 1998 US data.

6. Monetary policy is considered by many to be a crude or blunt instrument of policy because it works through changes in interest rates and money supply, which must then filter through

into the economy; fiscal policy, by contrast, is deemed to be more precise in that tax changes can be directed to specific targets.

7. The selection of a Governor of the Bank of Canada in 2000, who had come from the public service, where he had been a deputy minister and worked closely with several cabinet ministers, led to concerns about the Bank's future independence from day-to-day political exigencies.

8. Ontario experienced both tax cuts and growth after the election of the Conservative government. But correlation is not causality: the high growth was a direct consequence of the accelerating growth in the United States, to which the Ontario economy is closely tied. The tax cuts, and supply-side policies, in fact, reduced growth in Ontario below what it would have been by simply 'piggy-backing' on the US experience.

9. Much attention was paid by the world press to the 'retreat' from the welfare state in Sweden. This is shown by the decline in the ratio from 1989 (60.2 per cent) to 1994 (54.0 per cent) and 1995 (54.2 per cent). However, there has been a steady increase since 1994 so that the estimated figure for 2002 (56.5 per cent) is actually greater than that of 1984 (55.8 per cent).

10. US income tax rates are lower in general, but these are offset by high social security payments.

11. Though we do not discuss them here, the UN also produces a gender-related development index (GDI) that uses the same variables as in the Human Development Index, but adjusts them for gender differences; and a gender empowerment measure (GEM), which measures economic power and decision-making, political power and decision-making, and power over economic resources for both men and women. In 2000, Canada ranked eighth in the GEM, with Norway, Iceland, Sweden, Denmark, and Finland holding the top five places.

    Social indicators also are beginning to be used domestically. The Canadian Council on Social Development, for example, has produced a Personal Security Index (PSI) since 1998. This measures annual changes in the security of Canadians in terms of three dimensions: economic, physical, and health security. The PSI is broader than the GDP, and combines both objective and subjective indicators (CCSD, 2001b).

12. This drop was attributable to an increase in the life expectancy rate for Norway and Australia and a small decline for Canada. There was also an increase in educational enrolment for Australia.

13. For these purposes, the income poverty line is defined as 50 per cent of median disposable household income.

# SUGGESTED READING

Guest, Dennis. 1997. *The Emergence of Social Security in Canada*, 3rd edn. Vancouver: University of British Columbia Press.

McGilly, Frank. 1998. *Canada's Public Social Services*, 2nd edn. Toronto: Oxford University Press.

Rice, James J., and Michael J. Prince. 2000. *Changing Politics of Canadian Social Policy*. Toronto: University of Toronto Press.

    The first two of these books are the standard historical studies of the development and structure of social welfare in Canada. They offer the detailed history that is not provided in this text. The third book contains much useful historical information, though the primary focus is not historical.

Jackson, Andrew, and David Robinson, with Bob Baldwin and Cindy Wiggins. 2000. *Falling Behind: The State of Working Canada, 2000*. Ottawa: Canadian Centre for Policy Alternatives.

    This is an excellent and detailed review of major economic and social trends in Canada, written from a progressive perspective. The text is consciously 'data-heavy' to provide a ready reference source, and the authors anticipate that the content will be updated in future on a regular basis.

McQuaig, Linda. 1995. *Shooting the Hippo: Death by Deficit and Other Canadian Myths*. Toronto: Penguin Books.

This book challenges the dominant discourse about the priority for deficit reduction at the expense of everything else.

Statistics Canada, Income Statistics Division. Various years. *Incomes in Canada*. Ottawa: Statistics Canada Catalogue no. 75–202–XIE (electronic version) and Catalogue no. 75–202–XPE (paper version).

This annual report from Statistics Canada contains virtually all the relevant data on the distribution of incomes in Canada. It is essential for anyone interested in income inequality, both current and historically.

Statistics Canada. 2001. *Income Trends in Canada*. Ottawa: Statistics Canada Catalogue no. 13F0022XCB, 21 Feb.

This CD-ROM contains income tables for Canada, 10 provinces, and 15 census metropolitan areas covering the period 1980–98. Its historical perspective is invaluable for examining trends over time.

Statistics Canada. 2001. *The Assets and Debts of Canadians: An Overview of the Results of the Survey of Financial Security*. Ottawa: Statistics Canada Catalogue no. 13–595–XIE

This report contains the first data on the distribution of wealth (assets) in Canada since a previous report in 1984. Wealth is distributed far more unequally than incomes, and it is an area about which we knew little prior to this report.

Swanson, Jean. 2001. *Poor-Bashing: The Politics of Exclusion*. Toronto: Between the Lines.

Written by a long-time anti-poverty activist, this book explores inequalities in Canada, including a discussion of how poverty often is associated with other forms of oppression, such as sexism and racism.

# Approaches to Social Policy

P art II of this book (Chapters 2and 3) develops and explores a new definition of and approach to social policy. In it I question the traditional distinction between economic and social policy, particularly the pervasive assumption that the former is primary, and the latter a secondary add-on.

I shall suggest that rather than social policy being considered a poor relative of economic policy, economic policy should properly be thought of as a subset of social policy. In a broader definition of social policy are incorporated notions of class, gender, race, and age, leading to a structural or systemic analysis of issues such as feminism, ethnicity, and aging. Such a definition is also normatively neutral in that it rejects any idea of necessary or inherent benevolence in social policy.

The dominant paradigms today consistently claim that social policy is less important than economic policy, and represents a drag on economic growth, which is the primary aim of public policy in a market economy. I suggest to the contrary, that conceptually economic policy is but a small subset of a broader social policy, and that the evaluation of economic initiatives should use the same normative criteria as are applied to traditional social programs. Values and choices underlie what we commonly think of as economic policies in the identical manner—they stand at the base of social policies.

I begin with some previous approaches to social policy that place it alongside economic policies. Some of these view the concepts as complementary, in that social policies promote economic growth, while others view them as opposites—social policies represent a drain. But, in all cases, economic growth is the primary goal, while social policy represents an external factor to aid or impede. We also consider the structural approach to social policy using a class-based analysis, in which social programs will be provided only to the minimum extent necessary to ensure the resilience of the capitalist system.

My conceptual definition of social policy distinguishes it from economic policy on the basis of one crucial criterion: while the former is marked by *interdependence* among the members of a group, economic policy is based on *indifference* among individuals. Interdependence can have a positive (or benevolent) vector, which produces the caring and consensual social policies so prominent in the mainstream literature. It can have a negative (or malevolent) vector, which leads to conflict among groups based on variables such as class or race and social policy outcomes marked by opposition and difference. Or, the interdependence can decline until it approaches zero, at which point it becomes indifference, the hallmark of the economic market. Economic policy thus becomes a subset of social policy.

We look at a number of issues arising from our definition, including the difficulty of actually identifying motivations; the meaning of social consensus and the implications of its absence; and the notion of redistribution as found in both economics and social policy. From this we develop a model of redistribution that not only relates to the empirical data on redistribution, which we examined in Part I, but also serves as a guide to the empirical data in Parts III and IV of this book.

In Chapter 3, I further explore the relation of economic and social policy. I give considerable attention to the assumptions and limitations of the *residual* model of social welfare, an approach based on minimal governmental intervention in the economy, and that permeates most 'official' thinking today in Canada. I question the relevance of the market in the social welfare arena—whether all users of social services are *competent* (as the economic market assumes) and whether social services are like other goods and services we buy and sell in the marketplace.

I then look at the role of the family and the voluntary/charitable sectors within the residual model, and explore their crucial role in limiting the responsibilities to be incurred by the state. Work—paid employment—holds an absolutely central role in these discussions, and this as well is examined.

Part II concludes by assessing the overall relevance of the residual model, placing it alongside the *institutional* model of welfare, which is often—but not always—the preferred alternative approach to meeting social needs.

# CHAPTER TWO

# Defining Social Policy

*A society that provides no outlet for man's idealist passions is asking to be torn apart by violence.*

Colin Wilson, 1972[1]

## INTRODUCTION

*Social policy* is a term replete with emotional content but lacking an agreed-upon meaning. To some, social policy represents a form of charitable giving, either by government or individuals, a way by which we help the less fortunate and those who are needy, usually through no fault of their own. To others, social policy is self-help on a grand scale—a community coming together to address common and shared needs and concerns. More critically, social policy is viewed as the means of rewarding the victims of economic growth and mitigating the excesses of unrestrained capitalism: from this perspective, social policies serve as 'insurance' for a backlash against capitalist exploitation.

Social policy can also be a set of values, programs, and practices that bring us together (or, *should* bring us together) as a community, that relate to our shared experience, and that recognize our mutual interdependence. One's well-being is related to another's well-being. At the other end of the spectrum, social policies can be viewed as a set of programs for the poor and vulnerable, designed—depending on one's viewpoint—either to lock people into lives of dependency or to assist, temporarily, those who are dependent, as we direct them towards autonomy and independence.

Many approaches attempt to place social policy alongside economic policy, though the relation between the two is often unclear. Was the decision of the Harris government in Ontario to cut welfare rates by 22 per cent in 1996 an act of economic policy (to cut government spending and reduce the deficit) or a manifestation of social policy (to punish those dependent on the state)? Was the tax cut for the rich on the part of the new Campbell government in British Columbia in 2001 an element of economic policy (to stimulate the economy and reward individual incentive) or social policy (to reward their political constituency and widen the gap between rich and poor)?

For the practitioner, social policy may comprise the specific programs—such as child care or initiatives for the elderly or persons with disabilities—delivered by a particular government department or agency. Typically, the focus is on service delivery. But what about housing or corrections policy or labour-market related activities such as job training or workfare? What about Canada's defence policy, in terms of regional job creation or the impact on a local community of the closing of a military base? Indeed, what about the annual federal budget, the means through which we collectively pay for a wide array of services and programs?

# A LOOK AT SOCIAL POLICY AND ECONOMIC POLICY

## The Iceberg Phenomenon of Welfare

Much of the social welfare literature has not recognized the inter-relation between economics and social policy, as its focus has been on delivering services and meeting needs, without regard to the required financial resources and how they would be generated.

One important exception was a landmark lecture delivered by Richard Titmuss (1956) in 1955. Titmuss compared welfare spending to an iceberg, in which *social welfare* represents the visible tip. Beneath the surface lie the other parts of the iceberg: *occupational welfare* (benefits delivered through employment, such as occupationally based pensions) and *fiscal welfare* (benefits, delivered through the tax system, such as tax relief for RRSP contributions). Like the submerged parts of an iceberg, occupational welfare and fiscal welfare are both larger and less visible than the tip, social welfare.

This analogy suggests that social welfare represents but a small, though highly visible, portion of the total welfare picture. Social welfare spending ostensibly directs benefits from the rich to the poor (though as we have seen in Chapter 1, the reality is more complex). And as social welfare spending is highly visible, it is under constant scrutiny. Yet, the hidden part of the welfare iceberg—the package of occupational welfare and fiscal welfare—is much larger than that of social welfare; moreover, these benefits favour the wealthiest groups more than others as they flow disproportionately up the income scale; as well, they are substantially hidden from public scrutiny.

If all three types of welfare are taken together—the entire iceberg examined—we see that total welfare spending—occupational, fiscal, and social welfare together—redistributes from the bottom towards the top of the income scale.

The iceberg analogy also illustrates that the differences between social welfare and fiscal welfare are merely organizational, administrative, or bureaucratic. Social, occupational, and fiscal welfare can and should be explored within a common conceptual base and using the same analytic tools.

The implications of this analysis could have been quite radical had the ideas been developed further in later literature. Such an approach might have led to the early incorporation of economic policy and the tax system as central to the broader conception of social policy. Unfortunately, however, Titmuss returned to his earlier work on the personal social services, the tip of the iceberg. Though he guided the development of social administration for another 20 years, Titmuss had little more to say about the submerged part of the iceberg.

In Canada, David Lewis, a leader of the federal NDP in the 1970s, eloquently talked of 'corporate welfare bums', thereby turning public debate back towards Titmuss's iceberg. The massive tax savings received by holders of RRSPs and private pensions, and their profoundly regressive impact (Chapter 7) attest to the continuing relevance of Titmuss's occupational welfare. And today, in the context of rampant capitalism in Canada, it is hard to miss both the size and implications of a 'welfare iceberg' that has such a tiny social welfare component directed towards those at the very bottom.

## The Public Burden Model

A common approach to social policy is the 'public burden' model of welfare. Rooted both in the assumptions of capitalism and an American national ideology of individualism, it stresses the primacy of economic growth in public life.[2] Anything that interferes with this growth—specifically, welfare spending—must be firmly restrained. Public intervention may modify slightly the role of the economic market, but it can change nothing basic. A belief in a fundamental incompatibility between goals of equity and economic efficiency[3] leads to the assumption that welfare costs slow the engine of economic growth; social policy is the brake, which may be acknowledged as necessary, but only to be used abstemiously on the freeway of economic progress.[4]

Growth per se is considered to be a good thing: if the economic 'pie' gets larger, everyone can share in the new growth. This process is known as *trickle-down*, the assumption being that if governments promote economic growth, the benefits will ultimately filter down through all strata of society. Therefore, government policies to redistribute are both unnecessary and inefficient.

However, this view is weakened by the lack of empirical evidence to suggest that major benefits do actually trickle down. As we have seen, the last 25 years in Canada have been dominated by a market ideology promoting growth and a substantial retreat from the welfare state: the effect has been to widen the gap between rich and poor, creating more than a trickle (or even a cascade) and *up* rather than down.

## The Handmaiden Model: Investment in Human Capital

An alternate approach views social policy and economic policy to be complementary, and is often known as the *handmaiden* approach—Titmuss labelled it the *industrial achievement performance model*. From this perspective, economic policy is still primary; but social policy, rather than being a drag on growth, is viewed as conducive to and supportive of economic development. Expenditures on social policy can contribute to promoting economic growth, which remains the ultimate goal. That ever-growing 'pie', to be shared by all, remains the central image.

'Investment in human capital' is commonly spoken of in this context. Though the terminology implies the commodification of people, it was consciously chosen to reflect the parallel between investing in machines and investing in people. The essence of both investments is expenditure today in the expectation of a return tomorrow: just as we invest in a machine (physical capital) because we assume a return on this investment in the future, so too can we invest in people today (human capital) on the assumption of a return tomorrow. Indeed, much literature suggests that the financial returns to investing in people can far exceed those on investment in machines. Public investment in such human capital projects as public education, training, and child care yield consistent and dramatic long-term returns. The returns from public investment in basic literacy are, in purely financial terms, vastly greater than that on any other form of public spending.

The costs of investment in human capital are often immediate and relatively easy to measure. The returns accrue over time and are less amenable to ready measurement, but include (among many non-quantifiable indicators) the contribution to economic growth resulting from a more highly trained and more productive workforce.

Much social policy activity can be justified within the 'handmaiden' concept: for example, *Transitions* (Ontario, 1988), the only comprehensive review of social assistance conducted in Ontario, argued the case for higher welfare spending almost entirely in terms of investment. Rather than seeing welfare as supporting recipients in lives of dependence, *Transitions* viewed spending as investment, giving recipients the resources and skills to 'graduate' from social assistance to lives of independence and autonomy. These ideas became grotesquely distorted in later *workfare* programs in which recipients had to participate in meaningless make-work activities. The potential long-term benefits to individuals and to society from investment in education and training were lost in what became highly politicized programs to blame the poor.

A major difficulty with the handmaiden thesis is that if return on spending becomes the primary criterion for the allocation of resources, those groups from whom there is little or no return will tend to lose out. Thus, for example, young people or single mothers may do quite well, but the returns on disabled or elderly people can be small; or, severely alcoholic or addicted individuals may never generate any return on spending and therefore may be excluded from spending initiatives.

The Victorian Poor Laws (and the Elizabethan Poor Laws before them) distinguished between the 'deserving' and the 'non-deserving' poor, based in part on a morality of merit or worth. In essence, the handmaiden thesis re-creates this distinction, posited in terms of return on investment. The 'deserving' groups are now those from whom we can expect a return on our investments; the 'non-deserving' others can be symbolically or operationally consigned to some modern equivalent of the workhouse.

## Accumulation and Legitimation

Within the Marxian tradition there is a fundamental ambivalence about the state and in whose interest it acts, i.e., the 'relative autonomy of the state' (O'Connor, 1973). It is argued that the state acts in the interests, though not always at the behest, of the capitalist class or bourgeoisie. The role of the state is to foster conditions conducive to economic growth, which creates a surplus or profit appropriated by the bourgeoisie: this is the *accumulation* function of the state. However, the state must also ensure certain minimal levels of worker acquiescence to the existing economic order. This may require the state to carry out some notion of a broader social will. These *legitimation* activities, as they are called, will always be the minimum needed to prevent social unrest and the development of a working-class consciousness. Social expenditures are a burden, in that they reduce the surplus profits that would otherwise result from economic growth. Saville has described legitimation as 'the price to be paid for political security'.

There are practical difficulties in distinguishing legitimation from accumulation activities of the state. Is public spending on quality child care an investment in a healthy and productive future workforce? Or is the goal merely to maintain public quiet with the illusion that the state responds to the needs of the working class?

Often, social expenditure is viewed as serving legitimation goals and, as such, must be severely checked; social workers in their gatekeeper function often serve the purpose of limiting access to social spending and benefits (Mullaly, 1997; Carniol, 2000). However, Canada is an internationl anomaly, in that, historically, much government spending has been on accumulation. Panitch (1977) has argued persuasively that throughout Canadian history an active interventionist government has been the norm. From the early development of Canadian Pacific Railway through to the introduction of medicare, it has primarily served the accumulation needs of the bourgeoisie.

Some have argued that a state-run medical care scheme, free at the point of use, responded more to the needs of capital than to an ideal of collective caring. A healthy workforce is a productive workforce, and a healthy workforce can be generated at minimum private cost in a system in which the costs are not borne by individual employers as benefits to workers, but instead are passed on to the state and in turn to taxpayers. Unemployment insurance through much of its history ran large annual deficits, which Ottawa covered out of general revenues, thereby enabling employers to pass on the financial cost of a redundant workforce. The costs are socialized—passed to the state— to be collected through a tax system in which capital pays a very small share.

This ambivalence has led commentators (Gough 1981, 1999; Collier, 1997) to argue that the legitimation function may yield identifiable gains even under capitalism, as a result of pressure on the state through the organized efforts of working-class unions and their allies. Mullaly (1997) and Carniol (2000) both have shown how social workers can serve an important role in exercising this pressure. Through its legitimation function, the state will respond to group pressure (from unions) and implement, in part at least, the collective will—that which benefits working-class citizens and their allies. Others, arguing from a more traditional Marxist perspective, claim that such gains are inevitably trivial and illusory and that under capitalism the fundamental role of the state will always be to serve the interests of the propertied class. Only by fundamentally changing the structures of the state can the interests of the working class predominate, establishing true welfare within society.[5]

## BUILDING A DEFINITION: 'SOCIAL' AND 'POLICY'

Though we have seen a number of approaches towards social policy, the most useful definition, for our purposes, builds on Richard Titmuss's (1974) simple treatment of the term.

*Policy implies choice*, decision-making within a range of feasible alternatives. As Titmuss (1974) indicated many years ago, we have no policies about the weather as we are powerless to do anything about it: But we make choices—and therefore have policies—about how, or if, we respond to social concerns, from unemployment to homelessness to the environment. To do nothing, to leave the status quo in place, is a choice also and therefore a policy decision.

There are no inexorable imperatives on the public agenda. The mania to rapidly eliminate the deficit, which swept across Canada in the 1990s, was a value-based determination of priorities by economic and political elites, not some absolute. We, as a society, could have chosen not to eliminate the deficit, or to have done it more gradually. Each alternative—including the one that was chosen—carries with it consequences and costs. Different value systems lead to different weightings of benefits and costs. *Policy implies choice. There are always alternatives.*

Describing a social program as *unaffordable* means only that we are not prepared to raise the necessary revenues, either by raising taxes or by giving up something else; the *unaffordable* program simply resides far down our subjective list of social priorities.

Equally crucial, choice presupposes resources: we are all free to dine at the Ritz or to drive a Porsche, but some of us are freer to do so than are others. Choice without the resources to act on the choice is only theoretical choice, and theoretical choice, it may be argued, is not actual choice. Real choice—and hence, policy—is inextricably linked with prior decisions about the allocation of resources.

The term *social* is considerably easier to explicate for present purposes. Titmuss identified 'social' as the group, community, or collective with respect to which decisions or choices are made. If we combine the notion of *policy* as choice, and the definition of *social* as a group of two or more persons, we derive our working definition of *social policy*.

> *Social policy refers to choice or decision-making, with respect to some group, community, or collective (defined as two or more individuals).*

This definition contrasts with other decision-making processes, such as those of the private market, in which only individuals and their own needs are incorporated.

## Social Policy and Economic Policy

Our exploration of social policy proceeds by comparing and contrasting social policy to what we commonly view as economic policy. We begin our discussion by first considering a number of key assumptions that underlie the traditional economic market[6] and constitute the conceptual basis of traditional neo-classical economics. In Chapter 1, we read that these assumptions were applied during the Great Depression and failed to bring about the promised economic recovery. We now look more formally at these assumptions, although it is important to appreciate that these assumptions refer to a theoretical model only.

## The Assumptions of the Economic Market

*The focus of classical economics is on the individual.* In the absence of coercion, individuals freely engage in exchange relationships in which they buy and sell in the expectation that their well-being[7] will be enhanced. A group is nothing more than the sum of a number of individuals. Decision-making reflects the needs, wants, preferences, and resources of individuals.

*The model assumes a large number of buyers and sellers, with no individual able to exercise power over another.* This is known as the assumption of competitiveness. Prices cannot be set by any individual or group of individuals in collusion, because of the large numbers involved. Prices are the aggregate result of individual decisions of buyers and sellers, resulting from the impersonal workings of the market.

*Individuals pursue their self-interest and act to maximize their own well-being.* This follows directly from the foregoing assumption. Individual decisions can have no impact on the market due to the large numbers of buyers and sellers. Therefore, it is rational to tend one's own interests without particular regard to others. This is the assumption of *indifference*. Buyers and sellers have no feelings or interest—positive or negative—towards others in the market. Each is fundamentally *indifferent* (neutral) about others with whom she or he is considering a value-free transaction. If I have money, you have an apple and I am hungry, we may trade, provided no one else will give me more apples or a bigger or shinier apple for my money, and no one will give you more money for your apple. Both of us are merely seeking the best terms of exchange in order to maximize our own well-being.

*Individuals are assumed to be competent, i.e., to have both information and mobility.* *Information* implies full knowledge of the prices prevailing in the market, and what is being offered and of what quality. Will others selling apples offer them to me on better terms? Just how good is that apple you are offering? Are apples cheaper elsewhere in town? *Mobility* assumes that individuals are able to seek out and secure the best prices: if an apple is being offered more cheaply across town, it is assumed people can physically get there.

These conditions ensure that a single price will prevail in the market for a given quality of product. If a comparable apple is being sold more cheaply on the other side of town, buyers will know about it and easily and quickly get there to purchase it. Prices across town will then rise in order to ration the available supply. As there will be fewer buyers on this side of town, the price of apples here should drop. In due course, prices in the two locations will meet somewhere between the two original prices, and a single price will be in effect everywhere (allowing for differences attributable to transport and distribution costs).

It is clear that these assumptions are not always (some would say, rarely) upheld in practice. The best 'real world' pure market is a stock exchange, though even here the power of fund managers, the use of program trading, and the selective dissemination of information render it far from pure. A crucial question, then, is what, if anything, happens when such theoretical market assumptions do not relate to the real world. Does it matter? Are the assumptions crucial or can we modify—or even abandon—them? We return to this issue later.

## Indifference and Interdependence

To pursue our definition of social policy, we reiterate one of the central assumptions of classical economics: *indifference*, i.e., individualized decision-making, in which individuals act only with respect to their own needs, wants, or interests: A does not act in support of or in opposition to B, but pursues his[8] own goals, essentially indifferent to

B's existence. Social policy, by contrast, refers to collective decision-making, based on the needs and priorities of more than one person: there is some notion of 'group' such that A is no longer indifferent to B. Instead, A's choice must acknowledge and incorporate the fact of B's existence. This is known as *interdependence*.[9]

The major conceptual distinction between social policy and economic policy is the presence or absence of *indifference* and *interdependence*. Interdependence is not relevant to the economic market, as individuals are assumed to be autonomous. The unit of decision-making is the individual. The collective well-being is the sum of the well-being of all individuals, and is maximized when the individual's well-being is maximized. There is no community or society other than as the totality of its individuals. This view is epitomized by an infamous observation of former British Prime Minister Margaret Thatcher to the effect that there is no such thing as a society: there are only individuals and their families.

Supporters typically argue that the indifference of the market represents one of its greatest virtues. No one can understand what another individual wants or needs and to intervene on someone else's behalf is paternalistic and offensive. Such subjectivity in decision-making is highly capricious and therefore undesirable.

The opposing, traditional approach to social policy extends 'interdependence' beyond the simple recognition of another's existence, to a collective response to need. David Gil (1976), for example, has presented an 'underlying humanistic egalitarian democratic philosophy' as the basis to understand social policy.

Yet, a careful reading of our definition of social policy makes clear there is no inherent need for benevolence. Interdependence does not presuppose that A expresses or feels a positive concern for B or B's needs. Indeed, A might acknowledge B in order to exploit or exercise power over B. In other words, interdependence, which is crucial to our definition of social policy, can have either a positive or negative moral vector. Individuals can be motivated by concerns either of support and compassion, or of malevolence and exploitation. What distinguishes positive from negative dimensions of social policy is the motive for action that follows from the recognition of interdependence, the purpose for which A incorporates B's existence into A's decision-making.

Figure 2.1 presents a continuum of the motives for interaction among individuals. At one end of the spectrum, where individuals have positive or supportive feelings for one another, we see what has been labelled as the 'social conscience' theories of social policy. These follow in the mainstream tradition of Richard Titmuss.

Along this continuum, positive feelings weaken as we approach the centre, and cross to negative motivation, leading to conflict or exploitation (of individual or group). This approach is premised on social relationships being based on power, and a belief that those who have power use it to benefit themselves at the expense of others. One analysis based on the relative power of competing groups is a class analysis within the Marxian tradition; however, other conflict models also arise, based on gender, age, race, ability, sexual orientation, region, and nationality or immigrant status. This is an important step, because it suggests that studies in feminism, (dis)ability, anti-oppressive practice, and gerontology all can be approached from a common conceptual starting point, using a systemic or structural analysis within a social policy framework.

Motives Underlying Interdependence

| Negative | Indifferent | Positive |
|---|---|---|

| Malevolent (conflict) | Indifferent | Benevolent (consensus) |
|---|---|---|
| Social policy | Economic policy | Social policy |

**Figure 2.1  The Motives Underlying Interdependence**

Much early work in feminism, for example, challenged the ideas of Freud and his followers. But for many years now, feminism has used gender as a fundamental structural variable with which to analyze society. Studies in anti-oppression (Mullaly, 2002) probably always have been directed towards a structural analysis. Gerontology, on the other hand, is still often wedded to individual clinical studies of social functioning and pathology emerging from the medical model; the idea of ageism as a basic structural variable with which to approach a social analysis still commands limited (though rapidly increasing) interest. Work that combines more than one variable—as, for example, that of Cohen (1984) in her early and powerful study of women and aging—doubles the potential for a powerful structural analysis of intra-familial and intergenerational exercise of power.

There is, conceptually, a unique point along the continuum, where the motivation changes from positive to negative—a point at which the interdependence among individuals is mathematically equal to zero. There occurs a single point of transition where feelings among individuals are indifferent, neither positive nor negative. This point has been defined as the economic market, in which individuals pursue self-interested goals without concern—positive or negative—for others.

That there may be a point of zero interdependence is of crucial importance to our analysis. If there is a point at which interaction among individuals becomes zero (or indifference), that point is the basis of the economic market. Market exchange may thus be considered to be a subset of a more general social-policy exchange relationship. If the interdependence is based on feelings that are positive or negative, the exchange will be within the traditional social policy framework. However, if the feelings are of indifference, the exchange will occur within the economic market subset within the broader social policy universe.

Table 2.1 summarizes our analysis to this point. Social policy is a broad umbrella, of which one particular form is economic policy. The unit of analysis in mainstream economics is the individual, while that of social policy is the group (two or more individuals). The motive for the interaction in social policy is interdependence, which can be positive or negative (benevolent or malevolent). There is a point of zero interdependence or indifference, at which individuals, by definition, pursue their own self-interest. This constitutes the economic market.

**Table 2.1  A Summary of the Relation between Economic Policy and Social Policy**

|  | Economics | Social Policy |
|---|---|---|
| Unit of Analysis | Individual (n=1) | Group (n ≥ 2) |
| Motive for Interaction | Self-Interest | Interdependence |
| Nature of Interaction | Indifference to Others | Benevolent or Malevolent |

# ISSUES ARISING

Many issues, both conceptual and operational, arise from this approach to social policy.

## 1. Motives Are Hard to Determine

Attempting to identify the motives for social interaction—to distinguish between the benevolent, selfless, or altruistic act (the 'gift') and the self-interested or 'selfish' deed (the 'exchange')—is central to separating the benevolent social policy from the malevolent and the social from the economic. Is it possible to determine the reasons for interactions among individuals? Is a truly selfless act possible, or do self-interested motives lurk beneath the surface? Can we empirically identify these motives and can we draw meaningful distinctions between them?

Mainstream economics operates on an *a priori* assumption of indifference among individuals, so there is no particular interest in the motives for interaction. Individuals undertake exchange in order to enhance their well-being; otherwise they would not willingly engage in the interaction. Therefore, all exchange is self-interested, based on indifference, not benevolence or malevolence.

Researchers in psychology have attempted to explore the motives underlying altruism, a selfless act by one individual on behalf of another. They have investigated minor acts that are essentially costless to the individual performing them, such as an individual's readiness to give street directions or the time of day to an anonymous stranger. Other studies have tried to determine the motivation for donating a kidney, potentially a life-endangering act of benevolence.

In mainstream social policy the seminal work on altruism is undoubtedly Richard Titmuss's *The Gift Relationship* (1970), which attempted to determine why people willingly donate blood to some anonymous 'other' without compensation or direct reward—a 'middle-level' altruism in which there is an identifiable but small cost to the donor. One of Titmuss's goals was to argue the superiority of a voluntary donation-based system for both the giving and the receipt of blood. He compared this approach, used in Canada, Britain, and most other industrialized countries, to market-based systems of blood procurement used in the United States, where donors are paid for blood and users must purchase, replace, or privately insure.

Titmuss claimed that people have an altruistic predisposition—that they are ready to do an unreciprocated act of goodness for an anonymous 'other'. It was the task of social policy, he said, to provide the structures and framework within which people would be free to carry out their altruistic tendencies.

Later work (Lightman, 1981) looked specifically at lapsed donors in Toronto—those who had given blood at least once but then failed to return—and attempted to assess the quality or depth of this altruistic commitment. The data did reveal altruism or selfless motivation among those who chose to give blood, but found that this commitment was relatively weak: the basic readiness to give blood subsequent to a first donation was contingent upon favourable contextual factors—ease of donation, convenience of location and time, etc.

Blood donation as a prototype of an altruistic act of social policy has been challenged on the same grounds as were the psychological studies—namely, inference from a single case. While a useful and interesting contrast between private markets and non-market-based approaches, the wider applicability of the blood donation findings remains in question. Blood is seen by many as something that simply *should not* be a commodity, bought and sold like a pair of shoes. For practical and occasionally mystical reasons, people deem the donation of blood to be an opportunity to exercise civic and social responsibility, without undue cost to the donor.

These challenges carry substantial weight, and one is hard pressed to find another comparable case beyond blood donation. Even this one approach, if generalized, suggests welfare principles of private philanthropy, the individualized charity model.

Others have challenged this work more fundamentally, arguing that empirical research neither confirms nor negates any information about motives. Lightman (1982a, 1982b) used three different data collection methods (triangulation) to address the issue of validity or candour in response: we may say one thing but mean another. Individuals may donate blood out of enlightened self-interest, feeling that if they give today someone else will give tomorrow when they have need: a seemingly altruistic act becomes at least partially an exchange relationship. Today's 'gift' has become an investment or exchange in which people give blood today in order to get it back tomorrow (the insurance principle). As well, motives can be multiple or unconscious, and people may not know why they perform an act of altruism. People may give 'charity' for no reward or because they value the tax receipt, or related to their ethical or religious beliefs. They may also see this act as a way to prevent unrest in the streets and to maintain the social status quo (*to avoid social conflict*). As a group, donors may exact certain good behaviours from recipients in exchange for their 'gifts' (*social control*).

In Figure 2.1 the motives are presented along a continuum. Yet motives are rarely so unambiguous; motivation, both latent and manifest, is complex. While simplification may be necessary for analytic purposes, if most motives are a mixture of self-interest and altruism, what is the effect on the analysis?

If the existence of an altruistic motive cannot be empirically determined or denied, one falls back on assumption. Just as classical economics is based on an assumption of indifference, social policy can build on the assumption that people act from motives of altruism or malevolence, at least in part. The traditional literature does not argue or assume that people are motivated solely by altruistic concerns. Benevolent social policy chooses to focus on the development of social structures that will enable people to actualize their altruistic potential.

## 2. Social Consensus and the State

A central assumption underlying the development of the post-war welfare state was a broad societal consensus for social progress, but that was more than half a century ago. Since then, the notion has been questioned, both conceptually (Is it possible to think of society as an organic unity?) and practically, as memories of the Great Depression and the World War II bombings fade.

Conditions that lack a broad societal consensus have given rise to a conflict model of social policy: two or more groups in opposition to one another. Each group may experience internal cohesion based on common interests, such as economic class, gender, or age, but there is no overall social unity among the groups. Perhaps the very essence of feminism, anti-ageism, anti-ableism, anti-homophobia, and anti-racism is the belief that society is not a single unified body, but is instead comprised of disparate and often competing interests, in which some have power and the rest do not.

The need for broad social consensus explains the intense focus on social solidarity and social integration as essential to the development of a benevolent social policy. Kenneth Boulding (1967) in an important article more than 30 years ago, attempted to distinguish social policy from economic policy by arguing that the former was inherently an integrative system centred in institutions that create integration and hence consensus. The goal of social policy, in Boulding's view, is to foster integration and to discourage alienation, for the latter leads to the individualism and self-interest of the economic market.

A fundamental and operational challenge to the notions of social consensus focused on the role of public servants (including social workers) as agents of the state, mandated to implement social consensus. Studies have shown that public-sector managers pursue multiple goals, only some of which relate to the implementation of a consensual social will. Public servants may seek to increase the size of their departmental budget or the number of staff under their control, for example. As large organizations grow ever larger, they may tend to be increasingly driven by internal imperatives and less by an obligation to an increasingly remote outside world.

Perhaps the most powerful critique of the role of public servants (and politicians) emerged from the far right of the political spectrum, though others quickly jumped on board. Politicians, it was argued, aided by compliant public servants, make endless promises to the voters at election time, without adequately determining how these promises are to be paid for, i.e., they meet their own political and bureaucratic needs at the expense of the public good—if, in fact, the 'public good' exists for them apart from that which will win the next election.

The result is what O'Connor, writing in 1973 from the left, described as the 'fiscal crisis of the state': unrestrained state spending, in combination with an inability or unwillingness to tax sufficiently to pay for it. Increasing deficits would lead to loss of confidence in the economy and ultimately the complete breakdown of the economic and social system.

## 3. Redistribution and Economics

Mainstream economics is largely based on assumptions of benign self-interest and indifference to others: unless coerced, individuals engage in exchange relationships only if they perceive their well-being will be enhanced. The personal motives underlying such exchange are of no concern. Yet, much interaction among individuals and groups does not support this 'win-win' scenario—the essence of taxation, for example, is that A gains, but at the expense of B. Such redistribution in which both parties do not consider themselves better off creates an analytical dilemma for classical economics.

A common response is simply to declare redistribution as beyond the scope of the economist, and within the realm of the politician: redistribution is not relevant to the analysis of the economist. Clearly, such a response is inadequate for our purposes, as the very interactions that the economist does not want to deal with are to us of central interest.

A second response is to claim that there is no such thing as an unequal exchange as donors always receive some benefit, though perhaps it is intangible. If individuals choose to perform acts of charity or benevolence, the well-being of the donors is assumed to be enhanced by the giving; otherwise, they would not become involved.[10]

There is a recognized stream within mainstream economics that addresses issues of redistribution and well-being, though this is not central to the profession.[11] For example, the Pareto condition refers to a situation in which someone is better off and no one is worse off as a result of redistribution. This is referred to as a *Pareto preferred position* and might involve the redistribution that results from economic growth or organizational restructuring—provided that no one was ultimately worse off in absolute terms. These Pareto conditions clearly reflect very weak redistribution, in that the only requirement is that no one becomes worse off in absolute terms.[12] Equity in the broader sense is not addressed.

David Collard (1981) attempted to incorporate altruism into a standard economic analysis and to develop 'non-selfish economics' for 'rational economic man'; Collard *assumes* there is a residue of truly altruistic behaviour 'when all else has been separated out' and it is on this residue that he chooses to focus.

We previously considered an approach to social policy that assumed some altruistic component within human motivation. Collard, proceeding from mainstream economics, makes essentially the same assumption. Blending them, we may suggest that the typical motivation for interaction between individuals contains two coexisting elements, self-interest and altruism. While traditional economics focuses on the 'self-interest', social policy as we have conceptualized it would deal with the other, altruistic element.

### Benefit-Cost Analysis

A little further from traditional economics is benefit-cost analysis (BCA). The unit of analysis for BCA is the group or community rather than the individual of the economic market. BCA attempts to measure and weight the gains and losses of a proposed activity from the perspective of the community. Consider, for example, a factory that expels pollutants into the environment, the effects of which are felt only hundreds of miles away. In the traditional analysis of the firm, the damage need not be considered by the polluter, either for reasons of legal immunity or because it is not possible to trace the source of the pollution. This outcome is called an 'externality': the consequences of some actions are external (and therefore considered irrelevant) to the concerns of the doers. Externalities, which can affect persons positively or negatively, reflect costs borne by those who had no role in the decision that created the externality.

In a benefit-cost analysis, however, the interests of those downstream would be incorporated into the calculations. The question would be posed in terms of whether, on a community-wide basis, the benefits of the industrial activity outweigh the costs. This is known as an attempt to 'internalize the externality'.

In practice, benefit-cost analysis is difficult. Explicit decisions have to be made as to the relative weightings assigned to various interests. Many benefits and costs are hard to measure in a way acceptable to all parties. But for our purposes, it is the concept that is important; in its focus on a group rather than the individual, benefit-cost becomes a useful empirical methodology within a social policy framework.

## 4. Redistribution and Social Policy: The Goals

Because redistribution within the economic market occurs impersonally, as part of the exchange process, one need not consider its rationale, or goals. Within overtly normative social policy, however, both the rationale and goals of the redistribution must be scrutinized. Outside the market framework, the assumed interdependence of individuals allows—or demands—the pursuit of a wider range of overtly normative goals.

In this section, we consider some common goals underlying benevolent social policy. The language is familiar in daily discourse, but the meanings are not always clear. The most common goals traditionally include 'the meeting of needs', the pursuit of equity or equality and the more recent idea of social inclusion.

### Equity

There is an extensive literature in language and political philosophies that explores the meanings and implications of terms such as *equity, justice,* or *fairness.* Since the days of ancient Greece at least, we have attempted to develop absolute definitions, standards, or criteria by which specific situations can be determined to be *fair* or *equitable.* The debates are interesting, but are not particularly helpful in a discussion of redistributive goals within our social policy framework. All are prone to definitional ambiguity, with the result that one's use of 'fairness' or 'equity' often simply reflects one's personal value system.

In practical terms, *equity* often relates to experience in the workplace and tends to be relatively conservative, though there is no necessary reason for this. *Employment equity,* for example, essentially means an absence of barriers or impediments to employment and a requirement for fair or comparable treatment to all candidates for employment or promotion. Thus used, the term imposes no active requirement on employers to seek out candidates. Neither does it deal with existing or historical distribution of jobs, nor how equity is to be measured in a specific context. The approach would simply restrict employers from using discriminatory practices regarding those who appear in the workplace.

Similarly, *pay equity* essentially means 'equal pay for work of equal value' and once again employers are merely precluded from rewarding employees in unfair or discriminatory ways. Pay equity often uses job evaluations to assess actual job content to prevent 'inequities'. Comparisons are most effective when made within one setting. Problems arise when jobs such as nursing are predominantly of one gender and it becomes necessary to look to other jobs for comparability.

### Equality

The term *equality* conveys a greater sense of mathematically equivalent outcomes and is therefore a more controversial concept than equity. But equality also carries its own ambiguities in definition and measurement.

Some have questioned the desirability of equality as a goal for the redistributive activities of social policy. Others accept the general goal, but founder on the shoals of measurement and interpretation, for the term itself is subject to interpretation: equality can refer to process or substance; it can refer to opportunities or to outcome; and it can be measured empirically in various ways. Equality can be defined so that it protects the status quo or it can represent a radical agenda for change.[13]

At its most restrictive, equality refers to process and opportunity. Formal equality before the law provides the framework of certainty that is essential for the functioning of a market economy. Barriers must not prevent access to the law, under which all individuals must formally and without regard to personal characteristics be treated the same.

*Equality of opportunity* ensures that all individuals have the same chance in any setting and is intended to make the market work better. In the workplace, for example, it attempts to eliminate such extraneous and subjective considerations in employment decisions as an employer's preference to hire a less productive employee who is male or white over a more productive female or member of a minority group. Anti-discrimination legislation, the cornerstone of equality of opportunity, seeks to make the market work better by ensuring that hiring, compensation, and promotion are based solely on criteria of productivity. Blanket discrimination such as the exclusion of women from construction jobs would be prohibited as employers would be required to assess the capacity of specific individuals of both genders to perform specific tasks. Group exclusion, on any criteria, would not be permitted.

On occasion, the equal opportunity approach may sanction or require certain interventions. For example, this model would endorse Head Start programs for pre-school children, to offset a disadvantaged home life and to improve young children's personal skills and abilities in order to function better in a market economy. The goal would be to provide all children entering school with roughly the same chances and choices. Some children will work harder than others, due to innate differences in motivation, and some will ultimately be more 'successful'; but uneven economic outcomes are acceptable— *provided the starting line was the same for all*. This is an approach traditionally favoured by political conservatives.

Should a lack of child care be identified as a significant impediment to women entering the paid workforce, a program might be acceptable, provided its intent was to equalize employment opportunities. However, voluntary interventions such as an opportunity for counselling or upgrading would be preferable to imposed responses.

Far more interventionist is *equality of outcome* where the concern is less with process and more with substance. An analogy may be drawn to a race in which equal opportunity would focus on ensuring that all competitors have similar advantages at the start: what happens after the bell is rung, and who ultimately wins, is of no concern. Equality of outcome, by contrast, does not concentrate on ensuring that all start at the same point, but rather focuses on the outcomes—not the starting line, but rather the finishing line.

This perspective assumes that abilities are randomly distributed across populations: if some groups systematically succeed at the expense of other groups, it is because of preferred access to particular environments, to opportunities, supports, and resources. The likelihood of redressing such inequalities of opportunities is minimal, within a capitalist system. Hence, the recommended solution is to act *as if* opportunities were equal, which would lead to equal outcomes—and to focus on ensuring those equal outcomes.

Some argue that equal opportunity policies for employment can never be effective: anti-discrimination legislation deals with only the most blatant forms of abuse (just as a Head Start program cannot in practice fully offset a disadvantaged home environment). If men and women are equally productive in the absence of discriminatory barriers, statistics for men and women should reflect each occupying approximately 50 per cent of the jobs in any work environment (assuming large enough numbers). Thus, it would be appropriate to ensure this outcome through mandatory quotas if necessary, as voluntary goals and targets are unlikely to be effective.

Equality of outcome does not require *identical* outcomes, but can encompass both process and outcome (Tawney, 1931). It can refer to an individual's well-being as well as to actual resources. Thus, the term can be either objective or subjective, with the latter unlikely to lead to identical outcomes.

Critics of the equal opportunity approach would argue that formal equality before the law is not sufficient. The life socialization of persons from disadvantaged backgrounds would predict treatment in the courts inferior to that of the middle class. The vast majority of lawyers in private practice are neither trained for nor attuned to the particular needs of the poor. One can argue, moreover, that a legal system under capitalism places greater emphasis on the rights of property than on the rights of people, and the poor, by definition, do not tend to possess property. Certainly, much legal education and the compensation system direct most lawyers away from 'poverty law'. The only effective response is to establish separate legal aid clinics, staffed by lawyers knowledgeable in the legal problems that affect the poor, with compensation based on something other than fee-for-service. In this way the legal needs of the poor can be met in a manner comparable to the way fee-for-service responds to the needs of the middle class and rich.

Or let us consider access to post-secondary education. There are no formal barriers to entry and there are compensatory programs in place. In principle, all have equal access, or *equality of opportunity*. In reality, low-income students often are excluded by systemic and cultural considerations. The *opportunity cost* of attending university (the income given up by not doing paid work), which can easily exceed the direct costs, represents a major barrier to higher education to poor families.

The elimination of post-secondary tuition, often cited as a solution by student groups, would primarily benefit middle- and upper-income individuals who stay in school and do not go to work. Formal equality of opportunity then becomes inequality of outcome. To ensure true equality of opportunity, and hence of outcome, would entail the removal of all barriers: perhaps all students should be given salaries sufficient to cover both the direct outlays and also the earnings forgone. The payments would necessarily begin at the minimum school-leaving age, where opportunity costs become substantial.

Equality of opportunity, particularly of the formal nature, may do little to alter life chances. Therefore, a direct focus on outcomes may be necessary. Moreover, the case of higher education shows that increased equality of opportunity alone may worsen equality of outcome.

## Need

The concept of the *meeting of needs* lies somewhere between the definitional ambiguity of equity and the greater precision of *equality*. It is a fundamental building block in the human services and social welfare, notwithstanding—or perhaps because of—its definitional ambiguity. A child 'in need of protection' is the operative justification for apprehension in much of child welfare, while the Canada Assistance Plan, for many years the country's basic law on social assistance, specified only that an individual be 'in need or likely to be in need' for entitlement to benefits. Perhaps the vague meaning of 'need' was consciously chosen to give discretion to administrators or front-line workers to operationally define need in particular cases. The federal CAP legislation left much room for the provinces to determine who would qualify for benefits.

The differences among *need, want, desire,* and *preference* are rarely clear, though a need is of greater urgency than a want. Perhaps some conceptual line (or zone) could be drawn to separate the necessary from the merely desired, to begin to identify those basic or absolute needs to which everyone would have a right.

Some have argued that there is a limited range of absolute needs: first is the need for basic survival, either limited to the physical dimension or defined more broadly. Certainly the definition of basic survival is culturally bound: for example, in Third World countries it is typically defined as the minimum caloric intake necessary to maintain continued functioning, estimated at perhaps 700–800 calories per day. The second basic need is usually presented as autonomy, the right to function on one's own, free from undue interference. (Autonomy may apply to a group rather than to individuals, in which case the rights of individuals may be constrained in the name of group autonomy.) This notion is also problematic because autonomy can be defined narrowly (as in the *freedom from* outside interference) or more broadly (as in the *freedom to* do something).[14]

For example, food is necessary to basic survival, which constitutes a basic need, or right. Such a right creates a corresponding obligation on others to ensure that adequate and appropriate food is provided without conditions attached. Roy Parker has observed:

> The fact of being born into or recognized as members of a particular society itself brings entitlement to a defined standard of living and range of opportunities and implies a corresponding range of obligation for other members of that society.

Canada has signed virtually every international covenant referring to 'the human right to food' since 1966 with the International Covenant on Economic, Cultural and Social Rights (ICESCR) up to the World Declaration on Food Security (Rome, 1996). Yet, the rhetoric has not been matched by action; the termination of the Canada

Assistance Plan and the provincial cuts in welfare rates have increased hunger in Canada dramatically. Food banks, as Riches (1986) has observed, are one of Canada's major growth industries today.

Some argue to include housing as a basic need. The vast majority of housing in Canada is treated as a conventional economic commodity to be bought and sold in the market. However, if in Canada housing is deemed to be a basic survival need (which *should* be relatively non-controversial given Canada's climate), it constitutes a right. Hence, the right to housing should then not be subject to the marketplace but guaranteed to all.

At the other end of the ideological spectrum, the argument is made for a very narrow conceptualization of absolute needs: more rights lessen the incentive to maintain or attain self-reliance. The transformation of a want or a subjective need into a right, thereby requiring a societal response, becomes a 'dangerous heresy'.

From a structuralist or Marxist perspective needs are never absolute or the product of some exogenous value system or morality. Rather, needs are socially constructed by a value system moulded by the needs of capital. Capitalism creates 'false' needs essential to the continuing process of accumulation.

Needs always exceed the ability or willingness of an individual or society to meet them. In the short term, needs are often greater than a society's technical capacity to respond. The task then is to determine priorities among those needs and perhaps to attempt to find the elusive line of demarcation between needs (which entail a mandatory collective response) and wants (which can be left to individuals and the private market).

Notwithstanding its conceptual ambiguity, the centrality of need in public discourse calls for measurement. Some approaches perhaps require greater objectivity or certainty than is possible. The 'gap' model of needs, for example, makes explicit the value-based choices involved in identifying needs. Formally, almost mathematically, need is measured as the shortfall or deficiency between what is and what should be, where the latter delineates some desired state. *Should be* minus *is* equals *need*; while *is* can be identified with relative ease, defining *should be* remains fundamentally subjective.

Another approach is known as the 'harm principle'. A *need* is something the absence of which harms the individual. As in the 'gap model', need is a negative concept—the lack of something important.

The most common empirical approach to measuring needs is 'needs assessment', though the term itself entails no single methodology. Rather, it describes the systematic acquisition of information, from a simple subjective ordering of priorities to rigorous attempts at measurement. A needs assessment is often required by a potential funder to ensure that a need actually exists. Profoundly political, a needs assessment rarely reports that a need does not exist.

### Measuring Poverty

Nowhere are the practical difficulties in measuring need clearer than in attempts to define a poverty line in Canada (Ross, 2000; CCSD, 2001). Statistics Canada declines to use the term 'poverty line' because of its innate definitional ambiguity. Instead, it has produced the low-income cut-offs (or LICOs), as a de facto informal measure of the incidence of poverty, a cut-off below which people live in 'straitened circumstances'. The LICOs are relative measures, based on a comparison of the historical spending patterns of families at different income levels (Ross, 2000). A more recent indicator from Statistics Canada, the market basket measure (MBM), is also relative, but easier to understand, as it is based on a 'basket' of commodities and services that a low-income family might actually purchase. Using the LICOs, the incidence in child poverty in Canada was about 18 per cent (or one in five), but the MBM rate for the same year was only 12 per cent. This dramatic decrease of one-third in the recorded rate of child poverty—without any change in the conditions facing children and families—has led to considerable criticism of the new measure. Critics have alleged that rather than address the causes of child poverty in Canada, the government has instead redefined the terms so the same problem will look less grave in the eyes of the public.

As we see from Tables 1.5 and 1.6, international bodies tend to define the poverty line at one-half the median income in a country, an explicitly relative measure that is easy to collect at minimal cost. Chris Sarlo (1996, 2001), an economist working with the right-wing Fraser Institute, has tried to determine absolute poverty in Canada, based on his own interpretation of what a poor family needs; his measure, however, as relative as the others, simply positions poverty at a level that is meaner and more sparse.

### Social Inclusion

Traditional goals for redistribution tend to focus on substantive outcomes, such as raising the living standards of those below a certain line. More recently, the emphasis has shifted from content to process, arguing that merely redistributing money (or commodities) keeps recipients as recipients, albeit at a slightly higher standard of living. Redistribution of power and opportunities are needed, so that the marginalized or excluded may become full participating members of the community. Greater attention must be paid to social and economic rights as basic components of citizenship (or membership in the community). Much of this debate has revolved around the notion of social inclusion (or exclusion).

Duffy defines social exclusion as 'the inability to participate effectively in economic, social, political and cultural life . . . alienation and distance from the mainstream' (Oppenheim, 1998), while Graham Room (1995) viewed it as 'the process of being detached from the organizations and communities of which the society is composed and from the rights and obligations that they embody'.

The ideas of *social exclusion* come to us via the European Community, from earlier French academic literature dealing with 'les exclus'. The concept moves away from static notions of income deficiency: within the disability community, for example, existing income support programs are widely criticized because the payment of money is seen as ending society's obligation. Recipients need the financial support, but they also want to participate, to be involved in society. A disability cheque at the cost of exclusion is not an acceptable trade-off.

Oppenheim (1998) has identified four central advantages to focusing on the broader goals of social inclusion:

- Because social exclusion is about process, it can deal with the lived experiences of poor people. It is therefore far more reflective of their life realities than is a simple measure of low income. Social exclusion can deal with the social and economic conditions and the social institutions that lead to marginalization. Difficulties in the educational system, for example, may reflect the low income of the child's family, but there is far more at work in that child's life than a single poverty indicator can incorporate.

- Social exclusion offers breadth that can lead to wider goals. 'Economic security is not an end in itself but part of the achievement of a greater sense of well-being, active participation or common membership of our society.'
- Social exclusion takes into account issues such as loss of status, power, self-esteem, or expectations, which are associated with poverty, but are not included in the traditional indicators.
- Social exclusion is a relational term: one is excluded *from something*. This brings the rest of society directly into the analysis. It suggests that both the definition of the problem and possible solutions involve not only those excluded and the government, but all of us on a daily basis. In terms of political direction, social exclusion is far more dynamic, demanding that we all become immersed in the issues.

Moving from a conceptual understanding of social exclusion to a set of agreed-upon empirical indicators is daunting, and we are still in the early stages. Nevertheless, one of the early actions of Tony Blair as Prime Minister in Britain was to establish a Social Exclusion Unit, operating directly from his office. This gave the unit high bureaucratic and public visibility, while also recognizing the multi-dimensional nature of the issues. In Canada, in the summer of 2000, the Laidlaw Foundation began a major initiative on social inclusion.

## 5. Some Dimensions of Redistribution

In social policy, it is common to think of *vertical* redistribution, that is, transfers from those with greater resources (the rich) to those with less (the poor)—or vice versa. There are, however, not two income groups but many, and redistribution can occur in different ways along the income scale. Moreover, it is not only income that is subject to redistribution: one can also look at wealth or assets, or intangible resources such as opportunities or access or power.

Redistribution also occurs *horizontally*, to equalize outcomes among those at the *same income level*. The original family allowance program in Canada involved redistribution from families without children to families with children because the latter, at the same income level, incurred costs not borne by the childless.

Redistribution can also be viewed *intergenerationally*: dependence at each end of the life cycle is aided by contributions from those in between. Free and/or highly subsidized education, for example, or income through the Canada Child Tax Benefit, represents intergenerational redistribution to the young from everyone else. Old Age Security (OAS), the Guaranteed Income Supplement (GIS), subsidized housing, and reduced costs for drugs for seniors involve redistribution from all taxpayers to the old. In this 'intergenerational social contract', dependence in youth and in old age is supported through economic independence in the intervening years.

Figure 2.2 presents the results of a simulation using data for 1995. It illustrates the impact of all government taxation and transfer (benefit) programs at different ages. Individuals receive more transfers than they pay in taxes until 22 and after 63, while

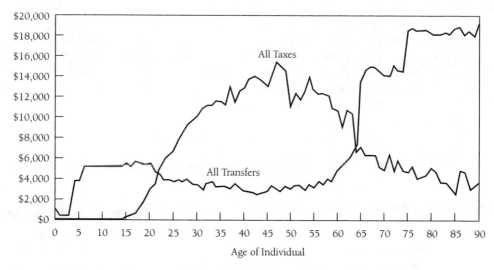

**Figure 2.2  Average Taxes and Transfers by Age, All Programs, 1995**
SOURCE: Hicks (1998: 42).

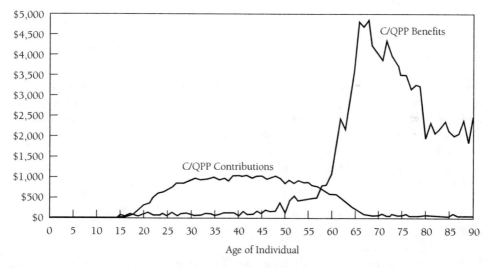

**Figure 2.3  Average C/QPP Benefits and Contributions, by Age, 1995**
SOURCE: Hicks (1998: 47).

between these ages they contribute more than they receive. Viewed as an intergenerational transfer, the population aged 22 to 63 is paying for the benefits received by the young and the elderly.

A similar analysis can be applied to a specific program: Figure 2.3 illustrates the payment (contribution) and benefit receipt distribution for Canada/Quebec Pension Plan, according to age.

Redistribution can also be viewed in terms of gender, in which income (or opportunity) is transferred from men to women, or vice versa. Women who work at home as
housekeepers and child-minders, typically without pay, redistribute earnings and earnings opportunities to men; child care programs often are intended to offset disadvantage and to permit such women to participate more fully in the paid workforce. The
redefinition of eligibility criteria for entitlement to Employment Insurance (EI) in the
late 1990s advantaged full-time workers at the expense of those in the part-time labour
force. The effect was to redistribute EI funds from women (who more frequently work
part-time) to men (who more frequently work full-time).

Geographic redistribution, particularly across provinces and regions, has been a central theme of Canadian history. Equalization payments from Ottawa to the poorer
provinces, differential eligibility for Employment Insurance based on an applicant's region
of residence, and decisions about where to locate prisons or military installations all
reflect imperatives to redistribute resources across the country to reduce the gaps between
the wealthy and the poorer regions. Debates concerning equalization choices have often
been acrimonious, among the most problematic of all federal-provincial issues.

## A MODEL OF REDISTRIBUTION

In Table 1.3 and Figures 1.3 and 1.4, we saw that people's final incomes were affected
by two influences on their market earnings: they receive cash benefits, which are transfers provided by government; and they pay taxes, which are transfers payable to government. Figure 2.4 presents a general model of social policy redistribution that
encompasses both these transfers. It is descriptive rather than explanatory, but illustrates that redistribution is a cycle: the upper portion refers to the allocation of benefits,
and the lower portion to the payment for these benefits. The cycle is represented as
closed, because those who receive the benefits are, in the aggregate, the same
people who pay for them.

The cycle also illustrates the two central questions that underlie all discussions
of social policy:

- *Allocation*: Who is to receive benefits (and in what form)?
- *Financing*: Who is to pay (and in what form)?

The model places equal emphasis on both the upper (receiving) and lower (paying)
portions of the redistributive cycle. Decisions about allocation of benefits and of payment
are, conceptually at least, independent of one another.

*Who benefits* (and how) and *who pays* (and how) both are central to the study of
social policy and both must be examined. They tell us about the degree of equity of the
redistribution, the net impact of specific actions and decisions.

At the left of Figure 2.4 is a circle labelled 'Redistributive Agents' (RA). This corre-
sponds to the mechanisms by which the above two questions are addressed. The most
common redistributive agency is, of course, government, which makes decisions both
about how to allocate benefits and how to pay for them; others, however, including

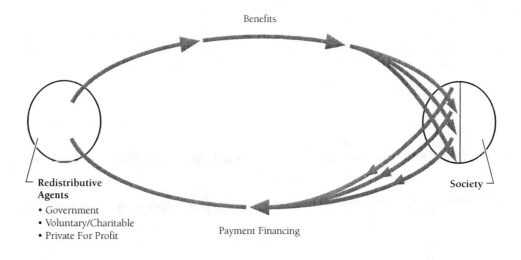

**Figure 2.4  A Model of Redistribution**

charities and the voluntary sector are also important to the redistributive cycle, and make comparable decisions within their areas of concern.

The spray of lines into and out of the box labelled 'Society' indicates that benefits can be allocated to, and funds drawn from, various sectors of the community. Those who benefit can be everyone, or only the poor (or rich), or only designated groups (e.g., children; people with illnesses or disabilities). All can pay or some will pay, and at variable levels.

Let us return to our example of post-secondary education. As we have seen, the case against tuition is often argued in terms of increased access for low-income individuals, because fees constitute a barrier that only middle- and upper-income earners can surmount. However, the story is more complex. If there were no tuition, the costs of university education would likely be borne by taxpayers, including those at low-income levels. An examination of who gets to university, and receives the benefits of free tuition, might reveal disproportionate representation from those higher up the income scale. Thus, the benefits would be disproportionately received by those with middle and higher incomes, while the payment burden is carried by all taxpayers, including those with low incomes. The net combined effect could be regressive, as those with low incomes contribute to the free university education of the middle and upper classes.[15]

As a further example we look at medicare, not empirically, but rather in terms of the model's capacity to identify the appropriate questions:

- On the benefits side coverage formally includes the entire population (though there is some slippage). However, overall use of insured medical services is disproportionately weighted up the income scale: although low income and poor health are statistically correlated, middle- and upper-income groups use more insured services, particularly those that are expensive, and they use them for longer periods of time.[16]

- On the financing side, each province funds its medicare program differently. If the funds come from general provincial tax revenues, the equity will be that of the overall tax system. In some provinces, partial funding comes from premiums, which are often regressive. Some provinces use a payroll tax, from which are excluded those without payrolls—the self-employed or those receiving interest, dividends, or capital gains: this, too, is regressive.

Combining the upper and lower portions of the redistributive cycle, in Figure 2.4, we observe that use of medicare is disproportionately weighted up the income scale and that funding is more complex to assess, though this would likely be mildly progressive. From this information, the overall net effect could then be ascertained (though we shall not do that here).

We could extend this type of model to compare medicare in different ways: to a privatized market model such as that of the United States; to some broader conceptualization of health that included what are now uninsured services, such as homeopathy. We might well find that the overall impact of medicare—both benefits and payment— is regressive, in that only upper- or middle-income groups benefit more than they pay. But we would likely also find the poor to be far worse off in a market-based system. The conclusion might be that while medicare, on balance, is regressive in its impact, it is far less so than in the United States. Medicare might then be seen as necessary to ensure that low-income households get access to insured medical services, even though they may subsidize the rich and pay more than their share of the costs.

# NOTES

1. This quote was found in the program for the play, *Love from a Stranger* (Agatha Christie), at the Shaw Festival, Niagara-on-the-Lake, Ontario, Summer 2001.
2. This is usually measured as gross domestic product (GDP), the value of all goods and services produced in the country during a year.
3. For a contrary view, see Jackson (2000).
4. The Macdonald Royal Commission (1985), the precursor of the free trade agreements with the United States, articulated this view, which became central as the agreements evolved.
5. The emphasis in Marx on economic factors as pre-eminent has led to criticism, as by Mishra (1985), that the analysis is over-determinist. Gramsci (1971) in particular has introduced an important role for the human agent, arguing that social systems can be modified independent of the economic base. Taylor-Gooby and Dale (1981) have described the welfare state as simultaneously both 'capitalist fraud and working-class victory'.
6. The 'economic market' to which we regularly refer is a theoretical construct, a process by which buyers and sellers of a commodity—goods or services, including labour—come together to buy and sell. The prices set in the market determine the terms or conditions of the exchange.
7. The concept of 'well-being' as used here need not refer only to monetary benefit, but can include psychic benefits as well.

8. Good Gingrich (2001) has suggested that '"he" 'deserves to be front and centre' in this context, because 'in neo-classical economics, "she" does not count, and her contributions are irrelevant and invisible . . . and "her goals" are not reflected in market ideology.'

9. Peter Leonard (1997) also refers to interdependence. As one way to confront popular and conservative notions of social welfare, he advocates a counter discourse—based on interdependence—in opposition to the dominant discourse of social welfare, which is that of dependence.

10. More formally, an individual's well-being (sometimes called utility in the language of the economist) can be postulated as a function, not only of the goods and services he or she possesses, but also as dependent on another's well-being (I am better off if you are better off). For those interested in the mathematics, we may assume two individuals A and B in which the utility of each is dependent on the various goods and services they possess (X), and in addition the utility of B is dependent on the utility of A (interpersonal utility).

$$UA = f(Xi,) \qquad (1)$$
$$UB = f(Xj, UA) \qquad (2)$$
$$\partial UA/Xi > 0 \qquad (3)$$
$$\partial UB/Xj > 0 \qquad (4)$$
$$\partial UB/UA > \text{or} < 0 \qquad (5)$$

In words, the utility of A is a function of the goods and services commanded (1). The utility of B is a function of both the goods and services, but also is a function of A's utility (interpersonal utility) (2). More goods and services increase the utilities of both A and B (3, 4), while a change in the utility of A will alter (either positively or negatively) the utility of B (5), the condition of interdependence.

11. See, for example, the project 'Equality, security + community: explaining and improving the distribution of well-being in Canada' (University of British Columbia, Centre for Research on Economic and Social Policy). Available at: <http://www2.arts.ubc.ca/cresp/>.

12. Some have lowered this threshold even further by suggesting that the gainers *could* compensate the losers, yet retain a surplus. Provided that the exchange creates a situation in which everyone could be better off with no one worse off, the Pareto conditions would be satisfied, regardless of what actual outcome ultimately emerges.

13. As long ago as 1931 R.H. Tawney labelled his call for extensive state action to limit the social and economic inequalities as a 'strategy for equality'. This was in many ways an early precursor of the post-war welfare state. Fifty years later, Julian LeGrand (1982) wrote *The Strategy of Equality*, which showed that inequalities in the four major spending areas—health, education, housing, and transport—either had not been substantially lessened or had widened under the British welfare state.

14. The ideas of positive and negative freedom (or liberty) are drawn from Berlin (1969).

15. We hasten to note that this argument is presented solely to illustrate the utility of the model; it is not an argument either for or against free tuition, which clearly involves more issues than are suggested above. See Lightman and Connell (2001).

16. Although the reasons for this disproportionate use are not presented in the model, the literature suggests that low-income groups tend to make less use of the expensive services of specialists and they also use less open-ended services, specifically psychiatry. Low-income groups tend to be more deferential and hence approach the medical model less aggressively, and they are often less articulate and vocal in demanding that their health needs be met. Furthermore, low-income workers may be less able to take hours off work to sit and wait in a doctor's office or hospital until they are seen.

# SUGGESTED READING

Jackson, Andrew. 2000. *Why We Don't Have To Choose between Social Justice and Economic Growth.* Ottawa: Canadian Council on Social Development.

This document addresses the perceived incompatibility between economic growth and equity, and argues that the two are fully compatible, and, as the title suggests, 'we don't have to choose.'

Statistics Canada. 2001. *Low income cut-offs from 1990 to 1999 and low income measures from 1989 to 1998.* Ottawa: Statistics Canada Catalogue no. 75F0002MIE00017.

Ross, David P., Katherine J. Scott, and Peter J. Smith. 2000. *The Canadian Fact Book on Poverty.* Ottawa: Canadian Council on Social Development.

Canadian Council on Social Development. 2001. *Defining and Redefining Poverty: A CCSD Perspective.* Ottawa: CCSD, Oct.

While Statistics Canada produces the data on low-income cut-offs (LICOs), it is the Canadian Council on Social Development that offers the most perceptive interpretation of what the numbers mean (and do not mean). Stats Canada itself provides a disclaimer in every report that it does not endorse the use of its LICOs as proxies for a poverty line. The Stats Canada report cited here provides data on both the LICOs and a competing indicator, the low-income measure (or LIM), over a 10-year period, as well as a detailed description of the methods used to arrive at them.

Titmuss, Richard. 1974. *Social Policy: An Introduction.* London: Allen and Unwin.

Reisman, David. 1977. *Richard Titmuss: Welfare and Society.* London: Heinemann.

Though Titmuss never wrote a comprehensive statement of his philosophy (as in a textbook), this posthumous compilation of the lectures he presented to the incoming classes at the London School of Economics is the next-best thing. Anyone interested in the field of social policy must have some awareness of Titmuss's impact. The book by Reisman is an early and largely sympathetic critique of Titmuss's work.

# CHAPTER THREE

# Social Policy and the Economic Market

## INTRODUCTION

In Chapter 2 we observed that an essential element in delineating social policy is interdependence among individuals, groups, and communities. Interdependence, seen as the extent of our mutual social obligation, can be construed narrowly or broadly: we can intervene early to assist those individuals, groups, and communities who are vulnerable or dependent as prevention, or later, to remedy or redress. We can focus on the few or include the many. We can assist reluctantly and for a short time only, or respond as a community in which there are ongoing shared rights and shared responsibilities.

In this chapter, we shall examine, more precisely, the relation between economic policy and social policy: we shall focus in particular on the *residual* model of welfare, which construes our collective social obligation very narrowly, and places great reliance on the private economic market as the optimal means to meet needs and allocate resources. We shall examine the assumptions that underlie the residual model, along with the implications for practice. In the residual model the role of the state is highly restricted: governmental involvement is seen not as a first line of response to social problems, but is considered as a last resort. Two intermediate stages are found. Between the individual and intervention by the state, first is the family, and second the voluntary sector. Only when the individual, the family, and the voluntary sector all break down or do not come into play is it acceptable for the state to intervene. Even in these limited cases the primary goal of state intervention is to build up the capacity of the individual, the family, or the voluntary sector to assume the responsibility. Thus, layers of responsibility occur, starting with individuals, proceeding to families, and subsequently to charities and the voluntary sector, with government having a temporary role only when all these resources have failed. The chapter concludes with a look at how work—paid market employment—serves a central role in enforcing the norms of residualism, and in ensuring the centrality of market consciousness in everyday life.

# LABELS

Figure 3.1 presents a continuum of responses to the concept of interdependence. Interdependence must properly be understood as lying along a continuum, but the literature often identifies only discrete points. The most common labels are 'residual', reflecting a narrow construction of one's social obligation, and 'institutional', conveying a clear sense of community responsibility. These terms were first introduced by Wilensky and Lebeaux in 1958, and amplified by others, most notably Richard Titmuss (1968b, 1974) and, later, Ramesh Mishra (1981), who added a point labelled 'normative' or 'socialist' at the end of his hypothetical continuum. (The latter term is probably more useful as there are strong normative elements at all positions.)

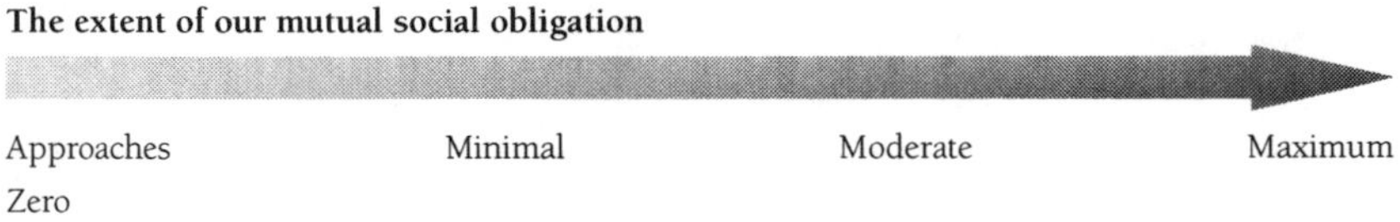

The extent of our mutual social obligation

Approaches               Minimal             Moderate            Maximum
Zero

**Figure 3.1 The Breadth of Benevolent Social Policy**

Other writers have labelled these discrete points differently. George and Wilding (1985) named their categories 'anti-collectivist', 'reluctant collectivist', 'Fabian socialist', and 'Marxist'. Fiona Williams (1992) described three distinct perspectives: anti-collectivism, social reformism (subdivided into non-socialist welfare collectivism; Fabian socialism; and radical social administration); and the political economy of welfare.

The most restrictive portion of the continuum is similar in all approaches; the theoretical point at the opposite end of the continuum typically goes beyond capitalism and the market economy. There is some question as to whether conflict-based models such as Marxism belong on the continuum at all. (We may recall that in Chapter 2, conflict-based models reflected a negative vector for interdependence in our continuum.) In every case, the categories reflect increments on a range of perspectives, from a very narrow to a very substantial (or even complete) sense of mutual social responsibility.

# RESIDUALISM

*The proper concern of social welfare is the individual. The individual is the best judge of his or her own welfare.*

The one conceptual end point along a continuum of declining interdependence is 'residualism' or 'anti-collectivism', with a severely limited view of interdependence.

Though residualism was originally a theoretical position in scholarly journals, in recent years, concrete programs, policies, and political proposals based on these values have been developed and implemented. Indeed, residualism is the dominant ideology of social policy in Canada today, high on the agenda of politicians and media barons. It is therefore necessary to devote much of this chapter to a full understanding of its meaning, implications, and limitations.

The basic premise of this model is a belief in the centrality of the individual and the private market, and in the responsibility of individuals to meet their own needs through their own resources whenever possible. We may label individual responsibility as a Level 1 (or primary or first-level) response, compared with Levels 2 and 3, the family and the community, respectively, that come into play when Level 1 proves inadequate, and which we examine below.

Individuals are held to be the best judges of their own well-being; no one else should interfere, except in certain narrowly delineated circumstances. The responsibility of others is severely limited in scope and duration, and is to be directed towards enhancing individual competence to function as autonomous individuals in the private market.

The 'group', or 'community', is strictly the sum of the individuals who comprise it; 'collective well-being' is simply the totality of the well-being of the individuals involved. If all people act to maximize their own interests, the welfare of all will be maximized. The state intervenes only as a last resort, and then strictly on a transitional and temporary basis. The private market works effectively and is the natural—and best—means of redistribution.

## Residual Welfare Model/Private Economic Market

Within the narrow range of the residual welfare model, the conceptual end point along our continuum in Figure 3.1 is situated where this decreasing interdependence approaches zero. We observed in Chapter 2 that the point at which interdependence reaches zero is the defining characteristic of the pure economic market, in which individuals pursue their own self-interest, indifferent to the well-being of others. The pure residual model (the conceptual end point of the continuum of interdependence) and the classical economic market (also the conceptual point at which interdependence becomes zero) become one.

> *Residualism is a set of values that conditions one's approach towards redistribution, while the economic market provides the technical means to effect this redistribution.*

As a result of this merging of values and means, the classical economic market (which is typically defined as a value-free arena in which to allocate resources and engage in exchange) acquires an overtly value-based counterpart; the residual model, a constellation of values that condition one's approach to social policy, acquires an operational forum through which to implement redistribution. The economic market becomes the best way to redistribute and allocate resources, and the residual value position embedded within the economic market becomes explicit. Technical efficiency 'marries' a set of values to shape a world view.

Residualism stresses the responsibility of individuals to meet their own needs: one's concern for others is severely restricted to enhancing their autonomy. The market is the optimal means through which to exercise this individual responsibility. It is only in the anonymous and impersonal market that individuals can freely choose their own needs/preferences/wants. Economics and residualism together present the market as the final arbiter of choice and freedom, the freedom of the individual being the ultimate goal and good in life. Nothing in this view can logically precede individual freedom and it is only through the economic market that this freedom can be assuredly actualized.

## The Market in Social Policy: The 'Best' Way to Provide

The claim that the market is the 'best' means by which to exercise choice and maximize individual autonomy is based in part on a view of what is 'most desirable'; i.e., that choice and the freedom for individuals to exercise choice without interference or restraint are, in themselves, the greatest goals for a society.

Also argued is that the market is the most efficient mechanism for decision-making in that it entails the least waste: no other allocative principle is more capable of ensuring that people get what they want, when they want it, and in the quantities they desire. The case is formally argued thus:

- Autonomous individuals can best decide what they want and, by definition, will maximize their well-being through the exercise of free choice.
- Any alternative system of decision-making can at best duplicate the choices that would have been made by the individuals acting freely.
- Individuals acting in the market are assumed to have considered and rejected any alternative allocative outcome; therefore, any other allocative outcome will be less desirable than that produced through the market.
- Any allocative system other than the market will produce outcomes that are equal or inferior to—but never better than—those generated through choice in the market.

Thus, and entirely tautologically, individual well-being is maximized through the exercise of free choice in the market economy.

The market is seen as efficient as it carries greater accountability and responsibility than any other form of decision-making. If individuals are dissatisfied with what emerges from a normative decision-making process, their recourse is persuasion—writing letters, lobbying, and voting. If individuals are dissatisfied with the market, they can take their dollars elsewhere. If enough buyers feel the same way, sellers will either alter their business practices or cease operations. Moreover, within a market context, individuals have recourse to the courts and legal accountability. Suppliers who face a potentially severe legal penalty will be more highly motivated in what they do. Any bureaucratic, voluntary, or other non-market-based system of allocation and redress is assumed to be imprecise, uncertain, and lacking effective accountability.

Market outcomes are also seen as most equitable, just, or fair. However, the market is not likely to produce equality of outcome, nor should it be expected to do so, for this is not a goal of market activity. George and Wilding's (1985) two classic liberal values—individualism (as distinct from a group-centred focus) and freedom (in the negative sense of freedom from interference, an absence of restraint)—inevitably will produce unequal outcomes because individuals have different capacities, resources, motivation, other personal attributes, and contextual strengths. Should the inequality produced by the market be unacceptable, the responsibility to address this lies directly with the actors in the political process.

### The Market and Stigma

At the outset of the post-war welfare state, the avoidance of stigma, which had characterized earlier forms of voluntary and charitable giving, was seen as a pre-eminent goal. Often this would be achieved through the universal delivery of services on a basis of full equality for all.

Yet any exchange or redistribution in which one person takes account of the needs of another is necessarily an exchange among unequals based on power: one party gives and the other receives. The 'gift' and the readiness to receive it carry with them the potential for dependence and the stigmatizing of the recipient (the 'spoiled identity'). Therefore, stigma can best be reduced or eliminated by the provision of services through the market, in which exchange is anonymous and impersonal, and conducted among equals.

## Two Critical Assumptions

Two critical assumptions underlie the belief in the market as the optimal means to meet needs: one of these refers to the capabilities of consumers, and the other to the distinct nature of social services.

### Assumption 1
*Individuals are able to exercise informed choice.* They have

- the information
- the mobility
- the competence (the intellectual capacity)
- the resources to make and act on informed choices.

The first three of these conditions—labelled in the previous chapter as assumptions of rationality—refer to personal characteristics of individuals; the fourth, the resource issue, relates to the ability to carry out choice.

Let us consider a single parent seeking child-care. She is assumed to be *informed*, to have all the facts needed to make a decision on the child-care options available in the local community, and the strengths and weaknesses of each: the flexibility of in-home care, the superior programming and increased socialization for children in daycare centres; the degree of comfort and specialized socialization with a parent or close relative as caregiver; the relative costs of the various types of care; their physical locations and proximity to the parent's home, work, or school, and so on.

*Mobility* refers to her ability to get from home to the child-care site and on to the day's activities, as any option is of little value if one cannot access it.

*Competence* implies that she can assimilate all the relevant information (including costs) and make informed decisions.

*Resources* presuppose that she has the time and money to acquire information and carry out her choice.

The perspective is illustrated by a story attributed to Margaret Thatcher, who could not understand why people did not buy all the Sunday papers (as did she and her husband Denis) to find various bargains, and then drive across London to purchase and store bulk purchases of household necessities.

Thatcher displayed no understanding that poor people often are unable to exercise informed choice. They may not have and cannot easily obtain full information: they may lack basic literacy, not know their way around a big city, or be unaware of quality differences associated with different prices. And they often lack the time and money to obtain such information, even if they appreciated its relevance to their lives. Nor do they always have the mobility to get to the bargains: poor people may lack access to child care, to cars, to money for gas, to cars large enough to transport bulk purchases, or the time to drive around a big city looking for bargains. Self-evidently, poor people do not have the financial resources to buy large quantities of commodities or the extra space in their homes to store goods, even were they able to acquire them. More basically, they may find the costs of newspapers beyond their means.

*The Concept of Capacity*[1]

The residual approach holds inadequate resources to be the major barrier to market competence; therefore, the preferred approach is to give money and permit the recipients to decide what to do. It is far better to give the single mother dollars and let her decide how she wishes to spend them than to have the state make choices about child care on her behalf.

In this sense, capacity to function in the market is assumed: the way individuals spend their money is held to be, by definition, the way that will maximize their well-being. Capacity is not generally seen as an empirical question to be tested.

Capability is often viewed dichotomously: individuals are either capable or they are not. For many legal purposes, this approach is necessary and probably desirable: we have a legal age at which to begin to drive, to drink, and to vote. Assessing each individual as to suitability to undertake these tasks is obviously onerous, and so we resort to a group or collective categorization.

Recently, however, both law and practice have begun to recognize that capacity is not dichotomous but a continuum, on which there are gradations of capacity and hence of ability to exercise informed choice. At certain times or for certain purposes, vulnerable people may be able to articulate their wishes clearly and persuasively; at other times and in other contexts, their capacities may be more restricted.

In most daily life situations, reality is more complex than a simple dichotomy:

- Capability must be assessed on an individual basis. Certain individuals may have restricted decision-making capacity, but entire groups do not: some seniors may have limited capacity for some decisions, but all seniors cannot be labelled incapable.

- Few individuals or groups are so lacking in capacity as to be permanently excluded from decision-making. People with psychiatric histories or frail seniors have good days and bad days; there are times and places and contexts in which their functioning is clear, and others in which their capability is more restricted. Even people in the early stages of Alzheimer's disease have times of lucidity. Moreover, capacity may be adequate in certain areas, such as personal care, but insufficient in others, such as dealing with financial matters. With respect to children, the courts increasingly reject simple splits, whereby, for example, a child of 15 cannot testify today, but tomorrow on her 16th birthday she suddenly is deemed capable. Judges question children at increasingly younger ages, and determine, on an individual basis, their ability to understand and respond. Creative innovations, such as testimony behind a screen or child-friendly courtroom settings, have led to children's views being accepted as valid and legitimate at far younger ages than was the norm.

Only a few years ago, many frail seniors, children, and other people with developmental or psychiatric disabilities were virtually excluded from the market economy and left to rely on the benevolent decision-making of state, family, or the volunteer sector. Today the public demands assistance and support in an increased and extended range of independent decision-making. Government responses often lag, as it is easier (and less costly) to offload responsibilities to families, but the trend towards increased decision-making for vulnerable people cannot be reversed.

### Assumption 2

*Social services are like other goods and services.* The residual approach assumes that social services are qualitatively not different from other goods and services that we buy and sell in the market: a free competitive market in educational services, health care, or child care is conceptually the same as a free competitive market in clothing or winter vacations. Sellers will compete for the business of consumers; those that best satisfy the wants of the public will thrive while those that do not will die.

In education, for example, institutions will display diverse philosophies and varying curricula: they will survive if they satisfy the market demands of parents/consumers. So too with child care services, or health-care providers, there is nothing unique to distinguish social services from any other goods or services found in the marketplace.

In an important lecture delivered in 1966, Richard Titmuss (1968) brought these two assumptions together as he discussed why health care cannot (or, more precisely, should not) be treated as merely another marketplace commodity. He illustrated how the 'purchase' of medical care was fundamentally dissimilar to the 'purchase' of, say, automobiles. Nearly half a century later, Titmuss's perspective retains surprising resilience.

## Level 2: The Family

To the extent that individuals are not capable of meeting their own needs (Level 1), it is assumed that the family will offer support. Within the residual framework, the individual is often subsumed within the family, with 'individuals and families' viewed together as the optimal decision-making unit. It is only when families break down that other systems may be expected to intervene.

Though the early social policy literature rarely discussed the composition of the family, it was inevitably assumed to be a traditional, two-parent unit, with the male at its head. The chauvinism and sexism implicit in this configuration were not actively embraced, but were nevertheless deeply embedded within the consciousness of the day.

There were, of course, numerous problems associated with the identification of families as the central pillars of society. First, a vast array of intra-familial matters became privatized, that is, removed from public view and not subject to wider scrutiny. Gender, and intergenerational relations—sexism, racism, ableism, and ageism—provided they occur within the family—become private concerns, outside the scope of public attention.

With the male typically defined as the head of the family, his authority over actions and decisions within the family are paramount, and the rights of the spouse and the children are secondary. Children and women are essentially the property of the male, without independent power or legitimacy. Just as the modern corporation is legally a single unit with a single head, so too is the family viewed as a single unit with the man at its apex.[2]

There is great reluctance within a residual framework to intervene in the family. For example, spousal and child abuse are matters of internal family functioning to be ignored by the state for as long as possible. There can be little or no preventive intervention. Typically the state can respond, if not after the abuse has actually occurred, then certainly only once the danger is clear, visible, and imminent.[3]

The emphasis on family presupposes a naive belief that the family will always be ready and able to help. In fact, the opposite is often the case. Residual social policy blithely assumes such family support, and because this support is assumed rather than assured, there is no broader collective obligation to intervene, even if the family is nowhere to be found.

The residual perspective holds that the family is more sensitive and responsive to the individual's needs than is the impersonal and intrusive state. While this is true in some cases, clearly, there is no reason why this should necessarily be the case. As Goodin (1985) has pointed out, the effect of a shift to residualism may be simply to replace dependence on the state with dependence on the family: the state applies its rules, however devised, consistently and impersonally; family rules may be arbitrary and capricious. In other words, within the family, there is flexibility—which can be good or bad, depending on how it is used. With the state, there is a uniformity of application that offers certainty, predictability and often an appeals mechanism, so the claimant has some rough idea of what to expect.

## Level 3: The Voluntary Sector/Communities/Faith Groups

When the individual is incapable and the family does not meet the need, responsibility falls to the local community and/or the voluntary sector. Because voluntary and charitable activities are willingly undertaken, they are often held up as models of collective responsibility at its best.

Though we shall undertake a more detailed discussion later, we may briefly note here that dependence upon volunteers carries essentially the same shortcomings as reliance upon family.

To the extent the community is the basic societal unit, a whole range of tasks and responsibilities are once again privatized: what goes on within the community is of no broader public interest. The community is assumed to be homogeneous and self-contained—inclusionary for those living within its boundaries and exclusionary to those outside. This gives rise to the view that social problems are not problems as long as they occur somewhere else.

Moreover, dependence on the voluntary sector is not without cost to the individual. Receiving a meal may require participation in a prayer service; a bed for the night may entail sleeping separate from one's partner. The power of community or agency may be exercised in arbitrary ways, and dependent recipients may have little option but to jump through whatever hoops are placed before them.

## Two Examples

The deinstitutionalization of people with psychiatric histories and community care for seniors illustrate how we have constructed elaborate social policy on the assumptions of the residual model and economic market—and how these policies have failed, because the theoretical assumptions are not fulfilled in practice.

Wolfensberger and others (1972) originally argued that deinstitutionalization or care in the community was therapeutically an advance in the treatment of psychiatric disability.[4] With active, ongoing support and involvement of family, voluntary agencies, and the local community, many patients could function much better outside large and dehumanizing institutions. Over the years, large numbers of patients have been discharged from institutions on the assumption that such supports would be available in the community. Occasionally, the approach has worked adequately, but more often the assumed supports have not been available or have been unable to cope with the demands placed on them.

Much the same story applies to our policies towards seniors. As the population has aged, society has not built institutions to house our seniors, nor developed comprehensive community-based services to enable them to live independently with dignity. The result, for both populations, has been increasing reliance on families and the voluntary sector (and the private sector for those with the means). Many difficulties arise when social policy depends on unpaid services provided by the family:

- *The family may not be available to render support.* Geographic mobility has led to families being located far from those who may need their help. Families dissolve and the members lose contact with one another. Elderly parents die, leaving adult children with developmental disabilities without adequate supports. Many psychiatric survivors live on or near the street, having long ago lost all contact with family.
- *The family may be unwilling to render support.* Just because people are related this does not necessarily mean they care about one another, nor does it imply that they will voluntarily respond to needs. Some countries have legislation requiring children to care for their elderly parents, although Canada is not among them; in any case, compulsion does not tend to produce quality outcomes.
- *The family may be incapable of rendering support.* Families face an unprecedented range of demands upon their time and resources, and there may simply be nothing

left over for elderly parents or a psychiatric survivor. Many families would be pre-pared to step in and help, but simply do not have the financial resources to do so. Families may also lack the technical skills, or the physical energy, to do all that is required of them.

- *The vulnerable person may be unwilling to become dependent upon family members.* Many people with psychiatric histories have severed contact with their families; frail seniors may not want to 'impose' on their children. The prospect of becoming physically dependent on their children is deeply discouraging and humiliating to many seniors.

- *Many families bring aging relatives into their own households, often at great personal and financial cost.* The woman usually bears primary care responsibility, both for her own and often her spouse's parents, while meeting the needs of her family and pursuing a career. This 'sandwich generation' is essential to contemporary social policy towards the elderly in Canada. While the approach was traditionally presented as embodying the presumed virtues of families so central to the residual model, all is not well on the home front. The emotional and financial costs to the 'sandwiched' women may be very high: nor do many seniors wish to become dependent (and potentially infan-tilized) in the homes of their children.

- *The voluntary sector, typically funded—and usually underfunded—by charitable dona-tions, is often incapable of filling the void.* As services are usually provided by volun-teers, there may be unevenness in delivery or no services at all. (We shall examine this issue in more detail in Chapter 9.)

Public policy regarding both seniors and psychiatric survivors is built on a set of assump-tions about the availability and superiority of family and voluntary resources. In the absence of these supports, public policy, much like the ostrich, buries its head in the sand, acts as if these supports were there, and simply ignores the evidence, while arguing that family and voluntary agencies should assume their proper responsibility (aided where possible by the for-profit sector). We have proceeded with an excess readiness to *assume* competence on the part of individuals, families, and communities, rather than undertaking the extensive and costly exercise of creating or enhancing their ability to cope in a market setting.[5]

## Level 4: The State

When all else fails—individual, family, community, and voluntary sector—only then is there a role for the state in the meeting of needs. But this intervention by government should be modest, a short-term transitional process directed towards enhancing indi-vidual capacity en route to independence and autonomy. The goal of the welfare state, said Alan Peacock (1966, 1977) many years ago, is to enable people to do without it. At some future point, at least in principle, the welfare state will no longer be necessary, when needs can be met and resources allocated based on the exercise of individual autonomy, supplemented if necessary by the family and voluntary sectors. The welfare state will simply wither away through irrelevance.

The characteristics of programs based on the theoretical assumptions of residualism correspond closely to what we see about us in Canada today:

- *Public services should only be provided as a last resort, after clear evidence that all other avenues of support have been exhausted.*
- *Applicants for social assistance are typically required to divest themselves of all assets and private resources in order to qualify for benefits.*

This may well include the sale of the car that might be required for the individual to seek or hold paid employment. In many places, able-bodied welfare applicants must produce a checklist signed by local employers that confirms they have been searching for work, regardless of the availability of jobs. The 'spouse-in-the-house' rule specified that if two people of opposite gender lived in the same premises, there was a presumption of financial support, regardless of the nature of the relationship. Though the Supreme Court of Canada has ruled this provision illegal, welfare 'police' in many places continue to snoop to ensure that women do not claim benefits when sharing premises with a man who, it is assumed, should be supporting her.

- *Eligibility for service should be construed very narrowly.*

As we saw in Chapter 1, the British Poor Laws drew a sharp distinction between the 'deserving' poor and the 'non-deserving' poor. The distinction was obviously fraught with moral judgements about worthiness, yet it remains, to this day, the underlying rationale for much public policy towards the poor.

While deservedness has always been delineated narrowly, in part to minimize claims on the state, in recent years the boundaries have shrunk even further. Single mothers with children, for example, were formerly deemed to be among the deserving poor; they were expected to raise their children, exempt from the more coercive aspects of welfare. However, single parents are no longer automatically deemed deserving. In Alberta, single parents are now generally expected to return to the workforce when the youngest child reaches six months.

Teenagers not living at home often are denied social assistance—unless there is compelling evidence of physical risk (abuse, assault) should they remain in their parents' homes. Such narrow qualifying conditions have led many young people either to stay in homes that are physically unsafe or to live on the streets. Likewise, tightening the qualifying conditions for long-term support for people with disabilities may exclude people with such disabilities as chronic alcoholism or drug dependence. They may wind up with nothing, living on the streets or in shelters.

When eligibility for social benefits is construed narrowly, fewer programs are offered to fewer recipients. The means test, usually the mechanism to determine qualification for income support, is often applied in order to deny rather than determine eligibility. Administrative rules and regulations further narrow the scope of what is to be provided publicly.

- *The assistance offered should be limited, whenever possible, to the provision of a limited range of opportunities and cash.*

The residual approach always prefers to assist people with cash, which maximizes recipients' choices and their responsibilities, while limiting the involvement of government and the community. If individuals spend their monthly welfare cheque on beer, that is their choice, and no one has the right to intervene. Giving people services (such as counselling), goods (such as a food basket), or credits (such as a voucher for clothes at a particular store) is seen as undesirable because these are paternalistic, may require an extensive state apparatus to deliver, and limit the freedom of recipients to identify their own priorities. (We return to this issue in Chapter 5.)

- *If the intent is to minimize dependence, then it may be desirable for service provision to be coercive.*

However, coercion is not compatible with free choice and personal responsibility. A major problem arises for residualists. These two competing priorities are often reconciled by suggesting that freedom is only available to those not dependent on the state, and that coercion is merely a means to the real outcome, which is autonomy and an end to the dependence.

There was a fundamental shift in principle in the nature of social assistance when the Canada Assistance plan (CAP) was terminated in 1995 and replaced by the Canada Health and Social Transfer (CHST). The absolute right to benefits under CAP was replaced in the CHST by a conditional—and coercive—entitlement. In practice, however, social assistance has always been coercive in nature, to ensure that a life of dependence remains unattractive.

Workfare is perhaps the best illustration of the current emphasis on coercion in social assistance today. Workfare is unpaid labour given *in exchange for* social assistance benefits. It is not job creation or training, or upgrading, nor does it include payment beyond the welfare cheque. Workfare is thus unpaid labour in exchange for the benefits. Workfare is stringently coercive in that it requires individuals to be at a certain place at a certain time (though it is largely indifferent as to what happens once they arrive) and the penalty for non-compliance is temporary loss of benefits, followed by permanent removal from the program.

- *Benefits and other interventions should be at a minimal level.*

Levels of intervention should always be low, to discourage dependence. Support at too high a level may deter the recipient from actively pursuing autonomy and independence. This approach reflects the Poor Laws' principle of *lesser eligibility*: benefits should always be sufficiently less than what individuals could earn through their own labour to encourage/coerce them to assume responsibility for their lives through paid labour. Today, welfare levels for single employables are substantially below provincial minimum wage levels for that same reason.[6]

Programs such as public education or health care (medicare) should also be provided at low levels, so as to leave maximum space for individual initiative (the private sector) as a top-up or supplement. Two-tiered health care and education would generally be good things.

- *The goal of all interventions is to maximize individual autonomy, usually through paid work.*

# THE CENTRALITY OF WORK

Within the residual framework the market is seen as the optimal means through which needs should be met. Paid work in the market is therefore absolutely central in this context. As one is responsible for meeting one's own needs and as paid work is the primary means for most people to generate the resources to meet these needs, a failure to work is seen as personal, familial, social, and perhaps ethical shortcoming.

Structural weaknesses in the economy, such as a lack of suitable jobs, are not acceptable reasons for non-employment. Instead the focus is on individuals and their presumed pathologies: laziness and voluntary inactivity threaten the moral and economic structure upon which residualism and the economic market are based. Therefore, severe penalties are applied for non-compliance with the work imperative in a market society, at least for those dependent on the state.

The expectation that single mothers should 'work' has been explained in different ways: in part it is structural, as work and welfare (formerly distinct solitudes) have become blended: movement occurs back and forth as work and welfare are 'mixed'. As well, women are no longer seen as dependants, but as individuals in the marketplace. More critically, the work expectations placed upon the single mother may reflect a moral stance: a punishment for failing to conform to the residual assumption of the traditional nuclear family as a central operating unit within society. Deviating from the social norm (and perhaps implicitly assuming culpability for the deviation) brings with it retribution in the form of an accelerated requirement to meet one's needs through the labour market.

## Wages and Housework

'Work' in the context of residual values typically refers to 'paid work', but most housework, including child-rearing, is unpaid, usually performed by women, and often in addition to paid work. Because it does not command a wage, housework is devalued. The 'man of the house', who typically has a better-paid job, holds the power and thereby commands respect (or at least deference); the woman, who may be working harder, has low status because she is partly outside the paid workforce.

Over a decade ago, this dilemma led to calls for housework to be compensated (known as the 'wages for housework' movement). However, philosophical debates within the feminist movement about both the desirability and the feasibility of paying for housework prevented the emergence of a unified stance. Some claimed that the proposal would increase income security for housekeepers and enhance the status of housework by treating it like other paid employment. Others argued that paying for housework would merely ossify a system that is inherently oppressive to women. Compensation would never be at an appropriate level, but the market exchange of money for work would legitimate a system that should be fundamentally altered. The only real solution, they argue, is to open more options to women, so that housework, if chosen, reflects a free decision rather than coercion and exploitation.

A more modest suggestion appears from time to time, and commands much support. Under this plan, housework would be eligible for coverage under the Canada Pension

Plan. A value would be placed on housework, comparable to equivalent compensated work, and be treated as income from self-employment. Individuals would then be permitted (or required) to contribute to CPP as does any other self-employed individual; or, perhaps, government would pay the premiums in recognition both of the broad social contribution of housekeeping and child-rearing and of the fact that many women in this position lack the resources to pay the premiums. As with other contributors, the standard CPP payments would be made at age 65, disability, or death.

## OUTSIDE RESIDUALISM: THE INSTITUTIONAL APPROACH

Outside the world of residual values overt normative choices for social policy-making become increasingly central. As the pure residual case conceptually reduces interdependence to zero, choices are exercised on the basis of an impersonal market mechanism. Introducing interdependence requires alternate systems of values, of which there are many, for the meeting of needs.

As we move from pure residualism in Figure 3.1, interdependence remains minimal at first, but at some point we pass to a fundamentally non-residualist or 'institutional' view of welfare, an intermediate range along this continuum of interdependence. The 'institutional' approach reflects a range of values, from near residualism to near socialism, and accounts for the largest portion of the continuum in Figure 3.1. The range of possible attitudinal sets comprising it is wide indeed.

Perhaps the most effective way to describe the institutional view of welfare is to identify a characteristic (such as 'reliance on the price mechanism') and assert that the institutional view has 'less' (or 'more' depending on the characteristic) than residualism, in a simple ordinal ranking—how much less (or more) can be specified only in particular contexts.

For example, as we move from pure residualism the central role of the market diminishes. So too does reliance upon family and the voluntary sector. In their place emerges a growing role for the state and its mandated services to meet needs. The range of services offered by the state increases as does the share of the population covered. Services are no longer restricted to a small group of poor or disadvantaged; no longer are the services limited or regularly means tested. Instead, a set of benefits is delivered by the state, or on its behalf, to a larger portion of the population, who would receive services as a right of membership in society, as an entitlement. The benefit levels would increase as the coercive drive towards self-reliance diminishes.

Mishra (1971) has observed that, in the residual model, the orientation of a service is 'coercive' while in the institutional model it would be 'utilitarian', meeting some socially recognized need. The characteristics associated with the institutional model clearly present a different package from that of residualism. The market is no longer the sole way of meeting needs. The market may remain relevant, to a greater or lesser extent, but normative values become increasingly important.

However, defining the substantive content of the institutional model of welfare beyond the above descriptions remains problematic. Perhaps it is best to view the approach as moving within a wide range between the end points in the middle area of the continuum.

At the upper end of the continuum one crosses another conceptual divide between institutionalism and some form of socialist society in which the market vanishes entirely and needs are met solely on the basis of there being needs. The means test and coercion no longer are relevant as everyone receives needed services at an adequate level as a matter of right. Mishra (1971) describes this model as 'solidaristic'. Clients are no longer 'the poor' (as in the residual model) or 'citizens' (as in the institutional model) but are now 'members of the collective'.

Though many models of the 'solidaristic' scenario have been devised, we shall not pursue it further. Not only is there a lack of agreement on its content in the literature, but residualism and the market represent the true battleground of the social policy process in the twenty-first century.

It is important to note that 'residual' and 'institutional' reflect prior value systems from which one approaches social policy. Programs and legislation are simply statements of laws or rules that are the outcome of prior normative choices. Programs also tend to reflect the pragmatic compromises essential to political life, and rarely reflect the pure models.

The right to social assistance was probably intended as a relatively pure statement of the institutional approach to need: the Canada Assistance Plan (CAP) identified 'need' as the sole criterion determining eligibility for benefits. Yet substantial coercive, punitive, and stigmatizing elements of residualism were always present in the process of determining whether need existed.

Medicare, to consider another example, has often been described as reflecting an institutional approach to health care, given its elimination of financial barriers to service and its view of health care as a right rather than a privilege. At the same time, medicare operates primarily within the traditional medical model, stressing cure rather than prevention. Moreover, not all health services are covered by medicare, and fees and privatization hover around the program.

The choice between a residual value stance and non-residualism turns on the intent of the interdependence. Is the purpose to compensate the 'losers' within a market context or does the goal represent a broader view of social interaction and collective responsibility? To what extent is the market the proper allocative mechanism and to what extent does one believe there are alternative, preferred, channels for the meeting of needs? In what contexts do we have a right—or, indeed, a responsibility—to limit the freedom of individuals to choose, act, and live as they wish?

Among those in the social services the institutional approach is often seen as the 'good guy' riding a white horse and carrying silver bullets while 'residualism' is the villain. Pinker (1979) has described this process:

> If social science students were not themselves collectivistically disposed they might pause to wonder why . . . the residualist always loses or rather why the institutionalist always wins at least the moral victory. What appears to happen is that the argument changes almost imperceptibly from a neutral description to an ethical indictment. Inexorably the residualist is identified—or rather exposed—both as an individualist and as an egoist, while the institutionalist is deemed to be inspired by a self-evidently superior form of altruism.

Clearly, residualism is not necessarily the villain, even to those who believe profoundly in the welfare state. The clinical concept of normalization, for example, represents a process by which disadvantaged individuals are encouraged to live 'normal' lives in the community to the maximum extent possible. They are assisted to cope in a market economy and to take responsibility for their lives, precisely in line with the residualist view. Supported employment for people with disabilities and community living for ex-psychiatric patients represent attempts by these groups to take responsibility for their own lives and to maximize their own choices and autonomy. Likewise the very term 'client empowerment' applied to users of social services, residents in public housing, and many other vulnerable groups illustrates a response to the failure of a big and not-so-benevolent welfare state. 'Power to the people' is perhaps a quintessentially residual statement in which autonomy and decision-making capacity of consumers are maximized.

Even Richard Titmuss carried a major thread of residualism (or classical liberalism) in his personal value system. Arguably the most important actor in the development of Britain's post-war welfare state, Titmuss was unwilling to argue for the elimination of private systems of health care and education. He profoundly believed that the superiority of state provision would become so glaringly evident that the private systems would wither away through irrelevance and non-use. Ending private systems through legislation was anathema to him, for he considered the state a danger to the pre-eminent goals of individual choice and freedom. To outlaw private health insurance, as Canada has done for services insured under medicare, would have been unacceptable to Titmuss. It was undoubtedly a major disappointment to Titmuss that the dual systems did not wither with time, and that both the British educational system and the National Health Service offer inferior levels of state provision precisely because so many of the upper and middle classes opt out to private systems.

While residualism may not be simply the villain in our cowboy movie, neither is it the hero. Critics of residualism deal with both its philosophical/ideological and pragmatic levels. Some argue, ethically or morally, that the market is not the means through which certain needs should be met. Hence, subjecting health care, education, or housing to market determination is wrong, regardless of outcome. There exist a range of basic needs with which everyone should be provided, as a matter of right, as the entitlement of membership in a society, and the market should neither enhance nor impede one's access to them. The disinterest of the market—its amorality—is considered to be normatively 'wrong', as it is by showing an active and positive concern for others that we fulfill our potential as human beings. The self-interested pursuit of one's own well-being can all too easily morph into unacceptable 'greed'.

Others have questioned the pre-eminence of free choice as *the* goal of social life, suggesting instead that choice is merely one means—among many—to attain ultimate goals. If a society decides that certain commodities or services are essential, then the receipt of these by all may be pre-eminent; choice and freedom would be merely means to a more important end—a certain standard of health or housing, for example. While choice in principle would certainly be desirable, so are many other social goals, some of which should take precedence.

Freedom has both a positive and a negative dimension but within the residual world only an absence of interference and restraint is considered relevant. Freedom in its more active sense means an ability to exercise and carry out choice, which critically presupposes adequate resources. In practice this means operational freedom for those with the resources and ability to act, but mere theoretical freedom for the rest. As noted in Chapter 2, we are all free to drive a Porsche or dine at the Ritz, but some are freer than others.

A different set of criticisms of residualism focuses not on morality and goals but on the operation of the market and its limitations in practice. Values ultimately are matters of personal preference, but the operation of the market system lends itself to empirical analysis. Such analysis reveals the limits in practice of the theoretical assumptions on which the model is built. In this view whether the market could potentially be made to work need not be answered as it is largely an irrelevant question. We observe the practice, and dismiss the actual functioning of the market as inadequate and unacceptable. It produces a world so far from that described by the theoretical assumptions as to make comparison futile. For example, the residualist world is excessively ready to assume competence on the part of individuals rather than undertaking the extensive and costly exercise of assuring their ability to cope in a market setting.

Within the market/residual framework, the unemployed fisherman in Newfoundland is assumed to be ready and able to move to Calgary and the single mother is assumed able to enter the paid workforce. It is their own prerogative to act on these available opportunities. If the fisherman lacks information or resources for mobility and if these can be generated, he should, rationally and in his long-term interest, move to Alberta; and if he chooses to stay in his home, he is free do so without any collective obligation on the part of the broader society.

In reality, people do not and cannot be assumed to act 'rationally' as the term is traditionally defined in economics; they do not always act in ways that are conducive to increasing their well-being, particularly when this concept is limited to material terms. Perhaps people *rarely* act this way. A range of intangible and unquantifiable goals motivate human behaviour, but these are to a large extent ignored in the market model. It may be far more 'rational' for our fisherman to remain in Newfoundland with the social supports of family and community than to plunge into the uncertain and hostile labour markets of Calgary or Vancouver.

Chomsky (Herman and Chomsky, 1988)—and more recently, Naomi Klein (2000)—has argued that in a world of monopolies the notion of free choice is illusory. Because our attitudes, preferences, and values are socially conditioned to the needs of capital, it is operationally impossible to generate a context-free process of choice within capitalism. The assumption of choice, so central to the market process, fades to irrelevance when values are moulded by context.

Powerful criticism is also directed at the family by residualism. By making the family central to decision-making, intra-familial issues are privatized and therefore ignored. Gender relations and intergenerational associations are seen as private matters beyond the scope of social policy interest. Thus, whatever the status quo might be, it is accepted, but with profoundly unacceptable outcomes. Feminism and structural gerontology, issues of racism, ageism, and ableism, and other serious social issues are effectively ignored within residualism.

# NOTES

1. Although the word 'competence' is widely used, the preferred term is 'capability' because it places greater emphasis on the individual's functional and behavioural capacity.
2. This helps to explain why women have fared so much worse than men in the shift towards residualism in Canadian society over the past quarter-century, as we saw in Chapter 1.
3. The recent change in mandate of the child welfare authorities in Ontario reflects the residual model: previously, child welfare agencies had a requirement to involve themselves with prevention and early intervention. In 2000, the agencies were required to redefine their mandate as child protection, which meant later intervention and apprehension only in the face of imminent danger. The government's actions reflected the privatization of child protection responsibilities within the family, buttressed by short-term cost savings, in the form of fewer and less qualified staff, despite empirical evidence that early intervention is always cheaper than later remedy.
4. There was also always a compelling financial argument that community care was cheaper than institutions. While the empirical case as to relative cost for the same quality of service has never been addressed definitively, community care usually proves to be cheaper than institutional care, because the quality of care is reduced.
5. A reverse situation can also occur where 'professionals' within institutions assume they know best how to treat psychiatric survivors/seniors/etc. even when their methods and theories are 50 years out of date.
6. This raises the question as to why a single employable person would choose a life on welfare with all its intrusiveness, if the alternative is employment at minimum wage with independence and significantly higher income. Such action would be fundamentally irrational. The answer, perhaps, is that these people are not, in fact, freely choosing to live off the state. The problem may be a lack of appropriate jobs rather than individual pathology.

# SUGGESTED READING

Baines, Carol, Patricia Evans, and Sheila Neysmith, eds. 1998. *Women's Caring: Feminist Perspectives on Social Welfare*, 2nd edn. Toronto: Oxford University Press.
  This is an excellent discussion of the conflicting roles and expectations faced by women attempting to provide care under patriarchy and capitalism.
Mishra, Ramesh. 1981. *Society and Social Policy*, 2nd rev. edn. London: Macmillan.
  This book contains perhaps the best description of the residual model, its characteristics, and its implications for practice. It also covers the institutional model of welfare and various other models (some of which are now outdated).
National Survey of Giving, Volunteering, and Participating. 2001. *Caring Canadians, Involved Canadians*. Ottawa: Statistics Canada Catalogue no. 71–542–XIE.
  This is the second national survey (covering 1999) on the extent and dimensions of voluntary activity in Canada. It is a rich source of data dealing with involvement by individuals in these activities.
http://www.welfarewatch.toronto.on.ca
  This Web site, jointly maintained by the Ontario Social Safety Network and the Community Social Planning Council of Toronto, contains a wealth of useful and important information on workfare (and other welfare-to-work programs), both in Canada and abroad.

Williams, Fiona. 1992. *Social Policy: A Critical Introduction*. Oxford: Polity Press, in association with Blackwell.

This book contains a valuable summary, overview, and categorization of the various mainstream and critical approaches to social policy. It also critiques many of these models for their lack of attention to structural variables such as gender and race, and attempts to incorporate these dimensions more centrally.

# Allocating Benefits

Parts III and IV of this book address the upper and lower vectors of the general redistributive model presented in Figure 2.4. Part III (Chapters 4, 5, and 6) focuses on the allocation of benefits, while Part IV (Chapters 7, 8, and 9) deals with the generation of needed resources. The three central issues in Part III are: how the benefits are delivered (Chapter 4), what is provided (Chapter 5), and to whom they are given (Chapter 6).

The question of how benefits are delivered leads to a discussion of privatization, commercialization, and welfare pluralism—all forms of alternate service delivery (or ASD). (We focus largely on for-profit approaches, leaving the voluntary sector to Chapter 9.) We begin by identifying two major rationales for commercialization—ideological and economic—and we note the various forms privatization can take, ranging from the outright sale of assets to deregulation and devaluing quality in the public sector. As we compare commercial and public delivery of services, we note the difficulties in measuring quality, and hence in ensuring standards in privatized services. This leads to the need for regulation and inspection for purposes of quality control, and these turn out to be difficult issues to address. We also note the distinct gender bias in privatization, which often results in increased unpaid home labour for women. Returning to the two original rationales, we conclude that the empirical case for commercialization—its allegedly greater efficiency—is essentially unproven in practice, often resulting in greater costs over time; the ideological case for commercialization is not subject to empirical assessment, as the fact of non-governmental delivery is the end in itself.

In Chapter 5, we examine the question of whether benefits should be delivered in-kind (as with education or medicare) or in cash. We look at issues such as paternalism, which underlies the decision to give benefits in-kind, and capacity (or competence), a necessary precondition for giving people money and letting them decide their own priorities. We consider the relative effectiveness of the two forms of provision, noting the stigma often attached to such in-kind benefits as public housing. We also explore efficiency questions such as economies of scale, and the lesser cost of Canadian medicare compared to the market-driven medical system in the United States. We consider vouchers, as a middle path between cash and in-kind provision, whereby consumers have constrained, but not unlimited, choice as to how to meet their needs. Examples of vouchers—from food stamps (used in the US) to legal aid certificates, educational vouchers, and even medicare—are explored.

Chapter 6 asks to whom benefits are to be given. We begin with the debate over universal allocation as compared to selective provision, again comparing in terms of effectiveness and efficiency. The issue of stigma recurs, alongside a practical focus on how selective eligibility is determined. There is a discussion of the guaranteed annual income (GAI), a conceptually pure way to meet needs while minimizing bureaucracy and administrative costs. And we ask why the GAI, so attractive to all points along the political spectrum, has never been implemented on a wide scale, while noting the results of limited GAI experiments in Canada and the United States.

When we look at government spending we discover that the simple concepts of universality and selectivity are no longer highly relevant. Cash benefits, particularly those delivered through the tax system, can be targeted to specific groups and recipients. We examine cash benefits that involve 'clawbacks' (or gradual benefit reductions) as incomes increase beyond identified thresholds, with a particular emphasis on benefits to seniors and children in Canada. We conclude that the simple dichotomies of cash/in-kind and universal/selective, while useful as conceptual starting points, must be modified in practice to address the complexities of program delivery in the real world.

# CHAPTER FOUR

# Allocating Benefits: Privatization, Commercialization, and Welfare Pluralism

*A society which depends on the incentive of private profit is doomed.*
George Bernard Shaw

## INTRODUCTION

During the last quarter-century, and particularly the last decade, Canada's post-war, welfare state has undergone significant shrinkage. Public provision of benefits has increasingly given way to reliance on families, communities, and the voluntary and charitable sectors, and an associated growth in the commercial or private for-profit sector. In this chapter we shall explore alternate modes of service delivery, focusing on the commercial sector and pluralistic approaches.

We shall begin by examining the case for privatization, posed in terms both of economics and ideology, considering the various forms of privatization, and discussing the central issues in the privatization debate. Questions of efficiency, of both quality and cost, loom alongside the recurring debate over competing ideologies or belief systems. Matters of accountability, irreversibility, and conflict of interest are addressed, as is the fundamental gender bias that permeates all privatization activity. If public services are to be privatized, there often arises a need for some form of state intervention to ensure the public interest is not sacrificed in the name of profits. Most commonly this takes the form of regulation or inspection.

Then we look at the forms of regulation, ranging from registration, through voluntary accreditation, to licensing and comprehensive regulation. The case for, and against, regulation is presented, followed by a brief discussion of welfare pluralism, as an alternate mode of service provision. The chapter closes with some limited evidence on the impacts of privatization.

Changes in the way we deliver services in Canada did not result from a sudden Thatcher-like change in the political and economic landscape. Nor was the result a dichotomous shift from public to private delivery of services. Canada has always had a

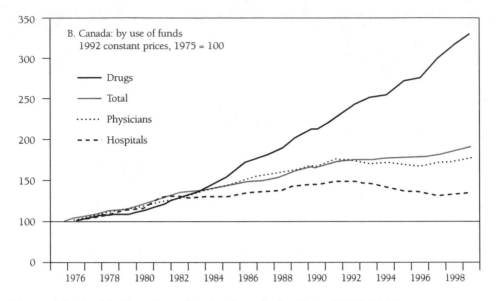

**Figure 4.1 Health-Care Spending in Canada, by Type, 1975–1998**
SOURCE: OECD (2000b).

substantial private presence in the social policy arena, and even today, the public sector remains important. We have had historically—and continue to have—a *mixed economy of welfare*, elements from both public and private sectors. Even in medicare, our most valued public social program, there is a large private presence, from for-profit labs to medical practitioners, entrepreneurs who work on a fee-for-service basis. In the 20 years following the introduction of medicare, the private share of health-care spending across Canada was about 25 per cent; by 1997 this had risen to 30 per cent. In 1998, Ontario's public share had dropped to 66.9 per cent and Alberta's to 69.4 per cent. Much of this increase in private spending (now more than one-third of all health-care spending) is attributable to the dramatic escalation in spending on drugs, which generally are not covered by medicare (CIHI, 2000). Figure 4.1 from the OECD (2000) shows this escalation in private spending since 1975.

Some group homes for vulnerable adults and children (including fostering programs) are operated on a for-profit basis; others are run by not-for-profit agencies or by the government. Since 1946 the federal government, through the Canada Mortgage and Housing Corporation, has been an important player in the housing area, partly as a guarantor of private mortgages. In some areas, public and private sectors coexist: long-term care facilities, for example, may be run directly by governments, sometimes at the municipal level; by charitable and not-for-profit agencies, often religiously based; and by large publicly traded multinational corporations. In Quebec, most nursing homes are operated directly by the provincial government.

In practice at both the service delivery and management levels, it is often difficult to distinguish the commercial organization from the not-for-profit. Many of the latter agencies experience pressure to generate 'surpluses', which are remarkably similar to the profits produced by commercial organizations. (Profit—or surplus—is the difference between revenues and costs. Increased profits result from increasing revenues or reducing costs.) Staff remuneration in not-for-profit agencies may include performance bonuses and may be conceptually identical to compensation systems in commercial organizations. Cost-cutting in the name of 'efficiency' occurs everywhere, regardless of organizational auspice.

The move towards privatization began as a slow pulling away from the structures and forms of the post-war welfare state, disillusionment with its outcomes, and disengagement from its processes. New forms of public discourse that talked of 'consumer empowerment' were incompatible with insensitive and rigid bureaucratic and political decision-making.

In its place, there emerged a new embrace of the market, with its promise of consumer sovereignty and control over decision-making. The reduction of bureaucratic control would also generate increased efficiency and effectiveness, which in turn would help address the emerging fiscal crisis of the state. Reducing the welfare state was seen as the way to cut government spending, thereby to reduce annual deficits and to generally put Canada's fiscal house in order.

In the early years, this loss of faith in the big welfare state led to a quest for more decentralized decision-making and service delivery. Local community control and citizen participation (as reflected in approaches such as *welfare pluralism*) seemed viable antidotes to the previous impersonal bureaucratic distribution of social benefits and programs. These alternatives did not constitute a full assault on the welfare state and all it represented, but could be seen as attempts to modify the impersonal edges while retaining the core values.

Inevitably, welfare pluralism raised the question, if government was to be restricted as direct service provider, why not cut back its role further? Why not bring the rigour and efficiency of the commercial market into the social welfare arena? Those who succeeded in private business could bring their thinking into the world of social welfare. Why not, in fact, treat the social services more like other commodities bought and sold in the marketplace?

At this point, the arguments move from a focus on outcomes to ideological debates of the merits of state provision of benefits. Lower taxation and a smaller public sector become ends in themselves, not merely means to efficiency and effectiveness, which in practice now become secondary goals. This leads directly to the residualist view that government should not provide any benefits or services, except as a last resort and on a temporary basis. While the place of the voluntary sector did not erode entirely, commercial for-profit approaches began to assume centre stage. What began as a gradual loss of support for the early welfare state acquired considerable momentum as the case for commercial delivery of services.

Undoubtedly this trend was accelerated by the Free Trade Agreement with the United States, and subsequently NAFTA, which gave to corporations legal rights that superseded those of sovereign governments. Commercialization, once introduced, becomes virtually impossible to reverse. (We shall return to this issue in the concluding chapter.)

By any criterion, Canada is increasingly marked by non-governmental forms of service provision. In this chapter, we shall examine some of these delivery modes, both in form and consequence. We shall defer our detailed discussion of the voluntary and charitable sectors to Chapter 9, although much of what is presented in this chapter applies to them as well.

# THE TERMS

*Privatization,* as Howard Glennerster (1985) indicated, is unrelated to particular ways of financing the social services: it is compatible with all funding arrangements. Rather, privatization refers to a mode of service delivery, outside the boundaries of government. The term is broad, and refers to a general approach rather than to a specific policy. It encompasses delivery by families, the voluntary sector, and for-profit businesses.

Market criteria (such as profit or ability-to-pay) may or may not influence the allocation of benefits. The sole condition is that service delivery must be non-governmental. *Commercialization,* a subset of privatization, refers only to services provided on a for-profit basis. *Welfare pluralism* refers to that form of service delivery in which the state is funder, but not direct service provider. Suppliers, either for-profit or not-for-profit, compete for the direct provision. Often the selection of direct service provider is delegated to a third party. Market criteria such as efficiency and the ability to satisfy consumers are relevant (though not always determining) in the choice of supplier. A pluralist approach is found in the practices of case management in which a worker assesses the client's needs and arranges for the requisite services. A child-care voucher, which carries with it a public subsidy and may be used at any 'approved' location, also reflects welfare pluralism.

# THE REASONS TO PRIVATIZE

There are two main reasons to undertake privatization:

- *economic,* usually issues of cost and efficiency ('the private sector can do it better'); and
- *ideological,* which reflects normative views about the proper role of the state ('government should not do it at all').

There is a third reason, *organizational independence,* which does not fit neatly under either of the two main categories and is less important overall.

## The Economic Case

This perspective usually builds on a general belief in the efficacy of the private market: it is better able to deliver services than is government. The rhetoric used is typically that of efficiency—the private sector can deliver more and better services per dollar spent; or, a given level and quality of services can be provided more cheaply outside government. The private sector is presented as being less bureaucratic, more flexible, and more ready to innovate, while government services are held to meet the needs of providers rather than of those being served. Privately delivered services supposedly will also respond to consumer needs and wishes in a way that the insensitive public service will not.

---

**Box 4.1  Effectiveness, Cost Minimization, and Efficiency**

---

The three standard evaluative criteria—effectiveness, efficiency, and cost minimization—must be distinguished from one another.

*Effectiveness* describes the extent to which a program's goals are met; it does not include any consideration of the costs of meeting these goals.

*Cost minimization* refers to the lowest dollar expenditure, per unit or in total. It assigns no importance to the quality of the service delivered.

*Efficiency* is an evaluative concept in that it assesses how well money is spent. It may be defined as the overall effectiveness or 'success' per dollar spent. An outcome will be most efficient if its effectiveness per dollar spent is greater than the effectiveness per dollar of any other competing activity. An efficient expenditure may not entail cost minimization: if spending on an activity increases slightly, but the effectiveness—the ability of the program to meet its goal—increases substantially, the efficiency would improve, even though more money is spent.

---

A variation on this theme has assumed great importance in Canada in recent years: privatization is now presented as essential to enhancing government revenues in a time of shrinking fiscal capacity. Selling off a public asset—whether Air Canada, Ontario Hydro, or public housing—provides a one-time cash infusion to government revenues, and may help balance a specific year's budget. But such actions—*selling the family jewels*—offer budgetary relief on a one-time basis only.

To privatize an ongoing service may liberate government from recurring expenditures. The costs of providing the service should be reduced if delivery is outsourced to a non-governmental provider. Some ongoing financial support from government may be required—perhaps an annual grant or subsidy—but this should be less than the prior cost. In other cases, government can divest itself of all future responsibility through privatization, though it may incur one-time costs such as severance. Whatever the details, the move to privatization should bring predictability to the budgetary processes of government, as fiscal targets can be set in advance, as are other expenditures.

## The Ideological Case

From this perspective, government simply should not be providing services that can be provided by the private sector (or government should not be providing services at all). Lines and limits of public responsibility will be clarified and the public service reduced. There is no issue of empirical verification, as privatization itself is the goal. The language may laud *making room* for the private sector or the virtues of private entrepreneurialism, but the case is normatively based, on a particular belief system about the proper roles of government and individual private responsibility.

The ideological defence of privatization also is based on breaking the power of public-sector unions. Extensive privatization in Britain during the Thatcher years was based significantly on animosity towards big unions. Privatized services are often non-union—

wages are lower than in the public sector—but unions are also seen as exercising too much political power and too much authority in regulating workplace practices that impede innovation. Thus, they must be bypassed entirely. Outsourcing service delivery to agencies or corporations beyond the control of public-sector unions is seen as the simplest solution to the problem of too much union power.

## Organizational Autonomy

Privatization is also alleged to offer greater organizational independence than is possible in the public sector. Bureaucratic rules and procedures offer little scope for professional autonomy and discretion. Therapeutic freedom, the right of counsellors to apply their professional skills and training as they deem best for their clients, requires a setting outside the control of government. Thus, many clinical social workers choose to leave the public sector and pursue private practice. Many alternative forms of helping are said to thrive better in the private sector: both the services and the way feminist counselling provides them, for example, could not be delivered as a direct government service. It is only in the private sector that the workers can obtain the freedom and flexibility to act in a suitably professional and sensitive manner. Family planning services based in the community can accommodate client needs more readily than as part of a large organizational structure. Hospices can offer an atmosphere and range of services over a longer term than are now considered acceptable to provide in a hospital.

The counter-argument addresses the resources and supports available in large governmental systems that are forfeited in the move to the private sector; and the claim that government provision is necessarily rigid and insensitive is empirically unproven. Flexible and accommodating public services are found alongside unresponsive and uncaring private-sector provisions. Therapeutic freedom may work to meet the needs of clients, but private providers can also ignore these issues and resist change out of indifference or through a focus on other personal or professional goals.

## The Forces of Competition

To the extent that privatization is based on an economic rationale, it should be subject to empirical verification—by comparing efficiency in the public and private sectors or by assessing the relative responsiveness to consumer wishes. If this is done, privatization will increase public-sector exposure to market forces through the introduction of competitive pressures.

When the case for privatization is not grounded in ideology, its driving force is *competition*, which requires service providers in the public and private sectors to increase efficiency, respond to consumer demands, and become more flexible and innovative. Without competition—as, for example, when a public service is sold or given to a single private operator with no other associated structural changes—an insensitive public monopoly may simply be replaced by an insensitive private monopoly, with no net improvement in public well-being. The only real change may be that theoretical public accountability is superseded by the non-existent accountability of a private provider.

> *Indeed, we may suggest that it is competition rather than privatization per se that should lead to desired social outcomes.*

Without competition, privatization may achieve little; in the presence of competition, privatization may prove neither essential nor desirable, as public services may prove superior using relevant evaluative criteria.

## FORMS OF PRIVATIZATION

Government activity in the economy and in society generally takes three forms: direct provision, subsidy, and regulation. Any of these may occur independently, or they can occur in combination. Government policy on pensions combines elements of all three: income to seniors is provided *directly* through Old Age Security or the Canada Pension Plan; private savings are *subsidized* through tax benefits offered to holders of RRSPs or registered pension plans (RPPs); and *rules* specify how private company pension funds can be invested.

Privatization will tend to dilute and reverse these same three forces. A withdrawal of *direct* provision may end a program, or outsource its delivery responsibilities; the removal or reduction of a *subsidy* will increase the cost to consumers and reduce the state's role in service provision; and easing or elimination of *regulations* reduces government's ability to protect the public interest.

Some of the forms privatization can take are:

- *Selling*. The direct way to privatize a service is for government to sell it, either to specific individuals or corporations, or through a stock offering to the public. This occurs most commonly with public assets or Crown corporations: the sale of Air Canada netted $700 million for the federal government, Petro-Canada $1.9 billion. Public housing is perhaps the most saleable asset in the social welfare field: the housing could be sold to sitting tenants (who might not have the resources to purchase it), to co-ops or non-profit housing providers, or to commercial landlords.[1] Other government assets can also be sold—surplus land lying idle, or the land under hospitals, schools, or government buildings.

  Sellng an asset involves a one-time budgetary gain that may help a government balance a budget or meet some other immediate fiscal target. However, there will often be higher continuing costs in the future, particularly if ongoing lease or rental arrangements are needed.

  Though there may be an ideological base for the sale of some assets, the revenue generated is usually a very important consideration for cash-starved governments.
- *Shutting down or cutting back*. Government can simply terminate a service or program, and the private sector will likely choose to meet at least part of the existing need. Programs can be ended to save tax money, in the belief that government should not be doing things, or to 'make room' for the private sector. English-as-a-second-language (ESL) programs can be shut down or child-care centres closed, or training programs terminated. Federal support for social housing was terminated in the early

1990s leading to today's housing problems in many cities, as the private sector did *not* step in. Services can be delisted from coverage under medicare, opening the door to their private provision. Cutbacks in subsidies to the arts mean the end to programs unless the private sector intervenes.

- *Freezing boundaries.* Limits can be set on an individual's usage of a service or on the aggregate service that will be publicly provided. In either case, excess demand can be met only privately. A ceiling on home-care entitlement, for example, forces those requiring more hours to rely on family, a limited voluntary sector, or an aggressive and expanding commercial sector. Provinces may choose not to insure new medical procedures or technologies under medicare, enabling providers to offer these on a for-profit basis. Licences can be required in order to deliver services, as in the case of nursing homes: if the issuance is frozen, people unable to get access will have to look elsewhere.

- *Devolution.* A government can devolve, or offload, certain responsibilities to another body, thereby ending its involvement. This process usually occurs between levels of government, or between government and an arm's-length agency or a non-governmental organization (NGO). There may not always be a financial saving, as ongoing subsidies may be involved, but the donor government will be liberated from day-to-day accountability. For example, the federal government has devolved many of its Aboriginal responsibilities to Native bands, and veterans' hospitals have been handed over to the provinces. Provincial governments can offload to municipalities, who, in turn, may pass the responsibility to households or a private provider. Devolution from one level of government to another is not really privatization; however, when the recipient is an agency or NGO, it would be.

- *Creating partnerships.* Government can choose to deliver services in partnership with the private sector, creating a mixed public-private model. The private sector may have skills that government lacks (such as the ability to run casinos) or may be prepared to provide capital that exceeds budgetary allocations (such as for the development of toll roads). Some partnerships, such as those that require social agencies to work with or to raise funds from the commercial world, in effect give the latter considerable power over agency decisions and directions in the future.

- *Devaluing quality.* If a government service deteriorates, those who can do so will move to the private sector. Less-skilled or demoralized public-sector workers, or workers with excessive caseloads, may deliver inferior services, thereby diverting some users to the private sector. Long waiting periods to obtain counselling increase the attractiveness of private practice; large class sizes, dirty schools, and a lack of specialized services, resulting from reductions in funding for public education, will lead some people to turn to the world of private education; a long wait for certain medical procedures such as an MRI scan causes some people to seek private medical care in the United States or in the 'grey' market, where private money (perhaps illegally) moves one to the head of the queue.

- *Contracting out.* Contracting with the private sector ensures government that certain services are provided, from a seasonal need for trucks for winter snow removal to group homes for troubled youth requiring specialized expertise. Contracting out can be accelerated through compulsory competitive tendering, in which services previously delivered in-house must be placed out for competitive bidding: garbage collection, for example, or home-care services can be provided by the lowest bidder who meets minimum quality standards. The problem, as we shall see, is that a contract awarded to the lowest bidder, subject to quality assurance, often simply goes to the lowest bid without adequate attention to quality. The goal in contracting out is more often to reduce the size of the public service than to save taxes.

- *Choosing to go private.* A purely ideological decision can be made to transfer a service from the public to the private sector. Justifications may be offered in terms of improved quality or lower cost, but the real motivation may be to reduce the size of the public sector.

  - *The case of prisons.* Traditionally, it was believed that the right to exercise coercive power should rest only with the state, so the custodial function of prisons should lie in the public sector. Likewise, when the correctional system was intended to rehabilitate, the state was viewed as the proper locus of responsibility. Today, however, prisons are largely 'warehouses', intended simply to keep convicts locked up where they can do no further harm and to protect the public. Prisons may also be unpleasant in order to discourage potential criminality, though rehabilitative goals are no longer considered to be particularly important. Nor is a state monopoly on the exercise of coercion any longer assumed: the growth of private security forces—particularly the large American-based firms—has made it relatively easy to privatize the operation of prisons. Any precise programmatic goals (beyond the custodial) are unclear and the presumed greater efficiency and lower costs of privately operated prisons have not been proven empirically. However, privatization does meet specific ideological needs: it reduces the size of the public sector, eliminates unions in the workplace, and reduces day-to-day public accountability. The approach also feeds a public desire to 'get tough' on prisoners, thereby enhancing any perceived deterrent effect of imprisonment.

- *Deregulating.* Government has always inspected, regulated, and licensed a wide range of services that it does not directly deliver, from child-care centres to taxis to clean water to long-term care facilities for seniors and people with developmental or psychiatric disabilities. Deregulation may lessen or remove explicit standards that service providers are expected to meet. There will typically be less inspection to ensure standards are maintained, and a concomitant easing of penalties for non-adherence. Compliance may become voluntary in practice, based perhaps on non-enforceable codes of conduct. As government's role as protector of the public interest is reduced, deregulation constitutes an important form of privatization.

## ISSUES IN PRIVATIZATION

The debate on privatization in Canada is part of the broader debate over the proper roles of the state and private markets. Privatization, as we have seen, brings about a transition in service provision from the public sector to the non-governmental sector, both not-for-profit organizations such as NGOs and for-profit or commercial operators.

Some objections to commercial provision of services do not apply to not-for-profits, while other concerns apply to any services provided privately.

## Ideology

Our history and traditions, together with some arbitrary decisions, explain what in Canada is considered appropriately private and what should be public. Apparently certain areas of social life—such as commercial surrogate parenthood and the 'rent-a-womb' phenomenon, on other than altruistic grounds—belong outside the market-place. But, where do we draw the lines? Or should nothing a priori be considered beyond the reach of the market?

In part such debates are grounded in ideology as to whether certain aspects of com-munal life should be provided by government or by another supplier. Often, however, ideology merely masks more tangible concerns. In our example of privatized prisons, for example, we presented a traditional view that coercive power should reside only with the state, to ensure constraints on the private use, or abuse, of power, and public account-ability for the exercise of force. Thus, perhaps, the issue is really one of accountability: and if public accountability ceases to be a matter of public interest, particularly for a group of marginalized people such as prisoners, then that argument against privatization loses some of its potency.

Gilbert and Terrell (1998) tend to downplay the role of belief systems in the decisions about privatization:

> There is a strong suspicion that the profit system is not morally compatible with the ethos of social welfare provision. Yet, moral objections would be difficult to sustain if it could be shown that profit-oriented agencies were the most effective and efficient means for delivering social services. If, on the other hand, profit-oriented agencies were shown to be less efficient and effective than nonprofit providers, moral objections would be unnecessary to deter the privatization of services.

They suggest, in effect, that the moral arguments about privatization are irrelevant and the debate is converted to one involving comparisons of efficiency and effectiveness. But are such comparisons possible? Can the factors involved be measured? Some empiricism crudely dismisses the role of normative considerations in decisions about privatization. Even if commercial delivery were more efficient and effective—a hypothesis that remains unproven, and to which we shall return momentarily—legitimate grounds clearly remain for opposition based on non-empirical considerations. Even were the debate posed in empirical terms, the size of the efficiency gap between the modes of delivery would be important in making choices.

Let us return to the earlier example of voluntary blood donation. When Richard Titmuss (1970) did his original study there was no rigorous way to test for 'bad blood'; therefore, not-for-profit systems of donation were seen to be preferable to commercial blood banks: altruistic motives were arguably more likely to produce good blood than those driven by commercial considerations. Today we can test for unsuitable donors, but the debate remains, now argued on moral grounds. Voluntary donation, as Titmuss claimed, gives people the opportunity to make altruistic acts, and reflects the view that we are a community rather than disconnected individuals in the marketplace.

Criteria for blood donation cannot be solely normative, for we still would not want to deal with the consequences of the well-motivated donor who gives bad blood. But neither can the debate be divorced from the normative considerations, and converted solely to comparisons of economic efficiency. It is to that efficiency that we now turn.

## Efficiency

Many people find the ideological debates about privatization profoundly uninteresting, and suggest that only empirical measures of effectiveness and efficiency are relevant. Which system will do the job better? And which can deliver more cheaply?

The empirical case for privatization is based on the premise that a constant quality of service can be delivered by a non-governmental provider at a lower overall cost, or that a better quality of service can be provided at the same cost. Measurement of cost is problematic, but seems minor alongside the obstacles to quantifying quality.

## Quality

Quality in the social services is hard to measure and even harder to ensure. Initially, we must identify desired outcomes and empirical indicators of quality that can be measured consistently and accurately (with reliability and validity), a task that is inevitably normative. Then, we must devise an operational system to ensure compliance with the required standards. To the extent the first task is straightforward, the second becomes easier.

Outcomes in the social services often are defined only vaguely, and there may be multiple goals, some unstated. What is the goal of a child-care program or a community-based initiative for psychiatric survivors? Often both long-range and short-term targets are ill-defined by design, in order to give maximum flexibility at the service delivery level. Many of these outcomes do not fit into simple measurable boxes or units. A lack of specific, quantifiable targets also ensures that penalties for non-compliance cannot be readily applied, as providers cannot be penalized for not meeting programmatic expectations that have not been set out explicitly. We shall return to the issues of inspection and regulation below.

In some cases, such as counselling or homemaker services, we often do not attempt to measure what transpires in the service delivery. Instead we measure time input—hours of service provided—as a proxy for program output, thereby forgoing any assessment of what actually occurs during a session. We assume, in effect, that the process is the outcome. This creates opportunities for providers to devalue (to cut costs on) the content of the service delivery. A less-skilled worker delivering an hour of inferior service still counts as an hour of service provided.

In other cases, we severely oversimplify the output in order to create measurable indicators. Standardized tests in the educational system illustrate this approach: the multiple, vague, and wide-ranging reasons for an educational system all are collapsed into a simple score on a multiple-choice test. Predictably, schools focus on those tests, at the expense of everything else. For-profit schools in the United States have found that passing rates in the tests may well improve, but what is not assessed (for which, of course, the schools are not compensated) is largely disregarded.

Nursing homes can be compensated on the basis of detailed clinical assessments of individual residents' needs. In Alberta a standardized assessment tool specifies the number of hours of nursing and other care required by each resident. If these identified indicators reflect what the nursing homes are paid to provide, then that is what they should deliver. This precise approach replaces earlier compensation schemes based on a flat per diem fee per resident, in which it was *assumed* that operators would deliver what was needed. The Alberta model, also used elsewhere in Canada, was introduced in the name of greater accountability and precision in payment, but a compartmentalization of care inevitably results.

Often the staff employed by the commercial sector will be less-skilled and less highly trained than their public-sector counterparts. They may be employed more flexibly, on an hourly basis, without the security of permanent employees. There may be fewer or no opportunities for upgrading or training and limited supervision, focused on fiscal accountability. The providers typically maintain that they are compensated to deliver specific services, and that it is their prerogative to make whatever labour arrangements they wish, provided their contracts are honoured. Indeed, one of the central aims of commercialization is to use lower-quality labour—to deskill—in those areas where staff could in any way be construed as overqualified for their tasks. Hence, registered nursing assistants (RNAs) may be substituted for registered nurses (RNs), and social workers with masters' degrees (MSWs) replaced by those with bachelors' degrees (BSWs), who in turn are replaced by social services workers with diplomas (SSWs).

Less-skilled, or less-motivated, staff may yield an inferior quality of service, though this outcome may only be identified over time. Continuity of care between worker and client is not a priority, so an ongoing relationship between the two is unlikely to develop, with adverse consequences particularly for frail and vulnerable clients.

Increased caseloads also result in lower-quality service. The time allotted for a specified procedure may be reduced. Unforeseen complications that take more time must be offset by abbreviated service elsewhere. The opportunity to assess clients holistically, to detect emerging problems that could be addressed more cheaply in a preventive manner, is eliminated. If workers choose to do tasks outside the job description, such as to water plants or make a phone call for a bedridden client, they are compelled to do so on their own time. The human interaction that is essential to the quality of life for a frail senior is largely eliminated.

This entire process may be labelled as the *commodification of care*, the application to the service sector of the assembly-line mentality and procedures that dominate the production of goods and commodities. The production of shoes or automobiles may be mechanized and accelerated, but comparable changes in the service sector have more severe and adverse consequences. Privatization's need for accountable and quantifiable output is a major force in the drive towards commodification of care today.

Privatization can provide a higher quality of service, often at lower cost, by selecting only the easiest-to-serve cases; those excluded will have to stay with the public sector, creating two tiers of service and two qualities of service. This process, known as *creaming* or *cream-skimming*, also occurs in the name of diversity and choice. Even if a private operator has a mandate to serve the entire population, creaming may still marginalize the difficult cases, in the hope that they simply will go away.

## Cost

Because cost is relatively easy to measure, it tends to become the focus in the analysis of privatization. Quality, being difficult to measure, is often simplified or ignored entirely. Thus, a comparison of relative efficiency tends in practice to become one of cost alternatives. Cost minimization may become the sole 'empirical' basis for comparison.

As we have just seen, the deskilling of a workforce is central to privatization. Clearly this has major cost implications for the service providers. There are major financial benefits to commercial providers who pay staff for only the exact hours worked (or, more accurately, for the exact hours assigned, as the staff may work in excess of this amount for no additional remuneration). Often there are no, or inferior, fringe benefits or pensions for the hourly-employed staff; and wages are inevitably below those in the public sector (though this gap is narrowing due to public-sector restraint). These short-term cost savings to taxpayers come at the direct expense of workers who receive inferior salaries and conditions of employment. The fact that many of these workers in the commercial sector are women, often recent immigrants and/or from minority backgrounds, cannot be overlooked.

Cost savings also are generated in the commercial sector through alternate service delivery modes, such as shorter time allocations for procedures, as noted above. They can also provide more beds per room in a residential facility, or fewer square metres of floor space per bed, or serve cheaper (and less palatable) meals that still meet mandatory nutrition standards. The evening meal in a residential facility may be served at 3 p.m. because the day shift leaves at 4.

Overhead costs also are generally assumed to be less in the private sector than in government. This is undoubtedly true in many cases, because there is less bureaucracy. However, overhead may be a function primarily of size: a large commercial provider and a large public-sector provider may well have comparable administrative structures and bureaucracies.

Compliance costs can be high in the private sector. These are the *policing* costs associated with identifying and measuring relevant outcomes, preparing and tendering contracts, monitoring performance and compliance, and imposing and justifying sanctions or penalties. The more complex the area under study, the more detailed the contracts and the more expensive the regulatory apparatus. Inspection and regulation are particularly costly because they involve ongoing labour costs, rather than one-time fixed expenditures. If inspection is to provide a serious incentive for providers to comply with the terms of their contracts, it must occur frequently and so will be costly, particularly if there is an appeals procedure. If inspections are infrequent, they will be cheap, but meaningless. Some inspections can be terminated, offloaded or reports made voluntary in order to lower costs, but the result—as was shown in the polluted water supply at Walkerton, Ontario—is that public health and safety can be put at risk.[2]

There is also an important time dimension to the costs associated with privatization. Major one-time costs can involve severance, usually paid by the state as it eliminates permanent staff. When privatization is undertaken because of its potential to ease a short-term budgetary crisis, as with the sale of a public asset, the Minister of Finance may discover that severance and other non-recurring costs greatly reduce the net proceeds of the sale: the state may end up without its asset and without its employees, but not much better off financially in the short-term. Over time, the loss of the asset may result in higher costs, as ongoing services are purchased from the private sector.

On the other hand, low short-term costs associated with privatization may rise dramatically once the public-sector competition is eliminated. A provider may *low-ball,* that is, submit a low bid, well below the costs of providing the service, in order to secure the contract and in the expectation that later additions to the contract to cover items not originally included will make the final contract comfortably profitable. (This operates in the same way as the cost of home renovations seems inevitably to rise after the contract is awarded.) Low-ball contracts also drive out the competition, so that when the contract comes up for renewal, there is no effective opposition to the current provider, who can significantly raise the contract price. In effect, government monopoly is replaced by private-sector monopoly, against the public interest.

If private providers are compensated on a per-client or per-service basis, costs to the state may rise as providers attempt to increase the number of clients or services. In a privatized prison (or group home or long-term care facility) the operator may receive fixed compensation plus a payment for each client-day. Clearly, there is an incentive for prison operators to maximize the number of compensated prisoner-days by delaying probation or parole. An empty cell generates no income. A public-sector facility, by contrast, experiences no such conflict, as its funding is not contingent upon high occupancy rates. Ultimately its total operating costs might be less than those with privatization.

## Accountability and Conflict of Interest

Privatization implicitly promises greater accountability, though of what and to whom is not always clear. The private sector is typically accountable to the consumers and to the shareholders/owners (or board of directors in the case of a not-for-profit organization). Government is also accountable to consumers, but also to the bureaucratic and political process.

Accountability to consumers typically implies the need to satisfy those using a service, lest they take their business elsewhere—if there are alternatives available. A single supplier monopoly, whether public or private, has little incentive to satisfy service users. If there is competition, any service provider must pay greater attention to meeting the wishes of the users. Competing suppliers are central to the philosophy of welfare pluralism, precisely because this brings the promise of greater sensitivity and responsiveness to the needs and wishes of consumers. When there is a third-party case manager who arranges for needed services, it may not be easy or possible for the dissatisfied client to go elsewhere if the service provider satisfies the case manager.

Mandatory clients, such as those in child welfare or the prison system, do not have the option of moving elsewhere for service. The ensuing lack of accountability may provide a reason to not commercialize a service, or perhaps there is simply no accountability to consumers in practice. In 1987, the federal government experimented with contracts for voluntary non-profit organizations to supervise all parolees from the correctional system. The John Howard Society of Ontario recommended that the voluntary non-profit sector not accept contracts to provide custodial and coercive services (prisons, jails, parole, and probation) because it put at risk the ongoing relationships with those who need and used the service. Meeting the incompatible needs of the funder and of clients at the same time was impossible (Lightman, 1991).

Service users can also demand accountability through the courts, though this can be time-consuming and complex, and with an uncertain outcome. Small claims courts in many jurisdictions can simplify and expedite the process. But in many cases, governments cannot be sued in the courts.

Accountability also occurs up the ownership or management chain in both private and public sectors. Corporations have a fiduciary responsibility to shareholders, which may make the needs of the owners and consumers incompatible. Priority is usually assigned to the goals of the owners (as reflected in the share price for listed companies) or of the incumbent management, when diffuse stock ownership limits practical accountability to shareholders.

Public-sector accountability must satisfy both administrative and political processes. Bureaucratic authority, in principle, goes all the way up to the minister's office and Question Period in the House. In practice, however, political accountability is often limited, and lines of responsibility are vague.

## Gender

One of the most predictable consequences of privatization is the feminization of tasks. 'New economy' jobs—entailing a deskilled workforce and part-time hourly paid jobs that may lack benefits—invariably are filled by women, disproportionately minorities and/or recent immigrants. Many of these women have advanced skills from their countries of origin that are not recognized in Canada; others, by virtue of their marginalized status, remain trapped at the bottom of the hierarchy. The jobs these women fill are in the *secondary labour market,* a term referring, not to a physical location, but to the inferior pay and working conditions of the work. Unions are absent or weak in this sector.

When jobs are privatized to the not-for-profit sector, the tendency to cut wages and benefits may be less strong, but there persists often a devaluation and feminization of the work. Many NGOs tend to pay their line staff, disproportionately female, relatively low wages, usually due to funding constraints. (Senior management positions in NGOs tend to be better paid, but also tend to be male-dominated.) Benefits and pension, if offered, will be modest. Unions are present in some cases, but they are generally of limited effectiveness (though recent inroads from large and powerful unions such as the Canadian Autoworkers or the Steelworkers may reverse this over time). Because programs delivered in the social services tend to be labour-intensive, wages and salaries comprise a large portion of overall budgets; when cutbacks become necessary, the obvious response is to reduce the compensation bill. Thus, women pay the bill for privatization in the not-for-profit sector, as they do in a more extreme manner in the commercial world.

In certain areas, such as health care, women use the system more than men. Privatization typically includes deinsuring services or not insuring new services, procedures, and drugs; consumers must cover resultant increased costs. However, women are less able than men to do so because they have lower incomes, and are less likely to work in settings that offer private insurance for services not covered by medicare. Thus, privatization of health care—or any other service that women use more than men—adversely affects women highly disproportionately.

## Irreversibility

Privatization is difficult to reverse. Once a public asset is sold, usually well below the cost of replacement, rarely is it reacquired into the public domain. The cost to repurchase an entire stock of privatized public housing would be massive and as the residents are primarily poor, opposition would be much greater than a tax-resistant public and press would countenance. For example, when garbage collection is privatized, the trucks inevitably are purchased by the new provider at a fraction of the true replacement cost. Moreover, a private provider develops knowledge and skills concerning the delivery of a program that may exceed that of government, which becomes difficult or impossible to replicate.

International treaties also limit the government's capacity to restore a privatized service to the public sector. Certain services such as medicare or public education, construed narrowly, were exempted from the original Free Trade Agreement (FTA) and the subsequent North American Free Trade Agreement (NAFTA) (though the extent and viability of these exemptions were questionable). But once the commercial sector is allowed to deliver any services in these areas, the entire field becomes open to commercial provision. The net effect is that once a service is privatized, it becomes prohibitively expensive to return it to the public sector.

## THE REGULATORY DILEMMA[3]

Regulation is a process, usually involving inspection, intended to ensure minimum quality and standards in the delivery of a service or the provision of a commodity. It occurs in both the public and private sectors, often as a next-best alternative where competition among suppliers does not or cannot work. When services are privatized, regulation is generally put forward as a way to ensure the public interest is protected.

Regulation is often deemed desirable when users of a service—whether vulnerable or frail, or involuntary clients—are unable to exercise the rights and prerogatives of consumers. Regulation is seen as a way to redress the substantial imbalance of power between those providing the service and those using it, so providers do not abuse their power and all conditions associated with the delivery of the service are satisfied. Advocacy and personal support are an alternative to regulation: vulnerable persons are assisted to identify their own needs and ensure they are met. However, as consumer-based approaches are unlikely to work in certain cases, the benevolent alternative of regulation is required.

Structural factors may create a situation in which marketplace competition does not occur: there may be a natural monopoly, as with the provision of clean water; or, the supply of services may be limited by technology (as with radio frequencies) or political preference. A legal limitation on supply usually occurs when each place (as in a child-care centre) carries a public subsidy: to keep down costs, the supply of places is limited by political decision. Where there is limited or no competition among suppliers, state intervention through regulation is appropriate to maintain minimum standards

In short, when consumers or market competition are unable to ensure quality, regulation with inspectors and inspections can require service providers to meet certain identified goals under pain of sanction. In practice, regulation does not always work smoothly. When delivery systems fail, whether in child care or in protecting the environment, there are almost automatic calls for better regulation to ensure that standards of public health and safety are met. But regulation is difficult, and can be costly; governments are reluctant to try, through bureaucratic means, to bring about what a competitive market would have produced. There are also different forms of intervention within 'regulation'.

## The Forms of Intervention

### Registration

The simplest and cheapest approach to protecting the public interest is through registration. Providers of a service must identify themselves to the public—usually municipal—authorities; providers may be given a permit to operate in exchange for a modest payment. Such permits involve no inspection, impose no substantive conditions, cannot be withdrawn, and will be given in unlimited numbers upon payment of the requisite fee. Generating revenue can be a significant outcome of permit issuance, though rarely is this the primary reason for action.

The main purpose of registration is to make providers known to the government. Other inspection systems (such as public health) may choose to investigate, but they cannot do this unless they know who is delivering what service where. Someone contemplating opening a group home, for example, might be required to register, so the relevant authorities (including child welfare) would become aware of what is planned. A rent registry would provide a listing of all rental accommodation and of the prices, information valuable to potential renters and other landlords.[4]

### Voluntary Accreditation or Certification

This is an affirmation that an individual or organization has done something (in the past) or meets certain standards (in the present). Usually the affirmation is by a non-governmental body such as an industry or professional association and the costs are borne by those directly involved. Accreditation has no legal force, and participation is voluntary. It does, however, offer potential consumers useful information about what they may be acquiring and may imply that those meeting the accreditation conditions render a higher quality of service compared to those who do not.[5] There may be unrelated reasons—such as the cost of accreditation or philosophical opposition to an accrediting college—why some providers choose not to be part of the process, and a lack of accreditation does not necessarily imply inferior quality. While certification may indicate that a service provider has taken a course or passed an examination, the link between this and quality of service is open to interpretation.

Accreditation can be withdrawn if standards are not maintained, and information about this may provide negative direction about what to avoid. Voluntary procedures, then, may convey information, but the interpretation is often ambiguous. Thus, they are most useful as marketing tools for industries or associations that wish to raise their standards and to be seen taking their self-imposed responsibilities seriously.

### Licensing

A licence represents official permission to do something: unlike registration, it also indicates that minimum standards have been attained. This may involve a one-time test, as with a driver's licence, or ongoing inspections, as in a licensed child-care centre. Licences may be given in unlimited numbers, or severely restricted, as with a taxi or a nursing home licence. When licences are both limited and transferable they can have considerable resale value. Such a licence is thus an asset, which carries with it property rights. Removing it amounts to expropriation and can occur only for cause, a process that is time-consuming, costly, and fraught with legal complexity.

### Regulation

The term 'regulation' as we use it refers to *comprehensive regulation*, a process by which standards are set by government, together with authority to monitor and secure compliance. Three conditions must be satisfied for comprehensive regulation to occur.

- mandatory minimum standards must be set;
- government inspectors must enforce the standards; and
- penalties or other sanctions must be available for failure to meet the standards.

As well, public funding to private service providers may be required with respect to low-income clients.

However difficult it may be to set quantifiable and measurable standards, a benchmark against which behaviour will be assessed is needed. It is possible to set standards and to provide neither meaningful inspection nor credible sanctions; in practice, then compliance becomes voluntary, as there is no real requirement for providers to stay in line. If providers are required to meet certain standards and clients lack the income required to pay for the services, then there may be a legal obligation for government to make up the deficiency. We shall examine some of these issues.

## The Case for Regulation

In general terms, there are three main reasons why we regulate, in either the public or private sectors:

- *To protect vulnerable persons*. Regulation can reflect a collective (and paternalistic) responsibility to intervene and protect consumers who are unable to look after their own concerns. The costs of regulation and the practical difficulties in effecting it successfully are typically downplayed by those promoting it as the best way to protect vulnerable people.
- *To protect service providers*. Regulation assumes standards and that those who cannot or will not meet these conditions should cease to be providers. By identifying specific

standards, regulation can protect compliant providers against both disreputable providers and unrealistic expectations from potential consumers.

- *For consistency.* As regulation requires that all providers meet the same standards, there is knowability and predictability for consumers. In some cases, regulation may require that every provider do the same thing in the same way, and for identical payment. The roles of professionals in these areas, such as public health nurses, are thereby clarified.

## The Case against Regulation

Apart from disagreements with the views expressed above, there are several additional arguments against regulation:

- *Disempowerment.* 'Perhaps the most compelling argument against extensive regulation' (Lightman, 1992) is that consumers of services are excluded from important decisions that affect their lives. Decisions are made and actions taken that presumably are in their best interests, but consumers have little or no say in deciding what is acceptable and what ultimately has been attained.
- *Decreased supply.* Regulations impose minimum standards on suppliers of services. Those previously operating below that minimum may experience increased costs and some suppliers will decide to close down. As a result the overall supply of services may decrease.

  This problem is particularly acute in the housing area. Many community groups regularly oppose minimum standards for residential accommodation, as their introduction will raise costs to those landlords who traditionally provide accommodation for people at the very bottom of the economic scale, the barely housed or the hard-to-house. Landlords, in communities where the supply of low-quality housing is small, may decide to upgrade to middle-class accommodation or leave the field entirely, if it is no longer economically viable to provide low-income housing. The argument is compelling. While regulation and standards aim to protect vulnerable persons and to improve the quality of their accommodation, the effect of introducing these standards may be to dehouse people. Is low-quality housing for many preferable to improved-quality housing for some, but no housing for others?
- *Higher cost.* Along with decreased supply, regulated standards also raise costs for those who continue to receive service, as suppliers will pass on increased costs to consumers. If consumers are on fixed incomes and unable to pay, the state would be expected to compensate; if it is unwilling to do so, some service providers may choose to absorb the additional costs, but others will simply ignore the new higher standards so as to avoid the additional costs.

  The regulatory process can also be very expensive to administer. Developing rules and regulations involves some expense, but the major costs are for ongoing inspection, for these are labour-intensive and continuing. A government may decide to save tax dollars by not inspecting, or only in a perfunctory manner. This will nullify the intent of regulation, as limited inspection removes any threat of meaningful sanctions and therefore any real obligation for providers to comply.

Compliance in practice becomes voluntary and the presumed benefits from regulation may disappear.

- *Technical problems.* As we saw above, quantification and measurement of outcomes in the social services are problematic. Quality, in particular, is difficult to assess for regulatory purposes. Standards with criteria that cannot be measured cannot be enforced.

  Some aspects of service—such as minimum staff-to-resident ratios in residential settings—are relatively easy to quantify, though 'cheating' on actual staffing numbers is possible: Overnight shifts, for example, are essentially unregulated as inspectors tend to go home at the end of the ordinary work day. Areas such as nutritional quality of food (or whether meals are tasty or even palatable) are even more difficult to regulate. 'Adding more water to the soup' describes the problems of setting reasonable regulatory standards, and of ensuring that they are met consistently.

- *Staffing/bureaucratic problems.* Regulation and inspection are carried out by people who, by definition, have weaknesses and limitations. Inspectors are expected to make informed judgements based on their expertise and training, yet they know that informal measures can often have a greater impact than strict enforcement. Often inspectors see themselves as educational and training consultants for service providers, rather than as police officers, handing out fines and penalties. Furthermore, inspectors tend to develop ongoing, collegial relationships with service providers, as they are relatively permanent players, while clients tend to come and go. Service providers can also develop concrete knowledge about the services and processes because they are on site continually, and inspectors may become dependent for information on those being inspected. When clients are poor, frail, or vulnerable, there can be class affinities between regulator and provider, while those ostensibly being protected are left on the outside, looking in. This is not to suggest overt collusion or corruption by inspectors (though these do occur), but describes a shared community of interest among 'professionals' in any setting. This process is known as *regulatory capture,* in which inspectors evolve into advocates for the service or industry they are supposed to police. This can occur in any regulated setting, in the telephone, water protection, or airline industries every bit as much as in a boarding house for psychiatric survivors.

- *The limits of sanctions.* Fines and penalties that are imposed can be challenged by service providers, though complex and time-consuming litigation serves no one's interests. Small fines may be viewed simply as a cost of doing business, and larger penalties often may be passed on to service users through reduced quality of service— *more water in the soup.* Ultimate sanctions, such as the suspension of a licence, are rarely applied because of the difficulties in finding alternative, and better, service providers. For example, if a nursing home licence is removed, suddenly frail residents have nowhere to live and no one to care for them. Because service providers are essential to a total service delivery system, they have sufficient power that they are virtually immune from severe sanctions.

For all these reasons, regulators will often reject sanctions in favour of more conciliatory approaches. More than a decade ago, the Ontario Ministry of Health abandoned penalties in its dealings with nursing homes. Charges laid against nursing-home operators in the province dropped from 497 in 1984 to 12 in 1988 to zero in 1989 and subsequently. In the last decade only one or two—there is some dispute—nursing home licences were removed. After the election of the Conservative government in 1995, inspections of long-term care facilities have been announced in advance, which converts them to something more akin to a tea party than a serious inquiry into the quality of care.

The ministry's view (through three governments representing three different political parties) has consistently been that enforcement is counterproductive and collegial relationships achieve more. The contrary view is that both a carrot and a stick are necessary; without the stick regulation becomes a system based on voluntary compliance, which is inadequate protection for vulnerable residents of nursing homes.

# WELFARE PLURALISM

Welfare pluralism attempts to address some glaring weaknesses of the big bureaucratic welfare state while stopping short of commercial for-profit delivery of service. This middle path, part of *the mixed economy of welfare*, combines governmental and non-governmental provision. A variant, *the third sector*, associated with the New Labour Party in Britain, stresses the role of voluntary, non-profit agencies, co-ops, and informal links of kinship and neighbourhood. In its early forms, welfare pluralism was limited largely to the not-for-profit sector, but it can also encompass the commercial world.

Welfare pluralism addresses the conflicts inherent in government's being both funder and provider of services: funders tend to restrain spending, while suppliers' primary obligation is to meet needs. The approach attempts to split these roles or, if they cannot be separated, to create a firewall (so the two roles function independently).

Welfare pluralism also confronts the impersonal nature of bureaucratic provision of services. Particularly when government is a monopoly provider, the incentive to respond to the needs of service users is minimal. As well, the overall tendency of public servants is to place their own needs and interests (or those of their political masters) ahead of those of their clients.

As a counterbalance, welfare pluralism retains government as funder, while introducing competition into the provision of social services. Government's role as provider of services is replaced, or supplemented, by a new role as *purchaser* of services from multiple suppliers who can be in both the commercial and not-for-profit worlds. In principle, government can be one of many competing suppliers who bid for contracts, provided the firewall is in place to keep distinct the roles of funder and service provider..

Often suppliers are not chosen by consumers spending cash, but by proxies, such as third-party decision-makers or vouchers. Decision-making is thereby decentralized, usually to the local or community level.

Case management represents a relatively pure application of the welfare pluralist approach: caseworkers arrange needed services for clients based on individualized assessments. The professionally determined needs of the client take precedence over the wishes of the client, who may not even be consulted. Payment for the services may involve a ledger transfer from funds administered by the worker on behalf of the client directly to service providers without involvement by the consumer.[6]

Canada's medicare is also 'pluralistic': government funds the system, which is supplied by competing physicians in both private practice and not-for-profit clinics. Payment goes from the funder directly to the service provider, bypassing consumers. Many European countries and Israel have competing health funds, among which consumers may be required to choose. The funds compete for members by offering different packages of services. Pluralism is also the basis of public education (parents are free to choose their child's school from the alternatives in the community) and of child care (the parent may hold a voucher that can be used at any approved centre). In these cases, however, decision-making is not delegated to some third party but instead is retained by the consumers.

Ideally, welfare pluralism would have the strengths of the market model, without its limitations. Certainly competition in place of government monopoly should improve service quality and efficiency, but only if suppliers respond, in part at least, to incentives. Choice may be limited to selecting among different suppliers offering the same product, even if it is packaged differently. The option of not using a service and spending the money on a greater priority is not available. Choice, then, is limited to the means; the end itself is not subject to choice.

Responsiveness and sensitivity to consumer preferences is also limited when there is a third-party decision-maker. A case manager may appreciate the clients' needs, but ultimately remains the one making important choices about clients' lives. It is not at all clear that a case manager's discretion in making choices is preferable to an impersonal government-based process. Discretion, as we have seen, can sensitively and caringly meet the needs of clients, but it can also exclude or marginalize clients. The fixed rules of a government service (such as welfare eligibility) may be preferred by users to the capriciousness of an agency worker.

Decentralization is undoubtedly one of the greatest attractions of welfare pluralism. Standardized services delivered by a hierarchical and centralized bureaucracy are replaced by smaller, more flexible units, responsive to local concerns and priorities. When decision-making at a local level and non-profit community-based agencies are strengthened, entire neighbourhoods benefit through participation and involvement. The needs of changing and diverse population groups can better be met with such an approach.

However, decentralization and local control can come at the expense of equity: communities that are well-organized and articulate will do well; those that are not will be further marginalized. The benefit will go to middle-class and urban communities, leaving the others behind. Though the use of a service will theoretically be determined by need rather than by ability to pay, unequal access by various communities may mitigate this goal. Indeed, not all individuals or communities want participation and involvement; people with very low incomes may be too busy trying to pay the rent to have time for what they see as middle-class indulgences such as participation. Local control for some can lead to systematic exclusion of others and to discriminatory practices that maintain the exclusion, as cream-skimming rejects costly and hard-to-serve clients.

When community participation does work, it can be the gateway to further progressive local political and social action. Once these processes begin, they can spread more broadly, resulting in greater involvement for political change and social justice.

Because pluralism replaces government jobs by employment in the private sector, it has been described as an attack on public-sector unions and a way to reduce public-sector employment. Certainly, it often substitutes insecure, temporary, and lower-paid jobs, typically with few benefits, for relatively secure and well-paid employment in the public sector. Women, as we saw earlier, bear the brunt of this downgrading. While this view reflects a general criticism of privatization, not specifically directed at welfare pluralism, the criticism has greater potency in this context as pluralism is presented as being progressive and enlightened, unlike the commercialization alternative.

## SOME EVIDENCE ON PRIVATIZATION

For those who believe in privatization as an ideological goal, empirical evidence is irrelevant: the shrinking of government is an end in and of itself. Many privatizations in Canada appear to be ideologically driven, as evaluations of privatized activities often do not occur, based on explicit political decisions.

Comparisons between the public and private sectors are difficult. For-profit schools typically score higher on standardized tests than do those in the public sector; but these schools cream-skim on intake and expel (or 'counsel out') problematic children, so the result is hardly surprising. Given its mandate to serve everyone, public education does not have the option to select only the best students. As well, average parental incomes are higher in the private sector, so the family environments (including home computers, private tutoring, etc) are more supportive. And as we noted earlier, commercial schools in the United States concentrate on areas that will be tested, to the detriment of everything else.

These operational difficulties lead some observers to conclude that no general conclusions can be drawn between commercial and not-for-profit service delivery in the health and social services. Certainly, generalizations are difficult, because even the findings of specific case studies are not always more broadly applicable.

Occasionally, however, for-profit (usually commercial) delivery of services is compared to government or not-for-profit delivery, usually in the health area, where the commercial sector is highly developed. In 1997, the government of Manitoba awarded a one-year contract to Olsten Health Services—a US-based corporation—to deliver 10 per cent of its home care services. Savings of up to $4 million were anticipated.

> When the contract came up for renewal . . . all services were brought back under public administration. This decision coincided with . . . FBI investigations of Olsten for alleged improper Medicare billing in the US. Other concerns about Olsten—and of privatization in general . . . included the claims that a privatized system results in lower wages that make it hard to attract and retain qualified caregivers; that it leads to a loss of control over standards, planning and administration, and thus to over-billing; that clients tend to be pressured to purchase additional costly, but unnecessary, services and products; and that it does not provide for an effective appeals procedure. (CCPA, 2000)

This same study (CCPA, 2000) reported on more than 20 studies comparing for-profit with not-for-profit health care in the United States. Four of the most recent studies all favour not-for-profit delivery. One of these found that the annual death rate was 20 per cent higher among patients with kidney disease treated at for-profit dialysis centres; they were also 26 per cent less likely to be placed on the waiting list for a kidney transplant than were those at the not-for-profit centres (Garg, 1999).

A study for the Alberta branch of the Consumers' Association of Canada (cited in CCPA, 2000) found that the growth of private cataract surgery clinics in that province has:

• increased public waiting lists;
• increased the cost of services, the price to patients, and the cost of health plan coverage;
• created conflict-of-interest situations that jeopardized both patients and taxpayers; and
• decreased public scrutiny, public accountability, and public control of the Alberta health-care plan.

Lightman (1992), serving as a one-person commission of inquiry, studied the impact of for-profit residential care homes for vulnerable adults in Ontario. No one knows how many people live in these unregulated homes, but an estimate prepared for the Commission suggested at least 50,000 residents. The settings include retirement homes for seniors and boarding/lodging homes targeted at persons with psychiatric or developmental disabilities. The Commission found widespread abuse—financial, physical, and emotional—and neglect, much of it directly attributable to the absence of a provincial role as protector. Though other provinces do not have as large an unregulated sector as Ontario, everywhere there are low-quality, often dangerous, residential premises for poor and vulnerable people that are not subject to rigorous and regular inspection and regulation.

A number of American-based multinational corporations have become major players in privatized social service delivery systems. Prominent among these is Accenture (formerly Andersen Consulting), which has worked with governments around the world to cut welfare caseloads and costs. NUPGE (2000), the National Union of Public and Government Employees, has produced what it describes as Andersen's 'Top Ten Major Screw-ups', including work for four American state governments, the government of Ireland and the National Insurance project in the UK, the Canada Department of Public Works, and the governments of New Brunswick and Ontario. In none of these cases did the expected cost savings and efficiencies emerge. Indeed, the state auditor of Nebraska stated, 'I've been auditor for six years now and this is *the most wasteful project I have ever heard of*. It's like pouring money down a deep, dark hole.'

In 1995 and 1996, New Brunswick's auditor issued consecutive reports criticizing an Andersen contract. The auditor said the government had paid the firm almost $1 million that it had not earned. Recently, citing ballooning costs, New Brunswick cancelled another contract with Andersen Consulting, this one to reorganize the province's justice system. According to the *Telegraph Journal*, the project was to have cost $60 million and saved the government $7 million per year; up to 15 per cent of jobs in the public system were to be cut and Andersen stood to make $9.2 million. The project cost ballooned to $144 million and the New Brunswick government had to pay $2 million just to get out of the deal. The federal government cancelled a $44.5 million contract with

Andersen Consulting in May 1995 after the firm failed to meet its contractual obligations and demanded that the contract price be doubled. The Ontario government hired Accenture to 'reform' the social assistance system in 1997, and the Auditor first 'red-flagged' the contract in 1998. In his 2001 Report (Ontario, 2001), the Auditor reported that it cost about six times as much to have Accenture to do work, as compared to public servants.[7] In the preceding year, the province had paid Accenture $193 million to revamp the social assistance system, but had realized savings of only $89.5 million.

Finally, we may look at an interesting, though tangential, example—a decision by Ontario's Ministry of Transportation to 'outsource' (privatize) the maintenance of 45,000 kilometres of roads in the province. The Provincial Auditor looked at the first four pilot projects and found that the ministry's claim of a 5 per cent savings in costs was based on an inflated estimate of the cost of work previously done by government employees. In fact, according to the Auditor, three of the four pilots were actually costing the government more money, and overall the cost savings were less than 1 per cent (Urquhart, 2000). A year later (Ontario, 2001) the Auditor criticized the ministry again, accusing it, in effect, of attempting to cover up the evident cost-saving failure of the outsourcing.

Do we conclude from this evidence that privatization never works, except perhaps for the commercial providers involved? There undoubtedly are many cases where commercial service delivery is cheaper (usually because of reduced labour costs), though the impact on quality remains unclear. Not-for-profit delivery, to which we shall return in Chapter 10, is often successful, because community groups can work more cheaply and in a more sensitive manner than government providers. But when the focus is restricted to commercial for-profit provision of service, the evidence overwhelmingly suggests that quality is rarely maintained and promised cost savings are often elusive or non-existent. The case for commercial delivery, it appears, may have to rest on ideology, an approach for which no evidence is either required or desired.

## NOTES

1. Much public or 'council' housing in Britain was enthusiastically sold off in the early Thatcher years: prices were allegedly set at levels beyond the capacity of sitting tenants, but well below market rates, providing large windfall gains for the politically connected who were able to step in and catch the bargains.

2. Inadequate inspection of the water supply at Walkerton, Ontario, in 2000, led to seven deaths and hundreds of illnesses, many of them serious. A year later, the Provincial Auditor (Ontario, 2001) criticized the Ontario government for its failure to conduct follow-up inspections on 'critical' deficiencies at provincially inspected slaughterhouses, suggesting significant parts of the food supply were at risk.

3. Parts of the following discussion were originally explored in *A Community of Interests: The Report of the Commission of Inquiry into Unregulated Residential Accommodation*, Ernie Lightman, Commissioner (Toronto: Government of Ontario, 1992).

4. Because care homes (retirement and boarding homes) have no provincial registration requirement in Ontario, their numbers, locations, and populations are not known. Occasionally a care home in Ontario comes into the public eye when there is an inquest into an unfortunate death of a resident in a home that no public agency knew existed.

5. For example, the hospitality industry association may assign ranking based on a number of stars (or other symbols) to hotels and motels, on a voluntary basis.

6. In contrast to this approach, agencies such as the Canadian Association for Community Living advocate individualized funding models, whereby dollars are attached to the client (as with case management), but it is the client who 'shops around' for the best package of services. This approach, based on a belief in consumer empowerment, can only be effective if funding levels are adequate and if the needed services are available for purchase.

7. Andersen Consulting rates ranged from $85 to $575 per hour compared to $28 to $70 per hour for comparable public-sector staff.

## SUGGESTED READINGS

Browne, Paul Leduc. 2000. *Unsafe Practices: Restructuring and Privatization in Ontario's Health Care*. Ottawa: Canadian Centre for Policy Alternatives, Nov.

Canadian Centre for Policy Alternatives (CCPA), with Pat Armstrong, Hugh Armstrong, and Colleen Fuller. 2000. *Health Care, Limited: the Privatization of Medicare*. Ottawa: Canadian Centre for Policy Alternatives.

Fuller, Colleen. 1998. *Caring for Profit: How Corporations Are Taking Over Canada's Health Care System*. Ottawa: CCPA.

Combined, these three recent studies from the Canadian Centre for Policy Alternatives produce a stark, and chilling, assessment of the state of medicare today. They are well written, easy to read, and very powerful.

Ismael, Jacqueline, and Yves Vaillancourt, eds. 1988.. *Privatization and Provincial Social Services in Canada: Policy, Administration and Service Delivery*. Edmonton: University of Alberta Press.

This volume examined the early implications of privatization of the social services in various provinces across Canada.

LeGrand, Julian, and Will Bartlett, eds. 1993. *Quasi-Markets and Social Policy*. London: Macmillan.

This edited volume examines welfare pluralism (quasi-markets) in several different areas of the social services (such as social housing, education, and community care). Most of the material is British, where the ideas were most fully developed during the Thatcher years, but there is limited reference to the US experience as well.

Lightman, Ernie. 1992. *A Community of Interests/Une communauté d'interêts*, Report of the Commission of Inquiry into Unregulated Residential Accommodation. Toronto.

The report of this Commission examined 'care homes' (boarding or lodging homes as well as retirement homes) for persons with psychiatric histories, developmental disabilities, or those who were seniors in Ontario. At least 50,000 vulnerable adults are estimated to reside in these settings that are totally unregulated by the provincial government.

Pitsula, James, and Ken Rasmussen. 1990. *Privatizing a Province: The New Right in Saskatchewan*. Vancouver: New Star Books.

This is an informative case study of ideologically driven privatization in Saskatchewan—and its consequences—during the government headed by Grant Devine as Premier. Several cabinet members wound up in jail.

Social Planning Council of Metropolitan Toronto. 1997. *Merchants of Care? The Non-profit Sector in a Competitive Social Services Marketplace*. Toronto: Social Planning Council.

This report by the Social Planning Council of Toronto examines the issues and practices of commercialization (for-profit service delivery) in that community. There is considerable case material.

# CHAPTER FIVE

# Allocating Benefits: What?

## INTRODUCTION

The architects of Britain's post-war welfare state wanted to ensure that benefits were actually received by the intended recipients, and with minimal stigma. Permeating their work were memories of the Great Depression and the Poor Laws when benefits were given grudgingly and in a highly personalized and demeaning manner. Two building blocks emerged: in-kind distribution and universal eligibility for benefits. These correspond to two questions in the upper portion of our redistributive cycle, developed in Chapter 2, where we considered the allocation of social benefits: *What* is to be provided and in what form, and *to whom* are the benefits to be given?

In this chapter, we shall examine the first of these questions. We consider the nature, implications, and normative rationales for the different forms of benefit allocation, and shall compare the main forms—cash or in-kind—in terms of standard evaluative criteria such as effectiveness, efficiency, and cost. Included will be analyses of paternalism, stigma, and capacity in decision-making. Vouchers will be introduced as a mid-point response, attempting to combine the best elements of both cash and in-kind provision. Several examples, ranging from legal aid to food stamps (in the US) to educational vouchers and child care, will illustrate the approach. In Chapter 6 we look at the other aspect of allocation: *who* is to receive? Chapters 7 to 9 explore the lower portion of the redistributive cycle, asking *who is to pay* and *in what form*?

Undoubtedly one of society's earliest forms of charitable activity was to deliver food to the worthy, but destitute, widow with small children. Today, one of the fastest growing areas of activity in the social welfare field is the food bank. We have come full circle: from 'food hamper to the deserving poor' all the way back to 'food hamper to the deserving poor'. We have attempted, but seemingly discarded, other approaches—money, without conditions or entitlements; money with programmatic conditions; money with sanctions; training; programs; opportunities; we have even flirted with the idea of giving the poor control over their own lives.

But we seem to be back to where we were a hundred—or many hundred—years ago: limited benefits delivered as tangible commodities to those truly in need.

## Food Banks

Nothing more graphically illustrates the collapse of our social safety nets in Canada than the emergence and rapid growth of food banks across the country (Riches, 1986).

Not many years ago, there was widespread agreement in Canada that people who were hungry were entitled to incomes sufficient to meet their basic needs. Organizationally, this was enshrined in the Canada Assistance Plan (1976–96), which specified being 'in need' as the sole condition for benefits, and provided money, rather than food baskets, to those in need. However, the amounts provided were often inadequate, and, in response, informal community-based alternatives emerged.

Among the most controversial were food banks, warehousing and/or food distribution centres where hungry people can receive food on a regular basis. Some banks offer predefined hampers; others permit users to choose among narrow sets of alternatives. In all cases, what is available depends in small part on private donations and in large part on corporations' surplus food stocks. Supplies, therefore, do not correspond to people's (especially children's) nutritional needs, but instead reflect what others wish to donate or to dispose of.

Canada's first organized food banks, in Alberta in the early 1980s, were directly copied from the United States, where food banks are a large and valued part of the voluntary sector. They are seen to reflect the best of local communities coming together, using a charity model, to help the needy without the intrusive hand of government. Because of their heavy reliance on volunteers and donations of food, the direct cost to taxpayers is slight. Corporations enthusiastically dispose of surplus food while receiving substantial tax benefits for their 'charitable' activity. The right of consumers to choose what they want to eat and to receive help without paternalism and pathos—their need for money rather than food baskets—has never been of great concern in America.

In Canada, by contrast, the spread of food banks created much greater ambivalence. It was blatantly obvious proof of the failure of the Canada Assistance Plan, an abdication by government of its duty to ensure that everyone has adequate income. Staff in food banks saw their role as providing band-aids, temporary emergency assistance to stop the hemorrhaging, but not a long-term solution. As early as 1989, the Metro Food Bank in Halifax announced that it would cease operations within five years, returning the responsibility to address hunger to government, where it belonged (Henderson, 1989). The paternalism and social control in distributing food was troubling even to those running these emergency warehouses; and the administrative inefficiency of providing food rather than cash assistance was evident. Moreover, were it not for the large numbers of volunteers, the food bank industry would not be viable. Food banks were not intended as fundamental cornerstones in Canada's safety net, yet that is what they became. Government has been permitted to ignore its responsibility to help the poor.

## Cash and In-Kind Benefits

The food basket is an example of delivering benefits *in kind*, that is, a system in which commodities such as food or housing, or services such as education, child care, or medical care, are given directly to recipients who meet pre-defined criteria. The major alternative delivers benefits as *cash*, usually by direct payments, but also through reduced liability for taxes (exemptions or deductions). Beneficiaries are then free to spend the money as they wish.

Decisions about *what* to give are more complex than the simple dichotomy between cash and in-kind delivery. One creative alternative, subject to much public debate in recent years, involves vouchers that can be exchanged for educational services, legal assistance, or, in the United States, for certain types of food (through food stamps). However, there exists a wider spectrum of benefit types. Some, such as power or access, are process-oriented and attempt to alter the fundamental structures of society, rather than merely to shift boxes of food from one person's kitchen to another's.

# TYPES OF BENEFITS

Gilbert and Terrell (1998) have identified six broad categories of benefit allocation. They differentiate them on the basis of transferability, the extent to which the benefit must be used by the recipient or can be reallocated to another, possibly in exchange for something else.

1. *Opportunities.* These are targeted benefits, directed to particular individuals or groups for their sole use. They often take the form of preferential or advantaged treatment (as in affirmative action programs), intended to redress past systemic disadvantage or exclusion. Opportunities also can be provided as rewards for past services or contributions (as in preferential programs for war veterans or seniors). Typically, opportunities are contingent: they may open doors to the receipt of other benefits, but are not of substantive value themselves.
2. *Services.* In this category are a wide array of activities, usually delivered by one individual (the provider) to another (the client). The benefit is not transferable, and is given on the explicit premise that it is what the client needs. Delivery of services is often done by social workers, and may be accompanied by complex (and expensive) bureaucratic or administrative arrangements. Services range from counselling and home care to education and medicare.
3. *Goods.* Some tangible in-kind commodities (such as food, clothing, wheelchairs, or baby cribs) may be readily transferable to others or converted to cash, though usually at a substantial discount; other commodities (such as housing) are less readily transferable. Such goods were the main form of benefit a century ago, and remain the preferred option for many individuals and charities today.
4. *Credits.* These include vouchers (as in legal aid), concessions (such as reduced rates for seniors), and rebates (including those through the tax system). Vouchers involve constrained choice, in that the benefit is received only if the recipient acts within

designated parameters, but within those boundaries there may be various alternatives. A daycare subsidy voucher, for example, must be used within specified daycare settings (usually licensed and inspected premises), but may be applied to any qualifying setting, thereby retaining a substantial element of consumer choice. Other vouchers may or may not be transferable beyond the intended recipient.

5. *Cash.* This most transferable of the benefit options offers the greatest consumer choice and is the simplest to administer. A guaranteed annual income (GAI), which assures a minimum income to eligible individuals, has often been embraced, across the political spectrum, as *the single* social program, to replace most of what is now on offer. Included in the category are both direct cash outlays and benefits delivered through the tax system, 'tax expenditures'—all credits, deductions, and exemptions, personal and corporate. (We shall discuss tax expenditures at length subsequently.)

6. *Power.* This reallocation of authority or control from one individual or group to another may involve consumer participation in service delivery. The Canadian Mental Health Association, for example, often requires that consumer-survivors (clients) sit on all boards and committees of the organization, though how much actual power this conveys is uncertain. Feminist counselling is organized horizontally rather than hierarchically, to minimize the power of the 'helpers'. The concept can extend more broadly to a system in which dependent people have control over their lives.[1]

To these six categories we may add a seventh, perhaps the obverse of opportunity, which entails a *requirement*, that individuals do something or meet some criterion—a negative benefit to, or sanction of, recipients.[2] Like opportunities, *requirements* do not convey substantive content, but are contingent, opening or closing doors to other benefits. A requirement may entail searching for work as a condition of receiving social assistance, or it may prohibit smoking in exchange for a bed in an emergency shelter.

Of the categories identified by Gilbert and Terrell (1998), the first four listed reflect what Tobin (1971) described as 'specific egalitarianism': any benefit in-kind moves towards some degree of equal access to the particular benefit but leaves untouched both access to other benefits and the underlying differences in capacity or ability to pay with no commitment to redress fundamental inequalities.[3] Hence, state intervention in particular areas for particular restricted (often political) ends is seen as a specific exception to the primacy of the market.

Power is clearly the most radical and progressive of the six categories, in that it alone attempts to address the causes of inequality. Within the broad category of *power* are a number of diverse goals including concrete benefits (such as gainful employment and the associated right to it) and more process-oriented outcomes (such as economic and social rights, status, access, or social inclusion).

These latter categories share a focus on a process to alter the fundamental structural relations in society, rather than merely to redress modest imbalances in final outcomes by altering the means through which resources are allocated. Redistribution of income, while necessary to some extent, is not sufficient: were the total wealth in Canada divided absolutely equally today among the total population, by tomorrow fundamental inequalities would have reappeared, unless the allocative systems and structures were simultaneously altered.

## Linking Cash and Other Benefits

The categories of benefits (whether positive or negative) are not mutually exclusive, and can be combined in various ways.

### From Canada Assistance Plan to Workfare

Under the Canada Assistance Plan, as we have seen, recipients were entitled to cash payments, without conditions, provided only that they were 'persons in need'. Theoretically, this was extremely progressive, in that it removed charity and coercion in favour of people's autonomy to conduct their lives as they wished. In practice, however, the provinces were given considerable discretion both to determine whether applicants were 'persons in need', and to impose conditions, such as a requirement that single employables engage in active job search. Official forms, signed by a number of employers, affirming that individuals had applied for work were the 'proof' that one was a 'person in need'; if one did not engage in job search, by definition, one could not be a 'person in need'. Thus, for many applicants, cash benefits were contingent upon meeting a *requirement* involving considerable social control.

When CAP was in place, in-kind benefits were attached to the receipt of CAP at various times, but always on an optional basis. Such add-ons might include opportunities— priority access to licensed child-care places or to training programs (for which the demand always exceeded the supply). Cash and in-kind incentives could top up social assistance for recipients attempting the transition from welfare to work: recipients could keep in-kind benefits, such as free drugs or dental cards, even after they began employment, or they could combine social assistance (cash benefit) with income from paid work (additional cash benefit) in ways that always ensured they were better off financially by participating in the paid workforce.

With the replacement of CAP by the Canada Health and Social Transfer (CHST) in 1996, the absolute entitlement to assistance was eliminated. Provinces were free to attach mandatory conditions or sanctions to the receipt of social assistance. The political discourse shifted as well: the 'deserving poor' had somehow become the 'indolent poor', who need coercive incentives to get their lives in order. The unrestricted cash payments under CAP were now considered 'passive' income support, as people allegedly were paid to do nothing—although this constitutes a fundamentally incorrect interpretation of CAP. In its place came the rhetoric of 'active' programming, in which people would be invited/encouraged/required to do specific tasks (in-kind benefits) in exchange for social assistance.

Cash payments through social assistance linked to in-kind requirements (benefits) involving some form of activity is the conceptual essence of workfare. Recipients are expected to participate in training or upgrading, search for jobs, and/or do volunteer work as a condition of—in exchange for—their income support (Gorlick and Brethour, 1998a, 1998b).

This conceptualization of workfare is fundamentally flawed. The dichotomy supposed between 'passive' welfare recipients sitting home and watching TV as compared with 'active' job-seekers taking control of their lives did not correspond to the realities faced by most people on social assistance. Skills development initiatives have always been dramatically oversubscribed and there has never been a need to formally tie participation to benefit receipt. Even the line between voluntary and compulsory participation is artificial: under CAP, social assistance payments for some were so low that any 'optional' add-ons that increased overall benefit levels were, in practice, compulsory; when the basic benefit is inadequate to live on, supplements may be voluntary in principle but mandatory in practice.

One senior civil servant actively involved in this area observed that the real goal of these new initiatives was the avoidance of idleness among the poor and dependent, while among the rich idleness remains highly desirable. Undoubtedly, this demonizing of the poor has met the political need of social control of the poor, by shifting the focus from systems and structures onto individual defect and pathology.[4]

## COMPARING DELIVERY MODES

How benefits can best be delivered depends, in part, on the underlying premises: Is homelessness fundamentally a problem of income deficiency or of inadequate housing stock? In other words, would greater income for low-income households suitably address the problem of homelessness? (Obviously, we think not, at least not in communities with tight housing markets.) Is hunger fundamentally a problem of income deficiency or of food production and distribution? Would world hunger disappear if adequate incomes were provided to all households? (The answer to this question, in Canada at least, tends to the affirmative.) Thus, providing people with sufficient incomes might allow them to meet their own nutritional needs in the marketplace, but would likely not resolve their housing problem, although in-kind provision might address it.

Normative considerations are important in decision-making about benefit provision; however, there is no general association between a particular value base and a preferred mode of service delivery. The early builders of the welfare state saw in-kind delivery as essential to the meeting of needs; the world they wished to replace was marked by inadequate housing, health, and education for the poor. The only certain way to meet these needs was to deliver them as tangible services. (The other component of this approach—universality—will be dealt with in the next chapter.) To these pioneers, the paternalism of this approach was acceptable, and such considerations as individual autonomy and the freedom to choose were deemed less important. These latter values remained high priorities to those favouring a residual value system, with minimal state intrusion.

In recent years many who formerly assumed paternalism was benevolent now tend to equate it with condescension or social control. They see a stigma or inferior status inherent in the receipt of in-kind benefits such as food hampers or public housing. These people, who typically hold to a more institutional value system (see Chapter 2), often advocate for cash payment. They argue for 'client empowerment' and freedom in the active sense of control over one's own life. Many urban black communities in the United States that fought for fully integrated education (a benefit in-kind) now favour educational vouchers that allow them to establish their own separate school programs, sensitive to local needs and priorities.

Those embracing a residual value system (Chapter 2) today tend to be the strongest supporters of the food bank system, because the approach replaces the oppressive hand of the state with voluntary neighbourhood activity. As well, residualism has adopted paternalism to ensure through meagre benefits and overt coercion that all helping activity is devoted towards ending dependence (and that support intended for children is not transformed into beer for adults).

Choosing a delivery mode for benefits involves more than problem conceptualization and normative stances. Of great importance are the answers to the central question of the 'in-kind' debate: *What is the role and adequacy of the market in social welfare?* The answers chosen will help determine those areas in which in-kind delivery of services may be preferable to cash transfers to recipients.

To the extent that the social services are similar to other commodities, and to the extent that consumers are competent to choose, presumably to give cash and to let those in need choose how to spend it would be preferable. When social services are unlike other goods and services or when consumers are not felt to be capable of informed choice, reliance on the market would be undesirable.

## PATERNALISM: 'FOR YOUR OWN GOOD'

*Paternalism*, in its simplest form, simply refers to a decision by one individual or group to interfere with the autonomous decision-making capacity of another individual or group ostensibly to enhance the latter's well-being. It is social control, presumably with a benevolent intent. External judgements are substituted for individuals' own wishes and priorities:

> *We know better than you what you need, even if that is not what you want—and we shall ensure that you get what you need. We interfere in your freedom for your own good.*

To constrain individual autonomy implies a greater concern with outcome than with process. Autonomous decision-making is subsumed in meeting some greater substantive goal.

In some sense, any decision by the state (or community) to restrict the absolute freedom of individuals involves paternalism: we install traffic lights and set rules for driving to protect motorists and pedestrians; we have public fire and police protection, and national defence, which individuals receive whether they want them or not; we require parents to educate their children to a certain minimum standard; through Canada Pension Plan we force wage-earners to save for their old age; through Workers' Compensation systems we require employers to insure against workplace injuries; through medicare we give people a package of health services without direct user charge. In each of these situations, the case for collective intervention must be justified on the basis of two distinct assumptions. One is technical and the other is ethical.

The *technical assumption* is that the state has the capacity to know better than do individuals what is in their own best interests. The state has better, or more, information than individuals, who would act 'unwisely' (because they lack this comprehensive information). For example, left to their own devices, many individuals would make inadequate provision for income in their old age because they cannot anticipate their future needs; in effect we do not trust parents to ensure that they will educate their children appropriately because they do not themselves possess the information and resources or have the capacity to do so, or because they do not appreciate its importance to the individual or to the larger society; people also may lack the information, resources, and capacity to provide for their own medical needs. In each case, we sanction collective intervention, because people do not, or cannot, acquire full knowledge.

Sometimes there are benefits to the community at large as a result of state intervention: basic education for all children is good because widespread literacy is necessary for the proper functioning of a democratic society; legal aid is needed for those appearing before the courts in order to ensure a fair legal system. A healthy population increases overall productivity, and there are public health benefits from the reduction in or absence of transferable diseases.

The *ethical assumption* is that society has the moral right to interfere with individuals' rights to conduct their lives as they wish. Provided no harm accrues to others and people are informed as to the consequences of their actions, why should individuals not be free to make their own decisions about saving for old age or insuring against illness? Why should people be required to pay for public fire protection if they can insure privately—or not insure at all? In some places, protection provided by the local fire department is an optional form of insurance, which people are free to purchase, or not, as they wish: in case of fire, help is provided only to those with coverage. What is wrong with this approach, provided people have good information about the choices available to them, and the consequences?

Both of these assumptions have been widely challenged. The state does not, in fact, always know better than individuals, and the ethical right to impose the collective will remains highly problematic.

Consider the experience with residential schools in Canada. Aboriginal children were forcibly removed from their homes, families, and communities to be integrated into the dominant white culture. The rationale was both technical—forced integration was the way to a better life—and ethical, based in moral judgements about parenting practices within the indigenous communities. The consequences of these decisions, in terms of abuse, failed assimilation, shattered communities, and loss of heritage, are still being felt by the affected individuals, their communities, and by society at large.

A decision by child welfare authorities to apprehend a child must be based on both technical and ethical assumptions: the worker must be assumed capable of deciding that a child is 'at risk', that the parents are incapable or unsuitable, and that there are no less intrusive alternatives available. Paternalism is central to this debate, as the decisions may involve stereotypes of class (or race, ethnicity, or single-parent status) in the determination of unsuitability: the arguments must be addressed in each case, as the facts are unique.

## EFFECTIVENESS

Before we can compare the effectiveness of cash and in-kind delivery of benefits, we must be clear on program goals. If the goal is to have a recipient actually receive a benefit, the most certain way to assure this is to physically deliver the benefit in-kind. Children are most likely to have good vision if we directly provide eye examinations and glasses, if needed. If we want children to be educated, we provide them with the schools, teachers, and supplies. If we want homes and lives to be protected against fire, we create a local fire department, paid for out of taxes.

Giving priority to certain program goals necessarily makes other goals secondary. Giving benefits in-kind assumes that effectiveness is primarily defined in terms of ensuring a benefit is received. Other goals—such as free choice on the part of the recipient—are secondary.

Voluntary organizations give hockey sticks to children to ensure that the kids have the opportunity to play hockey. If the price of a hockey stick was given to the parents instead, the money might be used to buy food or pay for housing. Thus, the donors decide, in lieu of the parents, what the children need most.

Some in-kind benefits, such as education, cannot be sold or transferred; others, such as prescription drugs, can be readily sold (though possibly at a fraction of original value), thereby negating the effectiveness target. Cash, by contrast, is not as effective in ensuring specific goals are met, as funds can be easily diverted, but cash maximizes the decision-making autonomy of recipients.

Offering a benefit in-kind does not ensure that it will be taken and used. Take-up rates for in-kind benefits vary, depending on access. Often benefits accrue disproportionately to the middle and upper classes, because the poor may lack information about the program, may not have the mobility to obtain it, or may not have the self-confidence or socialization to assert legitimate claims.

However, if the fundamental goal is to ensure the benefit is received, disproportionate use by upper-income groups is not a primary concern. Far more important is the recognition that the poor will utilize services more under medicare than if they were provided with cash, which typically would be diverted to more pressing needs, such as food, clothing, or shelter. Hence, the fact that the poor in Canada use medicare less than the middle or upper classes does not negate the fundamental premise that in-kind delivery for the poor is more effective than cash benefits.

# STIGMA

*Stigma* in the social services refers to the process whereby recipients of benefits are diminished, demeaned, or devalued compared to those who give or deliver the benefits (as was the case under the Poor Laws). The early developers of the welfare state held that to offer services as in-kind benefits to everyone, on the same basis, would go a long way towards reducing inequality in society. Today, however, stigma is used by service providers as a means of rationing and deterring use. By delivering services to which stigma is attached, it is hoped that usage (and hence overall cost) will be reduced. As well, stigma has become a form of social control, to keep recipients cowed and feeling subordinate.

Box 5.1, which tells the curious story of John Lennon's eyeglasses, shows that a benefit offered in-kind may be unattractive or highly desirable, depending on the context. If there is an option available that involves free choice, a two-tiered program may result. Recipients of the public benefit will carry a stigma associated with the benefit in-kind. But if the context changes, public perceptions will alter, and yesterday's stigmatized benefit may become much sought after today.

> ### Box 5.1  John Lennon's Eyeglasses
>
> For many years three specific types of eyeglass frames were available without charge
> as an in-kind benefit under Britain's National Health Service (NHS). They were imme-
> diately identifiable as 'NHS spectacles' and were largely used by the poor and mar-
> ginalized. Demand was modest, as there was a mild stigma attached to them. There
> was also a parallel private market where individuals paid high prices but were free
> to choose the styles they wished. In the 1960s, one of the NHS frames—wire-rimmed,
> the so-called 'granny glasses'—was worn and popularized by John Lennon of the
> Beatles. Suddenly there was tremendous demand for these NHS frames, as the stigma
> associated with their use was transformed into the ultimate in trendy imagery. People
> who had previously purchased more attractive frames privately now opted for free
> NHS frames, creating a huge upsurge in demand, far exceeding the NHS budgetary
> allocations for eyeglasses. Stigma was no longer an effective means to ration demand
> for eyeglasses. This created a budgetary and programmatic dilemma for the Labour
> government of the day: it was unwilling to provide free glasses for the middle classes,
> but was also unwilling to deal with the symbolism of removing a long-standing NHS
> entitlement to free glasses. The result? In a bureaucratic masterpiece of double-talk,
> the 'granny glasses' became 'temporarily unavailable', permanently.

Where there is no parallel private market, services (such as fire protection or public
libraries) are highly valued by those who use them across the entire community. Few
people would prefer a lower property tax bill (a cash benefit) if it meant no fire protection or libraries. This suggests that perhaps two tiers of benefit—a parallel private market with public services reserved for the poor—may confer an inferior status to in-kind
benefits rather than delivery in-kind per se. (We return to this in the next chapter when
we examine issues surrounding universality and selectivity.)

## Stigma in Housing

A powerful stigma in Canada today is that associated with residence in low-income public housing. Much (though definitely not all) of this housing stock is unappealing and
of low quality, and often physically cut off from nearby communities. Perhaps the housing is consciously made to be unattractive, to limit demand. Public housing meets a
narrow programmatic need of providing a place to live for those who otherwise might
be homeless. It fails, however, to meet broader programmatic goals: enabling people to
choose, with dignity, where to live, with whom, and in what way.

Some have argued that rent subsidies would solve the stigma problem, as recipients
would be free to address their own housing priorities. Unconditional cash payments are
advocated by those who see the problem as part of generalized income inadequacy. To
give money to the poor and allow them to meet their own housing needs as they see fit
would maximize consumer autonomy with least stigma.

Landlords often are reluctant to rent to people with low incomes, particularly to those who are on social assistance. The fact that the potential renters have cash does not make them less undesirable (or identifiable) in the eyes of the landlord. Their use of language, their bearing—indeed, even the geographic neighbourhood of residence—will mark recipients of social assistance.

In a slack housing market with a high vacancy rate, rent subsidies or unconditional cash payments might well substantially address the stigma issue: people could choose where to live and at what level. Low-income housing ghettoes would be less likely to emerge. (However, recipients of cash transfers might choose low-quality housing in order to buy more food for their children, or to buy food for more children.)

In a tight housing market with few vacancies, a different dynamic occurs: cash payments to large numbers of recipients bid up the prices of the limited stock of housing (as a way to ration); they do nothing to increase the supply of housing or to ensure that the cash will secure suitable quality housing. Thus, cash subsidies in tight housing markets are likely to disproportionately benefit landlords. Hence, rent controls are seen as a necessary complement to any system of cash assistance. But rent controls are most effective in the short term, and the only real solution to a tight housing market is to increase the supply of accommodation. The housing problem is not fundamentally one of income shortfall, but rather the problem is one of inadequate supply; and the only long-term remedy is to increase the supply.

We suggested above that while a benefit in-kind may tend to stigmatize recipients, cash appears to be 'stigma-free', as all money looks the same. But stigma may inhere in the socialized life experiences of the recipient, and in many contexts cash will do nothing to alleviate this inferior status. Thus, cash does not always eliminate stigma, as stigma involves wider life processes than merely whether benefits are delivered in-kind or in cash.

# EFFICIENCY

Cash is generally considered to be the most *efficient* way to deliver benefits. Once eligibility is determined, the organizational and bureaucratic costs are slight: cheques merely are issued (or cash payments made). In-kind benefits, however, involve administrative costs of acquiring or producing the benefit, assuring quality control, delivery, and oversight. These costs, in the aggregate, can exceed the value of the benefits.

Risks of conflict of interest, theft, or corruption probably are greater when in-kind benefits are provided. Service providers can be directed, or encouraged, to obtain products from specific suppliers, or to deliver through named parties. The opportunities for improper financial management are many, and the monitoring costs can be high. (There are also opportunities for theft involving cash benefits: creative accounting, non-existent recipients, and inadequate audit.)

## Economies of Scale

A powerful case for in-kind benefits involves economies of scale: as more of a benefit is produced or purchased, the per-unit cost goes down, through either the technical efficiencies of large-scale production or mass purchasing power. As a result, the per-unit cost is reduced below that which persons would pay individually. Mass production or purchase, however, typically involves uniformity, which presupposes consumer choice is unimportant or non-existent.

Large blocks of public housing were justified, in part, in terms of economies of scale: government as purchaser (and often, as builder) would be able to provide the housing at a lower cost per unit than individuals in the private market ever could attain. Choice was deemed to be unimportant. In practice, the presumed cost savings were often minimal or non-existent. It is not significantly cheaper, per unit, to build large amounts of housing all to a single plan than to construct smaller quantities with variation in design. Moreover, the inefficiencies of in-kind provision described above often outweighed any savings due to mass production and purchase. Finally, it was deemed that some choice in housing was desirable.

On the other hand, in-kind provision of drug benefits and pharmaceuticals has proven to be highly efficient. Most prescription drugs are produced by a few large multinational corporations, often protected by patents that delay the emergence of lower-cost generic alternatives. Many countries have chosen to include drugs as an in-kind benefit in their national health systems. Mass purchasing power obtains lower prices, generic substitutes are widely used, there is little or no advertising, and early intervention with drugs may be less costly than later treatment.

Canada, however, has chosen not to follow this path. Following the United States, we have given primacy to the interests of the multinational drug companies and private insurers over the provision of drugs as a universal in-kind benefit. The result, as we saw in Figure 4.1, is that drug prices have risen far faster than any other costs in our health-care system since the mid-1970s, and are responsible for much of the dramatic rise in overall health spending.

The objections to in-kind provision of drugs are partly ideological (consumer choice is minimized and the power of the multinationals challenged), and partly technical (large purchasers can err in their assessments of equivalence in clinical effect, or fall subject to corruption). However, if these possibilities are addressed, the case for in-kind provision is compelling.

Lower per-unit costs resulting from economies of scale do not necessarily lower total program costs: the costs paid by consumers (perhaps zero cost) are likely to be less than if they were purchasing the benefits themselves; therefore people may want more of the benefit, raising total program demand. Total program costs (the product of price per unit multiplied by total quantity) may well increase, because the increased overall demand may more than offset the lower per unit cost.

This argument is applied particularly to medicare. Because the service is provided as an in-kind benefit, without user fees, people allegedly use it more than they would if they had to pay for it directly. Undoubtedly many people, particularly the poor, do use medicare more than would buy private medical services. However, whether this is a good thing or a bad thing, whether there is 'abuse' or 'overuse', is a complex question to which we return in Chapter 8. Suffice it to say, however, that there is no empirical evidence to support 'overuse' or 'abuse', particularly by the poor, who use medicare more than the poor use market-based systems like that of the United States.

# Subsidies

Any program in which the price to consumers is less than that in the private market involves a *subsidy*, whereby the reduction in price represents the amount of public subsidy. A subsidy is a benefit in-kind because it lowers costs to consumers; is available only if individuals choose to use the particular services; and is not generally transferable. Subsidies can be widely applied (the costs of education) or they can be selective (reduced bus fares for seniors and child-care subsidies).

In practice, virtually all public services involve subsidies, from education, medicare, and most social services, child welfare, and child care, to services for seniors, minorities, and people with disabilities. Even prisons involve subsidies to the inmates. Anyone using these services, whether voluntarily or by compulsion, receives a subsidy. A universal subsidy lowers the price to all users while a selective or targeted subsidy is restricted to a specific group. Taxpayers pay part or all of the cost for these in-kind benefits, reflecting collective social priorities as determined by governments.

International trade rules have made subsidies controversial. In general, subsidies prevent a 'level playing field' and encourage a 'race to the bottom', whereby countries compete by offering ever greater incentives. These subsidies are widely used in producing goods (such as airplanes) that countries hope to export: the primary beneficiaries of the subsidies are the companies producing the goods (and their employees) and purchasers abroad. However, in recent years, large corporations have alleged that Canadian subsidies to public health care or education interfere with the rights of these businesses. With this bizarre, but increasingly articulated approach, the rules of international trade may prevent Canadian governments from subsidizing public education or health, because some believe they interfere with the profit-generating interests of foreign corporations. We return to this issue in the final chapter.

# Tax Expenditures

A *tax expenditure* is a cash benefit delivered through the tax system. Deductions, exemptions, credits, rebates, deferrals, or accelerated depletion allowances (for oil drilling) constitute tax expenditures, as they reduce taxes payable by somebody.

It is perhaps easiest to understand tax expenditures by way of example. Because of the child-care expense deduction on her personal income tax, Tova paid $400 less in taxes than she would if the provision did not exist or she did not use it. The public (including Tova) views this outcome favourably, in terms of lower taxes.

Conceptually, the same outcome could be attained in another way. If the child-care deduction did not exist, Tova's tax bill would be $400 higher. However, if the Minister of Finance authorized payment of a cheque for $400 directly to Tova to help with her child-care needs, her financial situation would be the same as if she had the deduction. But this direct payment would now be viewed as higher government spending.

In either case, Tova is better off by $400. The government spending is *direct* when a cheque is issued to Tova; the spending is *indirect* when it occurs through a reduced tax liability. In the current political climate, direct government spending is 'bad' and tax reductions are 'good', even though the financial impact in both cases is identical. Language use is always important in framing the discourse concerning tax policy!

There are several important characteristics of cash benefits delivered as tax expenditures:

- Tax expenditures are advantageous to government in that they tend to be relatively invisible, creating fundamental problems of democratic participation and accountability. Tax expenditures usually are buried deep in a government budget, presented, not as government spending, but as tax reductions. Few items in a budget are seriously debated in Parliament, and public accountability for tax expenditures tends to be minimal. The problems are particularly acute in the complex corporate tax system.
- The tax spending is targeted at those meeting certain conditions; the benefits flow directly and only to the recipients. There is no *spillover* effect, whereby benefits flow to others.
- Tax spending is administratively inexpensive, usually involving only an additional line or two on the relevant income tax form.
- Invisibility is also a problem because tax expenditures usually (though not necessarily) are regressive in impact.[5] The higher the taxpayer's income, the larger will be the gain. A $2,000 child-care deduction from taxable income results in different tax savings at different income levels, with those in the highest tax brackets (and having the highest incomes) saving the most. (We shall explore this further in Chapter 7.)

Issues of public visibility and accountability can become lost in the optics and politics of a situation. Suppose the Finance Minister announces in his budget a $2,000 deduction for child-care expenses. Cheers all around result in a 'good news' story, because everyone with eligible child-care expenses will now pay less tax. But what if that same Finance Minister posed his announcement in terms of tax spending—that in order to help families with child-care expenses, he will send a cheque for $1,000 to the richest Canadians and a cheque for $500 to those of more modest means? Regressive tax policy of this sort would be unlikely to earn the minister the same widespread approval. Yet the net effect is the same in each case.

## CAPACITY AND SUBSTITUTE DECISION-MAKERS

Giving recipients cash payments that they can spend as they wish centrally assumes *competence* or *capability,* the belief that people will make the 'correct' choices. For some, whatever people do is, by definition, a reflection of their preferences and priorities, and it is no one else's concern. This extreme position against paternalism holds that, if individuals choose, for example, not to pay for fire protection, that is their prerogative, and they alone will bear the consequences.

In general, however, there is a collective public understanding that for some people, in certain circumstances, the capacity for autonomous decision-making is restricted and some paternalism is needed. The operational challenge is where to draw the lines, and what to do on behalf of those deemed incapable.

Where competence is lacking, others must act. This may involve, as a last resort, appointing substitute decision-makers, either formally or informally. The goal of social policy intervention should be, as much as possible, to develop and enhance skills of capacity, to provide supports to assist people to make autonomous decisions.

Historically, we have had better systems of legal substitutes for property matters than for personal needs and care. This is not surprising, given that property and property rights are at the core of capitalism. A public trustee typically has sophisticated procedures to administer financial matters, but rarely do we have organized systems to protect personal care needs.

A few years ago Ontario proposed legislation to formalize a broad system of substitute decision-makers. Organizations representing people with developmental disabilities argued against the philosophical basis of the legislation. They take the position that we all need support, some more, or more frequently, than others. The *only* acceptable public policy intervention is to provide assistance and supports, whenever and to whatever extent needed. Given adequate resources, anyone, in principle, is capable of substantial action about how to live her or his life. Though there was pullback from this position in practice, the organizations remained firm to this as a statement of policy, principle, and ideology. Their philosophical position was buttressed by a fear that the legislation could make it too easy for families or the community to marginalize vulnerable people, to exclude them from any meaningful control over their lives, and from participation in society, by declaring them legally incapable.

The Advocacy Act, a creative alternative to substitute decision-making, was enacted in Ontario in the mid-1990s—and had the singular distinction of being the first program terminated by the incoming Conservatives in 1995.

## Ontario's Advocacy Act

This initiative, introduced by the NDP government, promised a system of social advocacy to some 600,000 vulnerable adults in Ontario (Lightman and Aviram, 2000). Just as legal aid was available to assist people in dealing with the law, social advocates would assist vulnerable adults in a wide range of non-legal issues (such as quality of care in nursing or retirement homes). The advocates would not make decisions on behalf of vulnerable people, but instead would give them help with information and support so they could make autonomous choices to the maximum extent possible. Central among their functions was to assist people (by giving rights advice) before they could be declared legally incapable.

The project never really had a chance. The government was committed to a wide-ranging and exhaustive consultation with grassroots community-based groups throughout Ontario, which took up much of the government's five-year term. The government did not decide until late in its term of office what would be the scope, mandate, and structure of the system or the number of advocates to be put in place. They also seriously underestimated the opposition to any activity that would provide independent advice to vulnerable adults. Health-care professionals, families, and operators of nursing and care homes mobilized against what they saw as unwarranted incursion on their decision-making. Finally, the government's ineptitude in guiding the legislation through the bureaucratic and political processes resulted in few tears being shed when the entire structure was abolished.

Nevertheless, social advocacy remains an exciting concept, because it accepts the dominant residual/economic market paradigm, while working to enhance the capacity of vulnerable people to function competently within its framework. Certain community groups, most prominent among them the Alzheimer Society and Friends of Schizophrenics, opposed the concept of advocacy because they felt the clients they represented were incapable of acting in their own best interests and needed protection from harming themselves. The Canadian Association for Community Living, representing people with developmental disabilities, enthusiastically embraced advocacy as an alternative to substitute decision-makers.

The tension between these competing positions was never resolved: there is both the need to respect people's rights to make their own decisions, even if these are 'incorrect' choices; and an equally compelling need to protect people from harming themselves or others. Social advocacy was intended to bridge this gap, to increase people's capacity to make their own decisions, with appropriate assistance, and to thereby lessen the need for legal substitutes. The debate was effectively terminated when the Conservative government abolished the advocacy program and gave responsibility back to professional gatekeepers and to families, regardless of their readiness or ability to assume the tasks.

# VOUCHERS

The voucher has been conceptualized as an intermediate response combining elements of cash and in-kind delivery. Typically (though not necessarily), the voucher is a physical document that gives to the recipient some choice within designated alternatives. The unfettered free choice of a cash payment is rejected in favour of paternalism: a specified need will be addressed, but a general income deficiency will not. At the same time, some choice is retained, giving constrained autonomy to the recipient, while meeting the ideological and/or administrative needs of donors. The element of social control is clear.

Some vouchers can be readily used by anyone holding them and are equivalent to cash. They can be bought and sold (including illegally and often at a discount), thereby circumventing the intended paternalism. Food stamps in the United States and emergency food vouchers given by Canadian welfare offices illustrate this approach. Vouchers also can be given to named recipients, and not transferable or negotiable: in these cases the vouchers are equivalent to in-kind allocation, with perhaps some element of choice.

The efficiency of vouchers is rarely considered, as constrained choice for recipients is typically the major (or only) policy interest. Substantial administrative costs may be incurred in determining eligibility (primarily because of the selective application of the benefit) and there are one-time start-up costs to ensure a market of sellers who will accept the vouchers. Costs associated with the use of vouchers depend on the complexity of reimbursement to service providers; usually, however, vouchers, like cheques, can be deposited for credit into a bank account.

Vouchers have been used more extensively in the United States than in Canada, because of the greater coercion and extraneous policy goals associated with their social programs.

### Food Stamps
Food stamps are undoubtedly the most extensively used voucher in the United States. The program enables designated low-income households to buy stamps at a substantially dis-

counted rate. The stamps are widely accepted at face value for a wide range of foods (excluding tobacco and alcohol). Food stamps thus serve as a general income supplement for poor individuals or families, while ensuring that state support is limited to nutritional ends.

Food stamps were introduced in 1961 in response to the agriculture industry's need to dispose of surplus produce, and the program has been delivered through the US Department of Agriculture (USDA) rather than through the welfare system. The primary program goal has been to distribute surplus food, not to meet the nutritional needs of recipients. Unlike the traditional welfare emphasis on limiting access, food stamps were widely available and used extensively. Indeed, before the Reagan administration cut back the program, it was estimated that one in eleven households was in receipt of food stamps.

Eligibility determination and distribution of food stamps lie solely with USDA, totally separate from welfare, and therefore without significant stigma. The coupons are negotiable by the bearer, and thus are equivalent to cash. Food stamps cannot be used for certain types of purchases: they are intended either to meet the nutritional needs of recipients, or to direct spending to the agriculture industry. In practice, the exclusions represent only a minor inconvenience as the precluded goods can be purchased with cash while the stamps are used for permitted items. In addition, there is a thriving resale market for food stamps, typically at a discount, determined by local conditions of demand and supply.

### Legal Aid Certificates

The right to legal assistance is widely seen as fundamental both to a democratic system and to a market economy. As such, there has always been a strong preference to deliver assistance in-kind to ensure no one is denied access. The earliest forms of legal aid were private charity delivered by individual lawyers to those whom they deemed worthy. Unrestricted cash payments that could be diverted to other uses have not been widely endorsed within the profession, government, or the public at large.

Currently, three models are used: legal aid certificates are true vouchers, exchangeable for legal services from any lawyer willing to participate. 'Public Defenders', a system widely used in the United States in which a salaried lawyer is available to assist those without private counsel, represents true delivery in-kind. Finally, legal aid clinics, also delivered as an in-kind benefit, are an innovative way to target legal assistance to the poor. Typically, clinics are located in low-income neighbourhoods and employ salaried lawyers who specialize in those areas of the law that most affect the poor.

Certificates are the preferred form of assistance for most of the legal profession. Eligibility may be determined by the law society using criteria independent of those used by other social welfare programs. The costs to determine eligibility thus are relatively high. Funding typically comes from the provincial government, which may apply pressure to narrow these criteria or to restrict the range of covered services. In Ontario, for example, legal aid is now difficult to obtain for non-criminal cases. A voucher naming both the eligible client and the designated problems or services is given to the individual, who is then free to use it to pay any participating lawyer.

The program contains strong elements of professional 'obligation' and social responsibility, seen by the law society as central to an individual's legal practice. Lawyers typically are paid a fixed fee for each case, which discourages long and involved proceedings in favour of rapid settlement, to the potential detriment of the client. As the compensation schedule is usually lower than most lawyers' fees, participation in legal aid is costliest for senior lawyers who command the highest fees in the private market. Many nevertheless participate in the plan, at least occasionally; but in practice the fee structure tends to exclude many senior practitioners from significant involvement.

Legal aid certificates are classic non-transferable vouchers: they are negotiable only by the identified recipient only for the identified purposes and cannot be converted to cash or any other use. Free choice on the part of consumers is constrained by the fee schedule, which may potentially challenge the goal of equal representation before the law. Tightening of the eligibility criteria and coverage in the face of governmental financial pressure has left many people without any legal representation, particularly of late in British Columbia.

### Educational Vouchers

Traditionally, there has been limited parental choice in public education at the primary and secondary levels in Canada, but educational vouchers represent a dramatic change. The idea began in the United States, promoted largely by Milton Friedman, but remained relatively unimportant until it became a central part of the George W. Bush agenda. In Canada, vouchers are used in the 'charter' schools of Alberta; in Ontario the tax credits announced in 2001 for parents using non-Catholic private schools are equivalent to vouchers.

In the purest case, each parent or guardian receives an educational voucher with a face value of their child's 'share' of the total public educational budget (the total budget divided by the number of children). Parents are then free to use the voucher at any educational institution—public, sectarian, or for-profit. This might be the local school, or one that specializes in mathematics, athletics, music, strict discipline, or religious instruction. Parents would have an absolute right to remove their children (and vouchers) from any school that did not satisfy them. Schools would receive reimbursement from the government for the total number of students multiplied by the face value of the voucher. Schools would survive solely on the basis of their ability to satisfy consumers. Thus, vouchers would introduce competition to education, setting up a 'marketplace' of educational philosophies and practices, replacing a monopolistic public system with one based on a vibrant pluralism.

There is no conceptual limit to the range of interests that could be accommodated. In the most extreme cases, schools would be accountable only to parents and for certain health and safety conditions. In most models, however, there is limited public input: minimal curriculum breadth (literacy, mathematics, etc.) and minimal quality control (perhaps as reflected in standardized test scores). Beyond these constraints, schools could use the money from the vouchers as they saw fit, identifying their own priorities.

In some cases, parents are permitted to supplement the face value of the vouchers to maximize parental choices, while undoubtedly entrenching a wide gap between the quality of education received by the rich and by the poor. In other forms, vouchers constitute full payment, and top-ups would not be permitted: all children would then receive the same per capita educational expenditure. Others advocate vouchers whose face value would vary inversely with income, so that the poor would receive vouchers for more money than would the rich; top-ups by the rich would be expected to roughly equalize total per capita spending on education.

The primary goals of the voucher approach are to maximize parental choice and responsibility, and to introduce competition into the educational sector, thereby presumably enhancing overall quality. The goals traditionally associated with public education—group socialization, social mix, and the development of well-rounded, generally educated graduates—are at best distinctly secondary.

Parental choice is not absolute. For example, we do not permit parents to decide whether or not to educate their children. Thus the issue is not whether vouchers give absolute choice to parents, but rather whether vouchers enhance choice in significant ways and whose choice will be increased. Clearly the articulate middle classes and the rich are more likely than the poor to have the resources—information, finances, and mobility—to be informed consumers. The more demanding groups will seek out and support certain schools, while others will be left behind to languish. Two-tier (and two-quality) education is almost inevitable.

This tendency may be aggravated if top-ups are allowed: the wealthy develop high-quality educational systems and leave public education to shrivel. Political resentment of and resistance to education taxes is likely to follow, as the more affluent opt out, leaving the public education system with a shrinking tax base and a clientele increasingly hard to serve. In both Britain and the United States, the rich and middle classes have largely abandoned public education.

If such an outcome is undesirable, the policy trade-off is clear: the right of some to spend their money as they wish must be constrained by their continued financial contribution to public education through taxes.

The opposite view became articulated widely during the 2000 American elections. Many urban black leaders became outspoken advocates of educational vouchers. Their communities had supported public education, but found that the wholesale abandonment of the public system by white taxpayers left an inferior and underfunded educational structure: claims of social mix and integration were self-evidently meaningless in the face of ghettoized residential patterns and failed busing. They saw vouchers as a way to seize financial, and hence programmatic, control away from remote and insensitive educational bureaucrats and the white-focused uniformity that permeates much public education. That these initiatives, if carried through, would re-create segregated educational systems was not seen as particularly problematic.

The middle classes in most parts of Canada generally have not fled public education. The alleged rigidity and insensitivity of public education are not widely experienced: and in the larger jurisdictions parents have some but not unlimited choice in selecting schools that meet their own personal philosophies and the interests of their children. One high school may develop excellence in music and another may become known for its arts program or its computers. One may promote strict discipline and require that uniforms be worn while another will not. Thus, parental choice can exist within the public system. Such an approach, in effect, creates a voucher system within public education—without the need for vouchers.

## Child Care

Child-care vouchers in Canada cannot be discussed apart from broader conceptual questions about the purpose of child care: Is child care an aid that enables mothers to participate in the paid labour force? Is it respite care for stay-at-home parents, so they can be better caregivers? Is child care primarily aimed at meeting the needs of the child as a form of early education? Is the need for help in securing suitable child care primarily a question of income deficiency or the result of inadequate supply?

Current practice in Canada reflects the ambivalence in the foregoing questions: the personal income tax system offers a tax deduction, which, in effect, defines child care as a work-related expense. The benefit is available only to those who receive receipts and can earn enough to pay income tax. As a tax deduction its value varies directly with income, so that the wealthiest taxpayers derive the greatest tax savings. Ottawa also provides cash assistance for most children with extra benefits for those in low-income families through the Canada Child Tax Benefit and its Supplement. The program assumes that parents receiving assistance are able and willing to locate suitable child care and are the best judges of their child-care needs.

Some argue that any government support should be limited to assistance with the costs of raising children, and hence should be directed towards all parents (or perhaps all low-income parents). Any assistance targeted to child care discriminates against parents who wish to look after their own children, or who wish to use informal and/or unpaid arrangements such as a grandparent or relative.

Many advocates of public child care argue against this view, claiming that cash assistance does not ensure quality child care. Low-income families are so pressed financially that any unrestricted cash payment may be shifted to other priorities such as food or rent. They may be left with low-cost and low-quality child care or no child care at all.

Child-care demand does not create its own supply: the fact that parents have cash with which to purchase child care does not assure that suitable places will be available. In many communities, despite financial aid, parents may be forced to accept inferior child care or forms of care that do not meet the family's needs or wishes.

Vouchers ensure that cash assistance is actually used on child care. Parents who qualify for help, usually through an income or means test, or as part of their social assistance, are given vouchers that can be used in any approved child-care facility where there is space. 'Approved' usually means the premises, whether child-care centres or in-home, are licensed and inspected. The value of the vouchers is usually set on a sliding scale, though 'full subsidy' still entails a daily fee to be paid by the parent.

While ensuring that the public support is restricted to child-care use, vouchers offer parents considerable choice: they can select child-care centres near their homes, work, or schools; or they purchase licensed in-home care. By limiting the vouchers to 'approved' premises, minimum quality standards are assured, at least in such areas as safety, nutrition, public health, and staff-to-child ratios.

## Medicare

The medical care systems of the United States, Britain, and Canada represent, respectively, the market, in-kind delivery, and a modified voucher system.

American health care operates on a for-profit market model. Limited assistance for the elderly and the poor has been provided in-kind through programs such as medicaid and medicare. The benefits are meagre, the quality of care often poor, and eligibility tightly restricted. The result is that more than 40 million Americans have no health insurance. For the vast majority of poor people, there is no significant assistance targeted specifically at health care; all problems are considered matters of income deficiency: any cash aid would inevitably be put to more urgent uses. The poor are unable to pay for their medical needs, nor are they able, as a rule, to obtain private insurance. Technically speaking, they are 'choosing to self-insure', which in practice means they do not insure.

In Britain, by contrast, the National Health Service (NHS) is delivered as a relatively pure in-kind benefit. Consumers 'sign on' to the practice of a specific physician, usually located near one's home. The doctor then serves as gatekeeper to the health-care system and is paid on a capitation basis. Changing doctors without changing residence is difficult, though not impossible. Historically, the primary policy goal of the NHS was to ensure medical coverage for everyone; thus the benefit is delivered in-kind. Freedom of choice for individuals to change physicians and to actively control their own medical care was considered less important than assuring that coverage was received.

Medicare in Canada treads a third path, though it is similar to Britain in that insured health services are directly provided to consumers as in-kind benefits. There is no payment at the point of use, and hence no financial barriers to the utilization of medicare services. However, Canadians are generally free to change doctors at will, and there are no limits to the use of medicare by individuals.

In practice this means that a Canadian's medicare card is equivalent to a health-care voucher. And like the classic voucher, medicare provides constrained free choice: medicare covers only designated services, and may exclude drugs, dental care, and alternative therapies such as massage therapy or homeopathy.[6] Private insurers are prevented by law from offering coverage for medicare-insured services. Still, large elements of choice remain (in contrast to the NHS) in the right of consumers to choose and change their physicians. Medicare is a unique form of voucher in that it contains no fixed maximum value: consumers are free to 'doctor shop' and physicians, who are generally paid on a fee-for-service basis, are free to see as many patients as they wish as often as they deem appropriate.

In-kind delivery in Canada is superior to the American market approach in its efficiency of delivery: according to the OECD, in the United States 13.6 per cent of GNP goes to medical care—high by international standards—yet the quality of service is mediocre for most and appalling for many. In Canada, 9.5 per cent of GNP is devoted to the medicare system, in part because there is no profit incentive for private insurers. In-kind delivery eliminates much of the advertising that is so prominent in the United States, and the overall administrative costs of delivery are slight. There is no means test for subsidy and no bad-debt problems exist for doctors, essentially reducing their billing and collection costs to zero.

On the negative side, the emphasis in Canada on ensuring free choice for consumers has rendered overall medicare costs difficult to control. Without limits on use by consumers and with flexible or no ceilings on billing by individual doctors, the total cost tends to increase year after year. But as Figure 4.1 demonstrated, drug costs, more than medicare, have led to the escalation in overall health costs in this country.

## NOTES

1. I.M. Young (1990) suggests that veto power be given to particular groups over issues that affect them directly. Thus, Aboriginal peoples would have veto power over decisions about land claims, while women would have veto power over decisions affecting reproductive rights.
2. *Requirements* can alternatively be viewed not as a distinct type of benefit, but rather as a *condition* that may apply to all benefit types.
3. Collard (1981) has referred to the 'overwhelming weight of impressionistic evidence' to support the view that people are less concerned with equality of incomes than with assuring reasonably equal access to the consumption of particular goods and services.
4. A serious commitment to training and job placement (whether labelled as 'workfare' or not) would be expensive, as American experience has shown. Substantial investments in supports such as child care would be required.
5. Tax credits, which also constitute tax expenditures, are not regressive in impact.
6. Medicare is a very expensive program to deliver: it contains no limits on the use of insured services or on the aggregate billings of doctors. Furthermore, while 'medically necessary services' as viewed in 1966 probably reflected a reasonable assessment of the state of medical care at the time, new models of delivery and new technologies have emerged in the intervening years, and these have not been adequately incorporated into the coverage provided by the provinces. Home care is undoubtedly part of any health-care continuum, and is often much cheaper than hospital-based care, but it is only partly insured. Likewise, drugs, which have increased in cost and in importance exponentially, as well as dental care, are often not insured through medicare. The available hardware associated with new medical technologies often lags seriously, as the provinces are slow to purchase.

## SUGGESTED READING

Childcare Resource and Research Unit, University of Toronto. n.d. *Child Care Vouchers: What Do We Know About Them?* Available at:
<http://www.childcarecanada.org/resources/CRRUpubs/factsheets/sheet5.html>.
This Web-based information sheet, and associated references, provides a valuable summary of the issues surrounding the child-care voucher debate.

Dobbin, Murray. 1997. *Charter Schools: Charting a Course to Social Division*. Ottawa: Canadian Centre for Policy Alternatives

Kalaw, Cecilia, Arlene McLaren, and Nadene Rehnby. 1998. *In the Name of 'Choice': A Study of Traditional Schools in BC*. Vancouver: Canadian Centre for Policy Alternatives.
These two books explore the shortcomings of 'choice' in a public education system. The first argues that 'charter schools' established so far in Canada have led to two-tier education based on income and social class; the latter found that 'traditional schools' in BC 'serve a desire by like-minded parents to seek refuge from the diversity—the perceived chaos—that must be served by public schools'.

Friedman, Milton, and Rose Friedman. 1980. *Free to Choose: A Personal Statement*. New York: Harcourt Brace Jovanovich.

This strong statement of the residual value system argues that choice (and the freedom to choose) is the pre-eminent goal of social life. The authors were among the earliest advocates of current 'New Right' thinking in the United States.

Riches, Graham. 1986. *Food Banks and the Welfare Crisis*. Ottawa: Canadian Council on Social Development.

This book placed the issue of food banks on the public agenda in Canada. The issues raised are even more urgent today than in 1986.

Stein, Janice Gross. 2001. *The Cult of Efficiency*. Toronto: Anansi.

This is the text of the 2001 CBC Massey Lectures, a critique of the all-pervasive emphasis on efficiency in the production and delivery of public goods.

<www.welfarewatch.toronto.on.ca>

This Web site, maintained by the Community Social Planning Council of Toronto, is the definitive Canadian source of information on workfare. It also reports on US experiences.

# CHAPTER SIX

# Allocating Benefits: To Whom?

## INTRODUCTION

In Chapter 5, we saw that the framers of the post-war welfare state considered in-kind distribution of benefits crucial to ensure that benefits were actually received by intended recipients; their parallel view held that universal allocation was the best way to ensure that everyone was covered. Universal programs entailed nearly 100 per cent coverage, and so there would be only one tier of service for everyone. Because all were included, it was assumed there would be widespread support for maintaining and enhancing the programs over time.

Both of the pillars of the Canadian post-war welfare state—Family Allowances and Old Age Security—were conceptualized on principles of universal coverage. By the early 1970s we had near-universal programs in a number of other areas: Canada Pension Plan, Workers' Compensation, and Unemployment Insurance, for those in the workforce; and medicare. A decade later, however, these programs, particularly those involving cash entitlements, came under serious attack. Posed in the language of directing assistance to those most in need and not 'wasting' money on those who could look after themselves, the case for selectivity came to the fore. Replacing universality with selective programs, in which benefits are targeted only to those who met specific predefined criteria, was presented as an important means to control the deficit and restore fiscal balance in Ottawa.

At the time, Chuck Rachlis (n.d.) saw the debate in different terms: 'the real aim of the pro-selectivity campaigns', he wrote, was 'the restructuring of the welfare state itself'. This ideological process had two steps, of which the move to selective allocation was the first. The second step entailed the elimination, or severe cutting back, of programs that now lacked broad political support because they were targeted to, and only used by, the poor.

By the beginning of the twenty-first century, medicare remained as the major universal federal program, though it was being starved by severe underfunding and growing for-profit activity. Provincially, public education retained the support of more than 95 per cent of Canadian families, yet even here middle-class and wealthy parents increasingly sought refuge in private schools and lobbied to finance their choices through voucher schemes and tax credits.

Today, the case for universality continues to resonate, though focused on a limited number of in-kind programs: medicare, perhaps the single social program distinguishing Canadian social policy from that of the United States; and child care, where the case for universality is so compelling that the debate will not go away. Otherwise, however, government—particularly the federal government—has shifted from universal in-kind programs to a narrower income distribution, typically delivered through the income tax system. Thus, the simple categories of 'universal' and 'selective' are no longer particularly useful. The questions today are no longer whether recipients are to be 'all' or 'some', but rather 'who among the some'.

In this chapter, we shall look at the evolution of the universal/selective debate in Canada. Decisions about who is to receive benefits comprise the second part of the upper half of our redistributive cycle (as developed in Chapter 2). As in Chapter 5, we shall use the standard evaluative criteria of efficiency and effectiveness to assess the merits of universality and selectivity. This will lead to a discussion of targeted benefits, directed towards specific deserving groups. We shall view the guaranteed annual income (GAI), which, conceptually, might resolve the debate by ensuring everyone a specific minimum income each year. We then proceed to look at government spending, including a discussion about tax-backs, or benefit reduction rates, as these determine who gets benefits. We shall look specifically at income support for seniors and for children and conclude the chapter with a review of some major current proposals to support children financially. We then move to Part IV of the book, and our discussion of the other side of the redistributive cycle, as we begin to explore how all these benefits are to be paid for.

# THE UNIVERSAL/SELECTIVE DEBATE

On an intuitive level, the terms 'universal' and 'selective' are straightforward: the former encompasses the entire population, the latter only a portion thereof. But the concepts themselves are ambiguous: When we refer to 'all' do we intend, literally, that the reference be to everyone? If so, perhaps only medicare would qualify as universal—and, even here, there are some exclusions. People newly resident in Canada are not eligible for coverage during a specified waiting period; and people who are homeless or transient may not qualify for coverage.[1]

More generally, 'universality' refers to everyone within a designated grouping. Universal programs typically include public education (covering children up to the minimum school-leaving age), Old Age Security (fully covering only those resident in Canada for at least 10 years and aged 65), and the Canada Pension Plan (covering only those in the paid workforce who earn at least $3,500 per year).

Many economists define universal programs as those in which the amount of benefit does not vary with the income of recipients, while selective programs are those for which the benefit changes as income changes: a systematic link between amount of benefit and income level makes a program selective; benefits independent of income are universal.

Universal programs in Canada have basically taken three forms:

- *In-kind* programs (medicare or public education);
- *Demogrants* (Old Age Security or the former Family Allowances);
- *Social insurance* (Canada Pension or Employment Insurance).

The latter two constitute cash benefits. Demogrants are unilateral payments from the Treasury (general tax revenues) to named groups of individuals, without regard to prior contribution. Social insurance programs link benefits to prior contribution, although not always based on sound actuarial principles.

Eligibility for selective programs is usually based on an individualized assessment, as with social assistance. Qualification tends to be discretionary, and there is little sense of entitlement on the part of recipients. Program take-up will be less than 100 per cent, so that that cost, in the short term at least, will be less than with universality.

## Effectiveness

As we saw earlier, the effectiveness of a program can only be assessed with respect to identified goals:

- If the programmatic goal is that everyone should receive coverage or benefits, then the case for universality is clear.
- If the goal is to minimize administrative delivery costs, the case for universality is strong, as there is no need to determine individual eligibility.
- If the goal is to minimize new public spending, then the short-term preference would probably be for selectivity, though over time the savings are less clear.
- If the goal is to target benefits and perhaps address diversity, then the case for selectivity may be persuasive.
- In a decentralized federal state, selectivity may be inevitable.

Clearly the most persuasive case for universality is that it ensures everyone receives the intended benefit and that everyone will be treated roughly the same. Everyone—including the affluent—has an interest in protecting and supporting such programs because they and their families use these programs.

The greatest threat to universal public education in Canada today is the movement of the middle and upper classes out of the system, towards private and 'charter' schools. If those able to do so opt out of universal public programs, the result will be two or more classes of services, and two tiers inevitably mean that one will be inferior to the other. It is often said, with considerable accuracy, that selective programs targeted to the poor tend to be poor programs. It is only by ensuring that everyone eligible is actually covered by a program that political support for high standards can be assured.

Moreover, when everyone participates in a program, shared interest is presumed to extend more broadly across the community, beyond the single common cause: more generic social cohesion should evolve over time. Universality is therefore an important mechanism in the broader quest for social cohesion and solidarity across the population.

Peter Findlay (1983) has talked of the symbolic impact of a universal program:

> To enact a program . . . universally is to state a commitment of respect and nurturance. It means that resources will be applied to meeting that commitment—taken from other commitments when necessary—and that the economic structure, social institutions, and political processes will be shaped to protect and maintain that commitment.

One of the purposes of the original Family Allowance program was to stimulate the economy and ensure that with the end of World War II the economy would not fall back into the depths of the Great Depression. A monthly demogrant from the federal government to each mother in Canada was intended to maintain overall purchasing power. However, the amounts involved were too modest to make a dramatic difference to individual households, although aggregated over all families in Canada there was a definite macroeconomic stimulus.

Today the economic goals of government are to reduce public spending in order to pay for tax cuts and to shrink the size of government as an end in itself. These goals appear to be met most effectively with selective and targeted programs that give benefits only to those who can show need, resulting in lower overall program costs at least in the short term.

There are costs associated with raising a child that all parents incur regardless of income level. A universal payment to parents would help offset these costs, while also recognizing there is a public interest in having children adequately cared for, a public investment in society's future citizens. As women tend to bear the largest burden in raising children, the Family Allowance cheque was made payable to the mother—an incredibly progressive decision in 1945. Though the amounts were not sufficient to grant a mother financial independence, they were nevertheless an important symbol of women's independent economic legitimacy, long before feminism became a viable political movement. The cheques were large enough to enable the mother to buy winter boots or a coat for a child, so the payment was not entirely symbolic.

The Family Allowance system was structured in Quebec to increase the payment for the third and subsequent children. (Similar programs operate in France and in Israel, where the explicit intent is to reward large families and perhaps to encourage procreation.) The incentives did have some modest effect in Quebec.

There are unavoidable costs associated with growing old; and perhaps everyone over 65 is entitled to financial support in recognition of a lifetime's contribution to society. Such considerations would apply to all seniors, regardless of income level, making a strong argument for universal payment. More generally, the case for universality is compelling in any situation in which assistance is justified on the basis of collective attributes for an entire group (such as age) rather than individual need or income deficiency.

At times, a program may be directed towards diversity needs: there may be special requirements for persons with AIDS or developmental disabilities, or for seniors in particular ethnic communities. Many of these needs will best be addressed through selective programs tailored to local values and priorities. Others, however, such as child care, can be accommodated within a universalist framework, designed to meet specific parental interests in particular settings, while maintaining an umbrella of universality.

### Stigma

The goal of social effectiveness is met when no one eligible for a benefit is deterred from applying because of stigma. Though the avoidance of stigma was a primary consideration at the outset of the welfare state, as early as 1979 the Canadian Council on Social Development argued that stigma was no longer a serious deterrent to accessing services. Certainly, stigma and the attendant social exclusion are too complex to be addressed solely through universal delivery of benefits.

Pinker (1979) noted that universal services tend to be more accessible and hence more used by the middle classes. He argued that the poor may be unwilling to utilize even universal services, having a life's socialization into the status of dependency. The costs—personal, emotional, and psychological—of becoming a 'recipient' may be higher than any perceived benefits. There is a sharp distinction between 'givers' and 'recipients', which universal services cannot offset.

Hence, Pinker suggested that specialized delivery systems might be required to reach some intended recipients, even for universal services; he also suggested that public resources should be directed to areas where the vulnerability and dependence of the poor—such as any imbalance of knowledge between rich and poor—would be least; and that anonymity at point of use could minimize the reluctance of the poor. His case example was the bus system in London: it should be free to users, as the poor took the bus more than the rich, and more than they rode the underground; and they did so with no sense of dependency or personal deficiency. Such an initiative would equalize access among classes and offer a universal program on equal terms to all.

Today, there is perhaps greater emphasis on the nature of the entitlement. If a benefit is viewed as a right, if numbers are great, benefit levels generous, and take-up rates high, applying for a particular benefit is likely to be seen as 'normal' rather than stigmatizing.

### Determining Eligibility

Application for a selective program today need not be stigmatizing or personally demeaning to the claimant. The various ways to determine eligibility for a selective program are not equally intrusive:

- A *means* test is personal and usually intrusive. It involves a calculation of an applicant's resources (income, wealth) and expenses. The difference between the two (positive or negative) equals the means or net resources available. The number of children in a household, and their ages, has often served as a convenient proxy for calculating expenses.
- An *income* test is simpler and merely requires an individual to report eligible income, without regard to expenses. Neither a means test nor an income test requires a personalized assessment (though it is more common with the former); the application for both can often be completed privately and submitted by mail.

- A *needs* test is the most complicated eligibility determination process. It typically involves an individualized assessment, conducted by a professional such as a social worker. It may entail evaluation of the applicant's capacities, using standardized testing instruments, and will suggest possible remedies, both cash and in-kind services. The needs test is considered the most precise approach and the most sensitive to the situations of individual applicants. It therefore permits and requires the greatest exercise of professional judgement and discretion and, therefore, is the least predictable and potentially most capricious alternative. Used carefully and with sensitivity, it may respond to an applicant's full range of needs; when used inappropriately, the needs test can be demeaning and exclusionary.

The Guaranteed Income Supplement (GIS) is a good example of a selective program that carries little or no stigma, yet has a high take-up rate. Of the 3.7 million recipients of OAS, just over a third (1.4 million) receive full or partial GIS. The application—as with the Canada Child Tax Benefit (CCTB) and the GST credit—uses an income test based on the previous year's tax return. Any process that uses tax returns to determine eligibility is likely to be impersonal, non-demeaning, and non-stigmatizing. Some programs, notably social assistance, cannot reliably use the previous year's tax return, as household incomes may vary widely from month to month or even more frequently. Individualized assessment, which can be potentially demeaning to the applicant, is therefore needed in these instances.

## Efficiency

The efficiency argument is traditionally used to justify selective delivery of benefits. Rather than providing benefits to those who do not need them, surely it would be more efficient to target the benefits to the intended recipients, recognizing that need varies with individual circumstances. There would be no waste or spillover—known as *seepage*—to unintended recipients. If the needy are the priority, resources should be directed to them.

A variant on this position suggests that universal benefits delivered to everyone equally do nothing to narrow the gap between rich and poor. A uniform payment to everyone raises the incomes of all by the same amount, but leaves the absolute gap unaltered. Only selective benefits, delivered to those at the bottom, can narrow differentials between rich and poor. If the goal is to narrow that gap, then selective programs are certainly preferable.

As well, universal programs, particularly if they are free at the point of use, will generate demand and encourage use beyond the levels that individuals would choose if they had to pay directly. Universal programs such as medicare allegedly foster *abuse*, that is, they cause people to use in excess of their need. We shall return to this issue at a later point. However, while universal entitlement may well induce people to use programs more, whether these higher levels are excessive, or abusive, remains an open question.

Precisely because they increase use, universal programs can be highly efficient over time. With medicare, for example, early access can enhance prevention, whereas remedy can be far more costly. If people were obligated to pay directly for medical care, the likelihood, particularly among the poor, would be to delay a visit to the physician. By the time they are forced by their illness to go, the costs to cure may be far greater than had they acted sooner. In this sense, then, early use of a universal service may be a highly efficient use of resources. Another similar example is universal free primary education, which is far less costly than later adult literacy training.

### Administrative Costs

At one time, the overhead costs to deliver a universal program were considerably less than those associated with selectivity, as there was no need to monitor, police, or assess eligibility. The costs of delivering the universal Family Allowance program were less than 1 per cent of total program costs; those of delivering selective social assistance could range up to 15 per cent of the total program. Today, the overhead costs of Employment Insurance or Workers' Compensation are high, compared to many other programs, because of the need for monitoring and policing.

The administrative costs to deliver a social benefit may be divided into three components:

- *Costs to determine eligibility*. These costs vary with the complexity of the eligibility determination process and with the degree of discretion on the part of the intake worker. An in-person application will always entail labour costs, though the personal interview is giving way to the previous year's tax return as a criterion for eligibility. In-kind programs such as medicare may still entail personal attendance, to generate a necessary photo card and prove eligibility by producing the required identification. Discretion for the worker is virtually non-existent, as acceptable forms of identification are non-negotiable.

  In general, the costs of determining eligibility are not necessarily greater for a selective program, nor will they always be substantial even if a personal interview is required. Professional discretion as a screening mechanism may entail substantial costs, but this approach is today largely limited to treatment-oriented programs. Costs to determine initial eligibility across different programs clearly differ, but such costs typically are not dramatic, and in any case they are one-time non-recurring expenses.

- *Ongoing costs to monitor eligibility*. These are the costs of policing to ensure that those who receive benefits continue to remain eligible to do so. For recipients whose status remains relatively constant, these costs are negligible: for example, after qualification for Old Age Security, one continues to receive the cheque until death. Likewise, the GIS involves minimal policing activity: people who are old and poor tend to remain so. Similarly, once individuals have received medicare cards there is relatively little monitoring to ensure continued eligibility, although some provinces' medicare cards have a fixed expiry date, necessitating periodic renewal.

  On the other hand, Employment Insurance, Workers' Compensation, and Canada Pension Plan disability benefits, which give universal coverage to the employed workforce, and social assistance, which is selective, all incur substantial monitoring costs to ensure continued eligibility. Recipients must either do something particular—for EI and social assistance one must search for work—or must be in a particular condition (for Workers' Compensation or CPP, one must be disabled). Cards signed by potential employers to verify that individuals are seeking work or medical forms completed by physicians are part of the monitoring process. These are also programs in which cheating is relatively easy, so there is also a political imperative to police rigorously.[2]

In all these cases, the need for monitoring and the costs of monitoring have little to do with whether a program is universal or selective.

- *Costs to deliver benefits*. For virtually all cash programs today, these costs are slight. With direct deposit to bank accounts, there is no need to cut and deliver cheques. In some communities, however, claimants must personally appear at a welfare office to get their cheques. This is supposedly to discourage 'phantom claimants', that is, recipients who may not exist, may be deceased, or are wintering abroad but still manage to cash their monthly cheques. These fraudulent claimants are few, and where personal collection is required the real purpose likely has less to do with fraud than with demeaning those dependent on the state.

### Gross and Net

Many cash benefit programs in Canada are subject to tax: any income received must be included in calculating one's annual tax liability to federal and provincial governments. Because Canada's income tax system is mildly progressive (as we shall see in the next chapter), recipients of benefits such as Old Age Security who have no other income pay no tax on what they receive; recipients of the same benefit who have other income will pay tax on all their income, including OAS, and thus they will retain, after taxes, only a portion of the original payment. The most affluent seniors repay their entire OAS (though for convenience they now receive no payments initially).

The overall effect of this tax liability is that payments that are universal in their application become selective in their impact: while everyone receives the same cash payment, the poor keep it all and the more affluent repay part or all through their personal income taxes. The final impact of the program is both somewhat progressive (the poor receive larger net benefits than do the rich) and selective (some receive more than others and some receive nothing).

Because everyone receives the same payment, there is no stigma associated with its receipt, nor is there any deterrent to discourage people from applying. All distinctions between rich and poor, between needy and affluent, occur impersonally and anonymously in each individual's tax return.

Why should benefits be delivered to individuals who, several months later, must repay part or all of what they received? Why not simply exempt them or assess, in advance, their net entitlement and deliver that? Since 1996, this has been done with respect to OAS: withholding is applied to benefits likely to be repaid. In other cases, however, it may be more efficient to deliver benefits universally and recover them selectively. To determine eligibility in advance may require a complex bureaucratic process at substantial cost; while the same determination is done at essentially zero cost after the fact. All that is involved is a minor change in the personal income tax form that requires a social benefit to be added to taxable income for the year. There are no additional administrative costs attributable to the social benefit.

Perhaps not enough of the initial benefit is recovered from those who do not need the money. It is argued that because our income tax system in Canada is only mildly progressive, even the richest Canadians pay back less than half of any taxable benefits they receive. Hence, the targeting of the benefit is inadequate, and resources could better be directed to the needy. This argument is compelling. However, as we saw earlier, the involvement of the middle and upper classes in a social program lends political support to its continuance and growth; were these groups to be excluded, it would become easy to marginalize both the program and the recipients.

More important, while the analysis of the problem may be correct (too much of the benefit is retained by the rich), the response—to convert to a selective program—is not the best way to proceed. If insufficient resources are recovered from those with higher incomes, the obvious solution is to increase the rate of recovery. The fundamental problem is not in the initial delivery of the benefits, but rather in an inadequately progressive tax system. We always have the option to make the income tax system more progressive, and thereby to recover more of the initial benefit from those who pay higher income taxes.

The current tax system singles out certain forms of income derived from social benefits for accelerated recovery. Anyone with a taxable income of more than $89,818 receives no Old Age Security (the equivalent of repaying the entire benefit), or anyone with a net income over $48,750 must repay part of any Employment Insurance benefit received.[3] Such singling out ensures high rates of repayment of the particular benefits, while leaving the tax structure unaltered.[4]

By singling out OAS or EI benefits for income tax purposes, Ottawa is effectively creating tiers of differing merit and differing legitimacy for different types of income. Though the reasons are never made clear, the entitlement to OAS or EI is somehow less resilient than the right to other forms of income. Social benefits become an inferior category of benefit, with Poor Law overtones, which one forfeits beyond a certain income threshold.

## Targeting of Benefits

Earlier in this chapter, one definition labelled universality as a benefit that did not depend on income. Benefits that vary with income level, by definition, are selective; and for each selective benefit it must be determined who gets how much. Such decisions are more important than the fact of their being selective, and are central to our understanding of most income support programs in Canada. Myles and Pierson (1997) have observed that apart from health care, CPP/QPP, Workers' Compensation, and some social services, *every significant Canadian social program is now subject to some form of targeting*.

Figure 6.1 helps us understand *targeting*, the process by which income benefits are directed at particular groups at the expense of other groups. In the diagram, income (the independent variable) is read off the horizontal axis; benefits (the dependent variable) are on the vertical axis. Both are measured in dollars.

We begin with the line UU, which reflects a universal payment, of value $OU, delivered to all households in the population. The payment is the same, regardless of income level; therefore the benefit line is horizontal.

In other cases, all of which are selective, there is a relation, usually inverse, between income level and the size of the benefit. The line describing that relation generally moves down and to the right, illustrating that higher income usually entails lower benefits.

Any given pool of money can be distributed in various ways: large payments can be given to the very poor, with middle- and upper-income groups receiving little or nothing; or, the payments to the poorest can be smaller, leaving more funds for those higher up the income scale. Let us start with the scenario represented by the steeply tapering

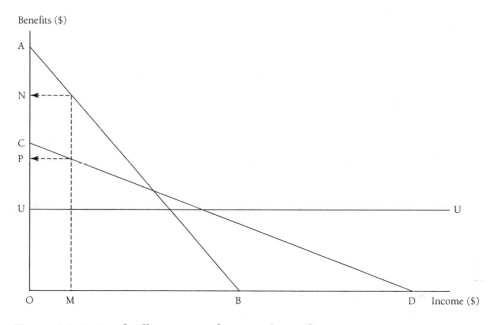

**Figure 6.1  A Simple Illustration of Targeted Benefits**

line AB: the maximum payment, $OA (representing zero eligible income), is substantial; the size of benefit drops, rather precipitously, as income rises, and at income level $OB, the benefit payment drops to $0. Households with incomes above $OB receive no benefit. From low-income level $OM, we follow the dotted line to N on the vertical axis and read the benefit payable as $ON.

An alternate program design scenario is represented in line CD, where the maximum benefit $OC is lower, but benefits are received much farther up the income scale, to income $OD. The slope of the line is more gradual, so that an increase in income results in benefits being reduced by less than in the first scenario. At income level $OM, the maximum benefit is $OP. Incomes between B and D receive modest benefits whereas they got none in the first scenario. The trade-off is that maximum benefits to the poorest are now lower.

A variant on these approaches can be observed in Figure 6.2, illustrating the effect of a *basic exemption*, where benefits do not decline as income rises. With incomes from zero to $OK (=EF), benefits ($OE) remain constant for all, but beyond income level $OK they decline as illustrated in lines FG or FH, terminating at income levels $OG or $OH. With income between zero and $OK, the maximum benefit $OE will be received. Beyond point K, benefits would reduce. Beyond income $OK, at income $OL benefits will total $OS (if the steep taper of FG is used) or $OT on the gentler slope of FH.

Points G or H, where benefits drop to zero, are known as the *break-even* points; point F, where benefits begin to diminish, is known as the *turning point*. The rate at which benefits are reduced is known as the *tax-back rate*, the *benefit reduction rate*, or the *clawback rate* and simply describes the amount by which benefits are *reduced, taxed back*, or *clawed back*[5] for every $1 increase in incomes.

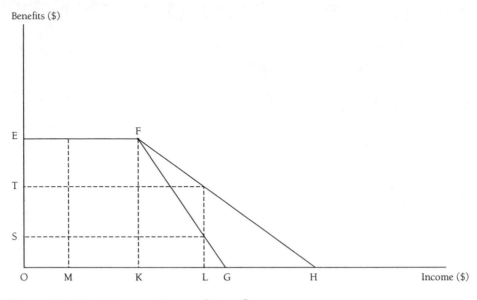

**Figure 6.2  Variations on Targeted Benefits**

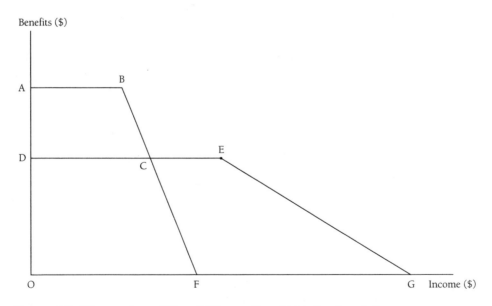

**Figure 6.3  Illustration of Two Different Benefit Reduction Schemes**

Figure 6.3 illustrates two schemes with different benefit levels and reduction rates. These are represented by lines ABF and DEG. The maximum benefit is higher in the first case (OA compared to OD), but benefits begin to decline at a lower income (turning point B versus turning point E). Total benefits terminate sooner, at income level OF rather than OG. Area ABFO reflects an approach that directs the greatest portion of the benefits to those with lowest incomes, while DEGO illustrates benefits that extend higher up the income scale. While spending represented by DCFO is the same in both cases, the policy decision is whether to channel higher benefits to the poorest (DABC) or to lower the maximum benefit but include those higher up the income scale (CEGF).

Policy and programmatic decisions influence the relation between income and benefits in the way they answer two basic questions:

- How steep should the tax-back or benefit reduction rate be? (Diagrammatically, how steep should the line slope?)
- Is there to be a basic exemption or does benefit reduction begin with the first dollar of earnings?

As we shall see, different income support programs in Canada reflect different types of answers to these questions.

## GUARANTEED ANNUAL INCOME (GAI)

The GAI has been presented as the ultimate universal program for income security: everyone would be covered under one initiative and almost all other social programs could be abolished. The cost savings in delivery of a single comprehensible system of income support would be massive.

The concept is simple. A target income, the *basic guarantee*, is set, usually based on family composition and size (number and ages of children). Those whose earned income falls below this threshold receive cash supplementation to bring them up to the line, usually through a negative income tax (NIT); those with incomes above the line pay tax as at present. The GAI is both the program name and the goal, while the NIT is the operational means to get there.

There are three critical concepts in a GAI scheme:

- *the guarantee level*, i.e., the income payable to those with no other source of income;
- *the tax-back or benefit reduction rate*, i.e., the rate at which benefits increase or reduce as other sources of income decline or rise; and
- *the break-even point*, i.e., the income level at which benefits decline to zero.

Figure 6.4 presents a simple form of a GAI. The horizontal axis, OM, reflects income from all sources before the GAI. On the vertical axis are the taxes to be paid or the benefits received through the GAI: above the horizontal axis taxes are due, while below the line benefits are received (i.e., negative taxes). The diagonal line, TDFK, represents the relationship between income and taxes paid or benefits received. The precise shape and slope of this line are the result of political decisions, but the slope will always be upward and to the right.

The diagram is interpreted by identifying the household income, the independent variable, on the horizontal axis, and then reading the benefits/taxes status as the depend-

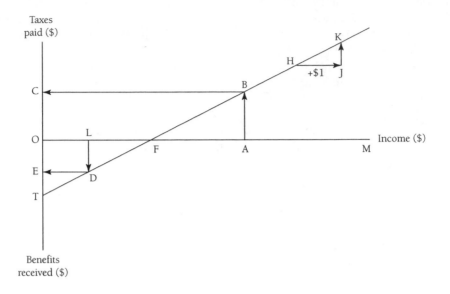

**Figure 6.4  Guaranteed Annual Income Using a Negative Income Tax**

ent variable on the vertical axis. Suppose, for example, a household has an income of $OL per year: from the diagram through point D, we arrive at point E on the vertical axis and the benefit would be $OE. Total household income would be $OL (from earnings) plus $OE (benefits received).

If the household income were higher ($OA), then taxes would be payable. From A we proceed through point B on the diagonal line to reach point C on the vertical axis. Taxes due would therefore total $OC. Total income would be $OA (from earnings) minus $OC (taxes due). Point F, income equivalent to $OF, represents the break-even point, at which neither benefits nor taxes are received or paid. All incomes below $OF receive benefits, in amounts declining as point F is approached; all incomes above $OF require the payment of taxes.

The tax rate in our diagram is constant, as illustrated by the slope of the diagonal line. If income goes up by amount HJ, then taxes increase by the vertical amount JK. The ratio of JK/HJ is known as the *marginal* tax rate: of each extra dollar earned (HJ), JK would be absorbed in taxes. Similarly, below the break-even point, F, the benefits received, or negative tax, would be the same. The rate at which benefits reduce is the *tax-back rate* or the *benefit reduction rate* (which, arithmetically, has the same value as the marginal tax rate).

Figure 6.5 shows how policy decisions influence the shape of the GAI. Line AB portrays a relatively low tax and benefit rate: as income goes up, the tax due or benefit received changes relatively little. A steeper tax and benefit rate is shown in line CD, resulting in a much greater increase in taxes payable (or benefits due). Line EFG shows how a tax/benefit rate need not be constant. In this example, the benefits increase or

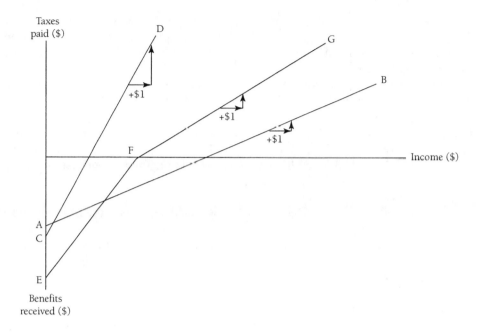

**Figure 6.5  Variants on a Guaranteed Annual Income**

decrease quite severely with a change in income for those with incomes below the break-even point: this means that if individuals increase their incomes (for example, through part-time work), their benefits decline substantially. The incentive to get paid work is therefore modest, as relatively little of the additional earnings can be retained. Conversely, if income drops, benefits make up a relatively large portion of the loss, so the decline in final income is modest.

For those with incomes above the break-even point, the tax burden is modest on line EFG. An increase of earnings results in a relatively slight tax increase, certainly less than the reduction in benefits experienced by their low-income counterparts. Line EFG reflects a decision that work/tax/benefit incentives for those with higher incomes (low tax rates) should be different from those with lower incomes (steep benefit reduction rate). In other words, policy/ideological decisions determine the shape of the diagonal tax/benefit line.

## GAI Experiments

The idea of a GAI originated with the American political right, as a way to reduce government bureaucracy and red tape and simultaneously to cut the costs of support for the poor. It was part of Richard Nixon's first campaign for president in 1960, endorsed by economist Milton Friedman, who had proposed the idea as early as 1943. Later, a GAI became part of Lyndon Johnson's 'War on Poverty': social reformers saw a GAI as a way to empower people, to give them greater control over their lives by reducing the discretionary power and intrusiveness of public servants. The first GAI experiment in the US began in 1968 in New Jersey, though for political reasons it was called a 'work incentive experiment' (Hum and Simpson, 1993). Later experiments in Denver and Seattle covered 4,800 families.

The Canadian Mincome experiment began in Winnipeg and Dauphin, Manitoba, in 1975 and was scheduled to run for three years. It involved 1,300 families and single individuals and included a rigorous research component. There were three tax-back rates and three guarantee levels. But, in 1979, Mincome 'died quietly' without producing a final report: 'the GAI concept itself had lost its allure' (ibid.). In the mid-1980s, the Macdonald Royal Commission called for a Universal Income Support Program or UISP (a form of GAI) but the Mulroney government acted instead on the Commission's other recommendation—free trade with the US.

Lloyd Axworthy's 1994 social security review considered a GAI only briefly and dismissed the idea. In late 2000, Prime Minister Chrétien, perhaps seeking a suitable legacy, revived the idea as part of an apparent 'cradle-to-grave program of guaranteed annual income' (Hum and Simpson, 2001). The idea, it seems, will never be acted upon, but neither will it go away.

## Why No GAI?

The operational details of a basic guaranteed annual income scheme are not complicated, and the concept has attracted both policy analysts and politicians across the political spectrum. The obvious question is that if the GAI is so attractive, why don't we now have one?

Myles and Pierson (1997) explored the politics of the GAI in both Canada and the US and found Canada to be considerably more receptive, for three reasons: (1) the shift to a system with elements of a negative income tax is smoother and more 'natural' in a country with a programmatic base in Beveridge's ideas; (2) ideological opposition to a GAI in the US is widespread; and (3) the American congressional system makes it relatively easy to block legislation. Resistance to a full GAI scheme certainly has political, policy, and methodological dimensions. The problems revolve around fear of excessive cost and the impact on work incentives. In brief, will people choose to work substantially less in the context of an income guarantee?

Methodologically, sampling and inference are problematic. However carefully chosen, can sample communities truly represent a wider population? Would findings from Winnipeg be applicable to Charlottetown or Calgary? Participants in the experiments knew they were part of large, carefully researched social experiments with considerable media attention. Did this awareness alter their behaviour? Would they have responded in a similar manner as unobserved anonymous citizens? More generally, can one infer from any grand social experiment, however meticulously designed and implemented, to a full population?

Politically, there is always fear of major change, and a GAI would entail a complete overhaul of the entire system of public benefits. What if it didn't work? What would it cost if low-income earners simply accepted the guarantee and didn't bother to work? In addition, though one single GAI program would be less expensive to administer than multiple programs, there was no consensus on the overall cost, as this would depend on the level at which the basic guarantee was set; and, not surprisingly, the optimal level was defined differently across the political spectrum.

Moreover, income situations can change quickly, and there would still be need for emergency short-term assistance, which a GAI could not address; this would reduce the anticipated savings. As well, what we have now could not be eliminated until the GAI was in place. During the transition, overlapping or duplicate systems would involve substantial waste. Also, there is the human relations/personnel element respecting large numbers of current employees, not to mention that many of those who derive substantial benefit from the current system would likely resist change. In short, the political, bureaucratic, and organizational issues associated with a fundamental restructuring represent perhaps a greater challenge—and risk—than any government would be willing or able to address.

Policy questions revolve around the issue of work incentives. Do they exist in practice? In what form? There are two conflicting economic hypotheses—the Income Effect and the Substitution Effect. People are assumed to compare the costs and benefits (both pecuniary and psychic) associated with work and non-employment[6] and determine how much extra work they are prepared to offer in response to a financial incentive. The Income Effect holds that an increase in potential earnings will lead people to buy more of all commodities, including non-employment, resulting in reduced labour force activity. The Substitution Effect predicts to the contrary, that increased earnings opportunities will cause people to substitute labour for non-employment.[7] Which of these will predominate in practice cannot be determined a priori.

Though economists and policy analysts cannot be certain about the relative impact of work incentives, ensuring they occur is essential to politicians. A mass social program in which large numbers of people would choose to take a guaranteed income to replace, rather than to supplement, paid work would be major political disaster. However unlikely such a scenario, no rational politicians would risk their careers for a GAI.

In their analysis of the Mincome data, Hum and Simpson (2001) reported that the reduction in work effort was modest—about 1 per cent for men, 3 per cent for wives, and 5 per cent for unmarried women, suggesting that fears of a GAI's adverse effect on work incentives are overblown. However, they did find that family structure altered. As in the US studies, families that had stayed together solely for financial reasons no longer needed to do so, as each individual could receive the GAI payment after dissolution. Hum and Simpson (2001) concluded that 'any future debate over the GAI is likely to shift towards the effect on family composition, rather than work disincentives.'

# A LOOK AT GOVERNMENT SPENDING

Earlier in this chapter, we observed that universality and selectivity are no longer particularly meaningful categories of government cash benefits in Canada today. Instead, targeting funds to particular groups appears more relevant. This leads us to a preliminary view of government spending activity, which we have noted is of two forms: direct spending, where government gives money to individuals; and tax spending, which produces the identical impact through reductions in tax payable. In this section, we focus on the former.

**Table 6.1 Net Expenditures, Government of Canada, 1999–2000 ($ billions)**

| | Net expenditure ($ billions) | Percentage of total net expenditure | Percentage of total program expenditure (excluding debt charges) |
|---|---|---|---|
| *Transfer payments* | | | |
| Seniors (total) | 23.4 | 15.3 | 20.9 |
| OAS | 18.1 | 11.8 | 16.2 |
| GIS | 4.9 | 3.2 | 4.4 |
| Spouses' Allowance | 0.4 | 0.3 | |
| EI | 11.3 | 7.4 | 10.1 |
| Other levels of government | | | |
| CHST | 14.9 | 9.7 | 13.3 |
| Fiscal arrangements | 10.7 | 7.0 | 9.6 |
| Other | 16.2 | 10.6 | 14.5 |
| Total transfer payments | 76.5 | 49.9 | 68.4 |
| *Crown corporations* | 3.0 | 2.0 | 2.7 |
| *Other programs* | | | |
| National defence | 10.2 | 6.6 | 9.1 |
| All other departments and agencies | 22.1 | 14.4 | 19.8 |
| Total | 32.3 | 21.1 | 28.9 |
| *Total program expenditure* | 111.8 | 72.9 | |
| *Public debt charges* | 41.6 | 27.1 | |
| *Total net expenditure* | 153.4 | | |
| *Other entries* | | | |
| CPP/QPP | 25.7 | | |
| Canada Child Tax Benefit | 6.0 | | |

SOURCE: Public Accounts of Canada Cat. No. P51-1-2001-1E.

Table 6.1 contains information on net federal government expenditure, based on the Public Accounts of Canada. For the fiscal year 1999–2000, federal spending totalled $153.4 billion, of which $111.8 billion (or 73 per cent) was direct program expenditure. There are four major types of spending activity:

- *Transfer payments* constitute by far the largest share, 49.9 per cent, of all federal spending activity, or about two-thirds (68 per cent) if we exclude debt charges. The figures include payments to individuals (seniors) for income support (15 per cent), as well as payments to provinces and territories (17 per cent). The latter 'fiscal arrangements' are long-standing measures to redress regional economic imbalances and payments under the Canada Health and Social Transfer.

- *Crown corporation expenditures* are minor, at $3 billion or 2 per cent of federal spending. As the number of Crown corporations shrinks due to government preferences for privatization, this budget item should decline even further.
- *Other program spending* includes all other spending by all other departments and agencies of government. National defence, at $10 billion or 7 per cent of federal spending, is the only individual entry of notable magnitude. In total, this budget line entails just over 21 per cent of net federal spending, or $32 billion.
- *Public debt charges*, including interest and other payments to carry the public debt, totalled $42 billion or 27 per cent of federal spending in 1999–2000.[8] It is not the size of the debt per se that is important, but the ability of the economy to carry that debt. Hence, we compare debt to gross domestic product (a common measure of the total economy's fiscal capacity). The OECD has recommended that a country's aggregate debt should not exceed 60 per cent of its GDP, an arbitrary but widely accepted measure. At the time of the fiscal crisis of the 1990s, Canada was above the 60 per cent level, peaking at 71 per cent in 1995–6, but for 2000–1, the figure was well below that, at 51.8 per cent.

Table 6.1 also shows how large and important income support is for seniors in Canada. For 1999–2000, the federal government spent $23 billion (15 per cent of total spending or 21 per cent of all program spending) in this area.

At the bottom of the table, we see that much less, $6 billion, was spent on the Canada Child Tax Benefit. This is not counted as direct spending in the Public Accounts; instead, it is recorded separately as an 'other entry', defined as a tax expenditure. This categorization is largely political: when the Minister of Finance talks of tax reductions (deemed to be 'good things' by the press and media), he can include the $6 billion Child Tax Benefit; his alternative would be to count the $6 billion as increased government spending (deemed to be a 'bad' thing). Clearly, the net effect on the recipient is identical, whether a dollar is spent directly on children or whether that same dollar is not collected in taxes due to the Child Tax Benefit.

Federal transfers to other levels of government total $26 billion, or 17 per cent of all federal spending, with $15 billion of this attributable to the CHST. These numbers attest to the extent to which Canada has become decentralized, particularly since, with few exceptions, the transfers are unconditional. Canada has been described as the world's most decentralized yet functioning federal state: Ottawa accounts for about 40 per cent of public spending, compared to some 60 per cent for the US federal government. Ottawa retains remarkably little direct responsibility for program spending, but serves, to a large extent, as banker to the provinces, which determine their own priorities. As nearly a quarter of Ottawa's spending (apart from debt charges) consists of transfers to other levels of governments, it is easy to see why consistent standards across Canada are increasingly difficult to ensure. It is virtually impossible for Ottawa to provide universal programs when so much of its direct spending merely consists of transfers to other governments.

## Employment-Related Spending

Two entries in Table 6.1 refer to federal spending as employment-related benefits—one for Employment Insurance (EI) and the other for the Canada/Quebec Pension Plan (CPP/QPP). The Public Accounts note an entry for $11.3 billion of direct spending on EI benefits, 7 per cent of the total. Elsewhere, under government revenues, is an entry reflecting the $18 billion in EI premiums that individuals and employers paid during the year. The surplus in the EI account, totalling some $6 billion, is available to Ottawa for general purposes, including deficit reduction or tax cuts.

Unemployment Insurance (UI) began as an arm's-length program built on sound actuarial principles. Until the severe cuts of the last decade, however, UI regularly ran a deficit, largely because those 'sound actuarial principles' were never implemented. Political needs never permitted benefit entitlements and premiums to be brought into harmony, and each year the deficit was covered by Ottawa from general revenues. In the last several years, however, premiums were increased and eligibility tightened, so that by 2000 there was an accumulated surplus of $38 billion in the EI account. Standard insurance principles would have turned that continuing surplus into either improved benefits or reduced contributions. Instead, Ottawa moved to incorporate the EI surplus into its general revenues

Both employers and employees have argued that the money belongs to them, as their premiums and reduced entitlements to benefits created the surplus. The money should be returned to them, through improved benefits and/or lower premiums. (The vocal business community prefers reduced premiums, of course, as businesses receive no direct value from benefit enhancements.) Ottawa merely notes that the EI revenues and expenses are separate entries in the federal accounts, thereby implicitly acknowledging that the surplus is 'owed' to the EI account. Yet, without the surpluses from EI, Ottawa would not have been able to eliminate the deficit when it did.

CPP/QPP benefits for 1999–2000 totalled $26 billion, with about $19 billion for the Canada Pension Plan and $7 billion for QPP. Though this money—and EI spending as well—is reported as departmental spending of Human Resources Development Canada (HRDC), the CPP money is kept in a distinct fund, managed by its own administrative system. In the 1990s it became clear that future CPP contributions from workers would not be sufficient to pay out the benefits due to the retiring baby boomers. To restore balance, Ottawa and the provinces jointly agreed to increase premiums over several years. For 2000–1, the fund was expected to have a surplus of over $3 billion.

Other solutions, such as delaying the age at which CPP benefits could be claimed, were considered politically unfeasible. Unlike EI, the financial problems with CPP were identified well in advance and were addressed in a professional and competent manner (though federal-provincial debate delayed any response for several years). Because the structures of EI and CPP are different, distinct treatments were possible: CPP benefits are determined for each individual, based on past earnings; contributors perceive that they 'own' their contributions as they do private pension contributions (though this is not technically correct). EI claims have always been subject to political expedience and premiums often were viewed as another form of taxation with no explicit link to specific benefits. Thus, while Ottawa easily absorbed the EI surplus, any attempt to claim a surplus in CPP would be far more controversial.

# Targeting Income Security

In this section, we trace the changes in the two major income security programs in Canada, directed to seniors and to children. Both began as universal entitlements, and both have evolved to targeted selective programs, the benefits of which are received and retained by only a part of each of these populations.

## Income Security for Seniors

As many seniors in post-World War II Canada had little or no private savings, there was considerable support for the universal Old Age Security (OAS) program when it was introduced in 1952. The only condition for entitlement was a minimum period of residence in Canada. The payment was large enough to enable an individual or couple to live in 'modest, but frugal comfort'. The payments were not initially taxable, thus constituting a 'true' universal payment. Today, OAS roughly follows the path in Figure 6.6. The full payment ($424 per month as of 2001) is received up to an income of $55,309. Beyond that, benefits diminish at a rate of 15 per cent, meaning that for each additional dollar of income above $55,309, benefits decline by 15 cents. At an income level of $89,818, benefits terminate entirely.

In 1967, the income-tested Guaranteed Income Supplement (GIS) was introduced for low-income seniors, mainly those who did not have benefits through the Canada Pension Plan. In some sense, the GIS was a substitute for the CPP. Because more than one-third of OAS recipients receive full or partial GIS, it is clear that many elderly people in Canada live

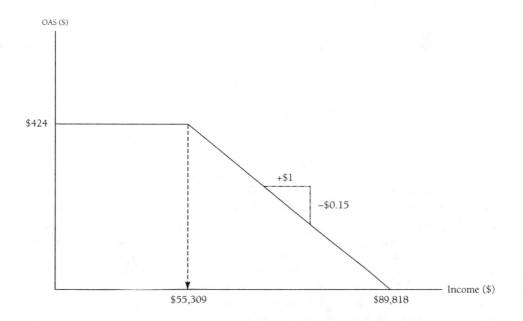

**Figure 6.6  Benefit Reductions in Old Age Security, 2001**

on little other than their government pensions. The GIS is clawed back severely, at 50 per cent, so that the benefit declines by 50 cents for every dollar beyond the eligible income ceiling. The maximum monthly payment of $504 is given only to those with no income other than OAS, and falls to zero at about $12,000 annual income for an individual and at about $16,000 combined for a couple. Until 1999, seniors had to apply for the GIS every spring, but since then the Canada Customs and Revenue Agency has passed on information from tax returns to HRDC, thereby eliminating this need.

The OAS has always been an expensive program, but until the 1970s it was widely agreed to be a necessary and appropriate expenditure. During that decade, however, concerns about runaway inflation and escalating deficits led governments to concentrate on cutting spending. Obviously, OAS was going to be a target. In 1977, more stringent residential requirements were imposed on OAS, though the numbers affected were slight. In 1983 and 1984, indexing of the benefits was introduced, but there was no impact as inflation in Canada dropped drastically. Then, after the election of 1984 that brought Brian Mulroney and the Conservatives into office, the Tories saw universality as an effective means to address the deficit and excessive government spending. In the budget of May 1985, the federal government proposed to partially de-index OAS (and other social programs) so that only inflation in excess of 3 per cent would be protected through increased benefits.[9] Seniors' groups mobilized and protested on Parliament Hill, and the government backed down.

In the 1989 budget universality in OAS was terminated. Everyone would continue to receive their monthly cheque, but the payments would be clawed back from those seniors with higher incomes. Since 1996, the government has withheld the amount of any clawback (based on the previous year's tax return), thereby ending what the National Council of Welfare (1999a) called the 'charade' of sending out monthly cheques and then reclaiming the money at tax time.

The 1996 budget proposed a new Seniors' Benefit combining the OAS, GIS, and two other minor credits for age and pension income. According to the Caledon Institute, over 90 per cent of single elderly women would come out ahead under the plan. But middle-income seniors, those with incomes between about $40,000 and $78,000, would be worse off. The new benefit was to redistribute income from couples to singles (because of a new family income eligibility criterion), and from middle- and lower middle-income seniors to the very poor. As high-income seniors already did not receive benefits, they would not be affected by these changes. There was tremendous resistance to the new plan from seniors (and others), and in 1998 the proposal was scrapped. The government had miscalculated the extent of political support and anger on the part of seniors with mid-level incomes, who would be worse off under the new plan while the very rich were unaffected. Redistribution from the middle to the bottom proved to be an unacceptable approach towards pension reform.

Table 6.2 presents information on the amounts and sources of income for different groups of seniors for the year 1997. For that year more than 40 per cent of women over 65 were poor, as opposed to 27 per cent of men and 7 per cent of couples. Virtually all seniors received Old Age Security, thereby actualizing the universal intent of the program. The non-poor received slightly more in government transfers than the poor, but they were considerably more likely to receive income from CPP/QPP, occupational pensions, and RRSPs. It is these benefits that largely distinguish the aged poor from the non-poor.

**Table 6.2  Sources of Income, Seniors in Canada, 1997**

| Group | Poor Unattached Women (65+) | Non-Poor Unattached Women (65+) | Poor Unattached Men (65+) | Non-Poor Unattached Men (65+) | Poor Couples (65+) | Non-Poor Couples (65+) |
|---|---|---|---|---|---|---|
| Numbers | 359,000 | 496,000 | 82,000 | 219,000 | 65,000 | 857,000 |
| Per cent receiving OAS and GIS | 98 | 99 | 96 | 99 | 91 | 100 |
| Per cent receiving CPP/QPP | 72 | 93 | 81 | 94 | 84 | 97 |
| Per cent receiving occupational pensions | 15 | 48 | 14 | 59 | 24 | 65 |
| Per cent receiving RRSP annuities | 3 | 22 | Sample too small | 18 | 6 | 29 |
| Total government transfers ($) | 11,808 | 12,370 | 11,784 | 12,694 | 16,324 | 18,818 |
| Total income, all sources ($) | 12,818 | 22,441 | 12,661 | 28,705 | 17,864 | 41,722 |
| Ratio, transfers to all income | .92 | .55 | .93 | .44 | .91 | .45 |

SOURCE: National Council of Welfare (1999a).

Among the poor, there are few differences between men and women in total government transfers or in total income: poor couples are not much better off, given that they must share the income. The final row in the table indicates how dependent poor seniors are on government transfers, which account for over 90 per cent of total income for men, women, and couples classified as poor. OAS/GIS comprise about two-thirds of total income for each group.

### Children's Benefits

Unlike Old Age Security, the original children's benefit, Family Allowances, was never intended to be a major component of household income. The payments were, in part, symbolic of the government's obligation to support children and to recognize that all families incurred costs to raise children. There was also a political advantage in that a government cheque arrived in the home of every mother in Canada each month. By the time the program was terminated in 1993, the maximum monthly stipend was $33 per child, which was neither trivial nor overly substantial. In households with two or three children the total was noticeable. A more serious problem lay with the failure of governments to index the amounts regularly (unlike OAS, which contained automatic indexing).

As we saw earlier, Canada is now one of very few industrialized countries that do not provide systematic support to parents in raising their children. Instead, we have had various initiatives and programs, many delivered through the tax system. The Refundable

Child Tax Credit (RCTC), introduced in 1979, is noteworthy because it was refundable, which meant that even a parent who paid no tax was eligible for the benefit. The program was delivered by the Department of Finance rather than by social services, thereby enhancing its status in the community, and payments were severely tapered towards those at the bottom of the income scale. In addition, the application process was anonymous and non-stigmatizing, as eligibility was based solely on the previous year's tax return. The cheques looked identical to the tax refunds received by the rich. At the outset, the RCTC caused great debate within the social welfare community. Many welcomed the program because it provided non-stigmatizing support to those in greatest need, and the take-up rate was high; others were troubled by the abandonment of universality in favour of an approach that was overtly selective. However, over time, the plan's supporters came to outnumber significantly its detractors.

While Ottawa was focusing on the new RCTC, the other forms of child benefits came under scrutiny. During the 1984 federal election, Brian Mulroney attacked universality in general, because payments ostensibly went to those not in need, but his particular focus was on Family Allowances. He asked rhetorically why his banker, who obviously did not need the money, should receive Family Allowance. The answer is that the cheque went not to the banker (who was likely male), but rather to his wife (McQuaig, 1993).

Although the Mulroney government sought to remove inflation protection from social benefits in the 1985 budget and was forced to retreat because of militant action by seniors, there was no comparable support for Family Allowances and the partial de-indexation held. Benefits were thereafter increased only for that portion of inflation in excess of 3 per cent per annum.[10] The 1989 federal budget proposed to claw back the full amount of Family Allowances (and OAS) from higher-income recipients. Many in the social welfare community argued for continued universality, thereby paradoxically urging the government to continue benefits to the rich, many of whom neither wanted nor needed public assistance.

Finally, on 1 January 1993, Family Allowances were ended, and no one appeared to notice. Benefits had already been clawed back from upper-income households, and for the others the payments were very modest. Henceforth, all federal child support, apart from a tax deduction for the receipted child-care expenses of working parents (which most benefited those with the highest incomes) would now be channelled through the Child Tax Benefit. In design, this new program followed the RCTC: there was a payment ($1,020 per year) for each child to an income ceiling ($25,921), and above this, a gradual reduction. As before, this design targeted the poorest families with a gradual reduction in assistance as incomes increased. There was also a 'working poor' supplement of up to $500 a family available only to those in the paid workforce.

The 1997 budget speech made one important change as a result of negotiations between Ottawa and the provinces. The renamed Canada Child Tax Benefit (CCTB) Supplement was specifically targeted to families with low incomes in the paid workforce: families on social assistance would receive the benefits, but the provinces would have the option to reduce provincial payments dollar for dollar. The provinces committed to reinvest any money saved in other programs directed at children, but there has been no formal system of accountability to ensure this. The central intent of this change was to reward families in the low-paid workforce and, by extension, to penalize those on social assistance. In other words, the program was now structured to provide a strong work incentive; and arguably, the focus was more on work incentives than on support for children (Lightman and Riches, 2000).

What had begun a half-century earlier as a universal program for all children in Canada had now evolved into a selective and somewhat coercive program to encourage participation in the paid workforce; child benefits had become secondary to work incentives. At the same time, the CCTB offers benefits far greater than anything ever contemplated for Family Allowances: the annual basic benefit, as of 2001, was $1,104 per child under 18 for families with incomes below $30,004. The benefit reduction rate was 2.5 per cent for families with one child and 5 per cent for those with two or more,[11] so the benefit disappeared at $74,000 income for families with one or two children. There is also a second payment, the National Child Benefit *Supplement* (NCBS), for low-income families, worth $977 for the first child, $771 for the second child, and $694 for each additional child. The NCBS has a high tax-back rate—11 per cent for families with one child; 20 per cent for those with two children; and 28 per cent for those with three or more children. The full supplement is paid up to an income of $21,214, and at an income of $30,000 (with three children or fewer) the NCBS payments terminate. Alberta and Quebec have their own payment schedules for the CCTB.

All provinces but Newfoundland, New Brunswick, and Manitoba exercise their right to claw back, dollar for dollar, the child benefit supplements of families on social assistance. Recipient families are no better off as a result, as the net effect is to transfer money from Ottawa to the provinces.[12]

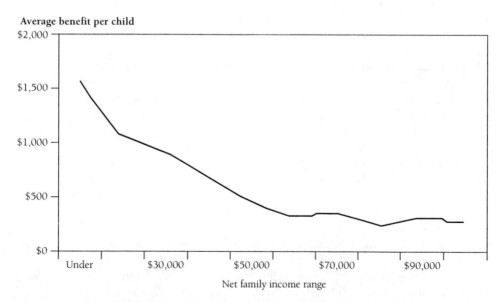

**Figure 6.7  Canada Child Tax Benefits Paid, by Family Income Class, Benefit Year 1998–9**

SOURCE: Canada Customs and Revenue Agency (CCRA), Total Child Benefits Paid by Net Family Income. Available at: <http://www.ccra-adrc.gc.ca/tax/individuals/stats/gb97/pst/ctb-e.htm>.

Figure 6.7 shows how the benefits of the CCTB are highly skewed down the income scale, as intended. For the benefit year July 1998 to June 1999 (based on the 1997 tax year), some 5.5 million children in 3.2 million families received over $5.7 billion. Nearly two-thirds (63 per cent) of the total benefit go to families with net incomes below the $25,921 threshold, and the average payment per child, $1,500, is considerably greater than that at higher income levels. Over 80 per cent of the total benefit is received by families with incomes below $40,000. Only 1 per cent of total payments goes to families with incomes over $60,000. This includes some 2,770 families with an average of 3.3 children and incomes over $100,000 who received a total of $2.5 million through the CCTB.

The fact that most provinces claw back the payments from families on social assistance is a major shortcoming of the program; however, for those who do receive the benefit, the targeting appears to be highly effective. Future increases in the payments should make a significant dent in the struggle against child poverty in Canada—*except for the poorest families who are on social assistance and whose benefits are clawed back by most provincial governments.*

## Some Proposals To Benefit Children

With one child in five living below the poverty line in Canada, there is a clear sense of urgency in the community (even if not within government) that action must be taken. There are many views on the design and underlying values of any future child benefits program, and the issue of universality appears again. Most current proposals involve support for families and view the benefit as a framework for a family income policy rather than as an extension of provincial welfare measures.

The Caledon Institute of Social Policy (Battle and Mendelson, 1999), building on the existing CCTB, calls for the consolidation of the basic and supplementary benefits. They advocate an immediate increase of the combined federal child benefit to $2,500 per year per child, with a gradual increase to a target of $4,000. The benefit would start to decline at family incomes of $25,000 and terminate at a family income of about $75,000, a slight increase. Families with incomes in the $20,000 to $50,000 range would be better off under these proposals, reflecting Caledon's awareness that political support for the program is needed from the middle class.

Campaign 2000 uses a broad life-cycle approach to child poverty (Novick, 1999). Like Caledon, it calls for the basic and supplementary child benefit to be consolidated, but with a more immediate target of a maximum benefit of $4,200 per child. Benefits would begin to decline sooner, at $18,000, and the reduction rate would be steeper. The net effect of Campaign 2000's proposal (which would cost an additional $8.4 billion when fully implemented) would be to target low and modest income families and, to a lesser extent, those with middle incomes.

The National Council of Welfare (1999b) takes a slightly different approach, calling for the government to end the provincial 'clawback' of the supplementary child benefit from families on social assistance. It also advocates an appeals mechanism for the Canada Child Tax Benefit and full indexation of both this program and the refundable GST credit.

At the other end of the political spectrum, the C.D. Howe Institute (Poschmann and Richards, 2000) calls for a non-refundable federal tax credit of $2,000 per child. The rationale is explicitly one of horizontal equity—to offset the unavoidable costs of raising a child. However, the $2,000 credit is non-refundable, and so is denied to those with low incomes who pay no federal taxes, although they presumably still incur costs to raise a child.[13] This study estimates that three-quarters of the $2.5 billion total cost of the proposals would be received by families in the $21,000–$75,000 range. Because there is no improvement for those at the bottom end of the income scale, most of the remaining 25 per cent ($0.625 billion) could be received only by families above $75,000.

Box 6.1 places the child benefits issue in a broader international context. The diagram illustrates the real-world complexity of targeting child benefits in Canada, the United States, the United Kingdom, and Australia (Battle et al., 2001).

---

### Box 6.1: Child Benefits in Four Countries

The graph shows child benefits (the CCTC and supplement in Canada) along with any tax expenditures directed towards children, but does not include other relevant programs, such as food stamps in the US or rental assistance in Australia and the UK, which can have a major impact on the living conditions of low-income families. The data refer to a one-parent family with one child under five years of age, deal only with federal programs, and are reported in US dollars, adjusted for national differences in purchasing power.

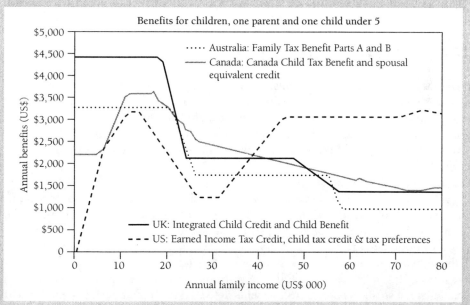

Benefits for children, one parent and one child under 5

---

The schemes for Australia and the UK are remarkably similar, though they were developed independently. In each case, there are three plateaus for benefits, corresponding to low-, middle-, and upper-income households. The tapers are very steep for incomes between $20,000 and $25,000 and again between $50,000 and $60,000:

in the UK, the benefit reduction rate is 45 per cent at incomes just over $20,000. Most single parents in both countries would find themselves on the highest plateau, with incomes below $20,000 and maximum benefits.

In Canada and the US the situation is different, as tax benefits are built into their systems. As a result, in each country benefits actually increase as income rises, when the tax benefits first kick in. In Canada this occurs over a relatively small range of low incomes, while in the US the Earned Income Tax Credit (EITC) increases benefits with income level for a narrow range of the working poor with incomes up to about $15,000. Alone among the countries, the US offers no benefits to those not in the paid workforce. The declining 'valley' for the US reflects the impact of the EITC, which tapers very severely and terminates at a low income, while the rise after the trough reflects the tax benefits that begin to have effect and produce the most generous benefits to families at high-income levels.

The graph for Canada shows a small plateau at the lowest income levels, as the CCTB covers all low-income families whether or not they are in the paid workforce. The modest upward slope shows the impact of the tax benefits that begin to be felt. There is no second plateau for Canada, but instead a long gradual decline in benefits, which is steeper initially (for low-income families) and then more gradual (for non-poor families). In the $25,000–$35,000 range, Canada offers the most generous benefits of the four countries.

# CASH, IN-KIND—UNIVERSAL/SELECTIVE

When we refer to in-kind programs, such as medicare or public education, many of the issues involved in the selectivity debate still resonate strongly. Only by ensuring that the middle and upper classes participate in and benefit from programs such as public education can popular support be maintained and high-quality programming delivered to everyone. The idea of stigma reappears when we talk of two-tiered delivery of services. As well, universal medicare is clearly more efficient than the market-based system of health care in the United States.

When we think of cash benefits, however, the ideas of universality and selectivity are no longer meaningful descriptors. The operative phrase today, in discussing cash redistribution, is 'targeting', that is, the process of directing funds up or down the income scale to designated recipient groups. Canada was among the first countries to redistribute income through the tax system, in the Refundable Child Tax Credit of 1979, and we remain, in the words of the Caledon Institute, a 'world leader in the use of income-tax delivered social benefits'. Cash benefits delivered through the tax system are neither universal nor selective in their original sense, but at different times and through different programs these benefits can be targeted to particular groups in a way that is efficient, impersonal, and non-demeaning. Many child welfare advocates continue to call for universal payments as a means of enhancing social solidarity and justifiably criticize the CCTB for its exclusion of families on social assistance. Yet, few are unwilling to work with the program: its underlying approach of redistributing benefits through the tax system and the targeting that this approach implies are widely accepted in the Canadian social policy arena today.

## NOTES

1. One of the federal conditions for cost-sharing of medicare is that there be universal coverage, which has usually been interpreted as referring to 95 per cent of the population: the other 5 per cent are assumed to be moving in or out of a province or do not qualify for specific reasons.
2. In reality, there is relatively little fraud in social assistance programs (see Morrison, 1995, 1998). According to the Ontario government's own data (Ontario, 2002), in 2000–1 there were roughly 53,000 'complaints' about individuals, and of these only 229 were referred to Crown attorneys for possible investigation.
3. The clawback rate for EI benefits is 30 per cent, which is high compared to all other social programs. Those claiming regular EI benefits for the first time are not subject to clawback.
4. As well, Ottawa's drive to simplify and demystify the tax system (often presented in terms of fewer tax brackets) is negated, as more sources of income are treated differentially for tax purposes.
5. When there is no basic exemption (as in lines AB or CD in Figure 6.1), the relation among maximum benefit (the point on the y-axis), the tax-back rate (t), and the break-even point (BE) is such that if two of the variables are given, the third is uniquely determined. In Figure 6.1, for example, $OA/t = OB$ or $OA = t \times OB$. More generally, maximum benefit divided by tax-back rate determines break-even point.
6. The economics literature refers to a choice between work and *leisure*. Jane McMichael (2001) points out that *non-employment* is a preferred term, as *leisure* 'has a popular meaning that does not usually evoke the image of caring for children, managing household work and searching for jobs.'
7. Formally, the substitution of work for non-employment occurs because the *opportunity cost* of an hour's leisure increases in response to higher potential earnings: that is, the income forgone by an hour's non-employment increases as a result of increased work incentives, so people will substitute work for non-employment.
8. The *deficit* (or *surplus*) refers to the amount by which annual spending falls short of (or exceeds) government revenues in any given year, while the *debt* represents the accumulated total of all past deficits. The debt is equivalent to a mortgage on a house, while the $42 billion interest payments would correspond to the carrying charges on that mortgage.
9. At 3 per cent inflation, benefits would not increase; at 4 per cent inflation, the increase would be 1 per cent (4 per cent minus 3 per cent); at 5 per cent inflation, the increase would be 2 per cent, and so on.
10. Shillington (2000b) has traced the marketing by governments of changes to the child benefits system since 1985. He argues that the two casualties of government marketing have been 'the truth and the poor': government often creates the illusion of increased support as a result of program changes in cases where there is none or overstates the extent of those supports.
11. That is, with incomes above the threshold, for each additional dollar of household income, benefits would reduce by 2.5 cents in families with one child and by 5 per cent if there were two or more.

12. Because the benefits are not indexed to inflation, families are worse off over time.
13. In order to ensure work incentives, they advocate a reduced clawback on a combined CCTC and GST credit 'restricted to those who fully exit welfare'. Regrettably, the authors weaken their case with their ideological reference to the 'culture of tax avoidance/evasion among the poor' without noting that the tax avoidance/evasion problems—and costs to the Treasury—are much greater among those with higher incomes.

## SUGGESTED READING

Battle, Ken, Michael Mendelson, Daniel Meyer, Jane Millar, and Peter Whiteford. 2001. *Benefits for Children: A Four Country Study*. Ottawa: Caledon Institute for Social Policy.

This is an excellent comparison of child benefits in Canada, the US, the UK, and Australia. Strengths and weaknesses of each country's approach are detailed.

Hum, Derek, and Wayne Simpson. 2001. 'A Guaranteed Annual Income? From Mincome to the Millennium', *Policy Options Politiques* (Jan.–Feb.): 78–82.

This short article describes the current situation with respect to a GAI in Canada.

McQuaig, Linda. 1993. *The Wealthy Banker's Wife: The Assault on Equality in Canada*. Toronto: Penguin Books.

This is an excellent discussion of the equality/universality debate in Canada, grounded in the political process. Highly readable.

National Council of Welfare. 1999a. *A Pension Primer*. Ottawa: NCW, Summer.

This report presents a clear overview of the pension situation in Canada. It will be readily understandable to the novice in the pension area.

Novick, Marvyn. 1999. *Fundamentals First: An Equal Opportunity for Birth for Every Child*. Toronto: Campaign 2000.

This report sets out the dimensions of a comprehensive response to the problem of child poverty in Canada, as developed by Campaign 2000. It uses a 'life-cycle' approach.

# PART IV

# Generating Resources

In Chapter 2, we posed the two central questions affecting social policy:

- Who is to receive what, and in what form?
- Who is to pay, and in what manner?

We then developed a model of redistribution that links service delivery with program financing. The model emphasized both questions, on both sides of the redistributive cycle, using the image of a closed circle to suggest that, in the aggregate, payers and recipients are the same people. But because those individuals who pay are not those who benefit, issues of reallocation and redistribution within the society—who pays and who receives—are of great importance.

In Chapters 4, 5, and 6 we examined allocation, the first question posed above. In Chapters 7, 8, and 9 we shall explore the second question, the financing of the social services. There are three general sources of financing for social and health services: government, users, and the voluntary sector.

*Government*

Government raises revenue directly through macro-level choices about levels of taxation and distribution within the society. Conscious government decisions determine what it will take (through direct taxes) and what it will not take (through tax expenditures). It also sets the context in which others can raise revenues, for example, by defining what constitutes a registered charity allowed to issue tax receipts to donors.

Taxes are, by far, the major source of revenue for government. Personal income tax is the most important, but there are other forms of taxation as well: corporate taxes; sales tax (such as the GST); excise and customs charges (relatively unimportant); payroll taxes (such as premiums for Canada Pension Plan or Employment Insurance). Government can also generate revenues by borrowing, usually by issuing bonds, or through inflation, which conceptually is equivalent to printing more money.

Government is distinguished from other sources of financing by two characteristics:

• Payment is mandatory. Whether one approves of the expenditure or wishes to participate is not relevant. We have a legal obligation to pay.
• Government spending transfers resources (money) from private to public uses. Our money is not put to uses that we individually choose, but according to the 'collective will', reflected in the actions of public servants and politicians.

*Users*

Users pay for a service only if they utilize it or expect to do so; non-users do not pay. Payment can be voluntary or mandatory, depending on the program. User payment generally takes two forms:

• *Fee*: payment at the point of use. It can be based on units of service, time, or complexity of process. An admission charge to a recreation centre, a road toll, and a fee paid for a health or counselling service not covered by medicare all are forms of user fees.
• *Premium*: payment in advance of use against later use, but not directly linked to specific usage. The 'administrative fees' charged by some physicians and premiums paid for coverage under medicare in some provinces, and for Employment Insurance, are user fees paid in advance.

*Voluntary Sector*

This category comprises several discrete sources of revenue for social and health services:

• charities (with legal status and charitable registration);
• lotteries and other forms of legal gambling; and
• other voluntary activity (without charitable registration), including donations.

Participation in these activities is not compulsory, and the beneficiaries are not necessarily those who pay.

Specific programs and initiatives can be financed by any or all of the above sources in any combination. Counselling at a voluntary agency, for example, may entail a user fee paid by the client (sometimes discretionary, and often subject to a means test), voluntary money provided through the United Way or agency fundraising, funding from government, perhaps through a purchase-of-service contract, a grant from a charitable foundation, either ongoing or for a specific project, and perhaps lottery proceeds. Today there is diminished access to ongoing or sustaining financing from government and increased project and contract-based funding. Agency workers often comment that they spend all their time 'scrambling' to secure money from multiple sources and filling out progress reports—and no longer have time to deliver services.

# CHAPTER SEVEN

# Paying Through Taxes

## INTRODUCTION

In this chapter, we examine the principles and the practice of Canada's tax system. We are particularly focused on the extent to which taxation can, and does, serve as an agent of progressive redistribution. We begin, however, with a general discussion of the goals and underlying values of taxation. We then discuss the two fundamental principles of taxation—ability to pay and the benefit principle—emphasizing that these reflect prior ideological choices about how taxes *should* be levied: one principle has no greater innate validity than the other.

Following this we look at data on the personal income tax system in Canada. We explore the impacts of such concepts as progressivity and regressivity, the distinction between deductions or exemptions and credits, and indexation, along with the idea of marginal taxation—why it is important, and how it works. Using data from the OECD, we shall see that the poor face confiscatory levels of taxation as they begin to undertake paid work. For example, in Ontario marginal rates of taxation potentially exceed 100 per cent, so that for an extra dollar of earned income, the low-income earner might lose more than one dollar in cash and in-kind benefits. We compare these taxation rates with the highest marginal rates faced by high-income taxpayers, which are now uniformly less than 50 per cent, federal and provincial combined.

We shall consider how the tax system treats child support payments compared to spousal support and how seniors are treated for income tax purposes. In Chapter 6 we introduced the idea of tax expenditures, and we now look at this area empirically.

The chapter then shifts to highlight tax reform in Canada, beginning with the Mulroney government and continuing up to the Liberal budgets of 2000, described as the biggest tax-cutting budgets in Canadian history. We shall see that although these were advertised as tax cuts directed to the middle classes, in fact the very rich derived the largest gains.

Finally, we consider two different approaches to budget-making in Canada. The first of these, the Alternate Federal Budget, is prepared annually by a coalition of social policy groups under the leadership of the Canadian Centre for Policy Alternatives and indicates how progressive outcomes could result from a different set of assumptions and priorities. We conclude with a look at the other end of the political spectrum, examining the flat-tax proposals that have been promoted by the neo-liberal interests in Canada and implemented for the provincial income tax in Alberta.

# GOALS OF TAXATION

There are a number of goals of any system of taxation, some more controversial than others. In large part, perceptions of the proper role of taxation reflect differing views about the correct role of government in society.

- *Raise revenue.* Undoubtedly, a pre-eminent goal of taxation is to generate revenue so that government can do the tasks it is expected to perform.
- *Alter behaviours.* Certain taxation decisions are designed to alter the behaviours of individuals or corporations. High taxes on alcohol and tobacco are intended to discourage consumption; a tax on non-renewable energy sources may aim to divert usage towards renewable sources. Taxes on 'junk food' but not on 'healthy' food hope to encourage healthier eating. Non-taxation of certain forms of income, such as that in RRSPs or RESPs (Registered Education Saving Plans), encourages people to save more than they otherwise might for their old age or their children's education.

  Tax incentives also can alter corporate behaviour. Industries can be encouraged to locate production in designated low-tax areas. The Canadian corporate tax system gives preferential treatment to the oil and mineral industries to encourage resource development. Efficiency can be encouraged through the non-taxation (or lower taxation) of innovations and technologies.
- *Redistribute income and pursue equity.* A controversial goal of taxation is redistributing income, particularly since, as we saw earlier, the term *equity* has no unique meaning.

Though there is no broad consensus as to what services government should provide, there is agreement on the need to raise funds for what tasks are undertaken. The role of government as a paternalistic agent in society, which we discussed earlier, now raises the question of whether (or to what extent) taxation *should* be used to alter behaviours and redistribute income. If one believes that government has a right or a responsibility to discourage unhealthy lifestyles or to encourage private savings for old age, then taxation incentives would be one appropriate way to pursue these goals. If one rejects the paternalism role of government in favour of self-reliance and individual responsibility, then one would not endorse such use of taxation.

Government 'minimalists' argue that 'social engineering' through tax policies is doomed, that raising revenue is the *only* rationale for taxation, and that this revenue should be used only for activities that individuals cannot undertake on their own.[1] Taxes should be designed to minimize interference with economic activities, not to alter individual economic decisions. They should not encourage people or businesses to do things they would not do in the absence of the tax.

Let us consider one example. When employers make contributions (which are compulsory and therefore constitute taxes) for Employment Insurance or Canada Pension Plan, there is an income ceiling beyond which no further premiums are required. For the year 2000, this limit was $39,000 for EI contributions and $39,600 for CPP yearly maximum pensionable earnings (YMPE). Once employees have reached these ceilings, no further annual payments are required from employers or employees. This ceiling is a disincentive to job creation—an employer will likely extend the hours of work of current employees above the ceilings (as no further EI or CPP premiums are payable) rather than hire new employees for whom contributions to the two programs are mandatory.[2] The optimal tax, based on the principle of *minimal interference,* would be one that would be neutral, that neither encourages nor discourages job creation.

## Equity in Taxation

The pursuit of equity in tax policy has two dimensions:

- *Horizontal equity*. Taxpayers who have the same financial capacity (income, resources, ability to pay) should pay the same taxes. Those at the same income level with differing needs (e.g., with and without children) should pay different taxes that reflect these different needs.
- *Vertical equity*. Taxpayers who have different financial capacity should pay different taxes. Vertical equity is a measure of how the total tax bill is spread across the different income classes. The notion of vertical equity, in effect, holds that wealthier taxpayers should pay higher tax rates, and is fundamental to the idea of progressive taxation.

Taxes can be *progressive, proportional,* or *regressive* in their impacts, as shown in Figure 7.1. With a *progressive* tax, taxpayers pay an increasing share of their incomes as these incomes increase. Thus, an individual with a taxable income of $100,000 would pay a greater share (percentage) of this income in taxes than would another with an income of $25,000. Income tax is the major progressive tax in Canada, though as we shall see, this progressivity is rather modest. Figure 7.1a shows that the average tax rate (total taxes divided by total income) increases as income level rises.

Because the line up and to the right in Figure 7.1a is continuous, each additional dollar of income will increase the average tax rate, albeit by tiny amounts. Since such an approach is not feasible in practice, we use *tax brackets,* as shown in Figure 7.1d. In place of a continuously rising tax rate, incomes are grouped into convenient steps, and all those in a single step pay the same rate. In the figure, incomes in the range OA pay no tax, while those in the range AB all pay an average rate of OE; those with higher incomes, between B and C, pay at a higher average tax rate of OF, and so on. The greater the number of tax brackets, the closer we get to a pure progressive tax, but at the same time, the greater is the complexity.

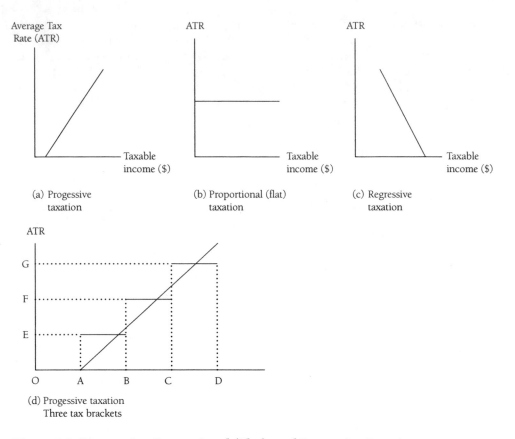

**Figure 7.1 Progressive, Proportional (Flat), and Regressive Taxation**

With a *proportional* tax, also known as a *flat* tax, all taxpayers pay the same tax rate, i.e., the same share of their taxable incomes, regardless of income level. Wealthier individuals will pay more dollars in total taxes, but the share would be constant for everyone. The horizontal tax line in Figure 7.1b illustrates this constant rate, regardless of income level.

On the other hand, with a *regressive* tax the rate of taxes paid decreases as incomes rise. The GST is a flat tax *in application*, in that everyone pays 7 per cent on all eligible purchases; but it is *regressive in impact* (with respect to income) because the tax is a larger share of a poor person's income than of a wealthier person's.[3] Hence, the share of income paid in GST decreases as income rises. CPP and EI contributions are also regressive beyond the ceiling for annual contributions—as premiums do not increase further, they represent a declining share of total income. For the year 2000, the maximum EI payment was $936, which represents a larger share of a $40,000 income than of an $80,000 income. Hence, beyond the ceilings for contributions, the premiums are regressive in their impact. Figure 7.1c reflects this with a line that slopes down and to the right, illustrating tax rates that decline as income increases.

# TWO PRINCIPLES OF TAXATION

There are two fundamental approaches to taxation: the *ability-to-pay* principle and the *benefit* principle. Both address the central question of the basis upon which taxes should be allocated, but they reflect different normative perspectives.

- *Ability-to-pay principle.* This approach is most closely associated with ideas of vertical equity and progressive taxation. It proposes that taxes be based on the taxpayer's ability to pay. Therefore, wealthier individuals would pay more. This is not a statement of the technical efficiency of a particular system of taxation, but rather a reflection of a particular value system.
- *Benefit principle.* This competing approach to taxation holds that it is right or correct or just that those who benefit from a public service should pay for it, while those who do not use it should not pay. Financial capacity is not relevant. Once again, this perspective does not reflect a technical analysis, but rather a particular value system.

Ability to pay implies that services should be paid from taxation, usually personal income tax, as it is the most progressive taxation vehicle available. The benefit principle favours user fees. These two principles clearly reflect the two value systems—institutional and residual—that we examined earlier. Residualists' emphasis on individual responsibility directs them towards the benefit principle, whereby users of a service pay for it and others do not. Institutionalists interpret responsibility in a more collective manner, supporting greater redistribution and financing through the tax system.

Any social program can, in principle, be financed through either approach. Medicare, for example, is largely financed through the tax system, reflecting our society's institutionalist view that we should all pay, according to our abilities; funding through user fees, reflecting residualism and the benefit principle, would ensure that those who use medical services would pay for them. (And/or those who wish to protect themselves against future medical costs would buy the necessary contingency insurance.) Toll roads and counselling require user fees, reflecting the view that those who use these services *should* pay for the benefits received: if we do not use the toll road, then we need not pay the fee.

Though the difference between these two competing perspectives may appear straightforward, we cannot overemphasize that they are ideological perspectives. Political commentators—and the taxpayer on the street—may argue that charges should be attached to a service *because those who use it should pay for it.* The position is presented as if it were some inevitable, inexorable truth. But it is not. The benefit principle represents a legitimate view as to how services could be financed, but it reflects a particular set of values and norms, nothing more. There is an alternative ideological position, which argues to the contrary. The two perspectives can be debated, but only as competing normative stances. There are relevant technical issues of tax policy in choosing between the approaches, but they are secondary to the normative debate.

As the welfare state is cut back, we see considerable movement from the ability-to-pay principle towards the benefit principle. Many services are adopting user fees to replace former support through taxes: increased student fees in post-secondary education; 'charges' levied on parents of primary and secondary school students; 'delisting' of insured services from medicare; charges at recreation centres that formerly were free to users; and paying for garbage collection by the bag rather than through taxes.

# TAX REVENUES IN CANADA

Table 7.1 presents information on government revenues in Canada, for all levels consolidated and for each level separately. Total revenue, all levels, was $351 billion in 1996–7; just under half ($155 billion) went to the federal government. Provincial/territorial revenues were slightly greater ($183 billion); local governments raised $41 billion.

Three major types of taxes are levied in Canada: income; spending; and property. The latter often serves as a proxy tax on wealth. At the bottom of Table 7.1, the 'other' category represents mostly revenues from the direct sale of goods and services by governments, as well as income from various government investments (including royalties from natural resources).

Of the three main categories, income tax—particularly the personal income tax—is the largest source of revenue for governments. In 1996–7, the personal income tax accounted for nearly one-half (44 per cent) of federal government revenues and one-quarter (25 per cent) of provincial/territorial revenues. In the aggregate, personal income taxes produced one-third (32 per cent) of total revenue for all governments in Canada.

Sales taxes, both the federal GST and provincial sales taxes, were the second greatest source of revenue, followed by payroll and premium charges, including contributions to EI, CPP/QPP, and Workers' Compensation, and then payroll taxes that are calculated as a percentage of wages and salaries and usually paid by employers.[4] Close behind were property and related taxes, which generate more than half (57 per cent) of all revenue at the local level. Corporation income taxes are a small share (7.6 per cent) of total government revenues, though they grew rapidly from $13 billion in 1992–3 to $27 billion in 1996–7.[5]

The $3.5 billion from lotteries represented only 1 per cent of total government revenues in 1996–7 (2 per cent at the provincial level). However, this amount was more than double the $1.7 billion collected in 1992–3. Its rapid growth suggests governments are increasingly reliant on gambling revenues right across the country. We return to this issue in Chapter Nine.

General property taxes are levied primarily by local governments, usually municipalities. They generated nearly $19 billion or 46 per cent of the revenue of all local governments in 1996–7. Property taxes, which are the major funding source for education in most provinces, are highly regressive in their impact, and increases in property taxes translate directly into higher rents.

Transfers from other (higher) levels of governments constitute some 15 per cent of total revenues at both the provincial and municipal levels.

## Personal Income Taxes

The personal income tax, governments' largest single source of revenue, is the only major tax that is even mildly progressive in impact, i.e., the only one encompassing the ability-to-pay principle. In concept, the calculation of tax liability is a relatively straightforward four-step task:

**Table 7.1  Consolidated Government Revenues**

| Source of Revenue | All Levels | | Federal | | Provincial/Territorial | | Local | |
|---|---|---|---|---|---|---|---|---|
| $ millions | 1996–7 | % of Total Revenue 1996–7 | 1996–7 | % of Total Revenue 1996–7 | 1996–7 | % of Total Revenue 1996–7 | 1998– | % of Total Revenue 1998 |
| Total Revenue | 351,317 | | 155,354 | | 183,442 | | 41,032 | |
| *Income Taxes* | 142,796 | 40.6 | 87,514 | 56.3 | 55,283 | 30.1 | 0 | |
| Personal income taxes | 113,750 | 32.4 | 68,521 | 44.1 | 45,229 | 24.7 | | |
| Corporation income taxes | 26,686 | 7.6 | 16,855 | 10.8 | 9,831 | 5.4 | | |
| Other | 2,361 | 0.7 | 2,138 | 1.4 | 224 | 0.1 | | |
| *Consumption Taxes* | 69,391 | 19.8 | 32,007 | 20.6 | 37,331 | 20.4 | 58 | 0.1 |
| General sales tax | 42,363 | 12.1 | 20,923 | 13.5 | 21,398 | 11.7 | 55 | 0.1 |
| Alcohol, tobacco taxes | 5,582 | 1.6 | 3,038 | 2.0 | 2,544 | 1.4 | | |
| Liquor profits | 2,519 | 0.7 | – | | 2,519 | 1.4 | | |
| Lottery profits | 3,517 | 1.0 | 51 | 0.0 | 3,465 | 1.9 | | |
| Gasoline, motive fuel taxes | 10,874 | 3.1 | 4,439 | 2.9 | 6,435 | 3.5 | | |
| Other | 4,536 | 1.3 | 3,541 | 2.3 | 969 | 0.5 | 3 | 0.0 |
| *Property and Related Taxes* | 36,983 | 10.5 | – | | 7,043 | 3.8 | 23,252 | 56.7 |
| General property taxes | 29,373 | 8.4 | | | 2,981 | 1.6 | 18,850 | 45.9 |
| Other | 7,610 | 2.2 | | | 4,061 | 2.2 | 4,402 | 10.7 |
| *Payroll, EI, CPP Premiums* | 37,076 | 10.6 | 22,658 | 14.6 | 14,417 | 7.9 | 0 | |
| *Transfers from Other Government* | | | 536 | | 27,732 | 15.1 | 6,304 | 15.4 |
| Other | 65,070 | 18.5 | 12,639 | 8.1 | 41,635 | 22.7 | 11,416 | 27.8 |

NOTE: Data for federal and provincial/territorial are for 1996–7 and for municipal are for 1998.

SOURCE: Statistics Canada, Public Sector Statistics, Catalogue no. 68-213-XIB.

1. We first calculate total taxable income. This is the most complex part of the exercise, as not all income counts the same and some income does not count at all, i.e., tax expenditures assign preferential treatment to certain forms of income. After all tax expenditures have been taken into account (usually as deductions from total income), the result is *taxable income.*
2. Second, we specify the tax rate or rates to be applied to taxable income. The provincial flat tax in Alberta has one rate for all taxpayers (plus a zero rate for those who pay no tax). The current federal system in Canada has four rates (plus zero). Reducing the number of rates does little to simplify the overall system.
3. Third, the tax rate (usually specified as a percentage) is multiplied by taxable income to produce the basic federal tax. This is what we owe to government.
4. Certain surtaxes and credits (including most provincial income taxes) are applied to the basic federal tax to increase or decrease the final amount payable.

### Average Tax Rates and Marginal Tax Rates

Table 7.2 shows the *average* tax rates paid at different income levels in Canada. The data, based on tax returns filed for the tax year 1997, present the total tax payable (federal and provincial plus surtaxes) as a share of total income (before deductions and credits). For all taxpayers, the *average* rate of taxation was 18.2 per cent, *before* the major tax cuts of 2000, which reduced tax levels even farther.

As the graph shows, Canada's personal income tax system is progressive. More than half of all taxpayers reported taxable incomes[6] under $20,000, and at this level the average tax burden is under 5 per cent. (But we should also note the high *marginal* rates that can face this group, as we shall see below.) More than three-quarters of all taxpayers in 1997 had less than $40,000 taxable income with maximum average tax rates of less than 16 per cent. The 8 per cent of filers in the $40,000–$50,000 range pay roughly the overall average tax rate of 19 per cent; at higher levels of income the rates increase, though there are relatively few filers at these lofty levels. For the 12 per cent of taxpayers with incomes above $50,000, the average tax rate is 26 per cent. The 0.8 per cent of tax filers who have average taxable incomes above $150,000 (and claim 10 per cent of all income in Canada) pay an average rate of 35.5 per cent.

Most discussion of tax policy does not focus on *average* tax rates, but rather on *marginal* rates. The *marginal* rate refers to the taxes paid on the last dollar of income and is important politically because of a concern that high marginal tax rates will discourage people from earning additional income (such as by working extra hours). This is known as the *disincentive effect* of high marginal rates of taxation.

Table 7.3 shows the federal *marginal* tax rates payable at different income levels as of 2001. The lower portion of Table 7.3 illustrates by example the relation between average and marginal taxation: individuals pay the lowest rate (16 per cent) on the first $35,000 of taxable income, so that at $10,000 taxes due amount to $1,600. At $50,000, individuals pay the lowest rate of 16 per cent on the first $35,000 and then pay 22 per cent on the excess above this amount. Total taxes are $8,900, which yields an *average* rate of 17.8 per cent. The person with taxable income of $70,000 pays 16 per cent on the first $35,000, 22 per cent on the next $25,000 (to $60,000), and then a rate of 26 per cent on the $10,000 balance up to the $70,000 taxable income. The average tax rate

**Table 7.2  Average Tax Rates, by Income Group, 1997**

| Income range ('000s) | 0–20 | 20–30 | 30–40 | 40–50 | 50–70 | 70–100 | 100–150 | 150+ | total |
|---|---|---|---|---|---|---|---|---|---|
| # of tax returns | 10,912,650 | 3,323,830 | 2,502,420 | 1,629,740 | 1,715,250 | 653,320 | 221,270 | 165,350 | 21,123,810 |
| % of all returns | 51.7 | 15.7 | 11.8 | 7.7 | 8.1 | 3.1 | 1.0 | 0.8 | |
| % of all income | 17.4 | 14.3 | 15.0 | 12.6 | 17.3 | 9.2 | 4.5 | 9.6 | |
| Avg. tax rate (%) | 4.78 | 12.46 | 15.78 | 18.91 | 21.74 | 25.15 | 28.77 | 35.50 | 18.16 |

SOURCE: Canada Customs and Revenue Agency, *Tax Statistics on Individuals* (2000), Basic Table 2: All Returns by Total Income Class.

**Table 7.3  Marginal Tax Rates, Canada**

| Taxable Income ($) | Marginal Tax Rate (%) |
|---|---|
| 0–35,000 | 16 |
| 35,000–60,000 | 22 |
| 60,000–100,000 | 26 |
| Over 100,000 | 29 |

| Taxable Income | Marginal Tax Rate | Taxes Due | Average Tax Rate |
|---|---|---|---|
| $10,000 | 16% | 16% of $10,000 = $1,600 | $1,600/$10,000 = 16% |
| $50,000 | 22% | 16% of $35,000 = $5,600<br>+22% of $15,000 = $3,300<br>TOTAL = $8,900 | $8,900/$50,000 = 17.8% |
| $70,000 | 26% | 16% of $35,000 = $5,600<br>+22% of $25,000 = $5,500<br>+26% of $10,000 = $2,600<br>TOTAL = $13,700 | $13,700/$70,000 = 19.6% |

SOURCE: Canada Customs and Revenue Agency.

here is 19.6 per cent. As long as the tax system is progressive, the average rate will never be higher than the marginal rate, so that people will always face a tax rate on any additional income that is higher than the average they are currently paying.

Notwithstanding the rhetoric in the press and in Parliament about Canada's allegedly excessive rates of personal taxation, Canada has a relatively flat tax system. Both marginal (Table 7.3) and average (Table 7.2) tax rates clearly show that the progression is liberal, particularly at upper income levels. The case for a flat tax, advocated by the neo-liberal parties, is substantially weakened by this reality.

The examples in Table 7.3 refer only to federal tax payable. There is also a provincial tax liability, which in all provinces except Quebec is calculated as a percentage of the federal tax. Most provinces are therefore bound by federal decisions regarding what constitutes taxable income and are limited in their ability to tailor the provincial income tax to reflect local priorities. But there are also minimal administrative costs. Quebec designs and delivers its own provincial income tax so it can pursue its own priorities, though it does so at the cost of a provincial taxation bureaucracy. Quebec residents also must complete two tax returns each year, one for Ottawa and a distinct one for Quebec City.

Table 7.4 presents the top marginal tax rates for 2001, federal and provincial, for a taxpayer in the highest marginal bracket, by province of residence. For salary income the top rates range from 49.2 per cent in Quebec to 39 per cent in Alberta, a difference of nearly one-quarter. (Dividends and capital gains, reflecting tax expenditures, are taxed at lower rates.) Not surprisingly, high-income individuals have responded to these disparities by moving their legal residence to low-tax provinces: people do not necessarily live year-round in Alberta, but they may establish official residence there for tax purposes. The consequence is that revenue is lost from poor, higher-taxing provinces to already wealthy Alberta. The strains on the federal state become aggravated.

**Table 7.4  Top Marginal Tax Rates, by Province, 2001**

| Province | Salaries (%) | Dividends (%) | Capital Gains (%) |
|---|---|---|---|
| Newfoundland | 48.6 | 32.0 | 24.3 |
| PEI | 47.4 | 32.0 | 23.7 |
| Nova Scotia | 47.3 | 31.9 | 23.7 |
| New Brunswick | 46.8 | 31.6 | 23.4 |
| Quebec | 49.2 | 34.1 | 24.6 |
| Ontario | 46.4 | 31.3 | 23.2 |
| Manitoba | 46.5 | 34.0 | 23.2 |
| Saskatchewan | 45.0 | 31.6 | 22.5 |
| Alberta | 39.0 | 24.1 | 19.5 |
| BC | 45.7 | 33.0 | 22.9 |

These rates refer to the combined federal and provincial taxes for a taxpayer in the highest bracket, by province of residence for 2001.

SOURCE: Canada Customs and Revenue Agency.

### Marginal Tax Rates for the Poor

For those at the bottom of the income scale, the disincentives associated with moving from social assistance to paid work may be substantial. Figure 7.2 shows the effective marginal tax rates for 1996 and 2000 faced by a one-earner Ontario couple in receipt of social assistance and with two children. The marginal rates rise dramatically, from under 10 per cent to nearly 80 per cent, while still at incomes below $10,000. At incomes up to about $35,000, the marginal tax rates are consistently greater than those faced by households with higher incomes (who are unlikely to be on social assistance). Above about $35,000, the marginal rates are essentially flat. The OECD indicates that these data do not include the loss of in-kind benefits such as extended health care, subsidized rent, or child care as incomes rise—which would raise the marginal rates for low-income households even higher, in excess of 100 per cent in some cases.

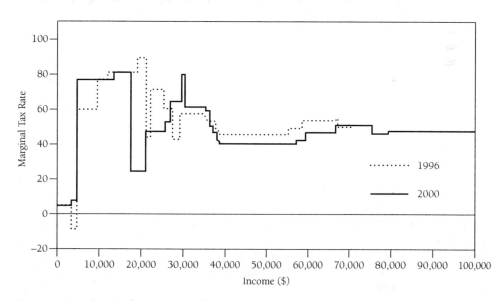

**Figure 7.2  Marginal Tax Rates by Income, Ontario, 1996 and 2000**
SOURCE: OECD (2000: 87).

The importance of these data cannot be overstated: low-income households in Ontario and elsewhere as well, in both 1996 and after the tax 'reforms' of 2000, face marginal tax rates that can readily exceed 100 per cent. In other words, individuals who choose to do paid work can lose more than one dollar in cash and in-kind benefits for every dollar they earn. The wealthy pay lower marginal tax rates and show no evidence of work disincentives; confiscatory levels of taxation are faced only by the poor. With marginal tax rates in excess of 100 per cent, why would anyone freely choose paid employment over social assistance? Yet, many people do—clear evidence that the commitment to the work ethic and to paying one's own way is highest among those with the lowest incomes.

*Different Kinds of Income*

An often cited Royal Commission of the early 1960s, known as the Carter Commission, called for all income to be treated the same, with no exemptions, deductions, or credits: 'a buck is a buck is a buck.' Had this advice been followed, the income base on which taxes are levied would have been much wider; there would have been fewer 'exceptions', which often meet the needs of special interests, and, arguably, the entire system would have been fairer.

Why are different forms of income treated differently for purposes of income tax? Wage and salary income and interest earned are treated directly as income. Income earned within tax shelters such as RRSPs or RESPs is not counted at all until it is withdrawn, to encourage people to save for specified purposes.

Other forms of income fall in between, typically being assessed for taxation purposes at less than 100 per cent of their value. These are *tax expenditures*: they reflect taxes not paid, and are equivalent to direct government spending. Capital gains, the difference between the purchase price and the sale price of an asset (largely profits, or losses, from transactions in the stock market) receive preferential treatment. Prior to the 2000 budget, 75 per cent of capital gains were included in calculating total income; the spring budget reduced this rate to two-thirds, and the autumn update lowered the rate further, to 50 per cent, the level in place between 1972 and 1988. (Prior to 1972, capital gains were not subject to tax in Canada.) Any income received through capital gains counts at one-half of its value for purposes of income tax. Likewise, dividends paid by corporations to shareholders receive preferential treatment: the effect is that for tax purposes, one dollar in dividends has the same after-tax value as $1.25 of interest income for a taxpayer in the highest bracket. Table 7.4 shows the differing marginal rates for salaries, capital gains, and dividend income for each province in 2001.

Table 7.5 shows the results of a simulation done by Statistics Canada prior to the 2000 budget to show the distribution of benefits that would follow if capital gains taxation were eliminated. The data refer to families, and show the increase in consumable incomes (that is, incomes after all compulsory deductions) from the elimination of taxes on capital gains. Of all benefits we have examined, the results are most strongly skewed in favour of the wealthiest families.

Approximately 3 per cent of Canadian families, those with incomes above $150,000, would derive more than half (56 per cent) of the total increase in consumable incomes, with a net gain of $2,756 per family. The families at the bottom derive little or no benefit, as they do not generally have capital gains: 76 per cent of families, with incomes below $65,000, derive a mere 13 per cent of the benefits. It is not until we reach a family income in excess of $75,000 that there is even a $100 increase in average annual income. The 9 per cent of families with incomes greater than $100,000 would reap a full 75 per cent of the benefit.

Why are dividends and capital gains taxed at a lower rate than wages or salaries? In part, the intent is to compensate for the greater risk associated with the stock market or a business, compared to receiving wages or interest on a secure investment. By diminishing the risk, Ottawa encourages people to invest in ways that promote overall growth in the economy.[7] More generally, political choices by government create tax expenditures whereby certain types of income are taxed at lower rates, and in most cases, it is upper-income tax filers who benefit.

**Table 7.5  Impact of Elimination of Capital Gains Tax**

| Family Total Income Group | Families (%) | Distribution of Families (000) | Distribution of Total Gains ($000) | Average Change in Final Income ($) | Share of Total Gain (%) |
|---|---|---|---|---|---|
| below $20,000 | 26 | 3,541 | 9,155 | 3 | 1 |
| $20,000–$30,000 | 15 | 2,100 | 18,899 | 9 | 1 |
| $30,000–$45,000 | 18 | 2,429 | 59,676 | 25 | 4 |
| $45,000–$65,000 | 17 | 2,292 | 113,588 | 50 | 7 |
| $65,000–$75,000 | 6 | 865 | 70,903 | 82 | 4 |
| $75,000–$100,000 | 10 | 1,304 | 160,377 | 123 | 9 |
| $100,000–$150,000 | 6 | 851 | 320,808 | 377 | 19 |
| $150,000+ | 3 | 343 | 945,653 | 2,756 | 56 |
| Total | 100 | 13,725 | 1,699,059 | 124 | 100 |

SOURCE: Statistics Canada, special tabulation done for Child Poverty Action Group and Canadian Childcare Education Foundation (Toronto, 2000).

Eliminating the tax on capital gains—or reducing it substantially, as the Liberals did in both budgets of 2000—results in dramatic increases in after-tax incomes for the wealthiest Canadians. It is also significant that when the federal government describes the gains that accrue to 'typical' families as a result of its budgetary activity, there is rarely, if ever, any mention of the impact of reduced taxation on capital gains.

## Deductions, Exemptions, and Credits

When all sources of eligible income are aggregated, according to the rules for each type of income, the sum is the *total income*. It is against this amount that deductions and exemptions are offset. Both deductions and exemptions are subtracted (deducted) from total income, resulting in a lowered *taxable* income (the amount on which we pay taxes). In impact, deductions and exemptions are generally regressive.

A tax credit, on the other hand, is applied after total taxes payable have been calculated, and its value is usually specified in dollars rather than as a reduction in taxable income. A credit can have an absolute value independent of income level or a value that varies inversely with income. A credit can be easily targeted to recipients with low incomes and will usually reflect progressivity: the lower the income, the higher the benefit.

The difference between exemptions/deductions and credits is fundamental to tax policy. Until the late 1980s, most tax benefits were in the form of regressive deductions and exemptions. As a result, the greatest benefits went to those who needed them the least. Beginning in 1979 with the Refundable Child Tax Credit, tax relief has shifted to credits, though a limited number of deductions remain. The easiest way to understand the difference between the two forms of tax benefit is by illustration, as in Table 7.6.

We begin with two individuals and a progressive tax system. Annie has a higher income and pays taxes at a higher marginal rate of 50 per cent; Sammie has a lower income and pays at a lower rate of 10 per cent. Suppose both individuals increase their incomes by one dollar. Because the tax system is progressive, Annie pays a higher rate,

## Table 7.6 The Regressive Impact of Tax Deductions

|  |  | *Annie* | *Sammie* |
|---|---|---|---|
| Marginal tax rate |  | 50% | 10% |
| Increase in taxable income (+$1) |  |  |  |
|  | Taxes due | $0.50 | $0.10 |
|  | Amount retained | $0.50 | $0.90 |
| Deduction from taxable income (–$1) |  |  |  |
|  | Taxes saved | $0.50 | $0.10 |
|  | Amount of actual loss | $0.50 | $0.90 |

50 per cent, that is, 50 cents in tax and she keeps the other 50 cents. Sammie is in a lower bracket and only pays 10 cents of that additional dollar, keeping the remaining 90 cents for herself.

Now let us consider the exact reverse situation. Both individuals now decrease their taxable income by a dollar. Both will now return to their status before they received the one-dollar increase. Annie will recover—not pay—50 cents in taxes (and will have to cover the other 50 cents of the loss on her own). The 50 cents she recovers comes from all taxpayers. Sammie, for her part, will now recover 10 cents in taxes, for a net loss of 90 cents.

A deduction or an exemption has the same effect as the one-dollar reduction in taxable income in our example. Annie, with the higher income, will save more money in taxes not payable than Sammie, with the lower income, as her taxes are reduced by a smaller amount. This is the symmetry of a progressive tax system: with increases in income, those in higher brackets pay a greater share than those below them, and with reductions in taxable income, they save a greater share. Hence, a given deduction or exemption provides the greatest dollar savings to the wealthiest taxpayers.

While our tax structure is mildly progressive as incomes rise, there is regressivity as incomes decline: the higher the income of the individual, the greater is the tax saving through deductions and exemptions. When a politician advocates increasing deductions in personal income tax, everyone who pays taxes will gain—and this is the point that will be emphasized. But those who have the most will benefit the most—a point rarely stressed in press releases. Individuals with low incomes will be happy to save $10 in taxes, but they will likely be unaware that their wealthier neighbours have just saved $50 on the same tax deduction. The government revenue not taken as a result of this deduction is a tax expenditure, which must be made up either in reduced public services (which may cost Sammie more than $10 to replace privately) or through some other form of taxation. We conclude that if the goal is vertical equity and a tax system based on the ability-to-pay principle, then tax deductions and exemptions are highly counterproductive.

A *tax credit*, on the other hand, is more straightforward and can easily be progressive in its impact. After the basic federal tax has been calculated, credits are subtracted from the total. Some credits are fixed in value: everyone meeting the criterion receives the same dollar benefit. Such credits are progressive with respect to income because they represent a larger share of income for a poor person than for a rich person. Other credits, such as the federal GST credit, vary inversely with income and are even more progressive in impact, as they decline in value beyond an income threshold. An important characteristic of tax credits is that they can be refundable, so individuals can receive the benefit even if they pay no taxes—a refund cheque from the government is generated. A deduction or exemption, by contrast, is usable only against taxable income and consequently is of no value if there is no taxable income.

### Taxes and Gender

Although Canada's tax system is formally gender neutral, certain provisions impact differentially on men and on women.

### Child-Care Expense Deduction (CCED)

We have previously observed that Canada is one of the few industrialized countries without a national child-care plan. Instead there are a number of aids, such as the child-care deduction on the income tax. Like all deductions, its value is greater the higher the income of the taxpayer.

**Table 7.7  Tax Savings, by Income Range, from Child-Care Expense Deduction**

| All Taxable Returns<br><br>Income Range ($) | Number<br>Claiming | Average<br>Allowance<br>per Claim ($) | Average<br>Tax Rate (%) | Estimated<br>Tax Savings ($) |
|---|---|---|---|---|
| 0–20,000 | 215,920 | 1,789 | 5.5 | 104.52 |
| 20–30,000 | 241,310 | 2,497 | 12.5 | 312.18 |
| 30–50,000 | 258,710 | 3,081 | 16.9 | 525.29 |
| 50–100,000 | 111,520 | 4,179 | 22.9 | 957.04 |
| 100,000+ | 9,270 | 4,333 | 33.3 | 1,443.00 |
| Total | 836,740 | 2,740 | 18.2 | 498.64 |

SOURCE: Canada Customs and Revenue Agency, *All and Taxable Returns with Allowed Child Care Expenses.* Available at: <http://www.ccra-adrc.gc.ca/tax/individuals/stats/gb97/pst/t08-all.htm>.

Table 7.7 estimates the value of the child-care deduction to taxpayers at different income levels.[8] Taxpayers with incomes in excess of $50,000 per annum claimed on average more than $4,000 for child-care expenses; the poorest taxpayers claimed $746. At incomes below $10,000, the average deduction lowers taxes by $6.71 per year; at incomes between $50,000 and $100,000, the savings approach $1,000 per year, and above $100,000 the average tax savings is about $1,450. Child-care and equity advocates have long called for this deduction to be converted to a credit so its impact will be more progressive.

The CCED conceptualizes child care as both an aid to participation in the workforce and as a problem of inadequate demand (too little money) that can be addressed through income supplementation. Both notions are narrow and miss the developmental importance of child care to parents and their children. The assumption that increased buying power will lead to new child-care places involves the traditional market view that higher demand creates response on the supply side. Giving parents more money will substantially address the child-care 'problem'. The child-care literature, however, is clear that increased incomes do not, in themselves, ensure an adequate response on the supply side.

The income tax system also treats child-care expenses as a form of work-related expense, like union dues or the costs of equipment. The deduction is available only to two-parent families when both members are in the paid workforce and to working single parents. In the former case, the deduction must be claimed by the parent with the lower income, usually the woman.[9] There are ceilings to the amounts claimed and the expenses must be supported with receipts and incurred to enable the claimant to do paid work. This conceptualization of child care as merely a work-related aid has, of course, been widely criticized: most fundamentally, the goals of child care should be viewed developmentally and construed broadly, rather than merely as a program to enable parents to enter the paid workforce.

In its taxation proposals, the Canadian Alliance advocated a uniform $3,000 deduction per child, available regardless of whether the parent works.[10] The intent, argued in the name of horizontal equity, was to equalize the situations of parents in and out of the paid workforce, i.e., that all families have costs associated with child-rearing. No receipts would be required.

Receipts for child-care expenses introduce a further class bias, to the disadvantage of low-income families. Upper-income taxpayers are more likely to use in-home care (such as nannies) or child-care centres, for which the provision of receipts is straightforward. Low-income parents are more likely to hire a neighbour or friend, for cash payment without a receipt. The lack of a receipt keeps many low-income parents from claiming a tax deduction to which they might be entitled, because of the informal (and inexpensive) care they often use.

### Spousal and Child Support

When spousal support is paid pursuant to a court order or written agreement, the payments are deductible from the income of the payer and taxable as income to the recipient. A court-ordered payment of $1,000, for example, might only cost the payer (who is usually a man) $500 on an after-tax basis if he is in a 50 per cent marginal tax bracket. The $1,000 is income to the spouse, and she is likely to have a lower income and may pay little or no tax.

Because of the deductibility, there is a substantial public subsidy in this arrangement: the man incurs a net cost of $500 but his spouse receives $1,000. The gap between what he pays and what she receives is bridged by taxpayers who provide the $500 to replace the taxes saved by the payer. There is a legitimate question whether the income tax system should be used to subsidize the support payments of upper-income taxpayers.

Moreover, in making award determinations the courts do not always consider the tax implications. If the payer is assessed as capable of paying $1,000 a month, this should reflect the net cost to him and therefore might entail a gross payment of $2,000 to the spouse. Similarly, if the recipient qualifies for $1,000 per month in support, the gross payment should be raised to provide for the tax liability she will incur on the income. The obvious solution would be to make neither payment nor receipt subject to taxes— no deduction and no inclusion in income—as happens with child support payments.

Prior to 1997, child support was deductible to the payer and included in the income of the recipient, producing the difficulties set out above. The courts often did not provide adequately for the tax implications of child support payments.

However, child support does not constitute income to the recipient but is intended to defray the costs associated with raising a child. In other words, the payee is no better off personally as a result. Nor should the public at large share in the payer's private costs through a deduction. Therefore, since 1997, such child support payments, made as a result of a court order, are neither deductible for the payer nor considered as income to the recipient. But the fundamental inequity with respect to spousal support payments remains in place.

### Taxes and Seniors

In our earlier discussion of seniors' benefits we saw that in the post-war years financial aid to seniors was given directly through universal Old Age Security, the Guaranteed Income Supplement, and some provincial supplements. Quite early, however, tax relief was offered to encourage individuals to provide for their own needs in old age.

Some of these benefits are tax deductions, others are now credits. All taxpayers 65 years of age or older can claim an age credit, intended to address horizontal equity and defray the universal costs associated with growing old. Over time, however, the focus shifted, so that above an income threshold benefits are reduced, and only the poor keep the total amount. Today the age credit is no longer an offset to the costs of aging, but an anti-poverty measure directed to seniors with low incomes: for those with income in excess of $26,284, the amount is clawed back at a rate of 15 per cent, reaching zero at an income of $49,824. This payment, and all our current patchwork of payments, might be redundant were there a comprehensive approach towards poverty and low income in Canada (such as a guaranteed income). In such a case we would no longer need assistance targeted to poor people who happen to fall in certain demographic categories (such as being old or disabled).

The first $1,000 of income from private pension plans (excluding CPP/QPP, OAS/GIS) may be claimed as a tax credit valued at $170. Though not regressive, this benefit can obviously be used only by those with private pension income, which excludes many of the poor. Its major rationale seems to be to encourage and reward people who have developed private pension plans. Canada/Quebec Pension Plan contributions can be claimed as a credit rather than a deduction, which enhances progressivity.

On the other hand, contributions to registered pension plans (RPPs, provided as an occupational benefit to employees in certain work settings) and to Registered Retirement Savings Plans (RRSPs) are deductions from taxable income. Both offer generous tax benefits to those who can use them: the maximum annual contribution to an RRSP is $13,500 per year, all of which is deductible from income. In addition, unused contribution eligibility from previous years can be carried forward to be claimed now or in future, and in certain cases one spouse can share the contributions of the other so as to reduce later tax liability. Overall, this means substantial after-tax savings for taxpayers in the higher brackets.

RPPs and RRSPs are regressive in two distinct ways: only those with substantial incomes have the surplus cash to put aside $13,500 a year (or more) in an RRSP. Most low-income earners cannot take advantage of the tax savings offered by contributing to RRSPs or RPPs, not to mention that they receive little or no pension benefits of any sort at their work. Second, because the contributions are treated as deductions from taxable income, the tax savings for a given RPP or RRSP contribution are greater for those in upper-income brackets.

Between 1991 and 1997, close to three-quarters of tax filers aged 25–64 contributed to either RRSPs or RPPs: nearly half (46 per cent) contributed each year during this period, and another 28 per cent saved 'regularly' (in four to six of the seven years). In 1997 these tax filers had their taxes reduced by nearly $4 billion through RRSPs or RPPs. This deduction is now among the largest and most regressive in the personal income tax. As income is the biggest factor in determining whether individuals will have RRSP or RPP savings, about three-quarters of those with incomes above $50,000 saved each year, while only a quarter of those with incomes in the $20,000-$29,000 range did so. Most (83 per cent) of those who did not contribute had incomes of less than $20,000; 60 per cent of non-savers were women though they were half of all tax filers. At all income ranges up to $80,000, women were equally or more likely than men to save through their RRSPs or RPPs, but because of their predominance in the low income ranges, the total savings (and taxes saved) were less for women than for men (Statistics Canada, 2001b).

**Table 7.8  Tax Savings from RRSPs, 1997**

| Income Range ($) | # Claims | Average Deduction per Claim ($) | Average Tax Rate (%) | Tax Savings ($) | Share of Tax Savings (%) |
|---|---|---|---|---|---|
| 0–30,000 | 2,073,340 | 2,019 | 6.6 | 133 | 7.4 |
| 30–50,000 | 2,181,080 | 3,520 | 17.0 | 598 | 35.1 |
| 50–100,000 | 704,540 | 6,252 | 22.7 | 1,419 | 26.9 |
| 100,000+ | 273,760 | 12,946 | 31.6 | 4,091 | 30.5 |

SOURCE: Canada Customs and Revenue Agency, All Returns with RRSP Contributions and/or Pension Adjustment Amount by Total Income Class.
Available at: <http://www.ccra-adrc.gc.ca/tax/individuals/stats/gb97/pst/t11rrsp3.htm>.

Table 7.8 estimates the tax savings (tax expenditures) resulting from RRSP contributions based on 1997 income tax returns.[11] As income goes up, so too does the tax deductible limit on RRSP contributions, so taxpayers with incomes over $100,000 claimed an average RRSP contribution of nearly $13,000. The lowest-income tax filers saved $133 in taxes on average, but those at the upper end of the income distribution saved, on average, more than $4,000. Those with incomes over $100,000 derived 30 per cent of the aggregate tax savings, while those with incomes below $30,000 received but 7 per cent of the total.

Richard Shillington (1999) has shown how income support programs targeted to the poor elderly can wind up subjecting them to marginal tax rates in excess of 100 per cent. For many seniors with low incomes, 'saving in a pension plan or RRSP is a mistake' as income from these sources can result in more than dollar-for-dollar reductions in means-tested programs such as the Guaranteed Income Supplement (GIS) and the associated provincial top-ups.

### Indexation and De-indexation

In 1974, the federal government began to index personal exemptions on the income tax, as well as the threshold values for each tax bracket. With rapid inflation in Canada, the rationale was that Ottawa should not receive 'windfall' (unanticipated) income solely as a result of inflation. If inflation was 10 per cent in a given year and if incomes went up by the same amount to compensate for this, taxpayers would have no greater purchasing power. However, the increase in income would move some tax-payers into higher brackets where they would pay higher rates of taxation. This process, known as *bracket creep*, describes incomes imperceptibly *creeping* into higher tax brackets, not because of anything that taxpayers or governments do. Solely because of the effects of inflation, some taxpayers find themselves in higher tax brackets and government reaps higher revenue. The indexation of benefits was intended to address this problem. As part of the expenditure control programs in the early 1980s, limits were put on indexation, and since 1986 indexing in many programs has been limited to inflation in excess of 3 per cent per year.[12]

The battle against de-indexation in Canada was led by Ken Battle, who coined the phrase 'social policy by stealth' to describe the invisible process by which taxes increased as a result of non-indexation. Battle estimated that partial de-indexation in the decade after 1988 forced an additional one million taxpayers to pay taxes solely because of *bracket creep*. In a report from the Caledon Institute, Battle (1999) described partial de-indexation as 'the hydra-headed monster of Canadian public policy'.

Finally, in the 2000 budget, Finance Minister Martin restored full indexation to the income tax system. Yet, the impact of restoring indexation is equivalent to increasing deductions for taxpayers and is therefore regressive (Lightman and Mitchell, 2000). In any case, as inflation is now very low, the overall cost of restoring full indexation seems minor. By the time indexation was restored the issue had become symbolic, focusing on the budgetary process and government transparency and accountability, more than it was a substantive objection to tax increases.

## Tax Expenditures

Although there are disagreements as to what constitutes a tax expenditure, the Department of Finance (2001) estimates that, in the aggregate, tax expenditures affecting individuals were some $104 billion in 2000; for corporations, the total was about $19 billion. As we saw earlier, tax expenditures dramatically erode the *tax base*, as certain types of income are taxed at lower rates or not taxed at all. If total revenues are to be held constant, higher rates of taxation are required on the remaining income. Alternatively, total government revenue will be reduced.

To reach a given revenue target, government can tax on a larger tax base at a lower rate or on a narrower base at higher rates. Commentators across the political spectrum consistently support widening the tax base, both in the name of equity and because a wider base would permit lower average levels of taxation. While some tax expenditures clearly serve socially desirable purposes, they should be acknowledged parts of a government's public spending agenda; other tax expenditures serve no public interest but merely reflect the influence of certain special interests.

Historically, most calls for reduction in taxation rates have been associated with widening the tax base (eliminating certain tax expenditures). The flat-tax proposal of the Canadian Alliance (which we shall examine later) called for a reduction in tax rates but with no widening of the tax base through the elimination of tax expenditures. Similarly, the massive reductions in tax rates in the federal budget and update of 2000 paid little attention to broadening the tax base. Both approaches, then, presupposed drastic reductions in government revenues and hence in government's fiscal capacity.

Table 7.9 summarizes some major tax expenditures in the Canadian personal and corporate tax systems.[13] The amounts in the table represent actual dollar savings to individual taxpayers—the revenue lost to government. The data refer to the federal system only.

Most of the personal income tax items in Table 7.9 are self-explanatory or are discussed elsewhere. The table also includes some of the more significant tax expenditures on the corporate side, but there are many others as well. Many of these are obscure and technical, but they may involve substantial amounts of tax revenues forgone. Two internal studies from CCRA (Beeby, 2001), reported by Canadian Press, showed that large numbers of Canadian businesses pay little or no tax due to their creative use of tax expenditures. Nearly two-thirds of all businesses in Canada with annual revenues of less than $15 million—up to 716,000 businesses in any given year—paid no federal tax between 1995 and 1998. About 6.5 per cent of giant corporations with revenues greater than $250 million, numbering about 41, also paid no federal tax during this period, and about 40 per cent of their subsidiary companies were also tax-free. A December 2000 study (Beeby, 2001) found that federal taxes paid by Canada's financial institutions (primarily banks) dropped by an 'astounding' $1.6 billion or 44 per cent between 1996 and 1998.

A fuller discussion of tax expenditures is beyond the scope of this study. However, each year the Canadian Centre for Policy Alternatives critically looks at both personal and corporate tax expenditures and makes a number of major recommendations through the Alternate Federal Budget. We look at this below. For now, we leave this topic by noting that not all tax expenditures are undesirable. Some, to be sure, serve broad social purposes, but all are sullied by the invisibility and lack of effective accountability in public spending decision-making.

# TAX REFORM IN CANADA

## Michael Wilson and the Conservatives

In 1987 Finance Minister Michael Wilson introduced major changes in the personal, corporate, and sales tax systems. He was following the US Tax Reform Act of 1986, which created only two personal tax rates (15 per cent and 28 per cent) (though additional higher rates were added under Presidents Bush and Clinton). Prior to the Wilson reforms, there were 10 brackets in the personal income tax; marginal rates rose from 6 per cent on the first $1,318 to 34 per cent on income above $63,347. Wilson reduced these to three brackets: 17 per cent on the first $27,500 of taxable income; 26 per cent between $27,500 and $55,000; and 29 per cent thereafter. Wilson also introduced a

**Table 7.9  Selected Tax Expenditures, 1995 and 2000, Estimated Forgone Revenues**

| | Estimates 1995 $ millions | Projections 2000 $ millions |
|---|---|---|
| *Personal Income Tax* | | |
| Basic personal credit | 17,650 | 20,445 |
| Registered pension plans (net) | 10,445 | 7,305 |
| RRSPs (net)[1] | 7,390 | 8,765 |
| Age credit | 1,270 | 1,285 |
| Pension income credit | 350 | 395 |
| Charitable donations credit | 975 | 1,365 |
| Political contributions credit | 10 | 17 |
| Non-taxation of lottery and gambling winnings | 1,155 | 1,635 |
| Child-care expense deduction (CCED) | 365 | 515 |
| Canada Child Tax Benefit | 5,240 | 6,930 |
| Attendant care expense deduction | S[4] | S |
| Disability tax credit | 270 | 310 |
| Deduction of meals and entertainment expenses | 97 | 75 |
| Employment Insurance[2] | 4,035 | 3,790 |
| CPP/QPP | 2,605 | 4,275 |
| Partial taxation of capital gains[3] | 405 | 1,390 |
| Employee stock options | 74 | 280 |
| Registered Education Savings Plans (RESPs) | n.a. | 135 |
| Small business (various) | 902 | 802 |
| *Corporation Income Tax* | | |
| Low tax rate for small business | 2,465 | 3,405 |
| Low tax rate for manufacturing and processing | 1,515 | 1,970 |
| Investment tax credits | 1,018 | 1,200 |
| Deductibility of charitable donations | 96 | 175 |
| Surtax on the profits of tobacco manufacturers | (–63) | (–70) |

NOTES:

[1] The entries for RPPs and RRSPs are net, meaning that the taxes charged on deregistration of plans have been subtracted from the totals. The tax expenditure, i.e., the deductions, for contributions and non-taxation of income earned while in the plans, amounted to $11.8 billion for 2000 for RRSPs. In other words, nearly $12 billion of public money was spent to aid middle and higher income individuals who had the resources to save in RRSPs.

[2] The entries for both EI and CPP/QPP include both credit for premiums paid by individuals and the non-taxation of premiums paid by employers.

[3] There was a major increase in tax expenditures in 2000 because of lowered rates of taxation of capital gains. There was also an assumption that more people capitalize their gains (sell their stocks) because of the reduced taxation.

[4] 'S' means total amount is small.

SOURCE: Canada, Department of Finance (2001).

5 per cent surtax on higher-income earners as a temporary anti-deficit measure (although it also retained some modest progressivity in a tax system that had been flattened by rate and bracket decreases).

In addition, Wilson introduced measures to enhance equity by eliminating or reducing many exemptions and deductions and by converting others to tax credits, which would be more progressive. Corporate tax rates were lowered and the groundwork was laid for the Goods and Services Tax (GST). The budget also constrained the broader purposes of various social initiatives (such as the age credit and OAS and EI benefits) and converted them into narrow income support measures by requiring repayment of benefits above certain cut-off income levels. Social programs previously aimed at large eligible populations were redefined as programs for low-income individuals; and, as we have observed, programs targeted to the poor tend to become poor programs.

## Paul Martin and the Liberals

The next structural changes in the tax system occurred after the federal budget was balanced in 1998. The 'Y2K budget' (as it was called) promised a 'children's budget', but during budget preparation this broad agenda was abandoned under pressure from the opposition parties in Ottawa, the provincial governments in Toronto and Edmonton, and the right-wing media.

Instead, in the spring of 2000, Finance Minister Martin introduced a tax-cutting budget, effectively abandoning the earlier commitment to children. The middle-income tax bracket would be reduced, in stages, from 26 per cent to 23 per cent, while the thresholds for the upper two tax brackets would be raised to $35,000 (from $29,590) and $70,000 (from $59,180). Capital gains taxation fell from 75 per cent to 66.7 per cent and full indexation was restored. As the deficit had been eliminated, the 5 per cent surtax on upper incomes— justified originally as a temporary anti-deficit measure—would be phased out. The basic corporate tax rate was cut by a quarter, from 28 per cent to 21 per cent.

In the October update, Martin introduced what he described as the biggest package of tax cuts in Canadian history. Tax rates were reduced further: the lowest rate was decreased from 17 per cent to 16 per cent; the middle rate, from 24 per cent to 22 per cent; and the rate for incomes between $60,000 and $100,000 was decreased from 29 per cent to 26 per cent. Incomes above $100,000 received no reduction in the basic rate, though by way of consolation the 5 per cent surtax was ended and the capital gains tax reduced from 66.7 per cent to 50 per cent. There were also modest enhancements to the Canada Child Tax Benefit.

These sweeping across-the-board tax cuts were presented as major gains for the 'typical' Canadian household. However, the Canadian Centre for Policy Alternatives calculated that, despite the Prime Minister's early promise to split the surplus evenly among spending, tax cuts, and debt reduction, only 2 per cent of the total surplus generated between 1997 and 2001 would go to social investments, while the remaining 98 per cent would be targeted to tax cuts and debt reduction. While all taxpayers benefited from the tax cuts, some gained more than others: the lowered tax rates and increased bracket thresholds were equivalent in impact to increased tax deductions and therefore were highly regressive.

## Big Winners and Little Winners

Table 7.10, drawn from the spring 2000 budget, shows the tax savings in dollars for four categories of taxpayer at different income levels.[14] The greatest tax savings accrue to those that have the most already—the higher the income, the greater the savings. The disparity is most pronounced for the single individual: savings for those in the $125,000 range are more than 10 times the savings for those in the lowest tax bracket. At the $125,000 level, the savings approximate $4,000, regardless of family composition.

**Table 7.10  Tax Savings (projected to 2004) for Different Taxpayer Types, from Selected Tax Changes in the Spring 2000 Federal Budget**

| Taxpayer Category | Income Level ($) | | | | | |
|---|---|---|---|---|---|---|
| | 15,000 | 35,000 | 60,000 | 75,000 | 100,000 | 125,000 |
| One-earner family of four | 2,549 | 2,061 | 3,074 | 3,853 | 3,513 | 4,093 |
| Two-earner family of four | 2,134 | 2,192 | 2,185 | 2,573 | 2,619 | 3,984 |
| Single individual | 329 | 899 | 1,888 | 2,785 | 3,345 | 3,925 |
| Single parent with one child | 1,157 | 1,586 | 2,375 | 3,287 | 3,420 | 4,000 |

SOURCE: Government of Canada, 2000 Federal Budget, Table A.7.10–13.

Let us consider a specific tax change—the rate reduction from 26 per cent to 23 per cent for those with incomes between $35,000 and $70,000, defined as those hard-working Canadians in the middle-income range. In the one-earner family of four, there is zero net benefit at incomes up to $35,000; at $40,000, the family is better off by $150 annually; at $60,000, they gain $750; and at $75,000 or higher, more than $1,100. When we consider the elimination of the 5 per cent high-earner surtax there was no benefit for the one-earner family under $75,000 income, though at that point they gain $2 on average; at $100,000, the gain is $364, at $125,000 it is $727.

These two changes account for much of the regressivity in the budget. Improvements to the Canada Child Tax Credit offset them slightly, but were of much less value than the tax table changes (depending, of course, on number of children); moreover, eligibility for the credit was extended up the income scale at the expense of enhanced payments to those below. Furthermore, in all provinces but Newfoundland, New Brunswick, and Manitoba, the supplement is 'clawed back' dollar-for-dollar from families on social assistance. Those with the greatest need, who are on welfare, receive nothing from the improved low-income supplement; instead the funds flow to the provincial treasuries to be used for other vaguely defined but ostensibly child-related purposes.

## Sharing the Pie

What the budget papers did not tell us directly is how the overall gains are shared across income brackets, how many taxpayers are at each level, and how the total surplus is shared. Prior to the budget's release, however, the Child Poverty Action Group and the Child Care Education Foundation commissioned Statistics Canada to run a number of simulations on the same model used by the Department of Finance to assess the equity impact of different tax cut scenarios on families (Lightman and Mitchell, 2000). One of these was close to Martin's eventual choices—and in tax policy, unlike lottery tickets, close is usually good enough.[15] Here is what the CPAG/CCEG study found:

- The 53 per cent of families with incomes below $40,000 received only 8.3 per cent of the total tax savings. Their after-tax incomes went up by less than 1 per cent on average.
- The 22 per cent of families in the middle-income range ($40,000-$65,000) received 23 per cent of the total savings. Average incomes increased by 2.7 per cent.
- The 24 per cent of families with incomes over $65,000 received 69 per cent of the savings. Of these, the 9 per cent of families with incomes over $100,000 gained 37 per cent of the benefits. Incomes increased on average by 4 per cent.
- Families with children under 18 received 41 per cent of the tax cuts; the other 59 per cent went to families and individuals without children. Among the families with children, three-quarters (75 per cent) of the tax savings went to families with incomes over $65,000; 21 per cent went to households in the $40,000-$65,000 (middle-income) range.

*In other words, of the total tax-cut scenario that was modelled, and which follows closely on the decisions subsequently made in the budget, only 8 per cent of the entire package (21 per cent of 41 per cent) goes to middle-income families with children under 18 years of age. Only 10 per cent of all the tax cuts go to families with children and incomes below $65,000.*

And the story gets worse. The impact of the reduction in the capital gains tax from 75 per cent to 67 per cent was not included in the tables attached to the budget papers. But using the Green Book of Taxation Statistics (as it was then called) we estimated this measure would remove approximately $1.1 billion from taxation, resulting in a revenue loss to government of $295 million–$350 million (based on the data for the 1996 tax year). More than half the total benefit (51.5 per cent) would accrue to individuals with incomes over $250,000; more than three-quarters (78 per cent) were received by individuals with incomes over $100,000.

*Clearly, the reduction in capital gains taxation represented a substantial windfall for the richest of the rich. Families with incomes below $60,000 received only 10 per cent of the total package.* We should also bear in mind that these estimates referred only to the spring 2000 budget, and not the autumn update with 'the largest tax cuts in Canadian history'.

## The Alternate Federal Budgets

Since 1995, a collective of social policy advocacy groups and unions, under the leadership of the Canadian Centre for Policy Alternatives, has produced an Alternate Federal Budget (AFB).[16] As the title implies, a different budget is put forward, based on a more progressive value system than that of the Department of Finance. Early on, when Finance Minister Martin was slashing spending to eliminate the deficit, the AFB argued that the deficit problem was not as severe as the government suggested, that a slower pace to eliminate the deficit (over a greater number of years) would achieve the government's goals with much less human cost, and that there were better ways to proceed than the mindless assault on government programs. When the deficit was eliminated, the groups pointed out that this had been accomplished, in large part, by cutting federal transfers to the provinces through the Canada Health and Social Transfer and by the 'theft' of the massive surplus in the Employment Insurance program (which belonged to those who had contributed premiums). The alternate budget has always advocated lowering interest rates to stimulate economic activity and has held that the Bank of Canada is responsible, in part, for low growth because of its policy of keeping rates artificially high. In light of the massive federal budgetary surplus and the even more massive social deficit that had been caused by the years of government cutbacks, the AFB for 2000 proposed a major new spending program to restore some of our frayed social capital.[17]

To pay for this new spending, the AFB set out a detailed financial plan, shown here as Table 7.11. There would be no increase in the overall taxation rates, nor a return to a deficit, but instead 'tax fairness', and the closing of many tax loopholes[18] would spread the tax burden more fairly. Alongside each item in the table is a brief explanation of what the tax change would entail. For example, tobacco taxes would be restored to their levels before the 1996 cuts; and the GST would be removed from books and magazines. A wealth tax would be introduced, expected to generate $3.1 billion in 2000–1. The AFB would eliminate many tax expenditures, both personal and corporate, including an end to the deductibility of expenses for political lobbying and for business meals and entertainment, and a ceiling would be put on the deductibility of corporate salaries. The preferential treatment of certain economic activities would end.

Though the values embedded in the Alternate Federal Budget have not, as yet, made their way into the corridors of power in Ottawa, the document has become an important component of the annual budgetary process in Canada. The AFB suggests there is a different path, a way to enhance growth with equity, to control government spending and distribute the tax burden fairly.

## The Flat Tax

There has always been ideological opposition to progressive taxation, though it was only in 1981 in the *Wall Street Journal* that the flat, or single, tax became popularized. The article generated a flurry of interest in the US, and later in Canada the idea gained credence after the election of the Mulroney government (1984) and as a major element in the platform of Canadian Alliance in the 2000 election. In Alberta, the provincial income tax, as of 2001, is flat, at 11 per cent, the first flat tax in Canada.

The concept of the flat tax is simple. Low-income individuals will be exempt from income tax entirely; everyone else will pay at the same rate. Figure 7.3 compares the flat tax, as proposed by the Canadian Alliance, alongside the income tax system in place as of the 2000 budget. (It does not include a second tier to the flat tax added by the Alliance just prior to the election or the changes in the autumn 2000 budget update). In the existing system, there is a basic exemption (credit) of about $8,000 while the Alliance proposed a basic exemption of $10,000. Hence, those with incomes between $8,000 and $10,000 would be removed from the tax rolls under the Alliance proposal. Above the basic exemption, the existing system rose through the three brackets (17 per cent, 26 per cent, and 29 per cent), while the Alliance alternative remained flat, at 17 per cent.

**Table 7.11  Summary of Alternate Federal Budget, 2000**

*Summary of Potential Revenue from Tax Changes ($ millions)*

| | | 2000–1 | 2001–2 | Explanation |
|---|---|---|---|---|
| **Tax Rates** | | | | |
| Consumption | Tobacco | 495 | | Restores tobacco taxes to pre-tax levels (accounts for 1996 partial restoration) |
| | GST on books | (47) | | Eliminate GST on all books and magazines |
| Wealth tax | | 3,104 | | Estimate revenue at 0.33 per cent of GDP, OECD range of 0.25 to 0.75 per cent |
| Financial institutions | Excess profits tax | | 474 | Tax on financial institution profit in excess of non-finance average rate of return |
| Personal income tax | Implementation of Campaign 2000 child benefit: includes elimination of earned income credit | (5,533) | (2,766) | $4,200 per child benefit, 10 per cent of income offset from $18,000 to $45,000; 5 per cent offset above $45,000 |
| | 50% increase in disability and medical credits | (378) | | 50 per cent increase in amounts of disability and medical credits |
| Restore full indexing of all tax parameters | | (225) | (900) | Full indexing costs $900 million per year: first year 2002 based on CPI increase in 2001 |
| **Tax Expenditures** | | | | |
| Personal | Employee stock options | 140 | | Eliminate exemption of 25 per cent of income from stock options |
| | Eliminate dividend tax credit | 201 | 604 | US-style integration of PIT and replace with CIT |
| | Capital gains farm exemption | 148 | | Eliminate $500,000 capital gains exemption for farm assets: allow rollover of gains within family |
| | Capital gains small business exemption | 465 | | Eliminate $500,000 capital gains exemption for small business assets |

| | | | | |
|---|---|---|---|---|
| | Full taxation of capital gains, personal | Eliminate 25 per cent exclusion of capital gains: replace with indexing of capital gains base from 2000 on | 89 | |
| | Full taxation of capital gains, corporate | Eliminate 25 per cent exclusion of capital gains: replace with indexing of capital gains base from 2000 on | 175 | |
| | End capital gains freezes, including family trusts | Various changes to personal income tax and corporate income tax to eliminate capital gains loopholes | | 300 |
| | Meals and entertainment | Eliminate deductibility of remaining 50 per cent of meal and entertainment expenses | | 105 |
| | Eliminate pension income credit | Partial offset for GIS increase | | |
| GST | Brokerage fees, etc. | Application of GST to financial fees other than bank service charges | | 190 |
| Corporate | Implementation of Mintz report | Corporate tax base-broadening measures as recommended in Mintz report: estimate is for Mintz measures not specified elsewhere, updated to 2000–1 | 2,384 | |
| | Surtax on foreign interest earnings | Part of capital markets regulatory package | | |
| | Meals and entertainment | Eliminate deductibility of remaining 50 per cent of meal and entertainment expenses | | 220 |
| | Lobbying | Eliminate deduction of lobbying expenses | | 50 |
| | High salaries | Limit corporate tax deductibility of salaries to $300,000 | | 50 |
| Administration | Collect taxes owed | Collect 10 per cent annually of $6.6 billion owed as estimated by Auditor General in 1994 | | 660 |
| *Total* | | | 59 | (55) |

SOURCE: CCPA (2000b).

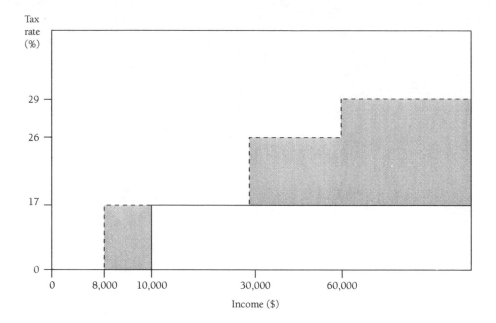

**Figure 7.3  Comparing a Flat Tax to the Status Quo**

Clearly, no taxpayer with an income above $10,000 would be worse off under the Alliance proposal, and above $30,000 (the threshold of the second bracket) everyone would be much better off with the flat tax. The savings that would accrue to taxpayers under the flat tax are represented by the shaded areas in Figure 7.3: the higher the income, the larger are the savings.

Shillington (2000) has calculated the impact of the flat tax. While 31 per cent of taxpayers have incomes below $20,000, they would receive 7.5 per cent of the total tax cut. Half of all taxpayers (54 per cent) have incomes below $30,000; they would receive 13.1 per cent of the total cut.

Table 7.12 shows that for incomes up to $30,000, the flat tax would be progressive: at $20,000, the tax cut constitutes some 2.4 per cent of total income; at $30,000, the cut decreases to 1.6 per cent of income. Above incomes of $30,000, the flat tax becomes steeply regressive. The tax cut at $100,000 income is valued at just under $8,000, or 8.0 per cent of income, and at $250,000 the tax cut is worth some $26,000, more than 10 per cent of income. Taxpayers with incomes over $100,000 comprise only 2.4 per cent of taxpayers, yet they will receive 29 per cent of the total tax cut. Kesselman (2000) looked at taxpayers with even higher incomes: at $600,000 income a taxpayer will receive a cut of 22 per cent ($75,000) in taxes; at $1 million in income the cut will be $129,000 or 23 per cent of taxes payable. Middle-income taxpayers would face a dramatic increase in their share of the tax burden, high-income taxpayers would pay dramatically less, and those at the very bottom would be better off since they would pay no income tax. This leaves the lower middle class to carry the load.

**Table 7.12  Impacts of the Flat Tax Proposal of the Canadian Alliance on Federal Income Taxes**

| Individual Income ($) | Dollar Value ($) | Value of the Tax | |
|---|---|---|---|
| | | As % of Previous Tax | As % of Income |
| 20,000 | 488 | 22 | 2.4 |
| 30,000 | 488 | 13 | 1.6 |
| 40,000 | 1,388 | 21 | 3.5 |
| 60,000 | 3,188 | 27 | 5.3 |
| 100,000 | 7,988 | 34 | 8.0 |
| 200,000 | 19,988 | 38 | 10.0 |
| 250,000 | 25,988 | 39 | 10.4 |

NOTE: This ignores the increased RRSP room and the reduced tax on capital gains.

SOURCE: Shillington (2000).

Although there has been a great deal of noise around the idea of a flat tax, the concept has never become mainstream. In the run-up to the 2000 election, the Alliance became concerned about the political saleability of a proposal that promised so much to the very rich. It added a second flat tier, a higher marginal rate of 25 per cent on incomes over $100,000. This was, however, to be only a transitional measure on the way to a single flat tax at the rate of 17 per cent.

The flat tax is traditionally linked to a general lowering of the total tax bill, so its proponents can claim, with accuracy, that everyone will pay less tax. However, total tax revenue is quite different from distributional impact, and it is the latter that the flat tax addresses. Higher or lower total taxes can be generated in a progressive or regressive manner, and the equity issue of the flat tax is unacceptable to many. The flat tax is promoted because it will be simple and readily comprehensible. Some US tax reforms would permit the ordinary taxpayer to a file a personal return on a postcard of only four lines: the first line would report total gross income from all sources; the second line would record specific deductions for marital status and/or children; the third would calculate taxable income as the difference between the first two lines; and the fourth line would calculate tax payable as a percentage of taxable income. Neat, simple, straightforward.

The problem, as we have seen, is that a simple tax is not necessarily a fair tax. Simplicity per se is not a primary concern for the income tax system, particularly given cheap and user-friendly software and electronic filing. Canada's tax system remains complex, and for those with substantial incomes the services of a competent accountant may be the best investment they can make. However, when tax liability is a function of one's access to expert help, rather than of one's income, clearly there is a problem with the total tax structure. That, sadly, is the case with taxes in Canada today. The complexity of our current system lies in the definition of taxable income—what counts and at what rate, and what deductions, exemptions, and credits the taxpayer can claim. The Alliance proposal left these matters basically unchanged. Neil Brooks (2000) points out that a shift to the flat tax would eliminate only two lines on the personal tax return.

It is more generally argued that lower tax rates (however attained) lead to increased growth and economic activity. Higher incomes for the rich, so the argument goes, 'trickle down' to the others, and people will respond to the enhanced work incentives. These arguments, however, relate to the general issue of lowering taxes[19] and are not relevant to a flat tax per se. There are many ways to reduce tax levels without incurring the regressivity of the flat tax.

Others argue that the flat tax would reduce tax evasion and avoidance, and would increase compliance: if taxes are lower, people more readily will pay their fair share. There is, self-evidently, no necessary correlation between levels of taxation and people's propensity to avoid or evade. More important, however, to argue that the tax system should be altered to encourage compliance is, in effect, to acquiesce to blackmail. If there is a problem of tax compliance, the obvious solution is to take direct measures, such as increased audits, rather than to change the rules to accommodate the rule-breakers.

The final issue in the flat-tax debate is the most fundamental. At its base, the case for and against the flat tax is ideological, and this debate turns on one's attitude towards progressive taxation and the social redistribution it implies. The case *for* the flat tax becomes the case *against* progressive taxation, redistribution, and the welfare state. As Neil Brooks (2000) has said, '*tax policy is quintessentially a matter of class politics, and progressive rates are, at least symbolically, a minor victory for the masses.*'

## NOTES

1. These are often called *public goods* and will be examined more fully in Chapter 8.
2. With respect to CPP, there is a basic annual exemption of $3,500 for which there are no contributions. CPP premiums are payable only on earnings above $3,500, which means the maximum annual contributory earnings are $34,100 ($37,600–$3,500).
3. Low-income individuals are likely to spend their entire incomes, so they effectively incur a 7 per cent per cent GST rate on the total amount (except for non-taxable items); higher-income individuals face a 7 per cent per cent tax only on that portion of their incomes which they spend—there is no GST on income not spent—and so the GST on total income is less than 7 per cent. Hence, the tax is regressive in impact.
4. Alberta has no provincial sales tax. As of 1998, four provinces (Newfoundland, Quebec, Ontario, and Manitoba) imposed payroll taxes either for general purposes or for specific uses such as health and/or education or worker training
5. Though corporations are legal entities, in reality they comprise a large number of shareholders who may receive profits or dividends; when this income is distributed to shareholders it is then taxed as personal income. Profits and dividends can be taxed in the hands of the corporation before disbursement, or as personal income when received by shareholders, but to tax the same money twice would constitute double taxation.
6. Unless otherwise indicated, all figures, tax brackets, etc. refer to taxable income as opposed to gross income.
7. In the United States, legislators observed that many capital gains resulted from speculation in the stock market rather than from providing long-term capital to promote economic growth. As a result, the US tax code now distinguishes between long-term capital gains (taxed at a lower rate) and short-term capital gains (taxed at a higher level, when the investment/stock is held for less than a specified period of time).

8. The information is drawn from the taxation statistics (Canada Customs and Revenue Agency, 2001). Although the marginal tax rates are conceptually required in these calculations, for convenience we have used the average rates. Each claim, which represents a deduction from taxable income, is multiplied by the average tax rate for the income level to give us an approximation of the probable tax savings. Since average rates are generally lower than marginal rates (as we saw above), the figures produced in Table 7.7 represent probable underestimates of the tax savings.

9. Of the 837,000 claims filed in 1997, three-quarters (75 per cent) were filed by women.

10. Under the Alliance flat-tax proposals, this provision would be worth $510 in federal tax savings ($3,000 × 17 per cent flat tax).

11. The figures include not only RRSP contributions but also pension adjustments (PA) that provide for individuals to make additional contributions to private pension plans. They have a similar effect to RRSPs in that they offer tax-sheltered savings.

12. See Chapter 6.

13. Tax expenditures are calculated separately for each entry, on the assumption that all else would remain constant if a specific expenditure was eliminated; in reality, a change in one item may induce behaviour changes elsewhere. Items coded 'S' mean the amount is small, while 'n.a.' indicates the information is not available. There are also tax expenditures associated with the GST/HST that we do not report here: items that are zero-rated (taxed at a zero rate), such as basic groceries, drugs, and medical devices (estimated tax expenditure of $3.9 billion for 2000), as well as exempt items such as residential rents. Tax expenditures can also be conceptualized as negative amounts. The surtax on the profits of tobacco manufacturers in Table 7.9 is a tax expenditure of -$70 million in 2000 (equivalent to a tax increase of this amount). Increasing this surtax would increase the negative tax expenditure.

14. The tax savings are based on the proposed tax reduction measures to 2004, including the tax table changes, elimination of the high-income-earner surtax, and enhancement of the Canada Child Tax Benefit. They do *not* include the reductions in capital gains taxes or the additional substantial tax reductions that followed in the autumn budget.

15. That is, all tax policy is based on projections and estimations about future behaviours and revenue flows—and a close approximation will inevitably give a good idea of the overall impact of any particular measure. We specified a basic exemption of $7,900, while Martin took $8,000; we both used a middle tax rate of 23 per cent, down from 26 per cent, and we both eliminated the 5 per cent high-income-earner surtax. However, the threshold for our middle tax bracket was $39,590, while Martin opted for $35,000; the upper bracket begins at $69,000 in our model and $70,000 in Martin's budget. All in all, this was a rather close approximation.

16. In Ontario and Nova Scotia, the latter beginning in 2001, alternative provincial budgets are also prepared.

17. This included $2 billion for national child care and early education services; $3 billion for health (including community care and a national drug plan); $5.5 billion for an improved child tax credit; plus new spending on post-secondary education, housing, improved eligibility for Employment Insurance benefits, and infrastructure and a new $1 billion Atmospheric Fund.

18. The concept of a tax *loophole* is interesting. The term has no formal or precise meaning, but usually refers to creative measures employed to reduce tax liabilities. To use a loophole is not usually illegal, though there are definite connotations of impropriety, in that the tax reduction measure *ought not* to be available. One person's loophole is another's legitimate use of the Income Tax Act.

19. This issue was discussed earlier in the context of work incentives and a guaranteed annual income.

## SUGGESTED READING

Brooks, Neil. 2000. *Flattening the Claims of the Flat-taxers*. Toronto: Osgoode Hall Law School, York University.

Kesselman, Jonathan. 2000. 'Flat Taxes, Dual Taxes, Smart Taxes: Making the Best Choices', *Policy Matters* (Institute for Research on Public Policy) 1, 7 (Nov.): 104.

These are powerful critiques of the flat-tax concept as put forward by neo-liberal interest groups and politicians and implemented in the provincial income tax of Alberta.

Canadian Centre for Policy Alternatives. (annual). *The Alternate Federal Budget*. Ottawa: CCPA.

Prepared annually by a coalition of community and labour groups working with the CCPA, the Alternate Federal Budget presents a critique of Ottawa's taxation plan and suggests a more creative alternative path.

Ontario. Fair Tax Commission. 1993. *Fair Taxation in a Changing World: Report of the Ontario Fair Tax Commission*. Toronto: University of Toronto Press in co-operation with the Ontario Fair Tax Commission.

This major inquiry, undertaken by the NDP government in Ontario, fundamentally re-examined the structure and goals of taxation in Ontario. The report is highly readable. The Commission also prepared reports on taxation in areas such as the environment, property tax, the GST/PST, wealth, and women.

Rosen, Harvey S. 1999. *Public Finance in Canada*. Toronto: McGraw-Hill Ryerson

Hyman, David N., and John C. Strick. 2001. *Public Finance in Canada: A Contemporary Application of Theory to Policy*. Toronto: Harcourt.

These are current mainstream textbooks used in public finance courses, and much of the content is very technical. However, the discussions about the theories and principles of taxation provide a useful background for understanding the tax system.

# CHAPTER EIGHT

# Fees, Charges, and Premiums

## INTRODUCTION

Fees and charges[1] are a means of financing social services as an alternate or complement to taxation. While taxes may reflect the ability-to-pay principle, fees and charges epitomize the benefit principle: if one uses a service, one pays for it *and it is normatively correct that one should pay for it*; if one does not use the service, one does not pay *and one should not pay*. Fees reflect the economic market: prices serve to allocate resources and consumers decide their own needs and priorities. In general, individuals would wish to use most public social services more than the state will provide (that is, demand exceeds supply). Therefore, access must be rationed, either by administrative decision or through the pricing mechanism.

As we saw in Chapters 5 and 6, collective decisions can determine who gets what benefit and in what forms. The alternate approach is to rely on the market: people make their own decisions about how to spend their money. If consumers pay directly for services, they should thereby demand choice and quality that meet their standards and criteria. The market reflects the preferences and priorities of consumers in a way that no alternate system of allocation can do. If they are dissatisfied with what is offered by a public provider, consumers can go elsewhere, into the private market, for example. This competition for the consumers' dollars should lead service providers to be innovative and creative, and increasingly efficient. That the poor cannot participate fully in this market activity is seen as a problem of income deficiency, which should be addressed through income redistribution. In short, fees and charges embody all the alleged strengths of the market model—and, as we shall see, they carry all the weaknesses and limitations as well.

Fees come in many forms. They can be paid at the point of use, such as an admission charge to a recreation centre; in advance, through insurance premiums reflecting an

actuarial link between the charge and the likelihood of a claim (as in Workers'
Compensation); or as simple compulsory payments to be recovered later (as in Canada
Pension Plan contributions). Fees can cover the full cost of providing a service, in which
case they may directly compete with the for-profit sector; or some of the cost, topped up
by a subsidy. They can also be a token charge (such as $1 per day for child care). Fees
can be imposed at a flat rate, with or without exemptions, or they can be variable (such
as the sliding scales used in many counselling agencies). Exemptions or reduced fees can
be targeted to individuals (usually with low incomes), to groups (such as seniors or
children), or to geographic areas (such as reduced or no entrance fees at swimming
pools or skating rinks in low-income neighbourhoods). Offering no exemptions or
reductions implies that other income support measures (such as welfare or food vouchers) will ensure access to needed services. Some fees are retained by the service providers
(such as the extra-billing fees of physicians); other fees are recovered by the state, as funder. Fees are imposed for both economic and ideological reasons.

   In this chapter, we shall examine some of the complex issues associated with fee-
charging in the social services. We begin with a brief discussion of the microeconomics
of fees, introducing the concept of elasticity of demand. To a large extent the impact of
fees depends on the sensitivity of consumer demand to price changes: Can consumers
go elsewhere if prices rise? And what are the implications if they do? We then look at a
number of contexts in which fees should not be imposed and examine in some detail the
five main reasons to charge fees. We consider also the actual fee-setting process, including the role of subsidies and discretion, and examine the other main type of fees—those
paid in advance of use, usually in the form of premiums, such as Employment Insurance,
Canada/Quebec Pension Plan, and Workers' Compensation.

## THE SIMPLE MICROECONOMICS OF FEES

A fee may be expected to raise the cost of a service: when price increases, people will buy
less of it. If the price of apples (or counselling) goes up, people will normally buy fewer
apples (or counselling sessions). However, in some situations this fundamental economic relationship does not apply. For example, people may actually buy more of something—a Porsche or advanced cosmetic surgery—if the price goes up, reflecting its
enhanced status value. In other cases, if the price change is minor or the service is
'essential' (such as bypass surgery), consumers may absorb additional fees, perhaps with
little fuss. Some services delivered by social workers are compulsory, often under court
order, and consumers therefore are not free to alter their usage patterns.

   For those familiar with traditional microeconomic analysis, Figure 8.1 portrays the
general impact of a new fee.[2] A fee raises the supply curve from line S1 to line S2. Assuming
an unchanged demand curve, the equilibrium point shifts from A to B. As the arrows
along the axes indicate, the price will increase and the quantity demanded will decrease—
how much depends on the slope (elasticity) of the demand curve. Distributional questions,
which consider whose use will decline (rich or poor, young or old, male or female, etc.),
are not addressed in this microeconomic analysis, which simply postulates that demand
will decline, given a price increase and a downward-sloping demand curve.

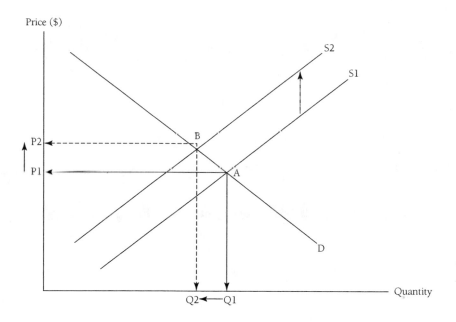

**Figure 8.1  The Simple Microeconomics of Fees**

## Elasticity of Demand

Fees are used, in general, both to raise revenues and to decrease usage; which goal is attained depends crucially on the sensitivity of consumer demand (i.e., how large the change is in the amount demanded) for a given change in price. This is known as the *elasticity of demand*: the greater the sensitivity to changes in price, the greater the change in usage; the smaller this elasticity, the less will be the change in use.

Figure 8.2 illustrates the effect on the quantity demanded and on total revenues of the same fee increase under conditions of low and high elasticity. If the elasticity is low (shown on the left), there is little change in demand in response to modest changes in price and a new fee will primarily increase revenue; that is, if quantity demanded remains relatively unaffected, the new, higher price increases total revenues (higher price times virtually the same quantity). If the elasticity is greater (shown on the right), there will be a greater decline in demand after the same fee is introduced and total revenues will drop (higher price times a substantially reduced quantity). In the first case, the main effect of new fees will be to raise revenues; in the latter case, total revenues and total demand (or usage) of the service both decrease.

The sensitivity of consumers to new fees—the elasticity of demand—depends, in general, on:

- *the price of the service*, before and after the fee is imposed. A fee for a formerly free service may decrease demand more than an increase in an existing fee. A slight fee increase should have less impact than a large fee increase.

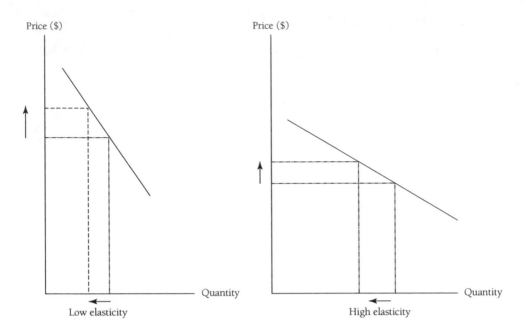

**Figure 8.2 High and Low Elasticity of Demand**

- *the prices of competing services*. Fees at a non-profit counselling agency must always be set with reference to those charged in private practice. Non-profit providers of home care may offer better-quality service than some for-profit providers (who tend to employ less qualified staff), but the relative prices may be important for many families. Non-profit child-care centres must set their rates in the context of both fees at for-profit commercial centres and rates for in-home care, both licensed and informal. In each of these examples, consumers may not choose among the alternatives solely on the basis of price, but for some individuals there will be considerable sensitivity to even small changes in price.
- *income levels*. The higher the income of the consumers, the less they will be affected by new fees; the lower the income, the greater the effect. Both absolute income levels and the relation of fees to income are relevant. For example, a 25 cent fee may have a great impact on few consumers, but a fee of several hundred dollars will have a major impact on many more.
- *tastes* and *preferences*. The priorities and wishes of consumers may lead them to use a particular type of service, which they will continue to use even if the charges increase substantially and there is a major effect on family income; others may have a weaker commitment to specific modes of care and therefore will be more price-conscious in their choices. For example, some users of child care or home care will always choose non-profit delivery for empirical or ideological reasons; thus, they will display little or no sensitivity to price changes in these sectors.

# THE REASONS NOT TO IMPOSE FEES

Before we examine the reasons why fees are utilized in the social services, let us consider why and where they are *not* appropriate. Undoubtedly, the most compelling argument against fee-charging is that the market does not work according to the traditional micro-economic analysis. Many of these issues have been presented earlier in this book, and build on the view that the social services are not like other commodities and services purchased in the private market.

## Public Goods

There is considerable consensus that charges cannot or should not be imposed in certain areas. Among these are *public goods*—services such as street lighting or national defence—for which specific beneficiaries cannot be identified. Public goods are marked by two general characteristics:

- *Non-excludability*. Individuals cannot be denied access to the benefits of the service or commodity. We all use street lights and public health, for example. Individual recipients, and the extent of their benefit, cannot be empirically determined, and it is not possible in practice to exclude some from coverage. Hence, the use of a pricing mechanism to determine usage is not viable.
- *Non-competition*. One individual's use of a service does not diminish another's ability to use it. In other words, quantities of the service are not finite, so they need not be rationed. An individual's benefit from the presence of street lights or the work of the public health department in inspecting restaurants does not lessen another's ability to derive a similar benefit.

In general, public goods must be paid for through taxes—public/collective payment for public/collective benefit. There would be no incentive for people to pay voluntarily for a service to which they cannot be denied access (known as the *free-rider problem*). The only resolution to this dilemma is that, as everyone benefits, all should contribute to the costs, whether through taxes or compulsory fees.

The boundaries of a 'public good' have been changing. Police services, for example, were once considered to be largely a public good, but the proliferation of private security agencies and the growing use of private-duty police officers paid on an hourly basis have converted policing into a mixed public and private good.

A variant on public goods would be *merit goods*, the use of which serves a broad public interest and for which fees would be counterproductive. For example, if child welfare services are to protect children at immediate risk, no public interest is served by limiting such services. Providing access to and information about birth control to teenagers may be socially desirable, but such a service would be severely impeded by fees. Primary education and basic literacy yield broad public benefits, while the major gain of an MBA is private. Fees should not ration access to the former, but at the post-secondary level there is a stronger case for their use. As with public goods, there are legitimate disagreements as to what constitute true merit goods, but widespread acceptance of their importance.

# THE REASONS TO IMPOSE FEES

When benefits and beneficiaries can be identified (unlike the case with public goods), fees become technically possible. When their introduction will not create inefficiencies (such as collection costs being higher than revenues), they may become feasible. When income distribution is not a goal (or is addressed in other ways), the case for the benefit principle becomes stronger. When there is belief in the efficiency and effectiveness of the market and in its capacity to reflect consumer preferences, fees can underpin this market.

Many years ago, Roy Parker (1976) developed five categories of reasons for which fees are introduced. Three of these—to raise revenues, to reduce demand, and to alter priorities—directly reflect the assumption that the market works, according to the economic analysis presented above. The fourth category—symbolism—may be the most compelling in today's political and economic climate, and the final category—to reduce abuse—warrants further discussion.

The reasons for particular fees are not always clear, and are often complex. Hospitals, for example, may attempt to impose 'hotel charges', ostensibly to cover the costs of food, etc. that would have been incurred were the patient not in the hospital. Is the primary goal to raise revenues, to deter abuse of the hospital system by ensuring that people are not better off financially, or to contribute symbolically to one's own care? The answer both determines and depends on the levels of fees and the system of exemptions and reductions. Let us examine Parker's five categories in more detail.

1. *To raise revenues.* In a context of severe government cutbacks, fees are usually introduced to generate revenue. As we have seen above, the amount of new revenue produced will depend in part on the elasticity of consumer demand. In some cases, substantial new revenues will result. Typically, however, revenue projections tend to be overestimated: small fees may not generate significant revenue and administrative structures may be needed to collect the fees and to determine eligibility for exemptions or reduced fees, resulting in lower net revenues than anticipated. Higher fees may significantly cut usage, as people are unwilling or unable to pay. Moreover, the higher the fee is, the greater the case for widespread exemptions and reductions, resulting in lower net revenues.

When government is under pressure to cut costs and reduce taxes, fees are attractive as a way of generating revenue, but raising revenue can be a short-term gain that entails substantial long-term costs and loss of revenue. For example, in 2001 the City of Toronto was faced with a severe budgetary crisis due to provincial downloading of responsibilities and the costs of amalgamating five municipalities into one. In response, user fees were introduced or extended. Council elected to sell home composters at $15 each, rather than give them away free, at an estimated total cost of $500,000. Each composter, if used regularly, diverts 100–200 kilograms of organic waste annually from garbage landfill sites. Free composters, which would have reduced home pickup and disposal costs, would have paid for themselves in 2–3 years. But since fees were charged, fewer composters were put into use, leading to higher program costs after the second or third year.

Fees at recreation centres had differed across the municipality before amalgamation and the new city sought standardization by extending and introducing fees. No fees were charged at 25 specified community centres in low-income neighbourhoods, and low-income individuals could apply to participate in one free program per session. Seniors were given discounts in most cases. Once the new fee policy was in place, there was a high demand for free programs (many directed to children), which resulted in long waiting lists. The take-up rate in paid programs was considerably below the expected 70 per cent: it was only 55 per cent in the fall of 1999, dropping to 43 per cent in the winter of 2000. The fees, described as modest by the politicians, were nevertheless greater than many families could or would afford. There was a revenue shortfall of $4.0 million in 1999, projected to rise to $5.1 million for 2000 (Toronto, 2000). As a way to generate revenues, community centre fees were clearly a failure. Undaunted, the city proceeded to introduce further new fees for certain children's programs in 2001.

Fees that deter people from seeking preventive services (such as child welfare prevention or inoculation against disease) inevitably result in higher remedial costs. In social and health services, prevention is inevitably cheaper and more effective than cure, yet fees that generate revenue in the short term can deter prevention and result in long-term costs that are inevitably higher.

Attempts to raise revenue are not usually targeted at the poor, who may well be exempt from the charges. Such arrangements are often presented in a 'Robin Hood tone' (Stoddart et al., 1993): more revenue, all of it drawn from those who can afford to pay, will be introduced into the system, and greater resources are seen as highly desirable. However, those who pay directly may tend to demand priority or preferential treatment, leading to two tiers of service. Some family counselling agencies employ explicit queue-jumping: those able and willing to pay full fees receive immediate service, while those eligible for reduced payment must wait. If the goal of charging the rich and exempting the poor is to redistribute costs according to ability to pay, personal income tax is a much more effective tool to this end.

2. *To reduce demand.* The other direct outcome of the traditional microeconomic analysis is that new or higher fees should make usage decline. The extent of the decline depends on the elasticity of consumer demand—the extent to which consumers are willing or able to forgo the service or to secure it elsewhere under more favourable conditions. As we have seen, the extent of reduced demand depends on the presence and terms of exemptions and reduced fees, as well as on the context in which fees are imposed.

At times, fees can be imposed to deter usage. During World War II women were needed in the workforce, and as a result public child care was expanded dramatically. At war's end, social norms dictated that women should return to their homes, while freeing up their jobs for returning veterans. In Britain (Judge and Matthews, 1980) many public child-care centres were shut down; others, particularly after the election of a Conservative government in 1952, began to charge full market fees. Those parents who could not afford the fees were means-tested. Because full fees became essentially the same in the public and for-profit sectors, those who could do so left the public sector—where the poor children were largely accommodated—and moved to the for-profit world of middle-class consumers. The high fees were explicitly intended to deter middle-class working women from using subsidized public child care, and to a large extent this goal was achieved.

The important question is not *whether* fees will reduce use, as in most cases there will be some measurable effect. Far more important are questions about the *extent* of the reduction and its distributional impact: *Whose use is reduced when fees are introduced? Is the impact greater on the poor than on the rich?*

Let us look at the experience with user fees in medicare. Between 1968 and 1971, Saskatchewan was governed by the Liberal Party, which introduced user fees of $1.50 per office visit to a physician. Before 1968, and after 1971, under the NDP, there were no such fees. The Saskatchewan experience is widely cited, because it is rare to observe a large-scale social experiment with a classic research design in which one could assess the change in use over time specifically attributable to fees. Beck and Horne (1971) found that the annual per capita use of physicians' services was reduced 6-7 per cent overall; however, among low-income people the decrease climbed to 18 per cent when fees were charged. Clearly, user fees had an identifiable and significant effect, particularly among low-income users. As Stoddart et al. (1993) note:

> For people at the same income level, user charges redistribute the costs of health care away from the 'healthy' and onto the 'sick'. . . . For people . . . who use the same amount of care, the same user charge places a greater burden relative to income on those with lower incomes.

Wealthy people pay more taxes and tend to be healthier than the poor:

> The healthy rich thus stand to gain the most from . . . user charges and the sick poor stand to lose the most. Viewed in this way, well-intentioned advocates of user charges seem more like the Sheriff of Nottingham than Robin Hood. (Ibid.)

In some cases there may be no deterrent effect, as people are unable or unwilling to reduce their usage. A charge of $2.50 per in-patient hospital day was imposed between 1968 and 1971 by the Saskatchewan Liberals, but this had no effect on hospital use. Consumers had little choice about using hospitals and few options but to pay the fee. Thus, while physicians' services were seen to be relatively elastic (meaning that people did without or deferred use in the face of user fees), hospital care proved to be relatively inelastic in that user fees did not significantly reduce use.

In some situations the deterrent may be limited. When a new fee is introduced there may be an initial 'shock' effect, but as people get accustomed to or cannot do without the service, old patterns of use may re-emerge. Some people may use a service for a while and then stop in the face of new fees. For example, eligibility for home care without charge may be limited to a certain number of hours per week, regardless of the extent of need; beyond the limit, full market fees are charged. Consumers may use the 'free' hours only and then stop, with the result that desirable or even essential care will not be received. There may be no overt intent to deter usage, but this outcome inevitably ensues, as was the case with the Toronto recreation centre fees after 1999.

3. *To shift priorities.* Fees can be introduced to alter priorities by changing the relative prices of competing services or goods. On the assumption that other aspects of services A and B remain unchanged, the addition of a fee to service A, but not to B,

should cause some users of A to shift to B—provided that A and B can serve as substitutes to some extent. The extent of the shift depends, as we have seen, on the size of the fee, the elasticity of demand (in this case for both A and B), the ease of substitution between A and B, consumer preferences, etc.

Full-cost fees in public child care after 1945 were imposed to alter usage patterns of the non-poor by causing them to move to the for-profit sector. Some counselling agencies charge high fees to clients without subsidy to divert them from the limited resources of the agency to private practitioners. In Toronto, there was an 80 per cent increase in registrations at five non-fee-charging recreation centres while registrations dropped where fees were introduced. More generally, the levels of charges in the not-for-profit and for-profit sectors influence patterns of use, particularly when consumers are uninformed about or indifferent to relative quality.

At times it is not the levels of charges in the two sectors but changes in the relationship of those charges that may induce movement. In home care or child care, for example, fees are often lower in the for-profit sectors because of lower labour costs (less qualified and/or fewer and/or more poorly paid non-unionized staff). Any increased fees in the non-profit sector may cause some shift to the for-profit sector among those with the weakest commitment to the non-profit principle and those with the lowest incomes. Conversely, the not-for-profits serve as an effective check on excessive fee increases by commercial providers.

In Ontario, until recently, home care was provided by both the Ministry of Community and Social Services (MCSS) and the Ministry of Health. Though there were theoretical differences in the services provided, in practice there was much overlap. Services provided through the Ministry of Health were insured services under medicare, delivered without user fee, with the physician as gatekeeper. In care provided through MCSS there was a long tradition of fee-charging on sliding scales. In areas such as home care/homemakers' services, consumers saw a broadly similar service offered in two ministries, one with fees and the other without. Needless to say, the behavioural patterns favoured the Ministry of Health (notwithstanding its tendency to medicalize what were often social problems), with MCSS a distinct second choice.

Charges may be imposed for services delivered in chronic and long-term care facilities while the same services carry no direct fee in an acute-care hospital. Thus, consumers attempt to remain in hospital, becoming 'bed blockers'. Back in the 1950s most medical services, including physicians' care and drugs, were provided without user fee in hospitals while the cost of medical care in the community was paid for by the consumer. Consequently, people entered hospitals, which were expensive to run, in preference to medical services in the community, which were cheaper to deliver but entailed direct costs to the consumer. Though the fees were not intended to alter usage patterns, they had that effect, thereby raising overall costs.

When municipalities impose user fees per bag for household garbage removal, the intent, in part, is to increase awareness of the amount of waste produced and of the potential for recycling and reusing. To some extent, 'tossing it out' can be replaced by recycling. However, if the fee is small, people may just pay it and keep producing garbage, particularly after an initial transitional awareness; alternatively, they may circumvent the fee by leaving garbage in public places, thereby creating potential health hazards and increasing costs.

4. *Checking abuse or overuse*. Conceptually, checking abuse is similar to reducing demand: each carries an expectation that new or higher fees will reduce usage. Abuse introduces the notion of a 'proper' amount of use, which is exceeded by some consumers, notwithstanding ongoing professional 'gatekeepers'. This 'overuse' is to be redressed through the imposition of fees.

Let us consider the components of the 'abuse' argument a little more formally, using Figure 8.3 as an aid. Fee-charging as an antidote to abuse assumes:

- There is an objective correct, proper, or optimal amount of use for a specific service.
- It is possible to identify and measure this point of optimal use (shown as amount Q2 in Figure 8.3).
- Current use (shown as Q1) exceeds optimal use, creating a condition of excess use, overuse, or abuse, all of which reflect unnecessary use.
- Excess use results from consumer actions and decisions.
- Consumers have the capacity and power to reduce use.
- Consumers would respond to user fees by reducing their use (shown by the arrowed lines in Figure 8.3).

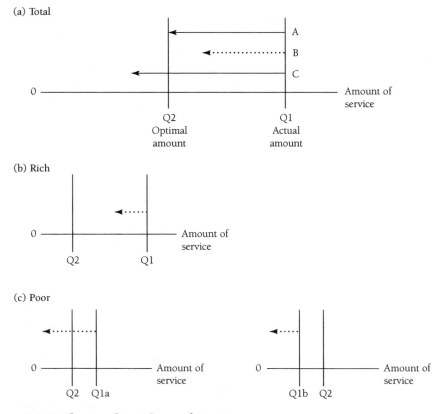

**Figure 8.3  Understanding Abuse of Services**

- Fees would reduce use precisely to the desired level (line A, in Figure 8.3a), and would not reduce use somewhat but not enough to reach the optimal amount (line B), nor would they reduce use below the optimal amount (line C).
- The reduction in use would not be spread evenly or randomly across all users, but would be targeted only at the 'abusers'.

This analysis assumes that the correct amount of use for any service or commodity can be determined empirically and that 'need' can be accurately and objectively measured for large groups of people. The important questions embedded in this view are left unanswered. *How* is the optimal amount of use to be measured and *who* is to measure it? Will this optimal amount be the same for everybody (as seems to be implied) or will it vary, and if so, what criteria will the assessment use?

It may be difficult, or perhaps impossible, to identify the optimal or ideal usage of a service. High use does not necessarily constitute overuse. How many visits to a doctor are too many? What if physicians encourage repeat visits, either to conduct thorough follow-up or because they are paid on a fee-for-service basis? If a parent takes an ill child to a doctor and the problem turns out to be trivial, is this an abuse of the system? Clearly, the parent lacks expert knowledge and the problem may require professional intervention. Is the goal of public policy to encourage parents to seek professional help early (because prevention is usually cheaper than cure) or to ration access and deter use? In a child welfare agency or counselling service, how would one even begin to determine the optimal amount of service?

It is our contention that there is no objective means to measure optimal usage of any social or health service. Usage patterns and needs are socially constructed, based on past use, user socialization, availability of resources, and use patterns of other services. For example, comparative data have shown differential rates for certain medical procedures, such as hysterectomies, in different communities. Do higher rates indicate medical necessity, or do they reflect treatment preferences of the physicians and/or their compensation structure? There may be abuse on the part of providers, but such findings would still not enable us to determine what the optimal rate of hysterectomies should be.

The capacity and willingness of consumers to reduce specific usage patterns are limited. Fee-charging should reduce overall usage, but it will not in situations where demand is non-responsive to changes in price or when the service provider (such as physician or parole officer) determines the required amount of service use.

Finally, no set of fees can guarantee that use is reduced, precisely or even approximately, to some predefined level. Our understanding of elasticity is limited, and attempts to predict the effect of fees—as with the Toronto recreation charges—can be highly inaccurate. In addition, overuse by some consumers may be symptomatic of 'hypochondria', a psychological need for the service, which will ensure continued use regardless of the cost considerations. Those who make substantial use of the service without real need are *least likely* to decrease their use, despite any financial penalties in the form of higher fees.

There is an alternate scenario. Let us assume there is an optimal amount of use as shown by Q2 in the Figures 8.3b and 8.3c, and we shall examine the distributional impact of fee-charging on the rich and on the poor. In Figure 8.3b, the rich may reduce usage by a modest amount, as shown by the dotted arrow moving to the left. As the rich tend to be relatively price insensitive, the reduction in use may be non-existent[3] or modest (as shown in the figure), but usage may remain in excess of the optimal amount.

For the poor, the introduction of fees may reduce usage levels substantially (high elasticity), as in Figure 8.3c. Current usage among the poor (Q1a) may be greater than desired; however, as the poor tend to have less access to services, current usage may equally well be less than the optimal amount (as shown in the bottom diagram where current use, Q1b, is to the left of , i.e., is less than, the desired amount Q2). In either case, a significant reduction in use should result from the fees, which may situate the recipients below—or further below—the optimal use levels.

In short, the rich are likely to be less affected by fees and may well continue to overuse or abuse a service. The poor, on the other hand, show greater sensitivity to price increases and are likely to decrease their usage, placing them (further) below the optimal levels.

Some provincial governments impose a 'parental contribution' fee on parents for their children in residential treatment facilities. A comparable charge in Britain has been identified as 'a hangover from the mid-19th century belief that [fees] would prevent abuse of the reformatory and industrial school system' (Judge, 1978). In other words, fees were introduced to ensure that parents did not abuse the reformatory system in order to abdicate their parental responsibilities. Perhaps the same ideas are in force in Canada (Lipovenko, 1984). Small fees may be attached to prescription drugs for those people on social assistance to deter unnecessary use (just as user fees were intended to eliminate unneeded visits to physicians). Low-income households may not purchase needed medications: use levels will be reduced, but this tells us nothing about patterns of abuse.

5. *Symbolism.* This rather vague term may be the most interesting and the most important reason for understanding fee-charging. It moves from traditional economics to ideology and values. It suggests that people should pay fees, that it is ethically correct that people contribute to the costs of services they receive, and that fees represent paying one's way and not accepting charity.

The importance of symbols cannot be overstated. Looking again to history, debates in the British Parliament after World War II focused on how to pay for seniors' residential accommodation. It was important that charges be levied on municipally-run housing 'so that any old persons who wish to go may go there in exactly the same way as many well-to-do people have been accustomed to go into residential hotels' (Glennerster, 1985; see also Judge and Matthews, 1980). Free accommodation would resonate of the pre-war charitable system and the Poor Laws, while paying one's way carried with it dignity and self-respect. The solution involved a bureaucratic transfer: money was paid by one department (as income support) to another department (for the provision of housing), but through the resident, so that control and independence were seen to be honoured.

The absence of user fees ('extra-billing') in medicare has long been the central symbol of our national commitment to universal health care. Indeed, more recently this commitment to medicare has emerged as the pre-eminent symbol of a unique Canadian identity. The case for fee-charging, in part to increase physicians' incomes, was clothed in the symbolism of paying one's own way for one's own health-care needs.

Symbolism can also reflect professional views on the role of fees as a treatment issue. The charging of fees and discussions concerning this may become important treatment tools. As Koren and Joyce (1953) argued a half-century ago, 'What the patient does with fees can be tangible evidence of his attitude, resistances, and acting out, and that exploration of behaviour can be utilized . . . in terms meaningful to the patient.' One strong advocate of fees (Seldon, 1977) argues as follows:

> In some circumstances a free or low-charge service may produce higher quality from dedicated social workers, nurses, etc. . . . But their feelings should come after those of their clients, who may prefer to pay as customers rather than receive as beneficiaries or supplicants.

Some claim that if people pay even a token amount for something such as counselling they will value it more highly, as a market purchase rather than a handout. The fact of payment, not the amount, converts a charitable transfer to a market exchange, and we are socialized to value things we purchase and, therefore, own. Payment should therefore lead to a greater sense of engagement and commitment by clients.

An opposite argument, which nonetheless accepts the psychological importance of the market exchange, claims that what we pay for is ours, to do with as we wish. Thus, if we are paying directly and choose to waste the time of the clinician, that is our prerogative. The therapist is paid in an exchange relationship, and like the purchase of a pair of shoes, nothing more is owed to the provider beyond the agreed-upon fees. A third view argues that the client's engagement depends on a variety of issues, of which the form and amount of payment are minor.

The impact of fees and their effectiveness in enhancing clinical outcomes have not been widely tested, yet the belief in the value of fees and of clients paying their own way remains strong within the clinical community. This belief leads to one of the deeper divisions within the social welfare community in Canada. Those most concerned with ensuring access to services tend to view fees as a deterrent; those most focused on treatment issues tend to favour fees as a valuable clinical tool. The two paths, regrettably, do not appear to meet.

## SETTING FEE LEVELS

Decisions about how to structure fees and/or exemptions are driven by both ideological and economic considerations. The purpose of fees and exemptions is to generate income while ensuring that access is not impeded by a financial barrier; thus, the decision may be to favour low-income users and at the same time retain the service as formally open to all.

Some fees, such as a user charge on prescriptions for seniors, can be set by government and applied uniformly. Other fees, set by agencies, can respond more flexibly to individual needs. Revenue targets for fees may be set: ideology may require that everyone make some token payment, regardless of income level, while economic factors may dictate some recognition of demand elasticity. What share of total agency revenue is to be provided by fees may be mandated by a funder. Some agencies, particularly feminist agencies, do not use a traditional fee schedule; instead, they ask clients to indicate the amount they feel comfortable contributing, though everyone may be expected to pay something, largely for symbolic reasons.

Typically, revenue targets are missed, as the fee reductions and exemptions in the fee structure reduce overall revenues. As most agency fee schedules are intended to be applied in a flexible manner, more concessions than intended may occur, particularly as clients are increasingly drawn from low-income populations. Counselling fee revenues at Toronto's Jewish Family and Child Services, for example, dropped from $104,000 in 1990 to $76,000 in 1995 (Landa and Kay, 1996).

Fees charged to clients are normally determined in three steps:

- Gross income of the individual or family is calculated.
- Expenses and other allowable deductions are subtracted from gross income to yield net income.
- A sliding scale is applied to net income.

Each of these steps entails choices. First, how is gross family income calculated? What counts and what does not? Are all assets (car, home, family mementoes) included? How does the agency deal with child and spousal support? Second, how are allowable expenses and deductions defined? Child and spousal support are problematic, as is personal debt, such as car loans and credit card debt.[4] Mortgage payments and high rental costs for housing also must be factored in. Individuals' spending patterns may exceed their capacity to pay the bills: by allowing such expenses is the agency acquiescing in 'inappropriate' or 'unwise' spending, which may be part of the reason why help is being sought? Other questions related to this complicated issue include the following. Is written proof of income and expenses required, or is affirmation sufficient? Do agency workers on occasion conspire with clients to reduce income and/or increase expenses so as to reduce fees? *Should* workers enumerate expenses to ensure clients are claiming all expenses to which they may be entitled? Does the entire process simply work to the benefit of middle-class clients who tend to have expenses to claim?

Some agencies use only gross income to determine whether service users qualify for a reduction or waiver of fees—expenses are not considered in calculating fees. Others use family size (not the number of persons seeking assistance) as a simple proxy for overall household costs: fees are then determined using a grid, with family income on one axis and family size on the other. Table 8.1 illustrates this type of arrangement, as used by the Family Services Association of Toronto.

Finally, the taper of the fee schedule—the sliding scale of fees—illustrates the most subjective aspects of the process. At what income are full fees payable? Do full fees pay the total cost of service? Is there an implicit subsidy for all users? Do full fees exceed the cost of providing the service, to provide a subsidy to other users? How quickly do fees decline as income drops? At an income half the full-fee threshold, would fees also be 50 per cent? Are fees to be waived outright in some cases, or will there always be some minimum fee charged? If the latter, what is the minimum fee to be and at what income level does it move higher? Is the fee payable on each visit, or is there an overall ceiling for those with the lowest incomes?

**Table 8.1  A Typical Fee Schedule in a Counselling Agency**

| INCOME LEVEL | Family Size | | | | | | | | | Interview Rate | Group Rate |
|---|---|---|---|---|---|---|---|---|---|---|---|
| | 1 | 2 | 3 | 4 | 5 | 6 | 7 | 8 | | 5.00 | 5.00 |
| | | | | | | | | | Minimum Fee | 5.00 | 5.00 |
| 1 | 15,500 | 21,000 | 26,500 | 30,000 | 33,500 | 36,500 | 39,000 | 41,500 | | 10.00 | 5.00 |
| 2 | 18,000 | 24,500 | 30,000 | 34,500 | 38,000 | 41,500 | 44,500 | 47,500 | | 15.00 | 10.00 |
| 3 | 20,500 | 28,000 | 33,500 | 39,000 | 42,500 | 46,500 | 50,000 | 53,500 | | 20.00 | 13.00 |
| 4 | 23,000 | 31,500 | 37,500 | 43,500 | 47,000 | 51,500 | 55,500 | 59,500 | | 25.00 | 15.00 |
| 5 | 25,500 | 35,000 | 41,500 | 48,000 | 52,000 | 56,500 | 61,000 | 65,500 | | 30.00 | 20.00 |
| 6 | 28,500 | 39,000 | 45,500 | 52,500 | 57,000 | 61,500 | 66,500 | 71,500 | | 35.00 | 23.00 |
| 7 | 31,500 | 43,000 | 49,500 | 57,500 | 62,000 | 67,000 | 72,500 | 78,000 | | 40.00 | 25.00 |
| 8 | 34,500 | 47,000 | 54,000 | 62,500 | 67,000 | 72,500 | 78,500 | 84,500 | | 45.00 | 28.00 |
| 9 | 37,500 | 51,000 | 58,500 | 67,500 | 72,500 | 78,000 | 84,500 | 91,000 | | 50.00 | 30.00 |
| 10 | 40,500 | 55,000 | 63,000 | 72,500 | 78,000 | 83,500 | 90,500 | 97,500 | | 55.00 | 33.00 |
| 11 | 43,500 | 59,000 | 67,500 | 77,500 | 83,500 | 89,000 | 96,500 | 104,000 | | 60.00 | 35.00 |
| 12 | 46,500 | 63,000 | 72,500 | 82,500 | 89,000 | 94,500 | 102,500 | 111,000 | | 65.00 | 40.00 |
| 13 | 50,000 | 67,500 | 77,500 | 88,000 | 94,500 | 100,500 | 108,500 | 118,000 | | 70.00 | 43.00 |
| 14 | 53,500 | 72,000 | 82,500 | 93,500 | 100,500 | 106,500 | 115,000 | 125,000 | | 75.00 | 45.00 |
| 15 | 57,000 | 76,500 | 87,500 | 99,000 | 106,500 | 112,500 | 121,500 | 132,000 | | 80.00 | 45.00 |
| 16 | 60,500 | 81,000 | 93,000 | 104,500 | 112,500 | 118,500 | 128,000 | 139,000 | | 85.00 | 45.00 |
| 17 | 64,000 | 85,500 | 98,500 | 110,000 | 118,500 | 124,500 | 134,500 | 146,000 | | 90.00 | 45.00 |

NOTE: Fee increases when family income reaches the next income level.

SOURCE: Family Service Association of Toronto (2001).

## Subsidies

A subsidy is the complement to a fee: together they comprise the full cost of delivering a service. Implicit in a policy concerning fee-charging is a policy on subsidies. A subsidy can be provided to all users, i.e., the fees charged do not cover the full cost of providing the service. For example, public transit fares are usually set so that total revenue covers a specified portion—always less than 100 per cent—of the actual costs of operating the system. This required share varies from place to place, depending on political decisions about the extent of government subsidy to the system. Subsidies for public transit are justified, in part, on the basis of *externalities*, which in this case refers to the benefit to everyone if there are fewer people driving their cars, reduced congestion on the roads, lower levels of pollution, and less need for maintenance and construction of new roads and highways.

Subsidies can be provided to individuals or groups, similar to how fees are determined. Concessionary bus fares for seniors or students, for example, subsidize all members of these groups and are justified on the basis of need or perhaps merit (even though wealthy students and seniors ride the bus). Reduced fares for buses on weekends are designed to attract riders when demand is otherwise low: though the per ride subsidy may be high, the cost to carry additional passengers on existing buses is zero, so the reduced fares add to overall system revenues.[5]

Subsidies can also be used as a gatekeeping mechanism. To receive a reduced rate for child care in an approved setting, for example, the parent may have to obtain one of a limited number of subsidies. The subsidy is equivalent to a voucher, permitting access and also ensuring that the funder will cover the costs above what the user pays. The parent's fee is usually based on an income or needs test. Most users of child care must pay some token fee at least, symbolic of paying one's way.

Eligibility for child-care subsidy varies from province to province and may also involve the municipalities. In New Brunswick, for example, the number of subsidies is capped, and applicants qualify for a subsidy only after meeting a needs test (involving both income and expenses). Other criteria, such as geographic location and at-risk status of the child, are also considered. In Ontario, eligibility is also determined by a needs test and other criteria; however, subsidy levels vary as well with the cost of the service and with the municipality, which in practice sets maximum subsidy rates. Unlike New Brunswick there is no cap in Ontario on the number of subsidized places, but the same effect is achieved through a ceiling on the province's overall subsidy budget. In both provinces the number of applicants exceeds the number of subsidized places available, and a long queue results. A subsidy can be used in any approved setting, and all parents must pay a user fee, which varies with individual circumstances (Mason, 2001).

In Quebec, there are no caps on the number of places, and the government provides $5 a day universal child care to all parents who wish to use it (Quebec, 1999). In all cases, the subsidy is substantial, but fees do not vary with the incomes or needs of parents. In British Columbia, a scheme introduced prior to the 2001 election placed no cap on the number of subsidies, and applicants were required to undergo only an income test, which is less intrusive than a needs test. No criteria other than income were applied to the subsidy determination process in BC. The scheme was scrapped after the election of the Campbell government.

Child-care subsidies are usually considered to be part of the social assistance system, and can be capricious and even incomprehensible. A recent survey of the child-care needs of single mothers in three Canadian cities (Mason, 2001) found that some single mothers in the paid workforce turned down increases in salary because this would have entailed a loss of subsidy that was greater than the increase in salary. They would have been worse off overall had they accepted the increased salary: the marginal tax rate on extra earned income would have been greater than 100 per cent. (In Chapter 7 we noted that the highest marginal tax rates in Canada on wages and salaries, federal and provincial combined, are now less than 50 per cent in all provinces.) No one attempts to defend tax rates in excess of 100 per cent on the poor; they are simply a consequence of other Byzantine decisions that affect the lives of those on social assistance.

## The Use of Discretion

In some settings, line workers determine fees. They may use their administrative discretion to ensure the client gets the lowest fee possible, or they may wish to use discussion about fees as a part of the therapeutic treatment process. In other cases, the workers prefer not to deal with fee-charging and the responsibility is delegated to a specific intake worker (or receptionist).

Reduced fees are increasingly applied to groups rather to individual need: seniors or students may qualify for lower fees, irrespective of individual circumstances. Lower fees may be agency policy in low-income neighbourhoods, even though clients with higher incomes may be unanticipated beneficiaries. Agencies have come under increasing financial pressure in the last number of years, and consequently worker discretion in setting fees has been reduced. This may result in the applicable fee being determined impersonally from a chart such as that shown in Table 8.1.

The use of discretion by workers in setting fees represents an exercise of power. This discretion/power can be used for the client's benefit (which may or may not entail lower fees), but power can also be abused. There is always a risk that the value system of the worker will be imposed on the client, in the form of speeches about wise and prudent spending and not wasting money on lottery tickets or cigarettes. Such discretion, which may be used for good or ill, knowingly or unconsciously, may be seen by clients as an unwanted and inappropriate intrusion in their lives. Clear and transparent rules without place for discretion—which become akin to rights for recipients—may be preferred by both clients and workers.

## Virtual Fees

*Virtual* or *phantom* health-care fees are used in Alberta to make people aware of the true costs of services without incurring the deterrent effects of actual fees. In its simplest form, consumers receive annual statements detailing the medicare-insured services they have used, along with the full cost of each item. The intent is to raise awareness of the cost of services and to encourage the public only to use services when necessary. No actual bills are generated, nor are any payments made. As a consciousness-raising measure that touches on issues of abuse and symbolism without directly confronting them, the idea may have some limited value.

In some proposed versions of this approach, consumers would sign for each medicare service received as they do for a credit card purchase, thereby providing the basis of the enumerated regular statements. Still, no direct payments would be made for services. This approach is more empowering to consumers in that it gives them a degree of market sovereignty: if dissatisfied with the services, they have the option not to sign the credit card bill and the provider is not automatically paid. This might also modestly restrain excess billing practices by physicians as consumers must sign for services delivered (though it would also undoubtedly anger providers who have become used to automatic reimbursement). As a way to give consumers some market power and control, without incurring the deterrent effects of high fees, models such as these may have much to commend them.

A variant carries the market concept farther. Each year, everyone would be given a medicare credit of an agreed-upon amount, perhaps adjusted for age or other factors of vulnerability. Every medicare service used would be charged against this notional credit, so the balance would decline over time. If the full amount is used up, nothing happens: there is no barrier to further use and no charges are levied. However, if a credit remains at year-end, the individual receives that amount in cash. The aim of this approach is to discourage unnecessary use of health services without penalizing the poor or sick. People would be rewarded for not going to the doctor's office, but there would be no financial deterrents for high users of the system.

In practice, this model may well impose precisely the barriers it purports to avoid. Low-income households may avoid using medicare services because they prefer the cash at year's end, and thus they will forgo preventive health-care services. The 'hypochondriacs' are unlikely to reduce their use in favour of a cash payment at year's end, and the model restrains not even the most blatant overusers. Upper-income households won't pay too much attention to the annual credit and will largely act as they acted before. In fact, the only plus to this approach is its capacity to inform consumers of what health care actually costs. Whether heightened awareness translates into a reduction of unnecessary use or, indeed, whether unnecessary use even occurs to the extent it is a problem remains an open question.

## PREMIUMS AND SOCIAL INSURANCE

While most user fees entail payment at the point of use, premiums are paid in advance. Often, like private insurance, premiums are contingent payments, and benefits are received only under specified conditions. The practice, however, varies widely.

The three major programs we shall examine are work-related: (Un)employment Insurance (UI/EI), Canada and Quebec Pension Plan (CPP/QPP), and Workers' Compensation (WC). Each of these is funded to some degree by compulsory premiums paid by employees and/or employers. Because the payments are compulsory they are comparable to taxes, but unlike taxes the monies are earmarked, in principle at least, for the specific programs and not for general governmental purposes. However, there can be no binding commitment for future benefits with a government program, as no Parliament can bind a future Parliament and benefit details can be changed by simple legislation.

In each case—UI/EI, CPP/QPP, and WC—there is a historical tension between the principles of *private insurance* and those of *social insurance*.

*Private insurance.* Premiums are based on the actuarial likelihood of a claim, along with the amount, duration, and other conditions of benefit receipt. Given an adequate sample size, and a history of claims incidence, future usage patterns (and hence required premiums) should be predictable with considerable accuracy. Ideally, these calculations should be based on individual risk characteristics of employers and individuals. Some jobs (such as construction workers) will have a higher risk of making a claim through Workers' Compensation than others (such as university professors) and so should carry higher premiums; some individuals may be more likely to make claims (such as older workers in jobs requiring physical strength). To the extent it is empirically possible to link the likelihood of a claim to identifiable and measurable individual characteristics, premiums should be set accordingly. In practice, the identification and calculation of individual risk factors may not be possible—or desirable—and instead risk is based on group characteristics. This is known as the *pooling of risk*.

These principles of private insurance are reference points against which social insurance program design can be assessed. They stress individual (rather than collective) responsibility, in which individual benefits should be linked systematically with prior contribution. (This approach resembles the residual welfare model first introduced in Chapter 2.)

*Social insurance.* As there is an explicit element of income transfer or income redistribution in social insurance, there is no need (or desire) for individual benefits to be linked systematically to prior contributions; general government revenues are a recognized source of funding for that portion of benefit costs not covered by premiums. Thus there is a substantial role for government as an agent of collective redistribution. Benefits for individuals or groups can be set independent of claims history, and eligibility can be based on normative considerations in addition to, or in place of, actuarial risk factors. Because CPP and EI have always based their premiums on earnings, and earnings are independent of the probability of making a claim, the setting of premiums clearly falls into the realm of social insurance. Risks are pooled on a total group basis (virtually Canada's total working population) rather than on individual risk.

## Employment Insurance

Of the major premium-based programs in Canada, EI comes closest to the pure case of social insurance; at times income redistribution has been central to decisions about program design. In fact, Unemployment Insurance (UI, as it was originally called) has never used sound actuarial principles. The high point of UI as a social insurance program occurred in 1971, when regional and maternity benefits were added and eligibility conditions eased. UI effectively became central to Canada's income support system, filling gaps not addressed for political reasons through the Canada Assistance Plan (CAP).

These new benefits could have been insurable, and with appropriate adjustments to the premium structure all could have been covered using traditional actuarial principles. For example, the new regional benefit was based on regional unemployment rates and applied particularly in the Atlantic provinces. The likelihood of increased claims could have been offset by higher premiums, reduced benefits, or shorter eligibility for benefits in that region. But, in fact, the opposite occurred. Eligibility in the fishery, at one point, involved as little as 10 weeks' insured work; thereafter, benefits could be claimed for the following 42 weeks. This was known as the '10-42' rule. UI had become a non-demeaning substitute for social assistance in the Atlantic provinces. It was not stigmatizing to receive UI (because one had contributed to the fund), while being 'on the dole' carried stigma (because one was a recipient without having been a prior contributor).

UI also became a major component of Ottawa's program of regional income redistribution. Caseloads and, hence, costs were shifted from the provinces, which paid 50 per cent of social assistance costs through the Canada Assistance Plan, to the federal government, which paid 100 per cent of UI deficits. Income was transferred from those in stable, permanent employment across Canada (who made fewer claims on UI) to those with short-term work histories, primarily in the Atlantic region. UI was no longer really insurance, which entails risk, because in many cases the probability of filing a claim approached 100 per cent. Instead, it more closely approximated forced, highly subsidized savings: contributors paid premiums and then withdrew their contributions supplemented by payments from the federal government, which were far in excess of those contributions.

Benefits received through EI must be declared as part of taxable income. But since 1979, individuals with annual incomes in excess of $48,250 who receive EI are required to pay back part or all of their benefits at a high rate of 30 per cent: for every dollar of annual income over this threshold, 30 cents of any EI benefits received must be paid back through the personal income tax. This repayment condition fundamentally negates any adherence to private insurance principles, under which eligibility for benefits is independent of income and based solely on meeting program conditions (such as unsuccessfully seeking work). The clawback introduced *need* (as measured by annual income) into benefit determination, and by so doing it effectively converted UI to an income support program for eligible low-income workers who lost their jobs.

This change in focus for EI, similar to the changes in seniors' benefits, reflects government policy to gut social programs of broader social purposes and to replace these with narrow low-income eligibility criteria for potential claimants. Social programs, in effect, have become anti-poverty programs.

The cutbacks in UI/EI through the 1990s were severe: the proportion of the unemployed who had contributed and received benefits dropped from 87 per cent in 1989 to about 38 per cent by 2000. In 1996 Unemployment Insurance was drastically revised and renamed Employment Insurance (EI). Benefit levels were reduced and eligibility tightened further. Qualifying periods were changed from a given number of weeks to a number of hours corresponding to a full workweek (called the 'intensity rule'). Women, many of whom are part-time workers, were particularly affected by this change. As they now lacked the necessary hours to qualify, the female rate of successful claims after the 1996 changes dropped by 20 per cent, compared to a 16 per cent decline for men. The intensity rule was abandoned after the 2000 election.[6]

People who voluntarily quit work were denied benefits entirely. This introduced 'fault' into the system, by denying benefits to persons who voluntarily quit their jobs. The problem lay in determining the precise meaning of *voluntary*. Women who quit their jobs as a result of sexual harassment were at particular risk. Though the regulations explicitly protect the benefits of persons who quit because of sexual harassment, there are recurring concerns that this provision works to the systematic disadvantage of working women. At the very least, the women may lose their initial entitlement to benefits, as the onus is on the employer to specify the reason why a person left a job: the individual may then have to appeal in order to have the decision reversed.

No significant link was established between premiums and the incidence of claims. Instead, the 1990s were marked by major reductions in eligibility and benefit levels in order to build up massive surpluses in the fund. Premiums were not reduced, yet pay-outs were cut, and the basic structure of premiums based on earned income rather than risk remained unaltered.

UI had become a major program of income redistribution: funds were transferred from workers and employers, who paid the premiums, to all Canadians, who benefited when the surpluses were applied to the federal deficit. Employers and employees called for stronger private insurance principles, which would have entailed lower premiums (favoured by employers) and/or enhanced benefits (preferred by employees). In response, premiums were lowered and improved benefits (promised prior to the 2000 election to improve Liberal Party prospects in Atlantic Canada) were introduced. Nevertheless, the surplus remains massive (in excess of $6 billion for 2000), an important element in Ottawa's fiscal plan for balanced budgets, and premiums continue to bear no relation to claims incidence.

For the year 2002, employee premiums were $2.20 per $100 of insured earnings, that is, a tax of 2.2 per cent on earnings, down by five cents from 2001 and significantly below the peak premiums of 3.07 per cent in 1994. The maximum insurable earnings of $39,000 were slightly above the average industrial wage for Canada. The maximum annual employee contribution was thus $858 for 2002. Employers contribute 1.4 times the employees' share, producing a maximum annual contribution of $1,201.20.

Benefits today are complex. Eligibility is primarily based on the regional unemployment rate and the number of weeks worked. Other program parameters include full-time and part-time work, short-term and seasonal employment, the treatment of other income, such as severance pay or pensions, the denial of benefits for the first two weeks of unemployment, and the cause of the unemployment.

The maximum weeks for benefit receipt, a function of regional unemployment levels, varied in 2000 from 14 to 45 weeks. Benefits also depend on the proportion of prior earnings replaced by EI (known as the *earnings replacement rate*). This rate used to be 66.6 per cent of previous earnings (and up to 75 per cent in some cases), but is now set at 55 per cent (with some exceptions). The maximum payment in 2000 was $413 per week, subject to clawback at a rate of 30 per cent, for those with annual incomes over $48,750.

As of the 2000 changes, maternity benefits (which can now be claimed by either spouse) are no longer subject to clawback. While this change might seem progressive in that it no longer penalizes time off work for parenting, it has been severely criticized as an inadequate response to the shortage of quality child-care places in Canada. The child-care problem should be addressed by expanding supply of places, not by making it financially more attractive for a parent (usually the woman) to stay out of the workforce. Moreover, the benefit is targeted (and often gender-biased), as it is only available to parents who contributed sufficient EI premiums.

# Canada/Quebec Pension Plan

The Canada and Quebec Pension Plans stand at the opposite end of the spectrum from Employment Insurance. Though individual premiums are not actuarially linked to benefits, the plans are required to be financially solvent without government subsidy. Therefore, premiums have been adjusted upward to provide for expected future increases in benefits.

Both CPP and QPP began in 1966, but they had fundamentally different funding bases. The Quebec Plan followed the traditional private insurance model of full funding: for the first several years, the program only collected premiums. Only when the asset base was sufficient to cover anticipated future claims did the program begin to pay out retirement benefits. The asset base is large, providing the Quebec Pension Board with substantial resources to invest, particularly in activities that would be of particular benefit to Quebec. The investments are guided by sound principles and have generated substantial returns over the years. The Canada Pension Plan, by contrast, has been financed on a pay-as-you-go basis: today's premiums pay today's benefits, and there is no need for a large reserve fund beyond what is required for short-term claims. This enabled the Plan to begin paying out claims soon after its inception, without the need to build a large asset base.

CPP distributes retirement pensions, disability pensions (including those for children of disabled contributors), payments to surviving spouses, and a one-time death benefit. Unlike most other social programs, CPP benefits are fully indexed according to the Consumer Price Index. The retirement pension is more a matter of forced savings than of traditional insurance, as the probability of receiving benefits upon retirement is 100 per cent; however, the size of the benefit depends on the contributions of each individual. The benefits related to disability and death reflect conventional private insurance principles, in that the benefit is linked to prior contributions, and premiums reflect the likelihood of claims. However, the risks are pooled over the entire population. Therefore, individual premiums do not reflect the likelihood of individual claims, but total premiums do reflect all claims likely to be filed.

CPP is funded with equal contributions from employer and employee; self-employed individuals must pay both shares. From 1966 to 1986, each party paid 1.8 per cent of eligible earnings: the first $3,500 of earnings is exempt, but contributions are paid on the next $35,600 to a ceiling of $39,100 (for 2002), known as yearly maximum pensionable earnings. In the early years there were more contributors than beneficiaries, in part because of the relatively young working population, and substantial surpluses were accumulated.

CPP was required to keep cash on hand equivalent to four times the payments expected to be made in the following year. Any remaining surplus was loaned to the provinces as non-cashable 20-year bonds. This arrangement gave the provinces a stable outlet for their bonds at rates lower than in the open market. For the contributors to CPP, however, the interest on their invested money was less than what they could have earned with other investments.

In the late 1980s the number of eligible claimants increased rapidly and annual payouts approached premium income. Increased life expectancy and the approaching retirement of the 'baby boomer' generation were about to necessitate a great increase in premiums for the working-age population to cover dramatically increased payouts. In response, the provinces and federal government agreed to increase premium rates, which rose to 1.9 per cent (for each of employer and employee) in 1987 and hit 2.8 per cent in 1996. By 1993, CPP had to draw on its surplus for the first time, and by 1996 the payout reached $17 billion while premiums totalled only $12 billion.

By 1997, the chief actuary of the CPP reported that the CPP fund would be depleted by 2015 and that contributions would have to increase to 14.2 per cent (combined employer-employee contribution) by 2030. To forestall this, the federal government and provinces agreed to increase rates again, to 9.9 per cent (combined) by 2003, where they would remain for a number of years. For 2001, the premium rate was 4.3 per cent for each party (totalling 8.6 per cent), rising to 4.7 per cent each in 2002 and 4.95 per cent each in 2003. Overall benefit costs were reduced by about 10 per cent, largely through reductions in entitlements to disability and death benefits.

By this time, the provinces no longer had the same borrowing needs since they began to balance their annual budgets. Therefore, CPP could invest its surplus in equity markets to get higher returns for investors. An arm's-length body, the Canada Pension Plan Investment Board (CPPIB), comprised of investment professionals rather than political appointments, was created for this purpose. Investing prudently within specified guidelines, and for the longer term, the fund is expected to return approximately 4 per cent each year (plus inflation).

After 1996, as bond issues came due, each province was permitted one further rollover for an additional 20 years. However, all new surplus CPP funds received were to go to the new CPPIB. The Investment Board received its first funds in March 1999, and by the end of fiscal 2000 it had $2.4 billion in equity markets. In its first full year, the CPPIB earned 40.1 per cent return on its investments, largely because of the dramatic rise in global stock markets. The returns for subsequent years were substantially lower due to declines in the stock market. As of September 2000, the account balance for CPP was in excess of $41 billion, the vast majority still in provincial bonds, but over time the balance will alter as the provincial bonds mature and more funds flow to the investment board.

The alternative, decreasing premiums as better returns are earned on invested funds, does not appear likely because the demographic bulge remains a major concern. As well, the federal and provincial governments are content with the forced savings inherent in CPP to ensure that working people with modest incomes—the real target population for CPP —have adequate resources in retirement and do not have to call on public assistance in their older years.

Back in 1976, Richard Bird stated that the Canada Pension Plan 'is in a sense a fraud' because in the future Parliament can change any benefit structure. Bird wrote that:

> contributors to the CPP really purchase nothing but the same right to be at the mercy of future generations which they had anyway. . . . In reality all effective social security systems rest in essence on a sort of implicit social contract under which those at work are taxed to support those retired, in the expectation that when they too are retired, the next generation will do the same for them.

Bird argued, in effect, that CPP and Old Age Security (OAS) are more alike than meets the eye. Though benefits under CPP are linked to prior contributions while OAS provides a flat-rate benefit (to an income ceiling), both are fully contingent programs. A simple Act of Parliament could alter both programs in ways totally unanticipated by contributors. As CPP contributions are not irrevocably linked to later benefits, they are really taxes—compulsory payments to government. Benefits under both schemes are financed (totally for OAS and partially for CPP) through current taxation, though only CPP premiums are earmarked as such.

## Workers' Compensation

Workers' Compensation is closest to the pure insurance model, as premiums are directly linked to the incidence of claims. Because the program lies within provincial jurisdiction the details differ across Canada, but in general outline they are similar.

Workers' Compensation was first introduced in Ontario in 1914 and other provinces followed thereafter. This legislation was unique in that it emerged in response to pressure from employers, who feared that under the common law the courts might award unlimited damages to employees for injuries sustained on the job. Workers' Compensation met their need, removing the right of employees to sue their employers for damages while offering a modest range of administratively determined payments for specific work-related injuries. The program was entirely funded by employers through premiums based on the accident history of the industry. As a result, WC has been viewed historically not as a broad social policy advance, but as legislative protection for employers.

Today, firms are pooled into industry groupings, and premiums are assigned to each category based on its historical accident claims record; rates are adjusted annually. Table 8.2 illustrates premium rates for some industrial groupings in Ontario for 2002, along with the rate change from the previous year.

Because the program is entirely funded by employers, safety at work may be viewed as primarily the responsibility of employers. More important, the risk rating system is

**Table 8.2  Workers' Compensation Premium Rates, Ontario (preliminary, 2002)**

| Rate Group Number | Description | 2002 Premium Rate ($) | 2001 Premium Rate ($) | Change (%) |
|---|---|---|---|---|
| 030 | Logging | 11.85 | 12.04 | –1.6 |
| 590 | Ambulance services | 6.61 | 6.37 | 3.8 |
| 608 | Beer stores | 3.36 | 3.41 | –1.5 |
| 638 | Pharmacies | 0.45 | 0.46 | –2.2 |
| 845 | Local government services | 1.56 | 1.45 | 7.6 |
| 851 | Homes for nursing care | 2.49 | 2.45 | 1.6 |
| 853 | Hospitals | 0.81 | 0.81 | 0.0 |
| 858 | Group homes | 2.46 | 2.52 | –2.4 |
| 861 | Treatment clinics | 0.81 | 0.79 | 2.5 |

SOURCE: Workplace Safety and Insurance Board, Ontario.
Available at: <http://www.wsib.on.ca/wsib/wsibsite.nsf/public/Employers2002PRTable2>.

based on an average for an industrial grouping, not the performance of individual firms: individual firm ratings might encourage employers to dissuade injured workers from lodging claims with the Board, as the firm's subsequent year's premiums would rise. In pooling risks over an industrial grouping, the intent was to promote safer working practices for all firms. If this involved higher costs, all firms would be affected equally and none would incur an unfair advantage over another. For some firms the industrial grouping is obvious, but other allocations are less clear; and being placed in a higher or lower risk grouping can have a significant impact on the premium costs.

To consider one example, care and retirement homes provide a range of services: some approximate low-level hospitals (which have a relatively low assessment because of their favourable accident history); others are more like nursing homes, which have higher accident rates and, hence, higher premiums. A separate category for these homes would require a clear operational definition of what they are and do, but this does not always exist. Consequently, the risk assessment category ultimately becomes somewhat arbitrary, with associated cost implications for employers.

Benefits across Canada totalled $4.6 billion in 1997, covering some 400,000 cases of time loss and fatal injury. Individual payments are a percentage of previous earnings, currently set in Ontario at 85 per cent of take-home pay (after deductions) up to an annual insured ceiling ($60,600 for 2001). There is no limit to the duration of benefits, though provinces have begun to integrate long-term WC cases into Canada Pension Plan disability benefits.

Benefit eligibility and levels are determined administratively on a case basis by provincial boards, and the avenues of appeal are limited. There are regular complaints that adjudicators are too closely linked to the boards (and therefore to the employers as funders). There are also allegations that the boards rely excessively on a so-called 'meat chart', in which predetermined formulas set benefit levels for specific impairments. Certainly, in the view of many claimants across Canada, a sense of fair and impartial third-party adjudication is absent. Claimants have countered by forming their own political advocacy groups, such as the Union of Injured Workers (UIW).

## NOTES

1. A *fee* is a payment that reflects the full cost of providing a service, using traditional market principles. A *charge*, in Howard Glennerster's (1985:91) words, 'implies some rationale . . . other than pure pricing criteria. There is an implied tokenism and arbitrariness rather than . . . a theoretically optimal allocation of resources which pricing entails.' In practice the terms are often used interchangeably, as they are in this book.
2. Those unfamiliar with the supply-and-demand curve analysis can skip this paragraph and Figures 8.1 and 8.2. The essential concepts are explained in the text in non-technical analysis.
3. As indicated earlier, an increase in price may actually lead to increased usage by the rich, resulting from the enhanced status or snob appeal of a service associated with higher levels of payment.
4. We saw in Chapter 1 that Statistics Canada estimated that credit card debt in Canada exceeded $14 billion in 1999 while loans on owned vehicles totalled $29 billion.

5. Technically, the marginal revenue of an extra rider is greater than zero, while the marginal cost is zero.
6. 'The Intensity rule has not worked as planned', according to an official government Web site: <http://www.hrdc-drhc.gc.ca/common/news/insur/00-66.shtml>.

## SUGGESTED READING

Parker, Roy. 1976. 'Charging for the social services', *Journal of Social Policy* 5, part 4 (Oct.): 359–73.
    Though somewhat dated, this remains the definitive article on the principles of fee-charging.
Townson, Monica. 1997. *Protecting Public Pensions: Myths vs. Reality*. Toronto and Ottawa: James Lorimer and Canadian Centre for Policy Alternatives.
    An excellent analysis of the threat to public pensions (Canada Pension Plan) in Canada and the probable future direction governments will follow. Includes chapters on pension 'reform' in Pinochet's Chile, Thatcher's Britain, and US Social Security.

# CHAPTER NINE

# Volunteers, Charities, and Gamblers

## INTRODUCTION

In the preceding two chapters, we have seen how social programs can be funded through taxes and user fees. A third important source of revenues, which is outside government (though there may be dependence on government), is the 'voluntary' sector (also known as the 'third sector'). For present purposes, this includes voluntary action by individuals, contributions of charities, and revenues of legal gambling.

A small part of the total economy, voluntary action is extremely important in certain areas—the social and health services, recreation, and culture. According to the National Survey of Giving, Volunteering and Participating (NSVGP, 2001), 22 million Canadians, (i.e., 91 per cent of the population aged 15 and over) made financial or in-kind contributions to charitable and non-profit organizations between 1 October 1999 and 30 September 2000. More than $5 billion was donated to charities, an increase of 11 per cent over the estimate from a comparable survey in 1997. Some 27 per cent of the population 15 and over served as volunteers during 1999–2000—a decrease from 31 per cent in 1997. In the aggregate, these volunteers provided more than 1 billion hours of service, equivalent to 549,000 full-time jobs.

There are an estimated 175,000 voluntary organizations in Canada, of which just under half are registered charities. This status confers distinct financial and other benefits on both the organizations and those who contribute. These bodies do not merely top up strong government social supports; they have become central to the funding and/or delivery of many social programs.

Provincial governments now derive about 3.6 per cent of total revenues (before federal transfers) from legal gambling, primarily lotteries, casinos, and video lottery terminals (VLTs). Charities receive another $1 billion annually from gambling activities they are licensed to run themselves, as well as through grants from provincial gaming authorities.

These organizations and activities by individuals clearly make an important financial contribution to Canada's social welfare system. They are distinguished by three characteristics:

- Participation is voluntary.[1] Those who wish to contribute do so, while others do not.
- The activities occur outside the direct auspices of government. Participants may depend on government—for financial support, for registered charitable status, for example, or for lottery gambling grants—but day-to-day control and direction reside with those who participate.
- Activity is not equally spread across the society, but tends to concentrate in specific areas.

We begin Chapter 9 with a look at the voluntary sector in Canada: who donates money and who volunteers time. We consider both the advantages and disadvantages of relying on volunteers and charities to fund and deliver social services. We then proceed to examine charities and the Income Tax Act—the process and criteria for organizations to receive charitable status from the federal government, a condition that permits them unilaterally to offer tax benefits to donors. The limits on advocacy and political activity imposed by this charitable status are based on court precedents from nineteenth-century England; consequently, these limits are complex and difficult to apply in the twenty-first century. We then proceed to an examination of lotteries, casinos, and VLTs. We identify the advantages and disadvantages of reliance on gambling as a revenue source for government, and close the chapter with a brief note on First Nations gambling activity.

## THE VOLUNTARY SECTOR IN CANADA

Voluntary help to those in need is, of course, as old as society itself. Over time, many voluntary activities, such as the provision of education, became governmental responsibilities, though rarely exclusively so. Today, as the welfare state continues to shrink, the voluntary sector reappears as a central player in the meeting of needs: witness the growth of food banks and private schooling. Voluntary organizations can be found in and make important contributions to virtually every area of public life: arts and culture, sports and recreation, self-help, religion and spiritual activities, as well as traditional health and social services. Many of these areas would not exist without volunteers and their contributions.

Yet, the expansion of voluntarism is controversial. There is clearly a legitimate role for volunteers, but the extent of the involvement is questioned. When food banks become essential to feeding people in a modern and wealthy society such as Canada, surely there is something wrong with our collective systems of production, distribution, and support.

## Who Donates?

According to the National Survey of Giving (NSGVP, 2001), more than half (53 per cent) of Canadians aged 15 and over donated food to organizations such as food banks in 1999-2000; more than two-thirds (69 per cent) gave clothing or goods. Over three-quarters (78 per cent) gave money to charities, with an average donation of $259, an increase of 8 per cent over 1996–7. However, much of the money comes from few donors. One-quarter of all donors gave $23 or less, about 1 per cent of the total value of all donations. Twenty-five per cent of donors (who gave $213 or more on average) contributed 82 per cent of the total. Donation rates were highest in the Atlantic provinces; the highest average donation was in Alberta. The lowest rates were in British Columbia and Quebec, and the lowest average donation was in Quebec.

In 1996–7, over half of all charitable giving (51 per cent of the money or $2.26 billion in total) went to religious organizations, constituting 15 per cent of all donations (Figure 9.1). The average donation to religious organizations was $270, more than twice that given to non-religious organizations ($125). The largest number of donors (38 per cent) gave $773 million to health organizations, while 21 per cent of donors gave $504 million to social service organizations. Together, health and social services received 28 per cent of all money donated. Education, culture, international aid, and the environment received less than 10 per cent of donations from under 10 per cent of donors.

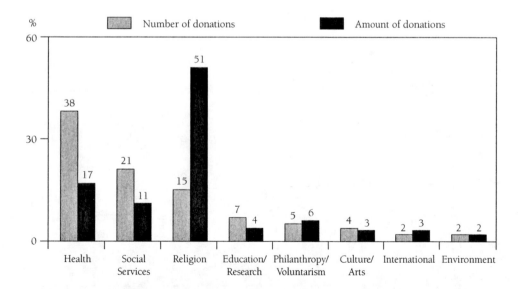

**Figure 9.1  Where Charitable Donations Go in Canada, 1997**

NOTE: Two per cent of both the number and the amount of donations were classed as 'other'. These included development and housing; law, advocacy, and politics; business and professional associations; and other organizations not classified elsewhere.

SOURCE: NSGVP (1998).

More than one-quarter of donors (29 per cent) gave to only one type of organization (based on Figure 9.1); 40 per cent of donors gave to three or more categories. By contrast, in 1999-2000, just under one-third (32 per cent) of Canadians donated 49 per cent of the total giving ($2.4 billion) to religious organizations. The average donation to religious organizations increased to $310, while that given to non-religious organizations also rose modestly to $140.

Slightly different information is available from the 1998 Survey of Household Spending of Statistics Canada (2000b). These data indicate that 70.9 per cent of households reported a contribution to charity in 1998, averaging $583. Religious organizations received money from 37.1 per cent of households (an average of $713), while 60.6 per cent of households contributed to non-religious charities (an average of $213).

Both rates of donation and average amount donated increase with household income. Donor rates rose consistently, from 63 per cent (average donation $142) for households with income under $20,000 to 86 per cent (average donation $529) from those with incomes over $100,000. When donations are viewed as a share of household income (Figure 9.2), however, the picture changes somewhat. In 1999–2000, average donations declined with income up to the $60,000–$80,000 range: those below $20,000 annually donate a greater share of their income than others. At higher income levels, there is a slight uptick. But it is clear that as a share of household income, the most generous donors are those with the lowest incomes.

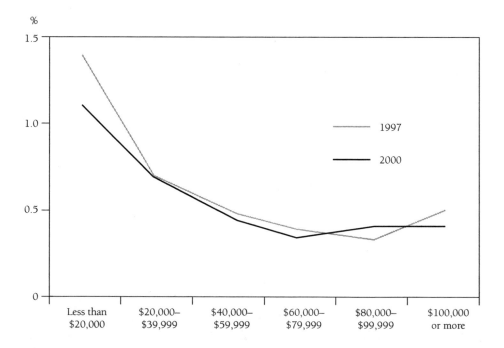

**Figure 9.2  Donations as a Share of Household Income, 1997 and 2000**

SOURCE: NSGVP (2001).

**Table 9.1  Rates of Volunteering and Number of Hours Volunteered, 1987, 1997, 2000**

|  | 2000 NSGVP | 1997 NSGVP | 1987 VAS[1] |
|---|---|---|---|
| *Rate of volunteering* | | | |
| Total population ('000) | 24,383 | 23,808 | 19,202 |
| Total volunteers ('000) | 6,513 | 7,472 | 5,337 |
| Volunteer participation rate (%) | 26.7 | 31.4 | 26.8 |
| *Hours volunteered* | | | |
| Total hours volunteered ('000,000) | 1,053.2 | 1,108.9 | 1,017.5 |
| Full-time year-round job equivalents[2] | 549,000 | 578,000 | 530,000 |
| Average hours volunteered per year | 162 | 149 | 191 |

1. 1987 Volunteer Activity Survey, Statistics Canada.

2. Assuming 40 hours of work per week for 48 weeks.

SOURCE: NSGVP (2001).

## Who Volunteers?

Table 9.1 shows the rate of volunteering and the number of hours volunteered in 1999–2000, compared with two earlier surveys. Whereas 5.3 million Canadians (26.8 per cent of the population 15 and over) had volunteered in 1987, the number rose to 7.5 million or just under one-third (31 per cent) of the population a decade later. In the three years to 1999–2000, however, there was a drop of 13 per cent—almost one million individuals—in the number of volunteers, to 6.5 million Canadians age 15 and over. Those fewer volunteers, however, gave more hours in 1999–2000: 162 hours, on average, compared to 149 hours three years earlier. The 1.05 billion hours volunteered represented a decline of 56 million hours since 1996–7. As with financial donors, relatively few individuals contributed the bulk of the hours: 25 per cent of all volunteers (1.6 million individuals) gave on average 188 hours or more, amounting to 73 per cent of all hours volunteered. One-quarter of volunteers gave 19 hours or less during the year, 1 per cent of all hours contributed. The highest rate of volunteering was in Saskatchewan; the largest number of hours volunteered was in the Atlantic provinces. The lowest rate of volunteering was in Quebec; the fewest average hours were in PEI.

The 1999–2000 survey (NSGVP, 2001) showed charities and non-profit organizations were increasingly reliant on a shrinking base of volunteers and donors: 9 per cent of Canadians (compared to 11 per cent three years earlier) were described as 'core supporters', donating 46 per cent of the total dollars and contributing 40 per cent of the total hours. 'What emerges is a portrait of a society in which most citizens provide modest, albeit important, levels of support to one another, but which also depends heavily upon the contributions of a small core of particularly engaged citizens' (ibid.). This core group is typically older, married, and religiously active; they tend to have higher incomes, be well educated, and have children between the ages of 6 and 17. However, this group appears to be declining in numbers, giving rise to serious concern of 'burnout' among the core supporters. The billion hours of volunteer activity and $5 billion in donations will not be easily replaced.

There is much speculation, though no hard data are available, to explain this shrinking core. Severe cutbacks in publicly provided social services have placed increasing demands on the voluntary sector, expectations that volunteers are simply incapable of addressing. Burnout seriously affects paid professional staff in many social agencies, and, one can assume, volunteers as well. Other causes may include the increasing demands of work and family, which leave less free time available, a decline in active religious participation, less need for young people to volunteer to gain workplace experience, and poor recruitment practices by many voluntary agencies.

## THE ADVANTAGES OF USING VOLUNTEERS AND CHARITIES

Perhaps the most obvious benefit of using volunteers and charitable organizations to deliver social services is the low cost.[2] Volunteers provide their labour either without charge or for a modest honorarium or direct expenses; they do not expect benefits and do not go on strike.

However, there are other reasons why volunteers and charities are preferred.

- Agencies outside government can do things that governments, for political or other reasons, cannot or will not do. Birth control, particularly directed to teenagers or younger children, and family planning were first delivered by NGOs, which have a flexibility and freedom not available within the public sector. This same distance frees government from any direct accountability for programs that many voters do not endorse. Agencies can also advocate on behalf of clients and work for political change in ways that government would not do, and might actively oppose.
- Voluntary agencies promote diversity and pluralism in areas (such as religion) where the state has no major direct role. They can show a cultural sensitivity to minority needs (ethnicity, sexual orientation, gender, ability) by virtue of being based in and accountable to diverse communities. NGOs represent the answer to the 'one-size-fits-all' charge against governmental service provision. By providing a greater range of services in a more flexible and timely manner, voluntary agencies often transcend the limits of bureaucratic professionalism.
- Such agencies can reflect local empowerment and control by promoting a philosophy of consumerism. Self-help groups, for example, are for those using a service without outside experts or professionals. The process and goals are determined by consumers, who can make important decisions about their lives without involvement by outsiders.
- Non-governmental service delivery reflects common views about the limits of the state. Certain areas—such as the arts and culture—have never really been embraced as direct governmental responsibilities in Canada (unlike in Europe, where they are part of government's central function). As a result, the not-for-profit sector raises funds and provides the services.

- NGOs reinforce current ideologies about reducing the size of the state. When a service is devolved from government, the public service is reduced and, theoretically, taxes could decrease. In an era when reducing the size of the public sector holds great political appeal, the attraction of assigning responsibility to the voluntary sector is obvious.

## THE DISADVANTAGES OF USING VOLUNTEERS AND CHARITIES

The most obvious drawback to volunteers and voluntary organizations is that lower cost can bring lower quality of service. Needs may be met unevenly, imperfectly, or not at all. Volunteers delivering meals on wheels, for example, may be elderly or retired, and on that cold and stormy February day they may not make their appointed rounds—precisely when the vulnerable recipients are most housebound and in greatest need of their meal delivery. Volunteers typically lack professional training and, however well meaning, may be unable to deliver the needed service.

There are additional concerns.

- Coverage may be uneven and equity may be lacking. Services may be provided only in certain geographic areas or only certain types of services will be delivered. Decentralized decision-making by volunteers regarding local needs and priorities may merely reflect the values and interests of the volunteers. What volunteers are willing to do will be done, but the rest will remain unaddressed. The greatest increases in volunteer activity in Canada over the last decade have been in the areas of environment and arts and culture. While these are obviously important, people across Canada remain hungry and homeless. Issues that are trendy may attract people and money, while more urgent concerns are left by the side.
- Fundamental needs may no longer be accommodated in a consistent and timely manner. Instead of people having income to buy food—or, even better, having the jobs to earn the income to buy the food—they are forced to rely on uneven and unpredictable food banks. What recipients receive depends on what others in the community choose to donate or on the surpluses in corporate warehouses. Volunteers replacing professional staff in hospitals may endanger both quality service delivery and, on occasion, even the lives of patients. An untrained worker on a crisis counselling line or in a hospice may cause great though inadvertent harm, and because the training of volunteers is inevitably brief, the outcomes are more uneven than in formal structured training programs.[3]
- Voluntary organizations may not always be flexible and ready to innovate. As they become older and more established, especially if they primarily receive public funds, they become subject to what Kramer (1981) called 'creeping formalization': bureaucratized and resistant to innovation. Voluntary agencies can also lose their ability to advocate effectively: many older, traditional voluntary bodies give little or no voice to the consumer.
- As those with higher incomes tend to give more, both in time and dollars, they acquire commensurate power and influence in identifying priorities. This privatized priority-setting carries a distinct class bias. An opera company or ballet may attract

volunteers and donations more easily than the after-school program for disadvantaged children. The poor simply are too busy trying to survive to be able to contribute either time or money on equal terms with the more affluent members of the community.

- Voluntarism represents a particular dilemma for women and for feminist theory. Some volunteers respond to needs previously unmet or dealt with privately in the home, or they may complement paid work. In such situations women as homemakers may receive emotional or physical support for their unpaid labour from volunteers. However, women as volunteers often replace poorly paid workers, who are often women as well. The net effect is that women as volunteers take jobs away from poorly paid, and often vulnerable, women as employees. The problem, for feminist theory, is to reconcile the exploitation of women who do unpaid work as volunteers with the exploitation of women who lose poorly paid jobs to volunteers. Moreover, the needs of those receiving services—males and females, and often the most vulnerable members of society—may not be addressed.
- Unions see volunteers as replacing stable, secure jobs founded on skill and training with unpaid, unskilled, and untrained labour. This is a process they generally oppose. They argue not only for the self-interest of their members, but also for the protection of the public interest and the needs of those receiving the services.

## The Paid Volunteer

There is a group of workers whose status and working conditions place them somewhere between volunteers and paid workers. They are often known as *paid volunteers*, though the label is inappropriate. They are overwhelmingly women, found in such areas as home child care (usually unlicensed) or fostering. They are paid a wage or fee, greater than expenses but less than full market compensation. The wage makes them workers, but the below-market levels of payment make them partial volunteers. The wage payment formalizes the relationship with the client, and may entail minimum standards or modest training; it allegedly helps the poor to undertake tasks as workers they could not do otherwise. Yet, the situation is profoundly exploitative of women as workers. As these tasks are often viewed as an extension of the woman's traditional unpaid parenting and housekeeping roles, the modest payments are presented as a significant step forward: modest pay is better than no pay. Full market compensation is deemed economically and socially unacceptable because of the high cost to taxpayers. The reluctance of taxpayers to pay for services they want translates directly into exploitation of vulnerable women who are expected to subsidize the lifestyles of their more affluent customers by accepting substandard wages.

Areas such as fostering, where the state pays for a public need to be met, may be distinguished from a field such as in-home child care, where the relationship is essentially private between buyer and seller of a service. Such distinctions miss the point that pay should compensate for the jobs that people do: the extent to which consumers are willing to pay is not used to determine other salary schedules and should not be applied to paid volunteers.

# CHARITIES AND THE INCOME TAX SYSTEM

Charities and voluntary giving are intimately linked through and with the income tax system. The status of a *registered charity* enables an organization to give donors tax receipts, which reduce their personal tax liability. There are also certain tax advantages for registered charities, such as exemption from income tax, and only they may obtain a bingo or lottery licence.

Of the estimated 175,000 voluntary organizations in Canada, about 80,000 are registered charities. According to the Canada Customs and Revenue Agency (CCRA, formerly Revenue Canada), taxpayers will save $1.4 billion in personal income tax and $201 million in corporate tax[4] in 2002 because of the deductibility of charitable donations (CCRA, 2001). This $1.6 billion in revenue forgone by the federal government will have to be offset by higher taxes in other areas or by reduced levels of total service. The vast majority of charitable giving comes from individuals: the taxes saved by corporate taxpayers amount to only 5 per cent of the savings through the personal income tax system.

Tax credits are an important inducement to making charitable donations. According to the NSGVP (1998), 41 per cent of donors indicated that someone in their household would be claiming a tax credit for charitable activities. Among small donors (under $40 a year), only 19 per cent indicated they would use the tax credit; among those giving $150 or more during the year, 80 per cent were planning to take advantage of the tax credit. For a small donation, the credit is minimal, so the low take-up rate is not surprising; at higher levels of donation, however, the credit is more substantial. More than a third of donors (37 per cent) indicated that they would donate more if offered a better tax credit, and this figure increased with the size of the annual donations. As the bulk of donations are given by a few donors, the total donated might rise significantly if the tax credit were enhanced.

When individuals donate[5] to registered charities, the receipts are credits that can be applied against taxes payable. All receipts in a given year are aggregated: a credit of 17 per cent (federal) is applied to the first $200, and a credit of 29 per cent is applied thereafter.[6] The taxes saved constitute tax expenditures, and are credits rather than deductions, so that everyone receives the same dollar reduction to taxes payable for identical dollar donations.

Suppose Tali donates $100 to a registered charity that cares for stray dogs and cats. She receives a tax receipt for $100, which converts into a credit of $17, so her federal taxes are reduced by $17. The registered charity is better off by $100. The net cost to Tali is only $83. Where does the other $17 come from? Clearly, from all other taxpayers, who forgo that $17 in taxes that Tali would otherwise owe. Conceptually, the federal government gives $17 to Tali, who passes it on to the charity along with her $83. The net effect is that by donating $100 to a registered charity, Tali has triggered a tax mechanism whereby all other taxpayers in Canada also contribute to her charity, to the sum of $17. If Sara objects to her tax dollars going to aid homeless dogs and cats, she has no recourse.

This process, of course, is not unique to charitable donations, but it is, as we saw in Chapter 7, simply a description of how tax expenditures operate. Unlike other tax expenditures, however, the charitable tax credit is activated by individual taxpayers who express personal preferences for particular causes or organizations. Were it operationally possible to develop a consensual ordering of collective social priorities in order to allocate public funds, the results would be unlikely to match what emerges from public spending through the charitable tax credit. Moreover, there is no upper limit to the public funds that can be allocated to a specific charity—there are fixed ceilings on the tax credits available to individuals, but no limit is set on the number of individuals who can make such contributions. Consequently, there is no limit to the total funds in the aggregate.

The result, once a charitable status is awarded to an organization, is the private use of public funds without public discussion or consultation. Causes that can generate the most funds through tax-receipted donations also receive the largest amounts of public money through the tax credit for donors. The organizations best able to market themselves, we need hardly add, are not necessarily those working in areas of the greatest social need or to which most people would choose to direct their tax revenues.

How, then, does a voluntary organization become a registered charity, and what does this status entail, aside from the right to issue tax receipts?

## Getting (and Keeping) Charitable Status

The Income Tax Act identifies three types of registered charities: charitable organizations (our primary focus), public foundations, and private foundations.[7] A charitable organization (or charity) can be registered by satisfying certain conditions determined by CCRA. These include an annual audit and a board, but the most relevant for us are the purposes for which the charity was established and the restrictions on what it may or may not do.[8]

A registered charity must serve a charitable purpose. While the Income Tax Act does not define charitable purpose, the courts have partly done so. The most often cited case, *Pemsel's Case*, from the British House of Lords in 1891 (with earlier roots in the common law of charity from Elizabethan England), identified four categories of charitable activity. These are still used by the courts and CCRA to determine if an organization should qualify as a registered charity:

1. the relief of poverty;
2. the advancement of education;
3. the advancement of religion; and
4. other purposes beneficial to the community as a whole (that the courts have identified as charitable).

Several essential points follow directly.

- The language is antiquarian in tone and the examples refer to casework, not to structural change: 'Organizations . . . for the relief of poverty . . . include . . . an orphanage' (Revenue Canada, 1977).
- The courts have held that political objects do not qualify as charitable purposes under any of these headings. An organization whose primary purpose is political change will not be registered as a charity.

- The courts have distinguished between education, a charitable object, and advocacy, often held to be political and, therefore, not a charitable object.
- The lines between these categories are vague. When does education become advocacy? How can a charitable organization not undertake *any* political activity, and what is the meaning of *political activity*? Charities have a treacherous path to tread, and if they falter they risk losing their charitable status and, with it, the right to issue tax receipts to donors.[9]

### Education and Advocacy

The advancement of education, for purposes of charitable status, must involve more than mere provision of information.[10] It may include training the mind, advancing knowledge or abilities, raising the artistic taste of the community, or improving a useful branch of human knowledge through research. But such educational activity must be reasonably balanced:

> all sides of an issue must be fairly presented so that people can draw their own conclusions. It is a question of the degree of bias in an activity . . . organizations must not rely on incomplete information or on an appeal to emotions. . . . The more controversial the subject matter, the greater the care the charity must take not to prejudge. (CCRA, 2000)

A 1988 case involved the Notre Dame de Grace Neighbourhood Association in Montreal, a community organization that focused on local social issues, access to community resources, and services to the disadvantaged. The courts held that its information and letter-writing campaigns, lobbying efforts, and 'defending peoples' rights' constituted political activity and were not educational within the meaning of the charity law. It was denied charitable status as a result.

More recently, however, a 1999 ruling from the Supreme Court of Canada expanded the meaning of education slightly. The current test is that there must be structure and genuinely educational purpose, a teaching or learning component, and a targeted attempt to educate others. But knowledge and education can take many forms. 'So long as [the purpose is] not solely to promote a particular view or political orientation, it may properly be viewed as falling within the advancement of education' (cited in Bridge, 2000). This recognition is helpful, but the line between education and advocacy remains blurred. Bridge gives the example of an organization devoted to health issues that advocates for new community health practices based on innovative models that have worked in Europe. Such activity might cross the line to advocacy and lead to denial of charitable status.

A draft paper (not yet incorporated into regulations) from CCRA (2000) identified four types of advocacy:

- To advocate on behalf of *individuals*. Examples include a developmentally challenged individual requiring a spokesperson to assist in the workplace or to gain access to community services, and a recent immigrant who may need an intermediary or translator. Such activities would be considered charitable in that they involve helping individuals in need.

- To advocate on behalf of a *group*. As a charity exists for the benefit of society as a whole, an organization promoting the interests of its constituents would not qualify as a charity. This might exclude community centres, self-help groups, or 'single-cause' bodies if they work only for the interests of the specific group they represent without any broader benefit to society as a whole.
- To advocate in order to change people's *behaviour*. Examples are anti-smoking campaigns and appeals to not buy fur, to use public transit, or to keep the family intact. In such cases, the courts would consider whether the advocacy takes the form of 'a well-rounded, reasoned presentation of the facts, or whether it is instead based on slanted, incomplete information and on an appeal to emotions'.
- To advocate to change people's *opinions*. Though examples are not given, this type of activity 'is unlikely to be charitable'.

### Political Activity

Charities have always engaged in political activities and, within limits, are permitted to do so. There are three broad categories of political activity:

- A charity cannot do certain things.
- A charity can do other things within limits.
- A charity is free to do still other things without limit in carrying out its mandate.

A charity cannot have a political purpose. It cannot support a political party or candidate, or promote a particular ideology. It cannot campaign to retain or change an existing law or policy. It cannot engage in partisan political activity that focuses on particular candidates or political parties. It cannot purchase tickets to fundraisers or give mailing lists to political parties. However, sponsoring an all-candidates' meeting or writing a balanced research document setting out the positions of the different parties would be acceptable. As the Canada Customs and Revenue Agency (2000) has explained, 'campaigning against "the government" can amount to opposing a specific "political party" depending on the surrounding circumstances.'

The *reason* why political purposes are deemed to be not charitable turns on another British court case, from 1917 (Bridge, 2000). Charitable activities must produce a public benefit. A political purpose—or an attempt to persuade the public on social issues—may or may not result in future in a public benefit. Because we cannot predict with certainty the outcome of political activity, the proper forum for such activity is Parliament. Such was the reasoning in 1917, and such remains official thinking today.

A charity is permitted to carry out political activity 'incidental and ancillary' to its charitable purpose. Such activity is subject to a requirement in the Income Tax Act, s. 149.1(6.2), that 'substantially all'—interpreted as meaning '90 percent or more'—of a charity's resources be spent on charitable activity. Thus, up to 10 percent of a charity's resources can be spent on permitted political activities.

A political activity must be both 'incidental' and 'ancillary' to the charity's main purposes. 'Incidental' means a minor or subordinate focus within the broader purposes of the charity's activities. 'Ancillary' means that the political activity must relate to and support the organization's purposes and must represent a reasonable way of achieving its goals. Thus, a hospital's campaign to avoid being shut down would likely not be acceptable political activity, while a campaign for greater funding for the hospital system as a whole might incur no difficulty. Publications, conferences, public meetings, or 'lawful demonstrations' would be acceptable within the 'incidental and ancillary' conditions.

Charities are free to engage in what is called 'government-related charitable activity' without limits as needed to carry out its purposes. Acceptable actions include a charity sharing its views and expertise with others 'in order to allow a full and reasoned consideration of an issue and not in order to sway public opinion or to bring pressure on a government' (CCRA, 2000); expressing an expert opinion in the media or to government; and conducting day-to-day business with government. The line between sharing views (acceptable) and influencing law, policy or public opinion (not acceptable) is obviously vague, and this would be determined primarily by the charity's intent in undertaking the activity. Thus, there is inevitably much scope for interpretation—and misinterpretation.

## The Problems

It is evident that the central difficulty with the law on charitable activity is its vagueness, its imprecision, and hence its lack of predictability. The seminal law is drawn from a British court case from 1891, with roots much further back in the Elizabethan Poor Laws. The disparity between contemporary needs and practices and an archaic legal context is profound. Charities often cannot know if an action will be deemed educational or political, and the consequences of misjudging can be severe. Even the 10 per cent rule is highly problematic, as government auditors may subjectively attempt to interpret retroactively the purposes of charity spending actions years after the event. Thus, many charities err on the side of caution.

Yet, charities are important participants in public policy debate. They speak for communities and often possess unique expertise about the impact of policies at ground level, in the daily lives of clients. They can't always wait to be asked for their views. As the state shrinks and charities are called on to carry more of the burden of caring for the vulnerable, their roles as spokespersons become ever more crucial. Being restricted to the delivery of services (as implied in much of case law) and being prevented—or severely restricted—in their efforts to bring about structural change can be deeply frustrating.

Paradoxically, tax laws permit, and even encourage, businesses and corporations to speak out on matters of public or private concern. Expenses associated with political representation and lobbying, in any form, are deductible from a corporation's taxable income and are therefore tax expenditures paid for in part by all taxpayers. Likewise, there are no limits on corporate use and deductibility of advertising that can be directed to overtly political ends (such as a billboard calling for the defeat of a government or the repeal of a piece of legislation). A charitable organization that calls for an increase in minimum wage or in welfare rates must be very careful not to cross into political advocacy, but a corporation that opposes such action can deduct all costs associated with promoting its position. This unequal treatment of political advocacy obviously impedes fair and balanced debate in matters of pressing social concern.

Charitable organizations respond to these tax constraints in a variety of ways:

- Some retreat, emphasizing casework and substantially abandoning any political action. As this book is being written, it is rumoured within the charitable community that Ottawa intends to clamp down hard on political action. Agencies that have never had difficulty are increasingly subject to investigation by CCRA. In response, some are abandoning long-held commitments to fundamental structural change.
- Some organizations have always maintained a split, accommodating two distinct legal entities—a charitable foundation, the purposes of which are fully compatible with the relevant case law, and a second body for overt advocacy. The pro-choice political action organization CARAL (the Canadian Abortion Rights Action League) has a sister charitable organization, the Childbirth by Choice Trust. The challenge, not always successful, has been to satisfy CCRA that the two bodies are separate.
- Other organizations embrace political goals and do not seek charitable status. Their literature typically warns potential donors that they are unable to issue tax receipts. In this way, they are free to pursue their mandates without constraint.
- Others maintain an advocacy role and argue (normatively) for the validity and legality of their actions in the context of their other work, typically related to clients who are served directly. The statement in the Social Union Framework Agreement (SUFA) that voluntary organizations should be part of the political and policy processes strengthens this perspective.
- Still other groups proceed by subterfuge. Political advocacy may be central to their mission, but without charitable status they would be non-viable financially. Unwilling to sacrifice either, they simply do what they have to do, hoping they won't be caught but fully aware of the consequences. Some try to 'launder' their money through safe charitable organizations, record advocacy on the books as service delivery, and adopt whatever other quasi-legal (or illegal) measures necessary.

Numerous mainstream organizations have, at different times, found their charitable status questioned. In 1984 the Canadian Mental Health Association, an eminently respectable body, was informed that it might not be satisfying the conditions for charitable status because its statement of purpose said that the CMHA should 'urge government at all levels to take legislative and financial action to further [the Association's] objectives' (Silversides, 1984). In 1990 (Grant, 1990) four animal rights groups, including both the Toronto and the Ontario Humane Societies, were put under review, allegedly because of their opposition to the fur industry—their campaigns to urge the public not to buy fur coats had led to a 20 per cent drop in business in one year. In 1996, *Briarpatch v. The Queen* was the first full hearing of a decision by Revenue Canada to deregister a charity. The Saskatchewan-based organization, with a focus on low-income people, had objectives including communications, media access, educational workshops, and breaking down barriers. Its main activity was the publication of a magazine, *Briarpatch*. The courts upheld Revenue Canada's decision to deregister because there was not sufficient 'continuity, structure and analysis' to qualify as education in the sense of training the mind. In 1999 (*Toronto Star*, 1999), Greenpeace was denied re-registration for the third time; its charitable status had been revoked a decade earlier.

Revenue Canada said that Greenpeace was not a charity because its activities had 'no public benefit'. The government argued that people could be sent 'into poverty' if lumber and paper mills were closed due to environmental hazards. Greenpeace responded by indicating that environmental protection creates jobs on a net basis, and stated that the denial of charitable status would not harm its fundraising activities—it did not rely on charitable status to survive.

As these examples indicate, government or corporate interests can always intervene in investigations of specific charities. As the losses in the fur industry suggest, when charities do succeed in their missions to alter people's behaviours, it is then that they run afoul of the tax people. As long as the charities have no particular impact, they will be left alone.

## United Way/Centraide

The first United Way was created in Denver, Colorado, in 1887; the first federated fundraising effort in Toronto was in 1918. Donating through the United Way is one of many ways in which people give to their community. At present there are 125 United Ways/Centraides across Canada. In 2000, they raised $328 million (or $12.99 per capita); allocations were made to 5,350 agencies across the country. The highest rate of donation was in Alberta ($18.87 per capita) and the lowest, excluding the territories, was in Quebec ($8.04). Some 32 donor organizations (corporate, labour, and employees) gave more than $1 million in 2000, mostly from employee campaigns in the workplace (United Way of Canada, 2001). In Toronto 62 per cent of all United Way revenues comes from employee campaigns, and only 29 per cent is corporate giving; the remaining 9 per cent comes from community special events and direct responses.

By collecting money from and speaking on behalf of the entire community, the United Way helps to create a culture in which voluntary activity is encouraged. Concern for the less fortunate changes from special-interest pleading by individual charities into a part of one's broad community obligations. In this way it is hoped that the initial donation of money will create a broader sense of involvement with and commitment to one's local neighbourhood. With its extensive use of volunteers, the United Way enables people to contribute to the social life of their communities.

The United Way also offers an efficient way to donate money to charity. Individuals do not have to choose among competing charities or respond to telephone or postal solicitations; they can make one contribution, confident that the allocations will broadly reflect overall community priorities. People are freed of the need to decide how to allocate their charitable contributions.

The United Way serves an important redistributive function within the community. In principle, at least, money is distributed to charities based on broad consensual priorities that reflect community needs. This results in more money flowing to small and less well-known organizations, representing groups such as recent immigrants or the poor, that would be unable to raise funds successfully on their own. To some, the greatest merit of the United Way is its redistributive function, whereby money is collected across the community and allocated, disproportionately to the contribution rate, to groups working with the poor and vulnerable.

On the other hand, questions have been raised. Although the United Way is decentralized—the United Way in each community across Canada has effective autonomy—certain themes do recur. The leadership tends to be drawn from the corporate elite, and the organizational style, therefore, tends to be conservative and cautious. While United Ways tend to acknowledge the inadequacy of voluntary donations to address deep social problems, on a daily level the organization is usually reluctant to challenge government directly. Its advocacy mission is very limited. A former mayor of Toronto has commented on the United Way in that city:

> Giving priority to fundraising, which requires good relationships with corporate leaders who also raise funds for [the provincial government], has meant the poor are falling behind. If United Way can't address this issue, it's clearly part of the problem, not the solution. (Sewell, 2001)

The efficacy of the fundraising is also not clear. While donors are encouraged to give once during the year, do they contribute more than they would in response to disparate requests? Perhaps donors think in terms of economies of scale and give less in one donation than they would if their giving was spread throughout the year. This issue remains empirically indeterminate.

There are also questions as to the United Way's ability to speak on behalf of the entire community. Small and new organizations, particularly those with a more overtly political orientation, are unlikely to be accepted under the United Way umbrella. Others, most notably the Catholic charities in many cities, have withdrawn to form their own faith-based counterpart, ShareLife, so they need not be part of an organization that gives money to Planned Parenthood or other groups promoting family planning, birth control, or women's right to choose.

A little publicized decision by some United Ways might seriously undermine its redistributive mission. United Ways in the United States found that donors were increasingly opting out and donating money directly to their chosen charities. In response, they introduced 'donor option' plans, whereby contributors to the United Way can earmark some or all of their donations to particular named charities. The privileged recipient agencies no longer need compete with other community priorities. Faced with a similar situation, United Ways in Canada followed suit and many now permit donor choice arrangements. Through the United Way in Toronto, contributions can be directed to any registered charity in Canada.

As long as the amounts involved in donor option plans are small, the earmarked contributions can be absorbed without altering basic priority-setting. But individual charities increasingly encourage donors to direct their United Way contribution to a named use. The United Way, in effect, becomes a conduit for money from individual donors to specific charities. For example, foundations attached to public schools are created, and parents are invited to use their United Way money to support the lagging quality of public education for their own children. Clearly, such a process will be most successful in affluent neighbourhoods.[11] In 2000, some $10 million of Toronto United Way money was directed through these donor preference plans. If, as anticipated, such arrangements expand in future years, the fundamental ability of United Way to redistribute to the less powerful will be at grave risk.

Some large charities do not need the United Way because they can raise funds successfully on their own and see no reason to share with the more vulnerable organizations in the community. They therefore do not participate in United Way drives. With donor preference plans, the United Way is responding to pressures from society, but these pressures reflect the fact that people may be losing their broad sense of community and want to support only certain causes. Yet, without donor preference options, United Ways might lose these donors entirely, as they might give directly to their chosen recipient, which can issue the same tax receipt as can the United Way. However, by embracing these private selective arrangements, the United Way is negating its central redistributive role in the community. Once again, charities representing the poor and vulnerable will be left behind.

# GAMBLING

Gambling is big business in Canada, a growing source of income for provincial governments, the not-for-profit sector, and private corporations. In 1996, the National Council of Welfare estimated that legal gambling in this country probably totalled between $20 billion and $27 billion annually (NCW, 1996). With the large revenues from gambling come equally large social problems and ethical dilemmas. The original Criminal Code of Canada, passed in 1892, prohibited all forms of gaming (gambling) but early amendments modified this outright ban. In 1900, small-scale raffles for charitable or religious purposes were permitted, and there was further easing of restrictions in 1906 and 1925. Charities and religious groups, with the field to themselves, could raise modest sums of money without difficulty.

In 1969, Montreal was faced with the need to pay for Expo 67 and the projected deficit from the 1976 Olympics. In a direct challenge to the Criminal Code, the city introduced Canada's first large-scale lottery with major cash prizes. The case made its way to the Supreme Court of Canada, which ruled against Montreal. In response, the Criminal Code was amended to permit federal and provincial governments, as well as charitable and religious organizations (under licence), to run widespread games of chance. The provinces and territories responded by introducing ticket lotteries and sweepstakes. In 1985, the provinces persuaded Ottawa to vacate the field in exchange for annual cash payments from the provinces to Ottawa so that today there is no federally run lottery. In 1989, when a further amendment to the Criminal Code permitted slot machines and other forms of electronic gambling, Canada's first permanent casino, in Winnipeg, introduced slot machines. A year later New Brunswick was the first to allow non-casino electronic gambling through video lottery terminals (VLTs) in stores and bars. Today, permanent casinos are found in all provinces but Prince Edward Island, New Brunswick, and Newfoundland, and VLTs have been introduced everywhere except British Columbia and Ontario.

A 1995 Canadian Centre for Philanthropy study found that 44 per cent of non-religious charities use gambling to raise funds (Hall, 1995). A 1999 study reported that 69 per cent of agencies receiving government grants from lottery proceeds considered gambling income very important to their organization's revenues (Berdahl, 1999). A recent estimate suggests there are more than 50 permanent casinos, 21,000 slot machines, 38,000 VLTs, 20,000 annual bingo events, and 44 permanent racetracks across Canada (Azmier, 2000). All represent lucrative sources of revenue for those who own or manage them.

## Lotteries

Lotteries vary widely in terms of prize values, chances of winning, and frequency. Draws such as Lotto 6/49 often offer winnings well in excess of $1 million; small 'scratch and win' or 'pull-type' instant-win tickets offer modest prizes. Some are run directly by government lottery corporations (such as Loto Québec or the Western Lottery Corporation), while others are licensed by governments to local charities, First Nations groups, and not-for-profit organizations for fundraising purposes. In 1992, lotteries accounted for about 90 per cent of government revenues from gambling, but by 1998 they had dropped to 35 per cent of the total. However, the absolute amount of money generated through lotteries has remained relatively flat, growing by 4 per cent between those years to $2.6 billion dollars.

Typically, about a third to a half of lottery sales represent net profits after all expenses and prizes. Provincial lottery revenues often go to provincial general revenues though profits may be earmarked for specific purposes. In addition, BC, Alberta, Saskatchewan, and Ontario have specific grant programs using provincial lottery profits that in 1998 directed about $175 million to charitable organizations. This total was expected to increase to nearly $400 million by 2001.

Bingos, raffles, and special-occasion casinos run under the auspices of charitable and not-for-profit organizations generated a further $762 million in profits in 1998. Most of these were of modest size and scope, such as pull-tab and break-open tickets. The sponsoring organizations apply for provincial licences to run these events and keep most of the profits, which may be shared with commercial operators who run the actual events. Provincial and territorial government derive little income from these events.

Combining the $175–$400 million in gambling grants with charitable gaming profits of $762 million, some $1 billion of revenue for charitable organizations is derived from people who gamble. This represents a substantial sum of money for a sector in which adequate funding is a chronic problem.

## Casinos

The first year-round Las Vegas-style casino opened in Winnipeg in 1989. In 1992, casinos accounted for only 1 per cent of revenue from gambling across Canada, but through the decade they experienced dramatic growth. By 1998, casinos surpassed lotteries as the largest single source of gambling revenues, yielding 39 per cent of the total. That year, $2.8 billion was bet at casinos, about 100 times the 1992 total.

Various management models are used in Canadian casinos. Some, such as the Winnipeg casino, are owned and operated by the provincial government, and the staff are provincial employees. The big casinos in Ontario are owned by the provincial lottery corporation, but management is contracted out to professional operators with casino interests elsewhere. Casino Rama ownership is shared by the Ontario government and the Chippewas First Nations band, which receives an inflation-adjusted annual fee of $4.5 million.

# VLTs

VLTs are like slot machines except that instead of a cash payout they print a credit slip, which is exchanged on the premises for cash. When the technology was developed to permit widespread introduction of video lottery terminals, it was inevitable they would spread across Canada. The Canada West Foundation (2001) has estimated that as of early 2001 there were an estimated 38,048 VLTs in 8,578 locations across Canada (except in Ontario and BC, neither of which has allowed VLTs). Excluding these two provinces, there is one VLT for every 293 adult Canadians, with over 40 per cent of the VLTs and nearly half the VLT sites located in Quebec. Newfoundland and Manitoba have the highest VLT-to-population ratios, with one machine for every 162 and 187 adults, respectively.

In 1992, VLTs comprised about 9 per cent of government revenues from gambling, but by 1998 this had risen to 28 per cent of total revenues—an increase of nine times, to $2.1 billion. For 1999–2000, 1.9 per cent of all provincial government revenues (before federal transfers) were accounted for by VLTs: Nova Scotia, Alberta, and Saskatchewan, each at 2.8 per cent, were the most heavily dependent.

It is estimated that for every $100 bet at a VLT there is a $30 profit. This translates into government profits of $1.6 billion in 2000. Commissions to retailer licensees totalled $561 million (or $15,000 per machine); with an average of 4.4 machines per site, the average annual profit per siteholder was $65,000 in 2000. The highest commission rates are in New Brunswick, where 47 per cent of VLT revenues go to the private sector, well above the national average of 26 per cent. The sum of retailer commissions and provincial revenues equals the values of the losses (or the cost of playing) attributable to VLTs. In 2000, the Canada West Foundation (2001) estimated that $7 billion was put into VLT machines across Canada. Payouts totalled $4.9 billion, resulting in a net loss to players of $2.1 billion, equivalent to $193 per adult per year in provinces that have the machines.[12]

# Big Money

According to Statistics Canada (Marshall, 2000), $8.1 billion was bet on some form of non-charity gambling activity in 1999, three times the $2.7 billion wagered in 1992. Gambling revenue exceeded $2 billion for the first time in a single quarter in the third quarter of 1999. Nearly 1 per cent of the overall increase in Canadian gross domestic product (GDP) between 1992 and 1998 was attributable to the gambling industry.

For the fiscal year 1999–2000, it has been estimated that $5.4 billion (3.6 per cent of all provincial revenues net of expenses) came from lotteries, casinos, and other forms of non-charitable gambling. Prince Edward Island was the least dependent, with 2.7 per cent of provincial revenues derived from these sources: Nova Scotia was the highest at 5.3 per cent. Azmier and Roach (2000) point out that this $5.4 billion in 1999–2000 nearly matches the $5.8 billion the provinces generated from alcohol and tobacco taxes combined, and '[i]f the current upward trends continue, gambling will soon outpace these revenue sources.'

Table 9.2 gives more information on who gambles in Canada, and how much they spend, by income level. Over three-quarters of households (77 per cent) reported that

### Table 9.2  Gambling Expenses by Household, 1998

|  | Total | After-tax income | | | | |
|---|---|---|---|---|---|---|
|  |  | Under $20,000 | $20,000 –39,999 | $40,000 –59,999 | $60,000 –79,999 | $80,000+ |
| Total households ('000) | 11,290 | 2,460 | 3,860 | 2,740 | 1,310 | 920 |
| Per cent reporting: Expenditure on at least one gambling activity | 77 | 63 | 79 | 81 | 84 | 84 |
| Government lotteries | 68 | 53 | 70 | 72 | 76 | 72 |
| Non-government lotteries, raffles, other | 34 | 18 | 31 | 41 | 45 | 51 |
| Casinos, slot machines, VLTs | 20 | 11 | 19 | 24 | 27 | 29 |
| Bingos | 10 | 12 | 10 | 10 | 10 | 8 |
| Average expenditure per spending household ($) | 460 | 315 | 405 | 470 | 715 | 590 |
| Gambling as per cent of total income | 0.7 | 1.5 | 1.1 | 0.8 | 0.9 | 0.5 |
| Gambling as per cent of total income (spending households) | 0.8 | 2.3 | 1.4 | 1.0 | 1.0 | 0.6 |

SOURCE: Canada, Statistics Canada (2000b).

they spent money on at least one charity or government-run gambling activity in 1998. Participation increased with income level, from 63 per cent of households in the lowest category to 84 per cent of households with incomes above $60,000. At 68 per cent of all households, participation was highest, by far, in government lotteries. Only 10 per cent of households played bingo during that year.

The average amount spent per household that gambled was $460, up from $425 two years earlier. The average amount spent increases with household income level, except in the highest income category, where it declined from $715 to $590. Far more important than the absolute amounts, however, is the gambling expenditure in relation to total household income. Spending constituted 0.8 per cent of total income for all households that gambled, but this share declines with income level. In households with incomes under $20,000 gambling comprised a not inconsiderable 2.3 per cent of total income, but in households with incomes in excess of $80,000, gambling comprised 0.6 per cent of income. On a regional basis, net spending on games of chance was greatest in the Northwest Territories in 1998, at over $700 per household. It is followed by Nunavut, where over $400 was gambled on average. The lowest spending was in British Columbia, at just under $200.

# ADVANTAGES OF GAMBLING AS A REVENUE SOURCE

Both governments and the charitable/not-for-profit sectors derive many benefits from the spread of gambling across Canada. Our examination of some of these is followed by a listing of some of the major drawbacks.

1. Gambling is *lucrative*. It generates in excess of $1 billion annually for charitable and not-for-profit organizations and a further $5.4 billion (in 1999–2000) for provincial and territorial governments. This represents 3.6 per cent of all provincial/territorial revenues (before federal transfers) and about 1.2 per cent of all charitable funding, roughly equivalent to all receipted corporate charitable donations. In general, this money does *not* replace other sources of revenue (particularly for government) but supplements the basic revenue sources. For charities, there may be some modest inverse relation between gambling revenues and individual donations, though the evidence is unclear.

2. Gambling is a *politically easy* way of generating revenues. Indeed, it is often described as voluntary taxation. It constitutes taxation in that payment to government is compulsory; it is voluntary in that individuals decide whether to gamble (and hence, whether to pay the taxes). Profits and expenses are taken off the top, and the pool available for winnings is based on what is left. In a 1999 telephone survey of 2,202 Canadians, nearly two-thirds of respondents (62 per cent) agreed with the statement 'gambling is a good way for governments to raise revenues because it is a form of voluntary taxation' (Azmier, 2000). Twenty-nine per cent of respondents 'strongly agreed' while only 32 per cent disagreed. 'Canadians view gambling participation as a choice. If people chose to over-contribute their share of tax revenue through gambling activity, this reduces the overall tax burden on the whole' (Azmier, 2000).

With gambling there is no equivalent to *taxpayer rage* or *voter resistance to taxes*, which has become so pronounced in Canada in recent years. Those participating in gambling understand and accept that much of the money wagered—over half in many cases—goes directly to government. There is no identifiable opposition to these 'taxes'. The same survey asked respondents to choose between increased taxes or more revenues from casinos, lotteries, and VLTs 'if (your province) needed to raise more money'. Over two-thirds (67 per cent) of respondents preferred gambling and only 19 per cent chose taxes, with the remaining 13 per cent opting for neither alternative.

The greatest support for the taxation option is in the Atlantic region (25 per cent), where sentiments in general are the most opposed to gambling. In contrast, only 8 per cent of respondents in Quebec preferred the taxation alternative. The demographic breakdown of responses is also revealing. There was a very dramatic positive association between education level and preference for taxes: support rose from 12 per cent among those with less than grade 12 to 47 per cent among those with a Master's degree and 60 per cent among those with doctorates. Among those respondents with household incomes over $100,000, 28 per cent supported higher taxes. In other words, the most educated and affluent Canadians may be most aware of the adverse social and economic costs of gambling, and are the most willing to rely on taxes to generate revenues for government. These groups argue against their own short-term economic interests, as they spend proportionately less on gambling than do the poor yet presumably would pay most of the tax bill.

3. Gambling is an *economically efficient* way of raising money. For the charities and not-for-profit organizations that receive provincial licences to run gambling activities, the operating costs are often negligible. If they contract with commercial operators, the latter will typically incur all costs (such as hall rental) in exchange for a share of the profits. The charity may be required to provide a number of volunteers to assist in actually running the event. With government lotteries, there is no need to collect taxes after the fact, as profits are drawn off the top. There are policing problems, particularly where large amounts of cash are involved, to ensure against skimming of the proceeds, but this is not believed to be a large problem.

4. Charities and non-profit organizations have *free use of funds* raised from gambling. These organizations increasingly receive funding through specific service contracts or fee-for-service arrangements with governments. Relatively little core or base funding comes without conditions. However, they are generally free to use gambling profits (though not necessarily the gambling grants) for any purposes, so they are often directed towards activities that cannot be funded in other ways. There is a comparable attraction for government: funds can be allocated on a discretionary basis for purposes that do not fit into existing budgetary allocations. As well, such spending can meet political needs that governments might have difficulty justifying in their legislatures.

5. It would appear that legalized gambling has wide *public support*. Opinion polls across Canada consistently support wide and easy availability of gambling outlets. They also hold that the bulk of the profits should go to charitable causes rather than to provincial treasuries (though, in fact, this is not the case). There is a long history of gambling to support worthy causes, and this tradition commands much support.

6. Legalized gambling is a relatively labour-intensive industry and creates *jobs*. Casinos create jobs in host communities, and there should be spillovers to entertainment, transportation, and hospitality, as well as to those supplying directly to the casinos. The revenues that small shopkeepers receive from the sale of lottery tickets keeps some of them solvent at a time when corner stores are rapidly disappearing. According to Statistics Canada (Marshall, 2000), jobs in the gambling industry more than tripled between 1992 and 1999, from 11,900 to 39,200. This net increase of 27,300 jobs represented 2 per cent of all new job growth in Canada since 1992, though in 1999 this employment represented only 0.3 per cent of all jobs in Canada. No good estimates are available of the jobs created in ancillary industries.

## DISADVANTAGES OF GAMBLING AS A REVENUE SOURCE

Just as gambling offers advantages to governments, charities, and communities, so, too, a number of disadvantages result from this 'easy' way to raise (and to lose) money.

1. To be sure, there are *ethical concerns* related to gambling. Governments appear to have no ethical problems with gambling as a source of revenue; they do not, however, tend to emphasize the amount of revenue generated or the impacts of the gambling. Instead, they quietly accumulate the income and disburse it as they wish. Many agencies and religious groups, however, have problems with gambling revenues. Certain religious groups, for example, have an ideological objection to gambling per se and,

consequently, a reluctance to use funds that come from improper sources. For many agencies, however, the absolute ethical problems are less than the concerns about the undesirable consequences of gambling.

2. Among the most common objections to gambling is that it is *regressive in impact*, as the percentage of household income spent on gambling is greatest among those with the lowest incomes. Statistics Canada (2000b) reports that gambling activity may be the most regressive form of household expenditure. Average *total* spending per household in the highest quintile (the wealthiest 20 per cent of the population) is 3.9 times that of the households in the lowest quintile. However, spending on gambling by households in the top quintile was only 1.6 times that of the poorest quintile of households. (By comparison, spending on recreation was five times greater in the wealthiest households, and on transportation it was four times greater.)

The finding is reinforced by taking a closer look at bingos. Though only 10 per cent of all households play bingo, involvement decreases with income level: participation is greatest among those with incomes below $20,000. The average expenditure among those participating in bingo was $700 per year, much greater than government-run lotteries ($251) or casinos, slots or VLTs ($432). Thus, bingo is a game disproportionately directed towards the households with lowest incomes, yet the average amounts spent are considerably greater than in other forms of legal gambling.

3. *Addiction to gambling* can become a serious problem. Individuals can develop a gambling dependency just as they can become alcohol or drug dependent, with concomitant adverse consequences: stress on the individual's marital and family relations; psychiatric and physical disorders; decline in job productivity and loss of employment; heightened incidence of multiple addictions, including substance abuse; and increases in crime and fraud. One study (Henriksson, 1996) estimated that each compulsive gambler costs society $56,000 on average. Anyone can be affected, regardless of income level or demographic profile.

According to the National Council of Welfare (1996), studies conducted by the provincial gaming authorities reported that 2.7–5.4 per cent of adults (totalling between 600,000 and 1.2 million Canadians) had gambling problems at the time they were questioned.

> The typical problem gambler in Canada is an unmarried man under the age of 30. Beyond this there is no clear pattern. It may well be that the profile of the problem gambler is becoming less distinct as problems appear in a variety of groups within the general population. (NCW, 1996)

Particular attention was paid to three groups of problem gamblers: adolescents, women, and Aboriginals. Though the quantity of research was limited, often restricted to one study or a single region, the findings with respect to young people were 'the most disturbing of the lot, because they suggest that governments are ignoring, if not promoting a new generation of problem gamblers' (ibid.).

Many agencies are reluctant to take gambling revenues from government because they feel it would make them complicit in creating problem gamblers. After all, as service providers they would be called upon to address, as clients, the very people whose money they received from gambling. The conflict of interest is too severe.

The response of government, in general, is to develop modest programs for problem gamblers, though these are rarely adequate to meet the needs. Some deal only with gambling, essentially ignoring the impact on the individual's environment. Funding tends to come directly from gambling profits rather than from provincial ministries of health or social services, thereby creating further conflicts for service providers.

4. Agencies that receive government funding from gambling revenues become *dependent* on government in a way they were not when they operated their own similar activities to raise funds. Before the rapid expansion of government-run gambling following the 1969 Criminal Code amendments, charities and not-for-profit organizations were virtually the sole providers of legal gambling activities in Canada. To compensate for crowding out these agencies, four provincial governments developed programs to share profits through gambling grant initiatives. These are often known as 'community chest' models, in some cases with ostensibly arm's-length bodies to allocate the revenues. For the receiving agencies, however, the freedom to generate their own money through gaming activities has been replaced by a dependence on the whim of government. Initiatives deemed unacceptable to the political branch of government, for whatever reason, might not be funded, regardless of merit. The freedom of using unencumbered gambling funds for new or creative initiatives can be replaced by a cautious institutional mentality to avoid rocking the boat.

In British Columbia, resistance to the community chest model has been widespread among social agencies because of a fear of political interference. Granting foundations, it is feared, might be given too much control over the activities of the recipient agencies, and this could lead to even greater government interference in their direct operation (Campbell, 2000). These fears came to pass with the politicization of the charitable grant-awarding Trillium Foundation in Ontario: Trillium formerly dispensed lottery profits to community agencies in a relatively non-partisan way. More recently, the Foundation has been stacked with political appointments, the executive director was fired, and the entire process came to be seen as part of the patronage apparatus of the Conservative government.

5. Questions have been raised about the long-term *stability and predictability* of gambling revenues for governments and for the agencies that receive this money through government. When gambling revenues started to yield substantial income to government, there was a reluctance to use revenues for core or spending activities, as the money came from unstable and uncertain sources that might decline or vary capriciously. As a result, lottery monies were often spent on visible projects such as building hockey rinks in small towns, while basic government services were in need. More recently, the pools of money available have introduced new competitors for the gambling dollars. These have included First Nations communities that have claimed sovereignty on their reserves, the National Hockey League, and for-profit companies offering gambling over the Internet.[13]

There is also some evidence that the public's appetite for gambling may be limited, if the relatively minor growth in lottery revenues after 1992 and the strong resistance to VLTs in many communities are a signal. This may create problems both for provincial governments, who have become dependent on gambling revenues, and for the charitable organizations that receive the gambling grants.

6. *Crime*[14] often is alleged to be related to the expansion of gambling activities. Although there is no clear empirical evidence of an increase in crime in communities that host casinos (Henrikson, 1996), this may reflect deficiencies in reporting and data collection. Key informant interviews with police officials in western Canada report that 'some forms of illegal gambling are flourishing because the activity has lost its social stigma' (Smith and Wynne, 1999). As well, both police and the courts are largely ignoring it. One Ontario respondent claimed that revenues from illegal gambling in the province were 34 times higher than legal gambling revenues (ibid.). Industry officials question these numbers, suggesting the police are arguing from self-interest to secure more resources for their own operations.

Locations such as casinos and racetracks may well serve as magnets for prostitution and money laundering; however, easy access to legal off-track betting and gaming premises may reduce the need for bookies and illegal card games. But we simply do not know the extent or cost of illegal gambling activities in Canada.

7. Legalized gambling may create some jobs, but for the most part these are *poor jobs*. Though the gambling industry—particularly in casinos—is labour-intensive, the jobs are typically of poorer quality. One study by Statistics Canada (cited in Strick, 1999) found that only 69 per cent of casino jobs were full-time, compared to 81 per cent in non-gambling work. In 1999, full-time hourly wages in gambling were $16.19 for men and $14.66 for women, compared to the averages of $18.58 and $15.32, respectively, for non-gambling industries (Marshall, 2000). The high incidence of part-time work and low full-time wages is associated with female employment: women held 56 per cent of all jobs in gambling, compared to 46 per cent of all jobs in other industries. (In 1992, women held 65 per cent of all gambling jobs.)

Spillover work in the local community is also uncertain. Except for hotels offering accommodation to out-of-town gamblers, there appears to be little additional benefit to local communities. In a city such as Windsor, even the accommodation gain may be slight, as many gamblers are day-trippers from the Detroit area. Furthermore, profits from the provincially run casinos tend to be retained by the provincial government, with little sharing with the host communities.

Strick (1999) has pointed out that the economic benefit to a local community depends not on how much casino revenue is generated, but on where the money comes from. A casino must draw at least 50 per cent of its customers from outside the immediate area in order to bring net economic benefit for the community. For the locals, spending in casinos may simply displace other spending that might have brought greater economic benefit to the community. (This is even more problematic with VLTs in small towns, as we shall see.) The casinos in Montreal and Winnipeg do not meet the 50 per cent criterion, while those in Niagara Falls and Windsor do: over 80 per cent of patrons and about 90 per cent of gross revenues in Windsor are estimated to come from the United States; in Winnipeg and Montreal, 75 per cent and 95 per cent of customers, respectively, were local.

## Video Lottery Terminals

VLTs are undoubtedly the most problematic element in the gaming picture in Canada and have been the focus of ongoing public concern. They have been described as the 'crack cocaine of gambling'. As the National Council of Welfare (1996) has stated, 'No skill or knowledge is required to play. A single "hit" costs very little, but playing tends to be addictive.'

VLTs are fast and easy to play, widely distributed in bars and restaurants, and particularly popular in small towns. The Canada West Foundation (2001) notes that printing out the winnings rather than paying out cash immediately 'has the effect of psychologically separating the player from the amount won/lost or wagered'.

VLTs were not introduced to Canada because the public wanted or demanded them. Rather, they were seen as another means of generating income for governments that were becoming insatiable in their quest for gambling revenues. But there was resistance. Initially, New Brunswick, Prince Edward Island, and Nova Scotia placed the terminals in locations such as bowling alleys, making gambling too available to young people and children. The remaining provinces located VLTs only in age-restricted (usually liquor-licensed) premises. By 2000, the Maritime provinces had fallen in line with this policy.

Between 1995 and 1998, several provinces placed limits on the number of VLTs permitted in the province and the number of machines permitted in any one location. (This ensured a lucrative return for those individuals currently operating the machines, as future competition would be restricted.) Though these caps were introduced in response to public concern about overly easy access to VLTs, the three Prairie provinces expanded the numbers of slot machines in licensed casinos after they imposed the cap on the VLTs.

There has also been extensive reliance on public consultation regarding VLTs, a process most unusual in the Canadian context. Municipalities in Manitoba, Alberta, and Prince Edward Island have conducted local referenda, and both Ontario and BC chose not to introduce VLTs after municipal voters indicated their disapproval. In May 2001 New Brunswick held a province-wide referendum on the removal of all VLTs: the decision was to retain them, albeit by a small margin. (Many local elections in Ontario in 1997 contained referenda on the establishment of Las-Vegas type casinos; more than 50 communities, including Toronto, London, and Peterborough, voted against, often by 2-to-1 margins.)

After 35 Alberta communities voted on the removal of VLTs in 1997–8, surveys reported people's reasons for their preferences. Among those who indicated they voted to keep the VLTs, two-thirds (66 per cent) cited 'freedom of choice' and the 'right to gamble'. This reasoning assumes that any harm associated with VLTs was freely accepted by players making informed choices. Given the generally conservative political orientation of Alberta residents, we may question whether 'freedom of choice' would be deemed as important elsewhere in Canada. Those opposed cited the high social cost of VLTs (29 per cent), the fact that VLTs are addictive (21 per cent), the fact that they personally know a problem gambler (16 per cent), and that VLTs lower the overall quality of life (13 per cent).

A national survey was undertaken in 1999 on Canadian gambling attitudes. Asked whether they would like to see more, or fewer, restrictions on gambling in their own province, respondents in Atlantic Canada were the most strongly against gambling: 60 per cent wanted more restrictions, compared to 34-49 per cent elsewhere. Atlantic Canada was also the most strongly anti-VLT, because of the social and economic costs to families. It came as a surprise when voters in New Brunswick opted to retain their VLTs in May 2001.

## First Nations Gambling

On-reserve gambling in Canada is permitted only by licence from the relevant provincial gaming authority under the Criminal Code. Currently, First Nations have the right to operate on-reserve VLT gambling in Manitoba and Nova Scotia. They operate casinos in Saskatchewan and British Columbia, and they share in the profits of Ontario's on-reserve Casino Rama. Many First Nations are seeking expansion of their gambling authority, including Criminal Code amendments to eliminate the requirement of provincial licensing.

Supporters of First Nations operation of gambling facilities emphasize the potential economic gains that they believe will accrue: increased tourism and other spillover benefits, new jobs, and direct revenues for the bands. On the other hand, gambling on reserves may create high levels of problem gambling (and alcohol addiction) within the bands and dependency on the part of the bands on gambling revenues, which may be transient as new or more attractive gambling venues 'steal away' the business. Existing economic activities and local incomes may also be harmed as resources and interest are diverted to the new gambling.

A national survey of attitudes towards gambling (Azmier, 2000) found considerable support for on-reserve gambling among the public at large: 52 per cent of respondents agreed with on-reserve gambling; only 34 per cent disagreed. Support was highest in Ontario (57 per cent), with other regions at 48–49 per cent. When asked if 'gambling creates opportunities for economic development on Aboriginal/Indian Reserves', 42 per cent of respondents replied in the affirmative. This suggests that while more than half the respondents supported on-reserve gambling, not all supporters believed it would bring economic benefits, presumably noting the social costs that might be involved.

## NOTES

1. Once a severe dependence on or addiction to gambling develops, the process may no longer be voluntary. But at the outset the choice as to whether to gamble is a free one. Recipients of social assistance may be required to volunteer through workfare-type programs as a condition of receiving their benefits. Such participation is coercive and not truly voluntary, and is not included in our discussion.
2. The voluntary sector, of course, does not rely solely on volunteers. There are paid staff, who can be well paid and unionized, though in general compensation levels are modest.
3. The 'career length' of volunteers in particular settings varies widely, so that overall it is often not worthwhile to provide lengthy and detailed training for volunteers.
4. Both of these estimates include a category known as 'gifts to the Crown'.
5. Donations can be either in cash or in-kind. There are occasional difficulties in assigning valuations for in-kind donations. Individuals can use tax receipts for up to 75 per cent of net income in any single year, but unused receipts can be carried forward to a future year. The 75 per cent ceiling does not apply in the case of 'gifts to the Crown'.
6. A charitable donation of $300 would receive a tax credit (reduction in taxes payable) of $63: 17 per cent of $200 (= $34) plus 29 per cent of $100 (= $29).

7. The first primarily carries out charitable activities; the latter two fund such activities. Private foundations are more tightly controlled (by a single family, for example) with more restricted sources of income. They are therefore likely to act according to the wishes of that controlling unit/family. Both types of foundations must spend at least 4.5 per cent of their assets (capital) each year.

8. There is an interesting discussion document from CCRA on the conditions for community economic development (CED) projects to qualify for charitable status. See CCRA (1999).

9. This problem is exacerbated by the Social Union Framework Agreement (SUFA), which calls for greater involvement of NGOs 'at the table'.

10. A 1977 information circular from Revenue Canada (1977: 2) stated that the advancement of education 'may include the dissemination of a philosophy . . . provided it is not pernicious or subversive of morality.'

11. An Ontario study based on a survey of 800 elementary schools (Brown, 2001) found that fundraising generated about $33 million in 2001. While the overall average was $9,940 (an increase of 39 per cent over three years), some schools raised as much as $100,000. The top 10 per cent of schools raised as much funds as the bottom 70 per cent combined.

12. Of course, only a minority of adults, many of whom live on fixed or low incomes, play these VLTs.

13. Over 50 countries around the world, including the United Kingdom, the European Union, South Africa, and the Caribbean and Australasian regions, permit legalized on-line gambling. An estimated US $2 billion is now spent on Internet gaming worldwide, an amount that more than tripled between 1998 and 2001.

14. Gambling can be categorized under three headings: *regulated games* (casinos, lotteries, VLTs, casinos, etc.), which typically operate with a provincial licence or are directly run by provincial authorities; *unregulated games* (card games with friends, sports pools, games of skill such as darts, Internet gambling, and stock speculation); and *illegal gambling* (bets with bookies or unlicensed VLTs).

## SUGGESTED READING

Bridge, Richard. 2000. *The Law of Advocacy by Charitable Organizations: The Case for Change*, prepared for Institute for Media, Policy and Civil Society. Vancouver, Sept.
An excellent summary of the law as it affects charitable organizations and their advocacy activities.

Canada Customs and Revenue Agency (CCRA). 2000. *Registered Charities: Education, Advocacy and Political Activities*. Ottawa: CCRA, RC4107E Draft #2, 19 May.

Revenue Canada. 1987. *Registered Charities—Ancillary and Incidental Political Activities*, Information Circular 87–1. Ottawa, 25 Feb.

Revenue Canada. 1978. *Registered Charities: Political Objects and Activities*, Information Circular 78–3. Ottawa, 27 Feb.

Revenue Canada. 1977. *Registered Charities*, Information Circular 77–14. Ottawa, 30 June.
These official documents from the federal government are essential reading for any registered charity concerned about its tax status or contemplating political action.

Canada West Foundation <www.cwf.ca>

A multi-year project on gambling in Canada has produced many detailed reports on the causes, impacts, and consequences of gambling in Canada. Most can be downloaded from the CWF Web site.

*ISUMA: Canadian Journal of Policy Research.* 2001. 'Volunteering', vol 2, no 2 (Summer).

This special issue of the journal presents a wide-ranging overview of many issues affecting volunteers, voluntarism, and the voluntary sector in Canada.

National Survey of Giving, Volunteering, and Participating (NSGVP). 1998, 2001. *Caring Canadians, Involved Canadians.* Ottawa:Statistics Canada, Catalogue no. 71-542-XIE

These two national surveys, conducted by Statistics Canada on behalf of several organizations that promote voluntarism, contain the most comprehensive data on charitable giving and voluntary activity in Canada.

# PART V

# Conclusion

In the final chapter we draw together many of the themes introduced earlier and look to the future. We begin with an assessment of the state of social policy in Canada today. The weaknesses and limitations of the big, impersonal welfare state are recounted in a context of globalization and transnational corporations. The outcome has been increasing reliance on families, communities, the third or voluntary sector, and, of course, the for-profit world. Earlier notions of community and collective well-being are at grave risk.

A central theme of this chapter—and indeed of the entire book—is that policy implies choice and that economic policy, viewed as a subset of a broader social policy, presents us with choices exactly comparable to those we face in designing the most modest of social programs.

Numerous constraints hinder the development of progressive social policy in Canada, ranging from tax-cutting obsessions in federal and provincial governments, widespread disengagement from participatory democratic processes, and a tightly controlled and highly conservative media to the Social Union Framework Agreement, NAFTA, and the globalizing forces of the World Trade Organization (WTO). But our hands are never tied: *policy—both economic and social—involves choice*.

Accepting the continuance of a primarily market-based economy as probable, even if not necessarily desirable, the chapter returns to an earlier theme of making the market work better. The premises underlying the market model are often merely *assumed* rather than *assured*, and a radical agenda of empowerment is here presented to assist vulnerable and dependent people to exercise all the rights and prerogatives of capable consumers in a market economy. This entails extensive personal supports for autonomous decision-making as well as adequate financial resources to make the theoretical market assumption of free choice real and meaningful to all in practice.

We then look at the outlines of what a new, welfare *society* in Canada might encompass in terms of both participatory processes leading to social inclusion and substantive outcomes to redress gross inequalities in wealth, income, and human resources.

The chapter then moves to the international stage, looking at the constraints—and opportunities—of globalization. We note that the models of NAFTA and the WTO do not represent the only way forward, but that there are alternative paths, including that of the European Community. *Policy—globally as well as nationally—involves choice*.

The book concludes by arguing that action must follow from choice. While the likelihood of making choices that differ fundamentally from those of the United States may not be possible for a small and economically dependent country such as Canada, there are always choices, in all policy decisions. There is always some room to manoeuvre, even if it is slight. And perhaps we won't know just how much space there is to exercise real choice until we make the effort and see what happens.

# CHAPTER TEN

# Looking Ahead

*If you believe you can spoil, believe you can fix.*
Rabbi Nachman of Bratslau

## INTRODUCTION

As we look back over half a century of welfare state activity in Canada, there is reason to feel a modest sense of accomplishment. At the same time, the speed and ease of retreat from what we achieved are cause for disappointment and concern.

We never developed comprehensive income security for all Canadians, as might have emerged from a guaranteed income, nor did we systematically address our other social needs. We never made the commitment to stable, secure, well-paying jobs for all, which would have obviated the need for many existing social programs, and we never acknowledged that under capitalism much of the welfare state is second best, far behind meaningful employment as the preferred path.

What we did, using government as our agent, was to cobble together a patchwork of programs, initiatives, and activities that, taken as a whole, offered a degree of protection to much of the population. And what we managed to accomplish was achieved while holding firm to the basic principles of capitalism and the market economy. We tinkered at the edges to make things a little better, but never confronted the fundamental inequities of the free enterprise banner. What we put in place was far superior to that offered in the United States or Japan, but distinctly less than was found in most of Western Europe.

We built incrementally from the end of World War II until the world energy crisis following the Yom Kippur war of 1973 between Israel and the Arab states, when the pendulum began to swing back. Indeed, the beginning of the end for our welfare state arrived before we had ended the beginning! No longer was there a general consensus to build together and to fill in the more incongruous gaps in the Canadian welfare state.

Governments began to talk of deficits and national debt, of runaway inflation alongside stubbornly high levels of unemployment, of looming threats to the currency and indeed to the capitalist state itself—unless government spending could be brought under control.

According to the neo-liberals, whose ideas came to dominate public discourse, the solution included severe restraint on public spending, an explicit link between the receipt of service and payment, the accelerated introduction of fees for public services, and the use of referenda to sanction public spending. The effect of this approach was to weaken seriously the concept of an altruistic social policy supported by a social consensus, replacing it with a more formal mechanistic delineation of the collective good as being that which people individually or collectively want and are prepared to pay for, either through voting for taxes or through the private market.

Undoubtedly, part of the success in recent years of the anti-social welfare crusade drew on a loss of public confidence in what the welfare state did—or did not—accomplish. Debates over high levels of government spending amid perceptions of waste and inappropriate targeting of public spending (which was often based on political considerations rather than on a clear understanding of needs) led to eminently fair questions about what the public got in return for the taxes spent on social welfare measures. Poverty was not ended in Canada, people were still homeless, and racism and discrimination did not abate.

There were other criticisms of the welfare state as well, at times emanating from within the ranks of its own supporters. The original welfare state, as developed in Britain, was highly bureaucratic, with little room for public or consumer input. Civil servants, cynically labelled as both omnipotent and omniscient, were assumed to know better what the public needed than the people themselves did—even if this was not what the people wanted. The post-war welfare state, as imported to Canada, contained these same central weaknesses of over-bureaucratization and relative insensitivity to consumer input.

While this world view may have been acceptable in the immediate aftermath of a world war that had been won by bureaucratic planning without particular public input, such an approach was widely unacceptable as early as the 1960s. The welfare state, as originally developed, had difficulty adapting to a changed public and political climate. Civil servants were now seen as cogs in a large bureaucratic machine, too detached from the public to know—or care—what the people thought or wanted, and far too concerned with enhancing their own empires within the public service.

The social democratic left—a loose phrase to describe the traditional supporters of the welfare state—was in some sense left holding the bag. As those opposed to the welfare state made great gains with their anti-statist message, the supporters had developed no viable alternatives to the status quo and thus were put in the uncomfortable position of defending a welfare state about which they, too, had serious doubts. Because 'big government' had earlier been viewed as the only agency with the capacity to implement social policy on a universal, non-stigmatizing basis, the social democratic left continued—for perhaps far too long—to support it, often solely for the lack of a feasible alternative. They (or 'we') tended to discount empirical evidence that has long made clear that the big welfare state did not and would not fulfill its early promises, as government redistribution often benefited the wealthy at the expense of the poor and middle classes. As shown in Richard Titmuss's original iceberg of social welfare (Chapter 2), the hidden or submerged parts—occupational, fiscal (and corporate) welfare—have become ever larger, with their highly regressive impacts, while we did not notice (or acknowledge) that the social welfare tip of the iceberg was melting away before our eyes.

With more modest goals, our welfare state at its height arguably might have succeeded. But these were not the benchmarks against which it was being assessed. When its supporters (through their enthusiasm) and its opponents (through their wish to eliminate) both attributed more grandiose expectations to the welfare state, more grand than could ever be achieved through the programs envisaged or delivered, then failure was essentially assured. With powerful opponents on a moral crusade, and with supporters who were often ambivalent, the post-war welfare state had little chance.

It is clear in retrospect that the early proponents of the welfare state underestimated the importance of pressure groups and public input in the development and delivery of welfare programs, while overstressing formal political accountability. The concept of 'social' cannot be simply operationalized in terms of the state (bureaucracy) or the legislature without listening to the voice of the broader community. Government bureaucracies became increasingly impregnable and inaccessible as the political and bureaucratic process, in all too many cases, came to be seen as simply pursuing its own private agendas.

> The social construction of altruistic public policies battling against egoistic economic policies, cf. David against Goliath, falls down if David is not all he is cracked up to be, is in the pay of Goliath, and the whole confrontation is staged to bolster the morale of the troops. (Walker, 1981)

Because its supporters were, for a long time, unwilling to write off the welfare state, efforts were focused on capturing (or recapturing) the state apparatus to serve once again as an agent of the collective will. In recent years, however, as the federal and even more the provincial governments pursued neo-liberal agendas, the prospect of the big and benevolent state acting as an agent of altruistic social policy has largely disappeared from the public radar screen.

For nearly 20 years governments in Canada talked the talk of deficit reduction but were unable or unwilling to walk the walk, and it was not until the infamous deficit-slashing budget of 1995 with its wide cuts to social programs, combined with the drastic reductions to Employment Insurance, that the fiscal house of Canada was finally brought in order. A deficit of $28 billion that the Liberals inherited in 1993 became a surplus of $20 billion by fiscal year 2000–1. The human price of this victory, however, was high. In March 2000, three-quarters of a million Canadians were using food banks, and 40 per cent of them were children. Lightman and Mitchell (2000b) interpreted the situation:

> For the last five years, Canada has engaged in all-out war against the deficit—the military analogy is always used in discussions about the deficit—and has succeeded . . . faster than many of us would have thought possible, or desirable. But there were casualties along the way. Services and programs that middle-income Canadians relied upon deteriorated or were eliminated entirely: public education is in crisis, and health care is in disarray. For upper income groups there is the option of the private school or the quick trip to the hospital in Buffalo; for the rest,

there is nothing. Incomes at middle and lower levels have been essentially flat for the past five years, but costs have gone up—new and creative fees where there were none before; the end of junior kindergarten in Ontario . . . resulting in the forced exit from the paid labour force for some parents and exorbitant private sector child care fees for others. The poorly housed have become marginally housed, or homeless. Children in Toronto live in sleazy motels. . . .

Throughout this war on the deficit, our upper income generals stayed home, relatively insulated from the fray below. It is the middle and lower income families who were the foot-soldiers in this battle—the 'grunts' as they were called in Viet Nam. They were told that once the battle was won, their day in the sun would come. A budget surplus would permit redress for all the damage done during the war. Jerusalem was just over the next hill.

Well, the war is over and victory declared. And Jerusalem is nowhere to be seen. The terms of debate have changed. Still there is no real money to compensate for the past cuts. The poorest are given little, as usual, with even their child benefit supplement taken away by rapacious provincial governments; the middle income households get maybe $10 or $15 a week (by 2004) and are told to fend for themselves in our newly privatized social world . . . (while) upper income taxpayers walk away with the gold.

It would be a mistake to attribute the effective end of Canada's welfare state to the imperatives of fiscal policy. Within the broad post-war social consensus that helped to develop our social programs, there were always points of dissent—individuals, groups, and provinces that did not endorse our collective social interventions. And coming north across the border was the incessant cry for individualism and the private market.[1] Through the 1980s the ideas of individualism increasingly filtered into the Canadian consciousness. The Free Trade Agreement of 1988 (later reinforced by NAFTA) accelerated the economic integration of the two countries—and with economic integration came a social fusion as well. Canadians watched American television and received their news from American wire services, or from domestic sources whose ownership usually tilted far to the right. The space for dissenting views, not only on the left but even near the middle of the road, became severely restricted.

By the time the deficit was 'conquered' in Canada, the terms of the national debate had fundamentally altered. What had begun two decades earlier as a technical response to the structural economic problem of deficit reduction had evolved into an ideological assault on the welfare stare and all that it stood for. Government spending became undesirable, not on economic grounds, but rather on purely normative grounds: people *should* look after their own needs; collective responses to social problems were *morally and ethically wrong*. The value base of residualism became the correct value base for Canada in the new century.

In this fundamental paradigm shift Canada was not alone, nor were we the only country to experience the impact of American ideological dominance and the tentacles of the large transnational corporations. Globalization became a seemingly irresistible mantra for the hegemony of the market. Yet, in this worldwide diffusion of rugged individualism, pockets of dissent remained and nagging doubts about the desirability of it all began to spread. Seattle, and the other global protests, talked to the need for a process based on legitimacy, openness, and transparency: world leaders could no longer go behind closed doors and divide up the global pie according to their respective strengths and appetites. The protests also challenged the fundamental premises of globalization itself: as Marx predicted so long ago, the continued aggrandizement of the rich, the accelerated exclusion of the poor, and the distance between them began to place stress on the very foundations of the capitalist state. The attacks on the World Trade Center and the Pentagon showed some of the consequences—and dangers—of globalization that had not been anticipated by its proponents.

Economic class and the hard, cruel reality of growing, grinding poverty in every society dismissed post-modernist notions of fluidity and uncertainty. Domestically, we saw the results of our embrace of the market: the gaps between rich and poor widened to levels unknown in this country since the days of the Great Depression, and these gaps—chasms, actually—were paralleled by widening differentials in income, power, and social inclusion between men and women, young and old, more able and lesser abled, immigrant and native-born, white and non-white, non-Aboriginal and Aboriginal. Social and health problems, ranging from senior poverty to tuberculosis, reappeared, years after we thought they had been permanently eradicated.

## POLICY MEANS CHOICE

In Chapters 2 and 3 we explored our definition of social policy, arguing that it represents a broad umbrella, subsuming within it what we commonly think of as economic policy. Economic policy is a subset of social policy, and all social policy involves choice: no absolute economic imperatives tie our hands and preclude debate over alternatives and options. Economic policy involves choices, just as do decisions about whether to allocate social benefits universally or selectively, as cash or in-kind.

When it became clear that the federal deficit would be eliminated, with the provinces not far behind, Prime Minister Chrétien promised that any future surplus would be divided into three equal parts: one-third to new spending, one-third to tax cuts, and one-third to paying down the accumulated debt—an attempt to reflect what he saw as the radically differing views among Canadians about future governmental priorities.[2]

A whole new set of questions appeared on the table. With the fiscal books in reasonably good shape and the Quebec situation relatively quiet, Canadians had an opportunity to contemplate and discuss the way forward. Would we attempt to create some new form of welfare society, building on the best of what we earlier had produced collectively? Or would we boldly continue on the path of the free market, minimizing government to the point of irrelevance?

Several major constraints influence this potential debate, which, regrettably, seems never to have occurred in Canada:

- The 2000 budgets of Paul Martin offered 'the largest tax cuts in Canadian history', largely targeted to upper-income Canadians. Chrétien's earlier agenda (if it was in fact that) was hijacked as the focus shifted to whether Ottawa would be able to meet its various existing spending obligations, without even contemplating new undertakings. The federal policy choice came down firmly on the side of tax cuts, at the expense of rebuilding our tattered infrastructure and restoring our social entitlements. With the shift to increased defence and security spending after September 2001, there seemed even less room for new social initiatives.

- The Social Union Framework Agreement (SUFA) between Ottawa and the provinces effectively tied the federal government's hands in regard to new federal initiatives in this country. The requirement for substantial provincial support before Ottawa undertakes a wide range of new spending activities has given great power to the conservative provinces (though this has been offset to some extent by SUFA's requirements that civil society be at the negotiating table). Ottawa is at risk of becoming nothing more than banker for provincial priorities. Believers in the importance of a strong central government in a federal state were dealt a potentially fatal blow.

- Reinforcing this limit on Ottawa's power from below is globalization from above. Both in the general sense and as manifest specifically in the Free Trade Agreement (and NAFTA), international obligations now severely limit Ottawa's ability to introduce new social initiatives, even were it able to secure the needed provincial support. Though it is now widely understood that medicare represents only part of the needed health-care system in Canada, complementary initiatives to add home care and prescription drugs would likely run afoul of the NAFTA constraints and would entail prohibitively high payments to US-based commercial corporations currently—or potentially—working in these areas.

- The media in Canada are among the most tightly controlled in the Western world. Older publishing empires—Thompson, Hollinger, Southam—have given way to newer conglomerates—Bell Globemedia, Shaw, CanwestGlobal, Videotron-Quebecor, Rogers—that cross the traditional lines between visual and print media, between entertainment and information dissemination. With the inconsistent exception of the *Toronto Star* (Torstar), virtually all private media ownership is conservative in orientation and corporate in its view of the public good. Even the CBC is careful not to offend its political masters. Dissenting voices (such as Web-based newspapers and magazines) exist but are often unheard, drowned in the sea of mainstream conservative views. Other major countries such as Britain, the United States, and France host a much wider array of political perspectives within their mainstream media.

- The parliamentary process in Canada seems at risk of lapsing into irrelevance: the continued lack of a viable Opposition, not only in Ottawa but in several provincial capitals as well, denies the accountability that every government should face. Government by opinion poll moves all parties in the same direction, and big money seems able to set political priorities more effectively and openly than in the past. There is little room for dissent, particularly from the centre-left. The effective demise of the NDP has removed the most articulate advocate for the welfare state and its programs.

- There has been a loss of what political scientist Henry Milner (2001) refers to as *civic literacy* in Canada: a general decline in civic involvement; less participation in community-based organizations; lower voter turnout; and reduced levels of political awareness. A broad disengagement from the electoral and political processes is the inevitable result.

## Four Scenarios

We have argued that the embrace of the market in Western countries has been based largely on an ideological faith in the supremacy of unconstrained market principles, notwithstanding empirical evidence to the contrary. Yet, the theoretical assumptions that underlie the market, as we saw in Chapter 3, are regularly violated in practice and rarely, if ever, are fully met in the real world. The assumption of mobility for the labour force would require that if people working in the fishery become unemployed in Newfoundland and there are jobs in Calgary, then they are both willing and able to transport themselves (and presumably their families) to take advantage of the opportunities. A single mother on welfare is informed of a job in her town and is assumed able to take it unencumbered by problems of transportation, child care, or limited work experience. The assumption of many sellers competing in a market must seem a cruel joke to the individual seeking affordable housing in Vancouver or, indeed, to almost anyone trying to 'shop around' for medical care. Nevertheless, governments increasingly are withdrawing from the provision of services, and consumers are left to meet their own needs through the private market.

Typically, there may be four responses when the theory of the market does not correspond to the real world:

- *If the theory doesn't fit the world, ignore the world.* This is the 'ostrich' response, by which the society symbolically puts its head in the ground and ignores what is happening. In the case of the single mother seeking child care, we simply assume she is able to make arrangements that are suitable to her needs. It's her problem, and the rest of us need not become involved. With respect to psychiatric survivors, we declare them competent consumers in a market economy upon discharge from hospital. We give them inadequate social assistance and a firm handshake, as we wish them well: definitionally competent consumers in a market economy. We proceed *as if* families are available, willing and able to help, and *as if* the beleaguered voluntary sector is able to meet the increasing demands in the face of dramatically shrinking fiscal and human resources. Thus ends our collective obligation, regardless of whether anyone is available to help, and despite the empirical evidence showing the damage done by our abandonment of vulnerable people.
- *If the theory doesn't fit the world, it doesn't really matter, because it's close enough.* In this view, the market assumptions need not be fully satisfied; rather, it is sufficient if they are adequately (or nearly or sufficiently) satisfied. They may be 'close enough' for practical purposes. In Chapter 3 we noted that Margaret Thatcher advised people to shop comprehensively for the best prices; yet, in practice, one need not have full information about all prices everywhere, but a sampling of prices, perhaps limited to one's own neighbourhood, would be good enough. In more general terms, the assumption would be that the private market adequately provides for most people, supplemented where necessary by *some* family support and voluntary activity. Those presumably few people who are excluded are either lazy (and therefore not worthy of our help) or not responsible for their dependence (and therefore deserving).
- *If the theory doesn't fit the world, forget about the theory.* In some cases we can decide that the market is not the correct way to make decisions or to exercise choice. We can

reach this conclusion on grounds of efficiency (private health care is wasteful and costly, as the US experience shows) or on normative grounds (it is morally or ethically undesirable to use the private market to meet certain needs). In the current struggle to protect medicare and to prevent the further intrusion of US-style for-profit health care, the market is rejected on both efficiency grounds (with massive empirical evidence in support) and on normative grounds (every legitimate poll in Canada shows the overwhelming majority of the population favours medicare over any alternative market-based approach). Also, we can simply decide that quality child care should be made available to all who desire it, outside the private for-profit sector. Perhaps it could be structured as a downward extension of junior kindergarten, available as a right and funded out of educational taxes. It would not be a commodity, bought and sold in the private market.

• *If the theory doesn't fit the world, change the world.* This is perhaps the least recognized alternative, but it is also the most radical in many ways. Given the overwhelming dominance of residual/market values in contemporary society, this may be the most viable and exciting avenue to redressing the vast inequalities in society. The approach holds that the market may not be the optimal allocation mechanism in society, but it is in place and represents the preferred redistributive mechanism for many; hence, the challenge is to make it work better. There are two distinct aspects to this argument. First, the market works better if we assist people to become informed and competent consumers; second, the market works better if an actual range of service alternatives exists from which consumers can choose.

As we saw earlier, the theoretical market assumptions about consumers are often not upheld. To make the market work better would entail substantial collective interventions, the introduction of programs and initiatives that recognize that people must have information; they must have mobility; they must have assistance, if desired, in assessing available alternatives; and perhaps most important of all, they must have resources to exercise meaningful choice. *Freedom to choose must be real and operational, and not merely theoretical.*

Thus, substantial spending (investment) on vulnerable people is necessary, specifically so they can function better as consumers in a market economy and exercise informed choice.[3] Resources must be distributed so we can all have the means to meet our own needs in the private market.

Operationally, this notion means fundamental change in how we approach vulnerability and dependence and address issues of oppression. It implies that psychiatric survivors would have a *right* to support and assistance to enable them to make their own decisions about how to live, rather than merely follow the dictates of an indifferent case manager or exploitive boarding-house landlord who holds the real decision-making authority. Survivors would also receive, as a *right,* incomes adequate to function in a market economy. Elderly people in long-term care facilities would no longer have their decision-making authority removed from them formally (through the appointment of substitute decision-makers) or informally (by offloading to families). Instead, they would receive support and assistance, from advocates and others, to maximize their capacity for autonomous action and decision-making. Health care must be equally accessible to all, without two tiers of service. All people vulnerable and dependent on the state would be entitled to incomes sufficient to live in acceptable circumstances.

The single mother with a small child would no longer simply be told to show up for workfare on the assumption she has secured safe and reliable child care; instead, she would be assisted, financially and personally, to make suitable arrangements. She would be provided with the information, mobility, and resources to make an informed decision about what kind of child care she would like; and the child care must in fact be accessible. She would face the same range of alternatives from the same base of competence and resources as her middle-class counterpart, and ultimately she would be able to make the same type of informed choice that would best address her own and her child's individual needs.

The second condition for effective market operation is that there be a range of service providers so consumers can exercise choice. A demand-side response (enhancing the competence of consumers) is not always sufficient: purchasing power alone will not generate adequate and quality child-care places or housing. In certain areas, government must provide services directly or ensure that they are provided. In other cases, the third sector (voluntary agencies) will play a crucial role in responding to the needs and wishes of consumers within a framework of pluralism.

Monopoly provision—the big impersonal government agency of the early welfare state years—is no longer acceptable in today's context of pluralism and consumer empowerment. To make the market work better, consumers must have control of the services and benefits they receive, and meaningful control presupposes the availability of alternative suppliers. To some extent, as the market assumes, choice does become an end in itself.

# A NEW WELFARE SOCIETY?

In considering the outlines of where we might go in future, we choose to talk of a new welfare *society* rather than a welfare *state*. In part the difference is semantic, to suggest difference from what we created in the past and found wanting; in part, however, the distinction is substantive, in that *society* is broader and more comprehensive than *state*, encompassing the wider community (including the third sector) beyond the formal systems and structures of state provision. Some dislike the term *welfare* because of its Poor Law connotations of dependence and the dole, preferring terms such as *well-being*, but we shall hold to the traditional label, using *welfare* in its more inclusive sense of *faring (or doing) well*.

Here we consider what a new and refocused welfare society in Canada might contain. We situate this discussion in a context of continuing capitalism and substantial adherence to the private market.

## Enhanced Capacity for Consumers

As a precondition for any new welfare society, there must be a serious commitment to make the market work better, as described in the fourth alternative above. In particular, there must be increased support to individuals so they can function better as consumers in a market economy (in addition to their other identities such as citizens, parents, or members of an inclusionary society who have rights resulting from these statuses). This first and most essential step would involve strengthening market mechanisms to result in meaningful empowerment of consumers. Such a process would include adequate resources to exercise real choice in the marketplace, along with information and personal supports to enhance the personal capacity of consumers. Lifelong learning, as Judith Maxwell (2001) has argued, would become a fundamental right. The change in our collective attitudes, our thinking about, and behaviours towards vulnerable people would be fundamental and dramatic.

Without these needed resources and supports, consumer sovereignty has no meaning; choice is only theoretical without resources to act and supports to make informed choices. And without informed consumers with adequate resources to choose, the entire market process becomes a sham and a meaningless exercise.

Empowered consumers, on the other hand, have less need for an overt paternalism by governments and service providers. There would be less need for government to provide direct services and less obligation on the part of government to regulate and inspect what is delivered. As we saw in Chapter 4, government regulation—in nursing homes, for example, or in water safety—is replete with difficulties, as regulators tend to identify with those being regulated, and the consumer is left on the outside looking in. Legal procedures, such as an enforceable residents' bill of rights in nursing homes, will often do more to ensure quality outcomes than will unenforceable and unenforced regulations.

## Jobs, Not Welfare

We must directly confront the reality that a meagre welfare state is not a substitute for meaningful, secure, and adequately remunerated employment. The key to individual autonomy in a market system is a suitable job. We must move beyond adding layers of bandages (through disconnected social programs) and begin to address the root cause of the problem (which is a lack of suitable employment opportunities). This demands a national commitment to an effective jobs strategy, whereby every Canadian who wants a job will be guaranteed access to suitable work. There are many ways to approach such an ambitious target, but what is important is to start—by articulating the commitment and by moving in a credible way to achieve this goal. And once the process starts, we shall quickly find offsetting benefits, many of them in the form of reduced needs for ongoing public assistance and support.

## Government as Funder

We have seen that Ottawa's role in the contemporary welfare state has increasingly evolved in the direction of funder, rather than direct service provider. The federal tax system, as a mechanism for redistributing income, has great potential to address equity concerns in an efficient, effective, and non-stigmatizing manner. Canada was among the first countries to recognize the potential of delivering benefits through the tax system and continues to use this approach in a creative manner. The Canada Child Tax Benefit, for example, could be a powerful and progressive tool in the fight against child poverty were the levels of payment higher and the supplement not clawed back by most provinces. Future advocacy would be well directed to removing the clawback more than on extending eligibility or increasing benefit levels for current recipients (a task more easily said than done, in a context of increasing neo-liberalism at the provincial level).

The difficulties with the tax system as a primary redistributive mechanism are two. First, as we have seen, the redistribution is not always progressive in its impact: much tax expenditure, including all deductions and exemptions, and preferential treatment of non-wage income, such as dividends or capital gains, directs huge amounts of tax money up the income scale, towards the rich and very rich. The tax system as a redistributive tool is conceptually neutral in its impact: it can reallocate resources up or down the income hierarchy. The political challenge is to attack upward distribution (particularly when presented as across-the-board tax cuts) and to focus instead on progressive downward distribution.

The second difficulty is that excess reliance on income tax may eliminate other desirable social goals. The clawback of OAS from upper-income seniors, for example, has converted a horizontally redistributive program reflecting the generalized greater needs of seniors into an income support program for poor people who happen to be old. (Poor people who don't happen to be old must find some other designated category, such as disability, in order to qualify for income support.) The clawback of Employment Insurance benefits from workers with annual incomes over the threshold is another example of the same problem: a program to insure against the risks of unemployment has been transformed into an income support program for poor workers who happen to qualify for benefits (that are now paid for by other workers, rich and poor, who haven't qualified). Program goals must be identified more clearly and with greater transparency; program structures must meet these goals. Income support goals should be identified as such and not presented as measures to address horizontal equity, and goals of horizontal equity should be supported by program designs that will serve these purposes.

In recent years, some provinces have begun to assume increasing control over their own income and corporate tax systems. In these cases, the issues are the same as those facing Ottawa.

## Ottawa as Limited Service Provider and Provinces as Service Providers

For over two decades Ottawa has been engaged in a serious and continuing effort to extricate itself from direct service provision. It has offloaded responsibilities to the provinces, the voluntary sector, Aboriginal bands, individual households, and the for-profit market. To a substantial extent, the federal government has succeeded in this quest, with results that often are unacceptable.

In certain areas, most obviously the provision of affordable housing and quality child care, we have seen that the market does not work acceptably: demand in the form of adequate incomes does not create its own supply. A major government role remains for either directly providing certain services or assisting the not-for-profit sectors to do so. Only Ottawa has the financial capacity to meet these Canada-wide needs, but its role must be greater than merely providing income support to needy Canadians.

In some instances, such as public education, health (as reflected in medicare), and the delivery of certain personal social services, Canadians have repeatedly expressed their preference for direct governmental provision. Yet, program parameters in these areas often do not correspond with conceptual needs. Medicare, to use the most obvious example, covers only enumerated insured services, while ignoring non-medicalized health services, alternatives, and drugs and under-insuring home and community care. There is no national consensus on what services should be provided directly by governments, or which should be protected against the grasp of the for-profit world, but attempts by government to privatize and devolve 'by stealth' (to use Ken Battle's term) should be resisted pending a fuller national debate, and efforts should continue to expand those areas in which current provision is deficient.

## Ottawa as Rule-maker and Enforcer

With the devolution of service delivery responsibilities, Ottawa now has a severely reduced role in ensuring that federal program standards are met and maintained. In fact, with the Canada Health and Social Transfer (CHST) Ottawa has given up all federal standards except for the five medicare principles and the prohibition of provincial minimum residence requirements for social assistance benefits. With the passage of the Social Union Framework Agreement (SUFA) Ottawa has ceded its right to exercise meaningful leadership and has become in effect merely one government among many.

Decentralization has tilted the federal-provincial scales so far in favour of the latter that we are now barely a functioning federal state with divided responsibilities and distinct areas of jurisdiction. Instead, Ottawa has become virtually a conduit that collects money from individuals and transfers the resources, without conditions, to the provinces, where the real decisions are made. This is an unstable and inequitable arrangement for a federal state. Either we go further and effectively terminate the federal state, with the remaining functions such as national defence and the Bank of Canada conducted only on sufferance of the provinces, or, alternatively, we redress the imbalances and restore greater authority to Ottawa. The latter is of course the preferred path, notwithstanding the provincial resistance that is certain to emerge. Such a rebalancing might entail modifying or abrogating entirely the SUFA; it surely would also require reconsideration of an asymmetrical federalism to recognize the legitimate aspirations and needs of Quebec, while not paralyzing Ottawa entirely.

The suggestion to consider abandoning the SUFA is not made lightly or without recognition of the many political realities and pressures.[4] At the same time, the idea does point to the direction we must take if Canada is to remain a viable federal state. I am not suggesting that either Ottawa or the provinces are definitionally the best or proper voice of the collective will: closer to home does not necessarily imply more representative of the public (and besides, municipalities are even closer than the provinces). What we require is the restoration of federal leadership, which has been lost through the SUFA.

This rebalancing would involve a return by Ottawa to shared-cost or other program designs to give it a greater say in how needs are met across the country. Arguably, medicare remains in place, albeit frayed at the edges, because the federal government continues to ensure adherence to the original program principles; and similarly, medicare is so frayed at the edges largely because Ottawa has abdicated its responsibility to enforce these principles and standards.

## An Increased Role for Local Governments, Agencies, and Not-for-Profit Providers

The most common response to the insensitivity of the big welfare state has been to turn inward and downward, to focus on communities as more appropriate agents to express the collective will. If consensus is no longer possible at a national level perhaps it may still be found locally, and the integration that Boulding (1967) believed to be so essential for social policy development may only be possible within a smaller, more manageable unit.

The strength of this 'small is beautiful' approach is that it may provide a setting in which the altruistic element of human motivation can emerge and grow. Yet, it is unclear whether the local community has the capacity to lessen alienation and promote social integration. In other words, would societal units that permit true involvement by individuals necessarily be so small as to be essentially irrelevant?

Of course, the big welfare state was originally created in response to social problems that could not be solved at a local level, and this reality may still exist. A small community may promote social consensus, but there is no assurance of benevolence. The local community may be (and often is) based on elitism and exclusion. Indeed, in dealing with social problems, from racism to pollution, there is much evidence to suggest that local communities are either incapable or unwilling to extend their benevolent gaze beyond their immediate boundaries. The NIMBY (not in my backyard) phenomenon, which appears to grow as the state recedes, reflects just such a parochial view.

To the social democratic left, big government was essential to carry out the welfare state promise. Though it clearly failed to fulfill the dreams of its supporters—perhaps, in retrospect, the original promise was too grandiose—the current response of turning to local communities undoubtedly carries a risk of returning to the very problems that originally led to the need for a welfare state. These remain deeply intractable dilemmas.

## A Reduced Role for the Commercial Sector

There are few documented cases of for-profit service providers in health and the social services actually delivering a better product at a lower price than the not-for-profit sector. Commercial providers can cut costs, at least in the short term, but this typically results from lower wages and inferior benefits for staff, along with reduced quality of service.

Decisions by government to offload responsibilities to the commercial sector are generally driven by perceived short-term cost savings (which often result in higher long-term costs) and/or ideological aversion to not-for-profit delivery. Future battles will be waged on the ideological front, as the empirical debates have been substantially resolved in favour of not-for-profit delivery. And ideological struggles are difficult to win when power in society is distributed so unevenly and access to the media is so narrowly controlled.

## Increased Reliance on Taxes and Less Recourse to User Fees and Private Payment

Two competing principles that underlie any system of taxation—the *ability-to-pay* principle and the *benefit* principle—were noted in Chapter 7. A preference for one over the other results from prior normative decisions about equity and progressivity. Any new welfare society must build on principles of progressive redistribution, or else there is no point to the exercise. The benefit principle and the values of residualism that accompany this belong to the private market, where consumers pay for use. The ability-to-pay principle, linked to the values of the institutional welfare model, links payment for services to personal resources: those most able pay the most, and those least able pay less.

A central theme of this book has been the need to focus on progressivity both in the delivery of benefits and in the generation of resources to pay for the programs. Progressive delivery can be more than offset by regressive generation of funds, yielding a regressive net effect overall. Therefore, the importance of the ability-to-pay principle must be emphasized again, for in practice this principle translates to an improved personal tax system without many of its more regressive elements.

## Reinvigorated Structures of Participation

Widespread disengagement from the systems and processes of collective decision-making seriously imperils any movement towards greater social inclusion based on fundamental human rights. Electoral reform that encourages and promotes diverse views is central. Indeed, perhaps it is time to consider some variant of proportional representation in our legislatures to replace the current 'first-past-the-post' model that often denies a voice to the majority, while electing candidates with as little as a third of the vote.

Yet, a revamped electoral system, while necessary, would not be sufficient. We also need new fora through which to determine and articulate the collective will. Community meetings, town hall events, and resuscitated legislative procedures can all help to reconnect alienated citizens to the underlying processes of social inclusion.

The courts and certain administrative tribunals stand somewhat apart from these general trends: they serve as emerging fields of debate, contested terrain, in the struggles for both participation and progressive outcomes. They offer communities and groups an avenue to challenge arbitrary and capricious decisions on the part of unresponsive governments and bureaucracies. Charter challenges, for example, serve an important educational and consciousness-raising function, even if they are ultimately unsuccessful; they keep issues on the table and in the public eye, while the politicians and bureaucrats wish they would simply disappear. Offsetting this, however, is the reality that the courts in Canada are generally very conservative in orientation, and dramatic substantive breakthroughs are rare.

International conventions and treaties, while not formally binding on sovereign national governments, can nevertheless exercise strong moral force. When Canada signs a treaty (as is done on a regular basis), the federal government is making a national commitment to address a need or meet certain standards. These obligations provide benchmarks, at the very least, against which our subsequent actions can be assessed. Regrettably, the politicians and senior bureaucrats often seem to treat the signing of international accords and agreements as psychologically and operationally disconnected from any later requirement to do anything. But as long as the formal commitments are in place, there remains room for questioning and challenge on the part of groups and communities. International obligations cannot be entirely ignored as long as local communities have voice.

# LOOKING GLOBALLY

Although the concept of globalization is generally viewed with disfavour—and fear—by those who hold social programs to be important, the term is neutral. Globalization, at its simplest, refers to a process by which smaller units of governance and/or decision-making are integrated into larger units that cross national boundaries on a wide scale. Economic integration is inevitably involved, and political and/or social dimensions may also be encompassed. Globalization may represent the next step beyond regional groupings such as NAFTA and the European Union.

This integration, in principle, can be progressive or regressive, beneficial or harmful to the public at large: there are different models and approaches upon which to build. NAFTA, for example, was conceptualized as an economic treaty to integrate the economies of Canada, Mexico, and the United States. It was based on market principles following the national ideology of the United States, and did not directly include social or political concerns. The European Union (EU), by contrast, was explicitly based on economic integration that included social concerns, leading ultimately to political integration. Built into the original EU treaties were progressive social protections for workers and high minimum standards, well in excess of those in Canada or the United States. (The generous social and workplace benefits were at the core of much anti-European sentiment in the Thatcher government and the British Conservative Party, which wanted to protect the existing lower levels of benefits.)

A noted media baron has suggested that Britain should withdraw from the EU and join NAFTA because of its greater adherence to market principles and admirably lower levels of social protection. I would suggest, in response, that Canada should withdraw from NAFTA and join the EU, for the very same reasons—higher levels of social protection and less belief in the unconstrained market. (Perhaps we could even arrange a trade—Canada for Britain—thereby satisfying both parties and extending each treaty across the Atlantic.) The important point, however, is not what country is in which arrangement, but that there are different models of integration and there are choices that every country faces. Policy, as we have repeatedly indicated, implies choice, locally, nationally, and globally.

Much of the commentary outside the corporate world is gloomy on the topic of globalization: it is seen as irresistible, leading inexorably to worldwide dominance by the market, with its inevitable widening differentials between the rich and poor, between the powerful and the rest. To a large extent these sentiments are validated by current experiences, particularly with respect to poor and developing countries. But this does not follow from any inherent evil in globalization; rather, the specific forms of globalization chosen are the problem. Globalization to date is based overwhelmingly on the American ideology of individualism and residualism and on the interests of the transnational corporations. In principle at least, there can be alternative forms of globalization emphasizing inclusion rather than marginalization.

NAFTA, the apparent prototype of current and future globalization, eliminates national barriers for most commercial transactions (though not for individual migration). As a commercial treaty, NAFTA leaves unaddressed the question of how to treat social programs. Though Brian Mulroney assured Canadians in the lead-up to the original Canada-US Free Trade Agreement that our social programs were safe, events have proved otherwise. There are certain narrow exemptions from NAFTA for public health and social programs, though over time these, too, may well become tradable commodities, identical to oil and gas. Once a protected service crosses the line and is sold commercially, the exemption falls and the service becomes fully subject to NAFTA's commercial provisions.

This debate recalls our earlier discussion about whether or to what extent social and health services are different from goods and services bought and sold in the marketplace. Certainly, Titmuss's view that health and, by extension, many other social services and programs are not market commodities is reflected by those who opposed NAFTA or who argued for generous exemptions from its provisions. The contrary view, which appears to be dominant currently, is that exemptions should be few and limited in impact, and that social and health services should be treated no differently from other marketplace commodities. Much emotion has been focused on culture and whether it is simply another marketplace activity or something qualitatively distinct and necessary to Canada's political and social identity. Equally important and powerful are the debates over our entire array of social programs, particularly medicare (which is protected from NAFTA) and health care construed more broadly, the status of which appears to be more ambiguous.

Once a substantive area becomes subject to NAFTA, it is essentially impossible for future governments to introduce new national social programs (without leaving NAFTA). Tradable commodities are protected under NAFTA as assets that cannot be confiscated or expropriated by governments without suitable compensation. Such compensation would necessarily include payments for loss of future earnings resulting from lost business opportunities. Future national programs such as for universal child care, home care, or pharmacare would require compensation for all lost future earnings opportunities by commercial providers operating in the United States (even if they had no presence in Canada). The astronomical cost would preclude major new social initiatives. In this way, a commercial treaty extends its reach to encompass social initiatives, and the earlier promise of a separation between these areas becomes meaningless. Any new welfare society activity in Canada will quickly run up against the wall of NAFTA.

Through the 1990s, Canadians substantially embraced the dominant ideology and accepted the inevitability of the market model of globalization. We were told of the limitless opportunities this new era would offer, and that the transitions, however painful, were a necessary price to pay for the glorious future. Alternative or dissenting views had little audience, given our deteriorating democratic system, reinforced by powerful media and corporate elites that defined and monopolized the single dominant discourse. Perhaps Paul Martin's deficit-slashing budget of 1995 was not merely intended to balance the budget, but also to bring our social programs down to what was offered in the United States, so Canada could effectively compete in the global market.

During this decade, Canadians were blinded by a narrowness of vision, by a lack of perspective. We did not look to, or think about, economic and social integration in Europe, where there were progressive social policies and protections, substantial redistribution from wealthy to poorer regions, and thriving economies. Economic growth and social protection were not incompatible in Europe, but instead were complementary. (The Public Burden model set out in Chapter 2, and currently the dominant paradigm in North America, did not reflect reality in Europe, but was a component, and consequence, of the residual value system of the United States.) Of course, Canada's ability to consider an alternate path has been severely limited by the extent of economic integration with the United States: it is difficult, or perhaps even impossible, to dance to a radically different tune under such circumstances.

Nevertheless we return to our recurring observation that policy implies choice, a point seemingly missed by Canadians as we were swallowed up into the giant maw of globalization. Globalization was not and is not inevitable. Globalization as manifested in its American-corporatist-residual forms was not and is not inevitable. The outcomes have been and shall be only the predictable results of particular economic and social policy choices.

The question for the future is a familiar question to us: How do we make choice real, and not merely theoretical? How do we create processes and structures in Canada that will enable us freely to choose our path to the future and to build our own welfare society, notwithstanding our great proximity to the United States?

A two-pronged response is called for. We must strive to build support and consensus for the idea of creating a new welfare society; and we must devise strategies to get from here to there. Resistance to NAFTA within Canada was largely a failure. But, paradoxically, resistance to globalization in its corporatist forms may have greater success. NAFTA was a trilateral arrangement with one large powerful player and two supplicants: it is difficult to resist a charging elephant. But on the global stage there are many players, and few are as dependent on the United States as Canada; many march to a different drummer. There are allies for this struggle to be found in the European Community, to be sure, but also elsewhere around the globe. There are increasing points of resistance to the mindless globalization of the market. The challenge for Canadians is to identify and to work with allies around the world (including the voices of dissent within the United States), and then to translate what we learn into domestic political policies.

The good news—as Seattle first showed—is that community groups can coalesce on a global scale. Computer technology and the World Wide Web are powerful organizational tools with which to challenge the global hegemony of the market. Traditional channels of communication and information dissemination, with their innately conservative biases, can be readily bypassed in favour of community-controlled and -operated alternatives. Public awareness of the damaging consequences of globalization is definitely increasing.

The bad news for Canadians lies in the effective demise of our democratic system and the loss of meaningful parliamentary resistance and opposition. Canadians either must revive the moribund democratic process, including the creation of a viable progressive party of the left (or centre-left), or, alternatively, they must develop mechanisms of governance that are community-based, likely issue-based, and that effectively bypass an increasingly irrelevant parliamentary system.

Street demonstrations, from Seattle to Quebec City to Genoa and beyond—even when violent—were inevitable, but they were also potentially useful. They were a predictable reaction to a sense of social exclusion and loss of control over our lives and to the vast inequities of globalization, American-style. The street action also drew widespread public attention to the decision-making processes of globalization, in which mostly white men in suits sat behind closed doors and divided up the world. The street action called for full and clear information to inform voters and create active participants in the democratic system. Demonstrators in the streets call for inclusion and protest against marginalization and oppression; they demand a process that is open, transparent, and legitimate. And they call for a reversal of the dramatically growing inequalities of power and resources, both domestic and worldwide.

Is it possible for Canadians to reverse our descent into market globalization and to build a new welfare society? Do we, at the end of the day, have the motivation and the capacity to act? Possibly not. But if we don't try, the outcome is inevitable.

## NOTES

1. While the United States briefly flirted with more progressive social ideas under the imagery of John Kennedy and the War on Poverty of Lyndon Johnson, the ignominious retreat from Vietnam led to an inward-looking America that lost its limited sense of community (Gardner, 2000).
2. In practice, the lines between Chrétien's three categories were blurred: we have seen that the Canada Child Tax Benefit, a $6 billion initiative, was framed as a tax cut so as to meet the political exigencies of the day.
3. The argument in this section is based solely on market principles. Clearly, investment in vulnerable people has broader benefits, based on criteria such as social inclusion and the enhancement of citizenship rights.
4. The beneficial feature of the SUFA, that it requires civil society to be a participant in the political negotiations between Ottawa and the provinces, must still be noted. The challenge is to ensure an operational mechanism for the SUFA that guarantees a diversity of voices is heard—particularly in the face of a tightly controlled media in Canada.

## SUGGESTED READING

McBride, Stephen. 2001. *Paradigm Shift: Globalization and the Canadian State*. Halifax: Fernwood.
   McBride examines the place of Canada in the drive to globalization and suggests strategies as to how we can potentially manage the interaction between Canada and globalization.
Mulvale, James. 2001. *Beyond the Keynesian Welfare State*. Toronto: Garamond/Irwin.
   This book examines the role of progressive Canadian social movements and organizations in maintaining a commitment to social welfare against a backdrop of globalization and the delegitimization of the Keynesian welfare state.
Savoie, Donald J. 1999. *Governing from the Centre: The Concentration of Power in Canadian Politics*. Toronto: University of Toronto Press.
   This examination of governance structures in Canada focuses on the concentration of power in the Prime Minister's Office and in a few central agencies such as the Privy Council Office, the Finance Department, and the Treasury Board.
Shrybman, Steven. 2001. *The World Trade Organization: A Citizen's Guide*, 2nd edn. Toronto: James Lorimer and Canadian Centre for Policy Alternatives.
   This progressive critique of the WTO includes an overview of the organization and the major decisions it has made. There is a new chapter on health care and other services.
Teeple, Gary. 1995. *Globalization and the Decline of Social Reform*. Toronto: Garamond.
   This widely read book, written in 1995 and revised in April 2000, examines the decline of social democracy and the potential for progressive social change within a context of increasing globalization.

**accumulation**

The role of the state is to foster conditions conducive to economic growth, which creates a surplus or profit that will be appropriated by the bourgeoisie. Within the Marxist framework, this is known as accumulation.

**basic exemption**

An income range where benefits are constant and do not decline in the presence of other income.

**benefit reduction rate**

Also known as *tax-back rate* or *clawback rate*. The rate at which benefits are reduced (or *clawed back*) as other income increases. A 20 per cent rate, for example, would mean that benefits are reduced by 20 cents for every additional dollar of other income.

**bracket creep**

The process by which incomes imperceptibly *creep* into higher tax brackets solely as a result of inflation.

**break-even point**

The income at which benefits drop to zero.

**clawback**

See *benefit reduction rate*.

**commercialization**

A subset of privatization that refers only to services provided on a for-profit basis.

**commodification of benefits**

The linking of social entitlements to participation in the workforce and the devaluing of social programs as useful in their own right.

**commodification of care**

The conversion of care into measurable, quantifiable units (for which a provider can be compensated); in other words, the application to the social services of assembly-line mentality and procedures.

**cost minimization**

The lowest dollar expenditure, per unit or in total. It assigns no importance to the quality of the service delivered.

**cream skimming or creaming**

The process by which only the best cases out of a larger population are selected, so as to give the best results. A for-profit school, for example, excludes difficult-to-serve students and so produces good results on standardized tests; social agencies may choose to serve only those clients with the highest potential of successful outcomes.

**debt (national)**

The accumulated total of all past annual national deficits.

**deduction**

A provision in the tax system that reduces the amount of income on which tax is payable. Usually regressive in impact and has the same impact as an exemption.

**deficit (or surplus)**
The amount by which annual spending exceeds (or falls short of) government revenues in a given year.

**demogrant**
Universal payment, usually cash, to everyone in a designated group (such as children or single parents).

**earnings replacement rate**
The share of previous earnings replaced by earnings-related social programs such as Employment Insurance.

**effectiveness**
The extent to which a program's goals are met; it does not include any consideration of the costs of meeting these goals.

**efficiency**
An evaluative concept in that it assesses how well money is spent. It may be defined as the overall effectiveness or 'success' per dollar spent. An outcome will be most efficient if its effectiveness per dollar spent is greater than the effectiveness per dollar of any other competing activity. An efficient expenditure may not entail cost minimization. If spending on an activity increases slightly but the effectiveness—the ability of the program to meet its goal—increases substantially, the efficiency would improve, even though more money is spent.

**exemption**
A provision in the tax system that exempts certain income from liability for taxes and thereby reduces the amount of income on which tax is payable. Usually regressive in impact and has the same effect as a deduction.

**fiscal policy**
The use by government of direct spending and taxation tools to achieve desired economic and social goals.

**free-rider problem**
There would be no incentive for anyone to pay for a service if payment were voluntary, and so some form of compulsory payment—whether through taxes or fees—is necessary. The phrase 'free rider' arises from the common example that if payment on public transit were voluntary, there would be no incentive to pay.

**gross domestic product**
The value of all goods and services produced in a country during a given year. GDP measures only those activities and commodities to which a monetary value is assigned (thus excluding, for example, housework and unpaid child care).

**guarantee level**
Also known as the *basic guarantee*. In guaranteed income discussions, the amount payable to those with no other source(s) of income.

**horizontal redistribution**
Typically involves redistribution among those with differing needs at the same income level to equalize outcomes. Thus, at the same level of incomes, those with children would have greater needs and thus would be entitled to greater benefits than those without children.

**income deciles**
Each decile represents 10 per cent of the population. If all incomes were distributed so that all individuals had the same income, each decile would contain both 10 per cent of the population and 10 per cent of total income. Because incomes are not equally distributed, the income deciles report on the extent of inequality. The deciles are important because they provide information on the distribution of incomes *within* quintiles.

**income quintiles**

Each quintile represents 20 per cent of the population. If all incomes were distributed so that all individuals had the same income, each quintile would contain both 20 per cent of the population and 20 per cent of total income. Because incomes are not equally distributed, the income quintiles report on the extent of inequality.

**income test**

The determination of eligibility for a benefit based on the applicant's (or the family's) income. Relatively simple and non-intrusive.

**Keynesianism**

An economic philosophy that argued the economy is not a self-regulating entity in which government should have only a very limited role. Instead, government has a major responsibility to regulate economic activity, to tax and spend in order to fight unemployment and recession. Keynesian ideas ended the Great Depression of the 1930s by assigning this active, interventionist role to government.

**laissez-faire economics**

The belief that the economy is a self-regulating entity and that the proper role of government was to stand aside. The events of the Great Depression in the 1930s showed the failure of laissez-faire economics, as the economy was not able to pull itself out of recession and restore full employment. Laissez-faire economics (also known as *traditional* or *classical* economics) remains the ideology of choice for the political right today.

**legitimation**

The state must ensure minimal levels of worker acquiescence to the existing economic order: this may entail minimal levels of social welfare provision, a process known in the Marxist framework as legitimation.

**liberalism**

The view that individuals should be free to do as they please with minimal or no interference from government. The term is associated with the work of John Locke, and does *not* refer to ideas of progressivity as in the American sense of 'liberal'. These ideas are associated with traditional or classical economics.

**means test**

The determination of eligibility based on the applicant's (or the family's) resources (income, assets) and expenses. Such a form of determining eligibility can be complex and intrusive.

**monetary policy**

The use by the Bank of Canada of changes in interest rates to achieve desired economic policies.

**needs test**

The determination of eligibility based on a professional, usually individualized determination. This can be based on resources and expenses as well as clinical assessments, and can be highly complex and intrusive.

**neo-liberalism**

Liberalism was discredited by its failure to address the Great Depression and was replaced by Keynesianism after World War II. When Keynesianism fell out of favour in the 1970s, liberalism reappeared on the scene (hence, *neo-liberalism*) and has remained a dominant paradigm since then.

**OECD**

The Organization for Economic Co-operation and Development (OECD), a Paris-based international body, 'brings together 30 countries sharing a commitment to democratic government and the market economy'. Members include the United States, Canada, Mexico, the major European countries, and Australia, Japan, and Korea.

**opportunity cost**

That which must be given up in order to do something else. Opportunity cost is not measured in dollars but rather refers to actual forgone activities. The opportunity cost of staying in school includes the income that would have been earned had a person gone to work.

**Pareto principle**

A redistribution of resources is preferred if someone is better off and no one is worse off as a result of the redistribution. This type of redistribution might follow from increased efficiency, for example, but would not address fundamental redistribution such as that of taxation, where one person's benefit is another person's loss. This very weak statement is perhaps the major contribution of classical economics to the debate on redistribution.

**paternalism**

A decision by one individual or group to interfere with the autonomous decision-making capacity of another individual or group, ostensibly to enhance the latter's well-being.

**pooling of risk**

An insurance principle by which premiums are based, not on the likelihood of a claim by a given individual, but rather on the likelihood of a claim by a member of a group.

**primary distribution**

The distribution of resources that results from the economic activity of individuals without direct government involvement.

**private insurance**

Individual premiums are linked actuarially to the statistical likelihood of a claim being made.

**privatization**

A mode of service delivery that is outside government. It may include not-for-profit agencies, NGOs (nongovernmental organizations), as well as commercial service providers.

**public goods**

Activities (such as national defence or street lighting) that individuals cannot undertake on their own and so must be provided, and paid for, collectively on a compulsory basis.

**registered charity**

A legal status that permits a charity to issue tax receipts to donors, but imposes certain conditions on the charity (including severe restrictions on advocacy).

**secondary distribution (or redistribution)**

The distribution of resources that results after the interventional activities of government (including payments to individuals or corporations and taxation policies).

**seepage**

The allocation of benefits to unintended recipients. Also known as *spillover*.

**social insurance**

A pooling of claimants and benefits such that there is no necessary actuarial link between individual premiums and the likelihood (duration, amount) of a claim being filed.

**stagflation**

A situation, first experienced in the 1970s, of simultaneous high levels of inflation and high unemployment. Previous thinking (including basic

Keynesianism) was based on assumptions that these two policy areas would not create problems at the same time. Government policy-makers did not know how to respond to stagflation.

**stigma**

In the social services, the process by which the recipient of a service is demeaned, diminished, or devalued.

**subsidy**

An arrangement whereby the price to consumers of a commodity or service is less than it would otherwise be in the private market, usually due to payments by government.

**targeting**

A process by which benefits are directed (or restricted) to certain categories of eligible recipients.

**taxable income**

The income on which we pay taxes, after subtraction of all deductions, exemptions, and credits.

**tax avoidance**

The arranging of one's affairs, within the law, so as to minimize tax liability.

**tax-back**

See **benefit reduction rate**.

**tax credit**

Applied after the calculation of taxes based on taxable income, this reduces the actual taxes payable. Often a flat rate reduction in taxes due, or the value can be inverse to income.

**tax evasion**

The non-payment of taxes that are legally due; it is against the law.

**tax expenditure**

A cash benefit to taxpayers that is delivered indirectly, through a reduction in the taxes that would otherwise be payable.

**tax return**

The tax forms completed and submitted by taxpayers. A tax *refund* is money given back to taxpayers as a result of overpayment in the initial tax return.

**turning point**

An income level at which the benefit reduction rate changes.

**vertical redistribution**

The redistribution of resources (incomes) up or down the income scale; typically, it refers to redistribution from those with greater resources (the rich) to those with less (the poor).

**VLTs**

Similar to slot machines, but instead of paying out cash, they print a credit slip that is exchanged on the premises for cash. Highly addictive and banned in British Columbia and Ontario.

**voucher**

A permit that entitles the recipient to acquire a commodity or service free or at a reduced rate from any eligible seller or service provider. The bearer has choice as to supplier, constrained within specified bounds.

**welfare pluralism**

A form of service delivery in which the state is funder, but does not directly provide the services. These are typically delivered by non-governmental providers, both for-profit and not-for-profit, who compete for contracts to deliver.

Arrow, Kenneth. 1963. 'Uncertainty and the Welfare Economics of Medical Care', *American Economic Review* 53, 5: 941–73.

Azmier, Jason. 2000. *Canadian Gambling Behaviour and Attitudes: Summary Report*. Calgary: Canada West Foundation, Feb.

_____ and R. Roach. 2000. *The Ethics of Charitable Gambling: A Survey*. Calgary: Canada West Foundation, 21 Dec.

Baines, Carol, Patricia Evans, and Sheila Neysmith, eds. 1998. *Women's Caring: Feminist Perspectives on Social Welfare*, 2nd edn. Toronto: Oxford University Press.

Banting, Keith. 1979. *Poverty, Politics and Policy: Britain in the 1960's*. London: Macmillan.

_____, ed. 2000. *The Nonprofit Sector in Canada: Roles and Relationships*. Montreal and Kingston: Queen's University School of Policy Studies and McGill-Queen's University Press.

Battle, Ken (Gratton Gray). 1990. 'Social Policy by Stealth', *Policy Options* 4, 2 (Mar.): 17–29.

_____ and Michael Mendelson. 1999. *How to Do a Children's Budget and a Tax Cut Budget in 2000*. Ottawa: Caledon Institute of Social Policy.

_____, _____, Daniel Meyer, Jane Millar, and Peter Whiteford. 2001. *Benefits for Children: A Four Country Study*. Ottawa: Caledon Institute for Social Policy.

Beck, R.G., and J. Horne. 1980. 'Utilization of Publicly Insured Health Services in Saskatchewan, Before, During and After Copayment', *Medical Care* 18: 787–806.

Beeby, Dean. 2001. 'Many companies pay little, no tax: Study', *Toronto Star*, 22 May.

Berdahl, Loleen Y. 1999. *The Impact of Gaming Upon Canadian Non-Profits*. Calgary: Canada West Foundation.

Berlin, Isaiah. 1969. *Four Essays on Liberty*. Oxford: Clarendon Press.

Bird, Richard M. 1976. *Charging for Public Services: A New Look at an Old Idea*. Toronto: Canadian Tax Foundation.

Black, R.J., P.E. Bryden, and J.F. Strain, eds. 1997. *The Welfare State in Canada: Past, Present and Future*. Concord, Ont.: Irwin.

Blake, Raymond B., and Jeff Keshen. 1955. *Social Welfare Policy in Canada: Historical Readings*. Toronto: Copp Clark.

Boulding, Kenneth. 1967. 'The Boundaries of Social Policy', *Social Work* 12, 1 (Jan.): 3–11.

Bridge, Richard. 2000. 'The Law of Advocacy by Charitable Organizations: The Case for Change', paper prepared for IMPACS, Institute for Media, Policy and Civil Society, Vancouver.

Brooks, Neil. 2000. *Flattening the Claims of the Flat-taxers*. Toronto: Osgoode Hall Law School, York University.

Brown, Louise. 2001. 'Fundraising gap creating two-tiered school system: survey', *Toronto Star*, 12 June.

Browne, Paul Leduc. 2000. *Unsafe Practices: Restructuring and Privatization in Ontario Health Care*. Ottawa: Canadian Centre for Policy Alternatives.

Caledon Institute of Social Policy. 1996. *The 1996 Budget and Social Policy*. Ottawa, Mar.

Campbell, Colin. 2000. *Non-profits and Gambling Expansion: The British Columbia Experience*. Calgary: Canada West Foundation.

Canada Customs and Revenue Agency (CCRA). 1999. *Registered Charities: Community Economic Development Programs*, RC 4143(E). Ottawa: CCRA, 23 Dec.

_____. 2000a. *Tax Statistics on Individuals*. Ottawa: CCRA.

_____. 2000b. *Registered Charities: Education, Advocacy and Political Activities*, RC4107E Draft #2. Ottawa: CCRA, 19 May.

_____. 2001. *Taxation Statistics, 1997*. Ottawa: CCRA. Available at: <http://www.ccra-adrc. gc.ca/tax/individuals/stats/gb97/pst>.

Canada West Foundation. 1999. *The Impact of Gaming Upon Canadian Non-Profits: A 1999 Survey of Gaming Grant Recipients*. Calgary: CWF, 20 July.

_____. 2001. *Video Lottery Terminals in New Brunswick*. Calgary: CWF.

Canadian Auto Workers. 2000a. *Tax Facts: Facts and Figures for the Battle Against Tax Cuts*. Toronto: CAW Research Department, Nov.

_____. 2000b. *Economic and Social Action*, vol. 6, no. 1 (Nov.).

Canadian Centre for Philanthropy. 2001. *National Survey of Giving, Volunteering and Participating: Fact Sheets*. Toronto: CCP, Apr.

Canadian Centre for Policy Alternatives, with Pat Armstrong, Hugh Armstrong, and Colleen Fuller. 2000a. *Health Care, Limited: The Privatization of Medicare*. Ottawa: CCPA.

_____. 2000b. *Alternate Federal Budget, 2000*. Ottawa: CCPA.

_____, British Columbia. 2001. *Rethinking the Tax Cut Experiment: BC Budget 2002 Brief*. Vancouver: CCPA-BC, 9 Oct.

Canadian Council on Social Development. 2001a. *Defining and Redefining Poverty: A CCSD Perspective*. Ottawa: CCSD, Oct.

_____. 2001b. *Gaining Ground: The Personal Security Index of 2001*. Ottawa: CCSD, 9 July.

Canadian Institute for Health Information. 2000. *Health Care in Canada, 2000*. Toronto: CIHI.

Carniol, Ben. 2000. *Case Critical: Challenging Social Services in Canada*, 4th edn. Toronto: Between the Lines.

Chappell, R. 1997. *Social Welfare in Canadian Society*. Toronto: ITP Nelson.

Clark, Christopher. 1998. *Canada's Income Security Programs*. Ottawa: Canadian Council on Social Development.

Cohen, Leah. 1984. *Small Expectations: Society's Betrayal of Older Women*. Toronto: McClelland & Stewart.

Collard, David. 1981. *Altruism and Economics: A Study in Non-Selfish Economics*. Oxford: Martin Robertson.

Collier, Ken. 1997. *After the Welfare State*. Toronto: Irwin.

Department of Finance. 2001. *Tax Expenditures and Evaluations 2000*. Ottawa: Department of Finance.

Dobbin, Murray. 1999. *Ten Tax Myths*. Ottawa: Canadian Centre for Policy Alternatives.

Esping-Andersen, Gosta. 1989. 'The three political economies of the welfare state', *Canadian Review of Sociology and Anthropology* 26, 1: 10–36.

_____. 1997. *Welfare States in Transition*. London: Sage.

Findlay, Peter. 1983. 'Social Welfare in Canada: The Case for Universality', *Canadian Social Work Review* 1: 17–24.

Freiler, Christa, Felicite Stairs, and Brigitte Kitchen. 2001. *Mothers as Earners, Mothers as Carers: Responsibility for Children, Social Policy and the Tax System*. Ottawa: Status of Women Canada.

Friedman, Milton. 1962. *Capitalism and Freedom*. Chicago: University of Chicago Press.

_____ and Rose Friedman. 1980. *Free To Choose: A Personal Statement*. New York: Harcourt Brace Jovanovich.

Fuller, Colleen. 1998. *Caring for Profit: How Corporations Are Taking Over Canada's Health Care System*. Ottawa: Canadian Centre for Policy Alternatives.

Gardner, Howard. 2000. 'Paroxysms of Choice', *New York Review of Books*, 19 Oct.

George, Vic, and Paul Wilding. 1985. *Ideology and Social Welfare*, 2nd rev. edn. London: Routledge & Kegan Paul.

Gil, David. 1976. *The Challenge of Social Equality*. Cambridge, Mass.: Schenkman.

Gilbert, Neil, and Paul Terrell. 1998. *Dimensions of Social Welfare Policy*. Boston: Allyn and Bacon.

Glennerster, Howard. 1985. *Paying for Welfare*. Oxford: Blackwell.

Good Gingrich, Luann. 2001. E-mail comments on manuscript. Kitchener, Ont.

Goodin, Robert. 1985. 'Self reliance versus the welfare state', *Journal of Social Policy* 14, 2 (Jan.): 27–45.

Gorlick, Carolyn, and Guy Brethour. 1998a. *Welfare to Work Programs: A National Inventory*. Ottawa: Canadian Council on Social Development.

_____ and _____. 1998b. *Welfare to Work Programs in Canada: A Discussion Paper*. Ottawa: Canadian Council on Social Development.

Gough, Ian. 1981. *The Political Economy of the Welfare State*. London: Macmillan.

_____. 1999. 'The Needs of Capital and the Needs of People: Can the Welfare State Reconcile the Two?', Inaugural Lecture at the University of Bath, 21 Jan.

Graham, John, Karen Swift, and Roger Delaney. 2000. *Canadian Social Policy: An Introduction*. Toronto: Prentice-Hall.

Gramsci, Antonio. 1971. *Selections from the Prison Notebooks*. New York: International.

Grant, Donald. 1990. 'Groups see fur lobby behind tax woes', *Globe and Mail*, 6 Apr.

Guest, Dennis. 1997. *The Emergence of Social Security in Canada*, 3rd edn. Vancouver: University of British Columbia Press.

Hall, Michael. 1995. *Charitable Fundraising in Canada*. Toronto: Canadian Centre for Philanthropy.

Hannant, Joan. 1989. *Privatizing Postal Services: The Implications for Women*. Ottawa: Canadian Centre for Policy Alternatives and the National Action Committee on the Status of Women.

Harvey, David. 1990. *The Condition of Postmodernity: An Enquiry into the Origins of Cultural Change*. Oxford: Blackwell.

Healy, Judith. 1998. *Welfare Options: Delivering Social Services*. St Leonards, Australia: Allen and Unwin.

Henderson, Rob. 1989. 'The Closing of the Metro Food Bank in Halifax', *Canadian Review of Social Policy* 24 (Nov.): 7–9.

Henriksson, Lennart. 1996. 'Hardly a Quick Fix: Casino Gambling in Canada', *Canadian Public Policy* 22, 2 (June): 116–28.

Herman, Edward S., and Noam Chomsky. 1988. *Manufacturing Consent: The Political Economy of the Mass Media*. New York: Pantheon Books.

Hick, Steven. 2001. *Social Work in Canada: An Introduction*. Toronto: Thompson Educational Publishing.

Hicks, Chantal. 1998. 'The Age Distribution of the Tax/Transfer System in Canada', in Miles Corak, ed., *Government Finances and Generational Equity*. Ottawa: Statistics Canada, Catalogue no. 68-513-XIE, 39–56.

Hum, Derek, and Wayne Simpson. 1993. 'Economic Response to a Guaranteed Annual Income: Experience from Canada and the United States', *Journal of Labor Economics* 11, 1, part 2 (Jan.): S293–6.

_____ and _____. 2001. 'A Guaranteed Annual Income? From Mincome to the Millennium', *Policy Options Politiques* (Jan.- Feb.): 78–82.

Ismael, Jacqueline, and Yves Vaillancourt, eds. 1988. *Privatization and Provincial Social Services in Canada: Policy, Administration and Service Delivery*. Edmonton: University of Alberta Press.

*ISUMA: Canadian Journal of Policy Research*. 2001. 'Volunteering', special issue 2, 2 (Summer).

Jackson, Andrew. 2000. *Why We Don't Have To Choose between Social Justice and Economic Growth*. Ottawa: Canadian Council on Social Development.

_____ and David Robinson, with Bob Baldwin and Cindy Wiggins. 2000. *Falling Behind: The State of Working Canada, 2000*. Ottawa: Canadian Centre for Policy Alternatives.

Judge, Ken. 1978. *Rationing Social Services: A Study of Resource Allocation and the Personal Social Services*. London: Heinemann.

_____ and James Matthews. 1980. *Charging for Social Care*. London: Allen and Unwin.

Kesselman, Jonathan. 2000. 'Flat Taxes, Dual Taxes, Smart Taxes: Making the Best Choices', *Policy Matters* (Institute for Research on Public Policy) 7, 1 (Nov.): 104 pp.

Klein, Naomi. 2000. *No Logo*. Toronto: Alfred A. Knopf.

Koren, L., and J. Joyce. 1953. 'The Treatment Implication of Payment of Fees in a Clinical Setting', *American Journal of Orthopsychiatry* 23 (Apr.): 350–7.

Kramer, Ralph. 1981. *Voluntary Agencies in the*

*Welfare State*. Berkeley: University of California Press.

Landa, Eva, and Teri Kay. 1996. Memo: To Budget and Finance Committee, Jewish Family and Child Services, Toronto, 22 Mar.

LeGrand, Julian. 1982. *The Strategy of Equality*. London: Allen and Unwin.

_____ and Will Bartlett. 1993. *Quasi Markets and Social Policy*. London: Macmillan.

_____, C. Propper, and Ray Robinson. 1992. *The Economics of Social Problems*, 3rd edn. London: Macmillan.

_____ and Ray Robinson, eds. 1984. *Privatisation and the Welfare State*. London: Allen and Unwin.

Leonard, Peter. 1997. *Postmodern Welfare: Reconstructing an Emancipatory Project*. London: Sage.

Lightman, Ernie. 1981. 'Continuity in Social Policy Behaviours: The Case of Voluntary Blood Donation', *Journal of Social Policy* 10, 1 (Jan.): 53–79.

_____. 1982a. 'Indirect Projection and the Validity Problem in Survey Research', *The Statistician* 31, 4 (Dec.): 321–31.

_____. 1982b. 'Technique bias in measuring acts of altruism', *Social Science and Medicine* 16, 18: 1627–34.

_____. 1992. *A Community of Interests/Une communauté d'interêts*. Report of the Commission of Inquiry into Unregulated Residential Accommodation, Ernie S Lightman, Ph.D., Commissioner. Toronto: Government of Ontario.

_____. 1995. 'Equity in Lean Times', in Daniel Drache and Andrew Ranachan, eds, *Warm Heart, Cold Country: Fiscal and Social Policy Reform in Canada*. Ottawa and Toronto: Caledon Institute for Social Policy and Robarts Centre for Canadian Studies.

_____ and Uri Aviram. 2000. 'Too Much, Too Late: The Advocacy Act in Ontario', *Law and Policy* 22, 1 (Jan.): 25–48.

_____ and Michele Connell. 2001. 'Student debt and access to higher education: An example from Ontario', *Canadian Social Work Review* 18, 1: 131–49.

_____, Christa Freiler, and John Gandy. 1990. 'A Transatlantic View: Privatisation, Canadian-Style', in Richard Parry, ed., *Privatisation*. London: Jessica Kingsley.

_____ and Andrew Mitchell. 2000a. *General Tax Relief: Impact on Canada's Families*. Toronto: Child Poverty Action Group and Child Care Education Foundation.

_____ and _____. 2000b. *Who Really Wins in the 2000 Budget?* Toronto: University of Toronto Faculty of Social Work.

_____ and Graham Riches. 2000. 'From Modest Rights to Commodification in Canada's Welfare State', *European Journal of Social Welfare* 3, 2 (July): 179–90.

_____ and _____. 2001. 'Canadian Social Policy at the Millennium: One Step Forward, Two Steps Back?', in Peter and Gary Craig Alcock, eds, *International Social Policy*. Basingstoke: Macmillan, 45–63.

Lipovenko, D. 1984. 'Ontario ceiling on CAS bills draws protests', *Globe and Mail*, 30 Oct.

McBride, Stephen. 2001. *Paradigm Shift: Globalization and the Canadian State*. Halifax: Fernwood.

_____ and John Shields. 1997. *Dismantling a Nation*, 2nd edn. Halifax: Fernwood.

McGilly, Frank. 1998. *Canada's Public Social Services*, 2nd edn. Toronto: Oxford University Press.

McMichael, Jane. 2001. 'An Investigation of the Determinants of General Welfare Assistance (GWA) Receipt from 1981 to 1994', Ph.D. thesis, University of Toronto.

McQuaig, Linda. 1993. *The Wealthy Banker's Wife: The Assault on Equality in Canada*. Toronto: Penguin Books.

_____. 1995. *Shooting the Hippo: Death by Deficit and Other Canadian Myths*. Toronto: Penguin Books.

Marshall, Katherine. 2000. 'Update on Gambling', *Perspectives on Labour and Income* 12, 1 (Spring). Statistics Canada, Catalogue no. 75-001-XPE. Available at: <www.statcan.ca/english/IPS/Data/75-001 XIE.htm>.

Mason, Robin, with Laurel Rothman and Pedro Barata. 2001. *Stacking the Deck: The Relationship between Reliable Child Care and Lone Mother's Attachment to the Labour Force*. Toronto: Campaign 2000.

Maxwell, Judith. 2001. 'Toward a Common Citizenship: Canada's Social and Economic Choices', *Reflexion* no. 4 (Jan.): 40 pp.

Miller, S.M., and Martin Rein. 1975. 'Can Income Redistribution Work?', *Social Policy* 6, 1 (May-June): 3–18.

Milner, Henry. 2001. *Civic Literacy in Comparative Context*. Ottawa: Institute for Research in Public Policy.

Mishra, Ramesh. 1981. *Society and Social Policy*, 2nd rev. edn. London: Macmillan.

_____. 1985. *The Welfare State in Crisis*. Brighton: Wheatsheaf Books.

Morrison, Ian. 1995. 'Facts about the administration of social assistance that criminal lawyers need to know', in *Charged with Fraud on Social Assistance: What Criminal Lawyers Need To Know*. Toronto: Law Society of Upper Canada, Continuing Legal Education Department.

_____. 1998. 'Ontario Works: A Preliminary Assessment', *Journal of Law and Social Policy* 13, 1: 28–36.

Mullaly, Bob. 1997. *Structural Social Work: Ideology, Theory and Practice*, 2nd edn. Toronto: Oxford University Press.

_____. 2002. *Challenging Oppression: A Critical Social Work Approach*. Toronto: Oxford University Press.

Mullard, Maurice, and Paul Spicker. 1998. *Social Policy in a Changing Society*. London and New York: Routledge.

Myles, John, and Paul Pierson. 1997. *Friedman's Revenge: The Reform of 'Liberal' Welfare States in Canada and the United States*. Ottawa: Caledon Institute of Social Policy.

National Council of Welfare. 1989. *The End of Universality Budget*. Ottawa: NCW.

_____. 1996. *Gambling in Canada*. Ottawa: NCW, Winter.

_____. 1997. *Child Benefits: A Small Step Forward*. Ottawa: NCW, Spring.

_____. 1999a. *A Pension Primer*. Ottawa: NCW, Summer

_____. 1999b. *Children First: A Pre-Budget Report by the National Council of Welfare*. Ottawa: NCW.

National Survey of Giving, Volunteering and Participating (NSGVP). 1998, 2001. *Caring Canadians, Involved Canadians*. Ottawa: Statistics Canada, Catalogue no. 71-542-XIE.

National Union of Public and Government Employees (NUPGE). 2000. *Living High on the Hog on the Backs of Ontario's Poor*. Ottawa: NUPGE, Apr.

Novick, Marvyn. 1999. *Fundamentals First: An Equal Opportunity for Birth for Every Child*. Toronto: Campaign 2000.

O'Connor, James. 1973. *The Fiscal Crisis of the State*. New York: St Martin's Press.

O'Connor, Julia. 1989. 'Welfare expenditure and policy orientation in Canada in comparative perspective', *Canadian Review of Sociology and Anthropology* 26, 1: 127–50.

Ontario. 1988. *Transitions: Report of the Social Assistance Review Committee*. Toronto: Queen's Printer for Ontario.

Ontario Ministry of Community and Social Services. 2002. *Welfare Fraud Control Report, 2000–2001*, 15 Jan. Available at: <http://www.gov.on.ca/CSS/page/brochure/fraud01.html>.

Ontario Office of the Provincial Auditor. 2001. *2001 Annual Report*. Toronto: Queen's Printer for Ontario, 29 Nov.

Oppenheim, Carey. 1998. *An Inclusive Society: Strategies for Tackling Poverty*. London: Institute for Public Policy Research.

Organization for Economic Co-operation and Development (OECD). 1998. *The Tax/Benefit Position of Employees: 1997*. Paris: OECD.

_____. 1999. *Revenue Statistics, 1965–1988*. Paris: OECD.

_____. 2000a. *Economic Outlook* 68 (Dec.).

_____. 2000b. *Economic Surveys, Canada, 1999–2000*. Paris: OECD, Aug.

Panitch, Leo, ed. 1977. *The Canadian State: Political Economy and Political Power*. Toronto: University of Toronto Press.

Parker, Roy. 1976. 'Charging for the Social Services', *Journal of Social Policy* 5, Part 4 (Oct.): 359–73.

Peacock, Alan. 1966. *The Welfare Society*, Unservile Paper No. 2. London: Merritt and Hatcher, for Liberal Party Publications.

———. 1977. *The Political Economy of Economic Freedom*. Cheltenham, UK: Edward Elgar.

Pinker, Robert. 1979. *The Idea of Welfare*. London: Heinemann.

Pitsula, James, and Ken Rasmussen. 1990. *Privatizing a Province: The New Right in Saskatchewan*. Vancouver: New Star Books.

Poschmann, Finn, and John Richards. 2000. *How To Lower Taxes and Improve Social Policy*. Toronto: C.D. Howe Institute Commentary No. 136.

Pushkal, Garg. 1999. 'Effect of the ownership of dialysis facilities on patients' survival and referral for transplantation', *New England Journal of Medicine* 341, 22 (25 Nov.): 1653–60.

Quebec. 1999. *Family Policy in Quebec*. Quebec: Ministry of Child and Family Welfare

Rachlis, Chuck. n.d. *The Right-Wing Threat to Universality*. Toronto: Ontario NDP Research.

Reisman, David. 1977. *Richard Titmuss: Welfare and Society*. London: Heinemann.

Revenue Canada. 1977. *Registered Charities*, Information Circular 77–14. Ottawa, 20 June.

———. 1978. *Registered Charities: Political Objects and Activities*, Information Circular 78–3. Ottawa, 27 Feb.

———. 1987. *Registered Charities: Ancillary and Incidental Political Activities*, Information Circular 87–1. Ottawa, 25 Feb.

Rice, James J., and Michael J. Prince. 2000. *Changing Politics of Canadian Social Policy*. Toronto: University of Toronto Press.

Riches, Graham. 1986. *Food Banks and the Welfare Crisis*. Ottawa: Canadian Council on Social Development.

Room, Graham. 1995. *Beyond the Threshold: The Measurement and Analysis of Social Exclusion*. London: Polity Press.

Ross, David P., Katherine J. Scott, and Peter J. Smith. 2000. *The Canadian Fact Book on Poverty*. Ottawa: Canadian Council on Social Development.

Royal Commission on the Economic Union and Development Prospects for Canada (Macdonald Commission). 1985. *Report*, 3 vols. Ottawa: Minister of Supply and Services.

Ruggeri, G.C., D. Van Wart, and R. Howard. 1996. *The Government as Robin Hood*. Kingston: Queen's University School of Policy Studies and Caledon Institute of Social Policy.

Sarlo, Christopher. 1996. *Poverty in Canada*. Vancouver: Fraser Institute.

———. 2001. *Measuring Poverty in Canada*. Vancouver: Fraser Institute, July.

Savoie, Donald J. 1999. *Governing from the Centre: The Concentration of Power in Canadian Politics*. Toronto: University of Toronto Press.

Seldon, Arthur. 1977. *Charge*. London: Temple Smith.

Sewell, John. 2001. 'United Way shirks its duty to the poor', *eye Magazine* (Toronto), 22 Mar.

Shillington, Richard. 1999. *The Dark Side of Targeting: Retirement Saving for Low-Income Canadians*. Toronto: C.D. Howe Institute, The Pension Papers, 30 Sept.

———. 2000a. 'High-income earners would cash in with Alliance flat tax', *Straight Goods* (Ottawa), 19 May.

———. 2000b. 'Two Casualties of the Child Tax Benefit: Truth and the Poor', *Policy Options Politiques* 67 (Nov.): 62–7.

Silversides, Ann. 1984. 'Revenue Canada queries charities' tax exempt status', *Globe and Mail*, 4 Apr.

Smeeding, Timothy. 2000. 'Income Inequality: Is Canada Different or Just Behind the Times?', paper presented to the 1999 meetings of the Canadian Economics Association, cited in Jackson et al. (2000: 38).

Smith, Gary, and Harold Wynne. 1999. *Gambling and Crime in Western Canada: Exploring Myth and Reality.* Calgary: Canada West Foundation, 20 Sept.

Social Planning Council of Metropolitan Toronto. 1997. *Merchants of Care? The Non-profit Sector in a Competitive Social Services Marketplace.* Toronto: Social Planning Council.

Statistics Canada. 2000a. *Income in Canada.* Ottawa: Statistics Canada, Income Statistics Division, Catalogue no. 75-202-XIE, June.

_____. 2000b. *Spending Patterns in Canada 1998.* Ottawa: Statistics Canada, Catalogue no. 62-202-XIE

_____. 2001a. *The Assets and Debts of Canadians: An Overview of the Results of the Survey of Financial Security.* Ottawa: Statistics Canada, Catalogue no. 13-595-XIE, Mar.

_____. 2001b. *Low income cut-offs from 1990 to 1999 and low income measures from 1989 to 1998.* Ottawa: Statistics Canada, Catalogue no. 75F0002MIE00017.

_____. 2001c. *Retirement Savings Through RPPs and RRSPs, 1991–1997.* Ottawa: Statistics Canada, Catalogue no. 74F0002XIB, 17 July.

_____. 2001d. *Public Sector Statistics: Financial Management System, 1999–2000.* Ottawa: Statistics Canada, Catalogue no. 68-213-XIB.

_____. 2001e. *Income Trends in Canada.* Ottawa: Statistics Canada, Catalogue no. 13F0022XCB 21 Feb.

Stein, Janice Gross. 2001. *The Cult of Efficiency.* Toronto: Anansi.

Stoddart, Greg, Morris Barer, Robert Evans, and Vandna Bhatia. 1993. *Why Not User Charges? The Real Issues.* Toronto: Premier's Council on Health, Well-Being and Social Justice.

Strick, John C. 1999. *The Public Sector in Canada: Programs, Finance and Policy.* Toronto: Thompson Educational Publishing.

Sutherland, Ross. 2001. 'Privatized home care in Ontario: An expensive model to avoid', *Straight Goods*, 11 May. Available at:<http://www.straightgoods.com/item434.asp>.

Swanson, Jean. 2001. *Poor-Bashing: The Politics of Exclusion.* Toronto: Between the Lines.

Tawney, R.H. 1931. *Equality.* London: Allen and Unwin.

Taylor-Gooby, Peter, and Jennifer Dale. 1981. *Social Theory and Social Welfare.* London: E. Arnold.

_____ and _____. 1998. *Choice and Public Policy: The Limits to Welfare Markets.* New York: St Martin's Press.

Teeple, Gary. 1995. *Globalization and the Decline of Social Reform.* Toronto: Garamond (rev. edn 2000).

Titmuss, Richard, ed. 1956. *The Social Division of Welfare: Essays on the Welfare State.* London: Unwin.

_____. 1968a. 'Choice and the "Welfare State"', in Titmuss (1968b).

_____. 1968b. *Commitment to Welfare.* London: Allen and Unwin.

_____. 1970. *The Gift Relationship: From Human Blood to Social Policy.* London: Allen and Unwin.

_____. 1974. *Social Policy: An Introduction.* London: Allen and Unwin.

Tobin, James. 1971. 'On Limiting the Domain of Inequality', *Journal of Law and Economics* 13, 2 (Jan.): 263–77.

Toronto, City of. 2000. *Recreation User Fee and Welcome Policy: Preliminary Evaluation.* Toronto: Economic Development and Parks Committee, Staff Report, 8 Mar.

*Toronto Star.* 1999. 'Greenpeace denied status', 7 June.

Townson, Monica. 2001. *Pensions Under Attack: What's Behind the Push to Privatize Public Pensions.* Toronto and Ottawa: James Lorimer and Canadian Centre for Policy Alternatives.

Turner, Joanne C., and Francis J. Turner. 2001. *Canadian Social Welfare.* Toronto: Allyn and Bacon.

United Nations. 2001. Human Development Indicators. Available at: <http://www.undp.org/hdr2001/back.pdf>.

United Way of Canada. 2001. Campaign Results, 2000.

Urquhart, Ian. 2000. 'Potholes in path to outsourcing', *Toronto Star*, 28 Feb.

Walker, Alan. 1981. 'Social Policy, Social Administration and the Social Construction of Welfare', *Sociology* 5, 1 (May): 127–50.

Walkom, Thomas. 2001. 'Big spending gets go-ahead thanks to war', *Toronto Star*, 11 Dec.

Wharf, Brian, and Brad McKenzie. 1998. *Connecting Policy to Practice in the Human Services*. Toronto: Oxford University Press.

Wilensky, Harold, and Charles Lebeaux. 1958. *Industrial Society and Social Welfare*. New York: Russell Sage.

Williams, Fiona. 1992. *Social Policy: A Critical Introduction*. Oxford: Polity Press, in association with Blackwell.

Wilson, Colin. 1972. *Order of Assassins: The Psychology of Murder*. London: Hart Davis.

Wilson, John, and Peter Hinton, eds. 1993. *Public Services and the 1990's*. Eastham, Wirral, Merseyside: Tudor.

Wolfensberger, Wolf, et al. 1972. *The Principle of Normalization in Human Services*. Toronto: National Institute on Mental Retardation in association with L. Crainford.

Yalnizyan, Armine. 1998. *The Growing Gap: A Report on Growing Inequality between the Rich and Poor in Canada*. Toronto: Centre for Social Justice.

Young, Iris Marion. 1990. *Justice and the Politics of Difference*. Princeton, NJ: Princeton University Press.